The world's best nude beaches and resorts

One thousand beautiful places for bathing naked

Published simultaneously in the UK and the US

UK publisher
Lifestyle Press Ltd, PO Box 1087, Bristol, BS48 3YD, UK
www.lifestyle-press.co.uk
info@lifestyle-press.co.uk

US publisher
The Naturist Society LLC, PO Box 132, Oshkosh, WI 54903, USA
www.naturistsociety.com
naturist@naturistsociety.com

© 2007 Lifestyle Press/The Naturist Society LLC

UK ISBN 978-0-9544767-3-1
US ISBN 978-0-934106-22-1

This book was researched extensively and written in good faith with the most up-to-date information available at the time of publication. All beaches listed are known personally to the authors, or have been recommended by naturists, or publicised by specialist websites, resort operators and tourist boards. Neither the publishers nor the authors accept any responsibility for any of the travel companies, resort operators and other organisations listed.

All details in this guide are liable to change and can not therefore be guaranteed. Neither the publishers nor the authors can accept any liability whatsoever arising from errors or omissions in this guide. We will publish updates on our website www.barebeaches.com – please let us know if you are aware of any details that need updating.

The listing of any naturist or clothing-optional location does not necessarily guarantee its existence or its ongoing suitability for nude use. Maps are provided for general guidance, not exact navigational information.

British Library Cataloguing-in Publication Data. A catalogue record for this book is available from the British Library

Authors
Mike Charles, Judi Ditzler, Nicky Hoffman Lee, Mark Storey, Nick Mayhew-Smith

UK advertising
Debbie Knowlson
Tel: +44 (0) 20 8488 9153 (UK)
debbie@manningblack.co.uk

US advertising
Carmen Hamm
Tel: (800) 886 7230 (in the US)
or +1 920 426 5009 (from abroad)
advertising@naturistsociety.com

Map designer
Emete Friddle

Thank you:
The authors would like to thank the countless naturists and travel professionals whose help and enthusiasm made this publication possible, especially Lee Baxandall, who inspired this series of guides. In particular big thanks for help on research and photography must go to Fiona Ashley, Jim Bailey, Cap'n Barefoot, Allen Baylis, Bill Bisbee, Malcolm Boura, Rod Burkey, Paul Carlson, Michael Cooney, Laurindo Correia, Cláudio Dias, Eros, Marv Frandsen, Marjorie Gersh-Young, Kay Hannan, Neil Hicks, Les Hotchkin, Laurie Jeffery, Debbie Jungwirth, Claudia Kellersch, Peter Knight, Bob Morton, Dale Musser, Bill Pennington, Suzanne Piper, John Purbrick, Paul Rapoport, Jeff Riddlebaugh, Kevin & Debbie Rudd, Morley Schloss, Bill Schroer, Jonathan Shopiro, Charlie Simonds, Dennis Craig Smith, Don Stanton, Camilla Van Sickle, Steve Thompson, Andrew Welch, Judy Williams and George Winlock.

■ Picture credits
Cover top: Arnaoutchot, France (Charlie Simonds)
Cover bottom: Caribbean (Kevin and Debbie Rudd)
Back cover: Bahamas (Chris A Crumley/Alamy)
Page one: Caribbean (Kevin and Debbie Rudd)
Page 5: Mallorca (www.radiantnude.com)

Where to bare around the world

Nude beaches and resorts

Introducing our colourful guide to all-over bathing

Welcome to the most natural way to enjoy just being you. Unlike other guides to beaches and holidays, this is the one that opens the door to the most adventurous and yet relaxing way to enjoy the natural elements. Why should a swimming costume come between you and the sea, sun and sand you've been waiting all year to enjoy?

This world guidebook is the culmination of several decades' work by a dedicated group of nude beach enthusiasts. It follows in the footsteps of a pioneering series of books called 'The World Guide to Nude Beaches and Resorts', published over five editions by The Naturist Society LLC in America. The title sold over 350,000 copies and went on to become a New York Times best-seller, under the careful guidance of author and nude beach advocate Lee Baxandall.

Now the concept has been fully updated in partnership with a European publisher, Lifestyle Press. Both specialise in exploring the modern bare beach scene. Today, nude beaches are a regular part of holiday life in Europe and America, with some of the most beautiful locations and the smartest facilities imaginable.

Long gone are the days when nude beach lovers had to hide themselves away on remote stretches of coast. Now you can choose from an almost endless list of all-over bathing experiences, from the glorious tropics to the invigorating Arctic (no kidding – see page 270).

We've done all the hard work researching the very best of these heavenly places and have come up with a list of 1,000. All that remains for you to do is spread out your towel, break open the sunscreen – and drop your swimming costume on the sand. You'll soon discover that the one you were born with is a whole lot nicer.

Can I take pictures at a nude beach?

(and eight other commonly asked questions)

Is photography allowed at naturist places?

Yes – up to a point. Like anyone else on holiday you'll want to come back with some happy reminders of your time in the sun. But other beach users might not want to end up in someone else's photo album, so don't point your camera at strangers. It's common courtesy on any sort of beach, but nude beach users might be even more sensitive and some countries have strict privacy laws too.

Naturist holiday resorts will almost certainly have their own rules about photography: if they don't give them to you with your welcome pack, just ask someone at reception.

▲ Smile please: but don't forget to check with the people in your viewfinder. Picture: Charlie Simonds

What about sitting on shared chairs?

Rest assured naturists put respect for others very highly. The universal code is to bring a towel, blanket or any other piece of material with you and simply place it between your bare buns and any public surface. You'll almost always have a towel with you at a naturist place anyway.

Will I get hassled if I strip off in public?

Although there is no absolute guarantee, a genuine naturist environment ought to be free of any unwelcome intrusion or hassle.

Naturist resorts are by far the safest and best protected places to enjoy a holiday in the nude. Hassle of any sort is very unlikely and any complaints would to be taken extremely seriously by the managers.

Beaches are of course less regulated but no-one should have to put up with anti-social or intrusive behaviour. Speak up for standards, and if a person doesn't respond to a polite word then by all means notify someone in authority.

Many nude beaches, particularly in southern Europe, have more women than men using them – a good sign that the beach is peaceful. But other places do get their unfair share of pests and for some beaches we've indicated where it's a particularly big problem.

What about holding a beach party?

A nude beach is exactly the sort of place to enjoy with a group of like-minded friends. But do remember other beach users, and avoid violating their peaceful relaxation with noisy beach games and the like. Playing music through speakers on a nude beach is particularly anti-social: if you are listening to music or the radio, don't forget your headphones.

▲ Where's the cafe? Nude beaches are often remote so don't forget your supplies. Picture: Juan Picca

What facilities will there be at the beach?

For obvious reasons, many nude beaches are more remote than ordinary ones. The chance of finding an ice cream salesman when you are half an hour's walk from the nearest road is very small (although surprises can happen!) Unless you're visiting a nude beach where facilities are specifically listed, bring all the supplies you need for the day, including food, drinks, chairs, towels, sunscreen and parasols. People mooching off others is just plain irritating in the best of circumstances.

Who needs rules when you're going naked?

Taking your clothes off doesn't mean complete anarchy has to follow. Nude beaches are sometimes only just tolerated by the authorities: the good behaviour of visitors will help keep them. So obey parking regulations and other rules about fires, camping, safe places for swimming and so on.

Isn't there a sexual side to nude beaches?

No more than on any other sort of beach. Overt sexual activity is completely illegal and in the context of a nude beach highly selfish and irresponsible as well. Nude is not lewd – and such behaviour is the quickest way to get a naturist beach closed.

Naturism is not about exhibitionism and any man who's tried it will confirm that sexual arousal is not an issue. A quick cover up with a towel would be easy enough in any case, but the fact of being publicly naked acts as a natural deterrent.

Do naturists look after their beaches?

Absolutely – one of the key aspects of naturism is respect for the environment. Some beaches have their own user groups who collect rubbish, while all nude beach visitors should take away their litter with them at the end of the day – plus a bit extra if possible. Nude beaches are sometimes the cleanest stretches of coastline as a result – a fact that park wardens and other people in authority can't help but notice.

Be particularly careful to avoid walking through environmentally sensitive areas such as sand dunes or nesting places for turtles.

▲ First-time nudists and single women alike happily enjoy hundreds of nude beaches the world over without any hassle at all – a good sign that everyone can join in the fun

Are nude beaches particularly friendly?

Many nude beaches attract a lively community of regulars, who might well give a cheerful nod to newcomers. But beyond that most beach visitors are there for the peaceful relaxation of getting back to nature. It's fine to make new friends in the right place and at the right time, but going to a nude beach is not really a social gathering. People shouldn't monopolise your time, especially when the welcome mat wasn't out in the first place. Respect for people's privacy is the key.

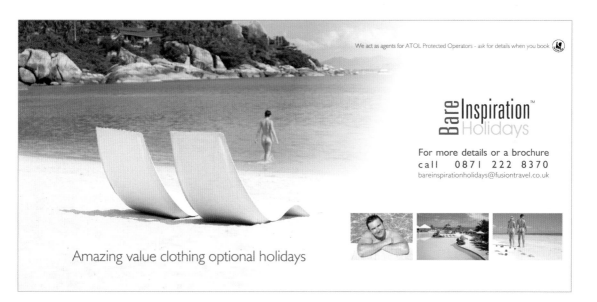

How to have a nude holiday

Wherever you want to go bare, there's a tour operator ready to help

Bare bathing on holiday involves going to a beach and taking all your clothes off. For almost all the beaches listed in this guide, it really is as simple as that.

When you want to organise your whole holiday around the absolute luxury of living naked by the sea, finding a tour operator has never been easier. The range of holidays gets better every year too, with quality and prices to suit both ends of the spectrum and everyone else in between.

Whether you want to camp in a pine forest by a sandy French beach or be pampered at a brand new resort in the Caribbean, there are travel companies ready to book your flight today. The choices include self-catering accommodation, campsites, caravan parks, private villas, log cabins and full-service hotels with spas. Some of these are simply near a local nude beach, while others are situated inside a fully naturist holiday resort – the ultimate place to enjoy a relaxing nude holiday.

What is a naturist resort?
Holiday centres, particularly those by the sea, are the most convenient way to get the most out of your precious few weeks' holiday each year. Apart from the lack of swimming costumes, they're much the same as regular resorts, but with a nicer atmosphere.

Indeed many people using naturist resorts are just regular holiday-makers who enjoy the freedom to relax naked for a week or two. They wouldn't consider themselves devoted naturists, just people who know a good thing when they see it and fancy doing something a bit special.

The other nice thing about naturist resorts is how family-friendly most of them are. European resorts in particular are organised around family holidays, with a huge range of activities, creative classes and even child minding services to let everyone get the most out of their stay.

When to go
The sun never sets on the world of nude bathing. At any time of day, in any season, there are plenty of beaches full of sunseekers, many of them escaping winter back home. For those of us living in northern Europe and North America – where the vast majority of nudists come from – there are some superb options in the Canary Islands, the Caribbean, and for those keen on a longer trip the sands of Australia, New Zealand and even South Africa beckon.

US naturist tour operators

Bare Necessities Tour & Travel
904 W. 29th Street
Austin, TX 78705
(800) 443-0405
www.bare-necessities.com

Caribbean Hideaways
2678 West Lake Road
Palm Harbor, FL 34684
(800) 828-9356
www.caribbeanhideaways.com

Castaways Travel
25701 Interstate 45 North #3A
Spring, TX 77380
(800) 470-2020
www.castawaystravel.com

Go Classy Tours Inc.
Palm Harbor Executive Center
2676 West Lake Road
Palm Harbor, FL 34684
(800) 329-8145
www.goclassy.com

Internaturally Travel, Inc.
PO Box 317
Newfoundland, NJ 07435
(973) 697-8099
www.internaturally.com

Vacation au Naturel
9360 Sunset Drive Suite 230
Miami, FL 33173
(800) 795-0031
www.vacationaunaturel.com

UK naturist tour operators

Peng Travel
UK's biggest naturist travel agent
Tel: 0845 345 8345
www.pengtravel.co.uk

Chalfont Holidays
European naturist resorts
Tel: 01494 580728
www.chalfontholidays.co.uk

France 4 Naturisme
Specialists in holidays au naturel
Tel: 0870 777 6837
www.france4naturisme.com

Bare Inspiration Holidays
Tel: 0871 222 8370
bareinspirationholidays@fusiontravel.co.uk

Canarian Dreams International
Canaries and Caribbean
Tel: 0870 770 5378
www.canariandreams.com

Island Seekers
Lanzarote and Fuerteventura
Tel: 0870 112 0555
www.islandseekers.co.uk

Sunseekers
Self-catering on Fuerteventura
Tel: 01403 738866
www.sunseekerholidays.com

Astbury Formentera
Experts on Formentera, Spain's Balearics
Tel: 01642 210163
www.formentera.co.uk

It's Natural
Self-catering at Vera Playa, Spain
Tel: 01354 661511
www.its-natural.net

Away with Dune
Worldwide holidays, Crete specialists
Tel: 0870 751 8866
www.awaywithdune.co.uk

Sunclad Homes
Vera Playa apartments, Spain
Tel: 01494 817170
suncladhomes@spanishcmail.com

Club Holidays
Holidays in the south of France
Tel: 01604 863300
www.clubholidays.net

Ann & David James Travel Ltd
www.capdagde.co.uk
Tel: 0844 484 5058

European naturist tour operators

Oboena Reisen
Large German naturist specialist
www.oboena.de

Internatuur
Dutch naturist tour operator
www.internatuur.nl

▲ Admiring the views at one of Europe's finest holiday destinations, El Portus in Spain. Picture by Charlie Simonds

The coolest nude places in the world

Want to wear your birthday suit somewhere really special? Try out our listings of the best beaches and resorts the world has to offer

Top 20 US beaches (alphabetical order)

Apollo/Playalinda Beaches, FL
Baker Beach, CA
Black's Beach, CA
Bonny Doon, CA
Collins Beach, OR
Gray Whale Cove, CA
Gunnison Beach, NJ
Haulover Beach, FL
Hippie Hollow, TX
Kehena Beach, HI
Lake Tahoe, NV
The Ledges, VT
Little Beach, HI (pictured right)
Lighthouse Beach, NY
Mazo Beach, WI
Red Rock Beach, CA
Red, White & Blue Beach, CA
Rooster Rock Beach, OR
San Gregorio Beach, CA
San Onofre Beach, CA

Top 10 US naturist resorts

Avalon, WV
Caliente, FL
Cypress Cove, FL
Desert Shadows Inn, CA
Laguna del Sol, CA
Lupin Lodge, CA
Mira Vista, AZ
Paradise Lakes, FL
Turtle Lake, MI
Valley View, CO

Top Canadian beaches

Crystal Crescent, NS (pictured below)
Hanlan's Point Beach, ON
Little Tribune Beach, BC
Oka Beach, ON
Wreck Beach, BC

Top Canadian naturist resorts

Club Naturiste Richard Brunet, ON
Domaine le Cyprès, QC
The Oasis, PE
Sunny Glades Nature Park, ON

Top 20 European beaches

Ada Bojana, Montenegro
Banana Beach, Skiathos
Bravone Plage, Corsica
Bredene, Belgium
Cala Macarelleta, Menorca
Les Grottes Plage, France
Leucate Plage, France
Meco Beach, Portugal
Migjorn, Formentera (pictured below)
Montalivet, France
Morfa Dyffryn, Wales
Paklina, Croatia
Plakias, Crete
Playa Risco del Paso, Fuerteventura
Playa Es Trenc, Mallorca
Sønderstrand, Denmark
Studland, England
Svanrevet, Sweden
Sylt beaches, Germany
Zandvoort, the Netherlands

Top 20 European naturist resorts

Arnaoutchot, France
Bunculuka, Croatia
Costa Natura, Spain
Eagle Peak, Spain
El Portus, Spain
El Templo del Sol, Spain
Euronat, France
Flevo-Natuur, the Netherlands
Gustavsberg, Sweden
Hotel Vera Playa Club
Koversada, Croatia
La Jenny, France
Magnolias, Gran Canaria
Pevors Farm, UK
Pizzo Greco, Italy
Riva Bella, Corsica (pictured above)
Rutar Lido, Austria
Solbakken, Denmark
Valalta, Croatia
Vritomartis, Crete

Top 20 beaches and resorts in the rest of the world

Abricó Beach, Brazil (pictured below)
Cable Beach, Australia
Cayo Largo, Cuba
Club Orient, St Martin
Eden Bay, Dominican Republic
Grand Lido Braco, Jamaica
Hidden Beach Resort, Mexico
Maslin Beach, Australia
Ocean beach, New Zealand
Otatoka beach, New Zealand
Paya Bay's Lil' Beach, Honduras
Plage Tarare, Guadeloupe
Playa Escondida, Argentina
Playa Sonrisa, Mexico
Praia do Pinho, Brazil
Samurai Beach, Australia
Sandy Bay, South Africa
Sorobon Beach, Bonaire
Swanbourne, Australia
Uretiti Beach, New Zealand

Chalfont Holidays

specialising in quality naturist holidays

We offer holidays tailor made to your requirements to these naturist destinations, and will organise the most convenient flights for you (acting as retail agents for various ATOL operators), car hire, accommodation and travel insurance. We are members of the Travel Trust Association (R6530) which will safeguard the finances for your holiday, and we have an ATOL licence (T7062).

Lanzarote Castillo de Papagayo is the only naturist village in the Canary Islands with several restaurants, bars and shops. It enjoys a remote position on the north east coast of the island. We can arrange holidays in the full range of apartments and houses on this naturist estate.

Gran Canaria Magnolias Natura is well situated to visit the famous Maspalomas naturist beach. This is a small estate of self-catering bungalows set in a tropical garden around an inviting pool next to a friendly bar restaurant... an excellent place to meet new friends and greet old ones.

Fuerteventura This island has the most extensive and widely used sand beaches for naturism. The new Monte Marina naturist apartments offers a great centre from which to enjoy those sun-washed shores. Or, enjoy the large salt water naturist pool nestled amongst the bougainvillea and palm trees in the middle of the apartment complex.

Kefalonia The Vassaliki Naturist Club has just opened on this stunning Greek island. The perfect place to enjoy the Mediterranean sun. It has a range of newly refurbished apartments and a large naturist pool and poolside bar. Mark and Samantha look forward to welcoming you.

The Algarve The naturist guest house Quinta da Vista, situated amidst orange groves and with a lovely pool, offers a great opportunity to explore the western Algarve and its several naturist beaches, Portuguese cuisine, and relaxed way of life.

Crete The Hotel Vritomartis is an idyllic naturist hotel. Everything about the hotel and grounds is delightful. Stroll down to its private naturist beach, sunbathe next to the large attractive pool, or treat yourself to a house speciality at the poolside bar, Sfakian pie.

Spain Near Javea on the Costa Blanca there are two welcoming naturist guest houses offering bed and breakfast and a restful naturist experience at different times of the year. Both have peaceful gardens and refreshing pools. El Escondite is also available as an independent rental in the summer months.

Austria Nestled in the Dachstein mountains at Ramsau, this naturist hotel provides a superb centre for winter snow sports and summer mountain walking. Enjoy the indoor/outdoor pool after a quick sauna, and indulge in great Austrian food in the upstairs dining room with a view.

Corsica This French island, 150 miles south-east of Nice, has the longest naturist beach in Europe with six naturist resorts to choose from. They offer different facilities and standards of accommodation, but all are a short walk away from beautiful sandy beaches and warm crystal clear sea water.

Turkey The elegant yacht, the Suzi Anna, offers a naturist sailing holiday around the magnificent remote and mountainous southern coast of Turkey. Based in the Gulf of Hisaronu, 25 miles from Marmaris, you can cruise into secluded beaches and sample Turkish delights.

Chalfont Holidays, c/o 196 High Road, Wood Green, London N22 8HH
Telephone: 0845 045 0987 Email: info@chalfontholidays.co.uk
Website: www.chalfontholidays.co.uk

▲ There's so much more to naturism than sunbathing. Picture taken on Mallorca, Spain's Balearics, by Charlie Simonds

For those who really dare to bare...

The local nude beach is all very well, but if your sunbathing needs a little excitement why not try our top 10 things to do nude before you die...

Go to le supermarché in your birthday suit

Well, it might not sound like the basis for a holiday. But for a truly complete naturist experience, stay at one of the full-size centres in France and live the way nature intended. Cap d'Agde, on the Med, is the world's biggest nude venue – it's an entire town rather than a beach resort. Meanwhile on the Atlantic coast, Euronat, Montalivet and La Jenny are all wonderfully well equipped holiday centres with all the conveniences of a seaside village.

Walk for a mile or more as nature intended

If space and solitude are your idea of naturist perfection, there is plenty of undeveloped coast around the world (see box on left). Put your clothes in the car, hide your key under a rock, and set off for a stroll along the sands with nothing but a light coat of sunscreen to keep you company.

Play beach volleyball without the kit

You can have great fun pretending to be a 1960s stereotype at a nudist resort – just pick up a volleyball and start playing. Many nude beach resorts, particularly the large centres in France and Spain, have a net on the sand and a host of willing participants ready for a match.

Parasail naked over a tropical beach

If you want to see what nudists look like from a bird's perspective, why not harness up for a beach sport you'll never forget. Visit the world-class nude beach and resort at Orient Bay (see page 30) and one of the beach sports centres will gladly let you have a go in your birthday suit.

Sunbathe in the nude at midnight

It is possible, on just one nude beach in the world, to sunbathe naked at midnight – but you'll have to travel to the Arctic circle first. Ursetvika beach in Norway (see page 270) is the only place regularly used by naturists above the Arctic circle, where the sun doesn't set around midsummer (21 June).

Camp wild beside a remote nude beach

Wake up to the sound of singing birds and rolling surf, and streak straight from sleeping bag to sea without wearing a stitch. It's back to nature at its most complete, and like the best things in life it's absolutely free – in every sense of the word. See the box on the right for some suggested places, and remember to follow good camping practice and local advice.

Skinnydip in one of America's hot springs

Even better if you have to hike to get there, soaking away your cares in the warmth of a natural mineral pool is a uniquely American way to enjoy the great outdoors. The country has more than a dozen such places listed in this guide, some in the wild and some that are managed. See page 102.

Cast off on a nude cruise or sailing trip

Out on the open sea, there's no one to see you're naked – a fact that many a sailor appreciates. You can even treat yourself to an entire nude cruise on a modern liner, thanks to some innovative US travel companies, or fix a smaller tour round the Croatian coast. Many naturist sailors have their own boat, or hire one for a holiday around the Mediterranean, Caribbean or other popular seas. Details of tour operators are in the box on the right.

Swim among the fish at a coral reef

Swimming naked in a warm sea surrounded by the darting colours of tropical sea life will imprint itself on your memory forever. There are nude resorts by a number of the world's top coral reefs, and some can organise snorkelling and diving trips for costume-free bliss (see box on right).

Don't keep it to yourself – bring a friend!

It's easy for some, and unthinkable for others: telling people you prefer to swim without clothes is certainly a good way to get a conversation going. It's not really a big deal in the great scheme of things and if someone you like gets a happy experience out of it, they will never stop thanking you!

WHERE YOU CAN BARE

Wild camping places

Cala de San Pedro, Spain (page 123)
Elafonissos, Greek islands (page 197)
Gavdos, Greek islands (page 195)
Koktebel, Ukraine (page 281)
Lulviksbadet, Sweden (page 267)
Otatoka Beach, New Zealand (page 298)
Serifos, Greek islands (page 201)
Ursetvika, Norway (page 270)
Werrong Beach, Australia (page 290)

(Note: if there's one thing that annoys narrow-minded officials more than bare bottoms on a beach, it's wild camping. If there's a clampdown at any of these places, do let us know.)

▲ **American dreams: Valley View Hot Spring. Picture: Michael Cooney**

WHERE YOU CAN BARE

Nude cruising and sailing operators

Bare Necessities Tour & Travel
Tel in US: (800) 443-0405
www.bare-necessities.com

Castaways Travel
Tel in US: (800) 470-2020
www.castawaystravel.com

Go Classy Tours Inc.
Tel in US: (800) 329-8145
www.goclassy.com

Naturist Cruise in Croatia
www.nudecruises.nl

Coral reefs and nearby nude resorts

Grand Lido Braco, Jamaica (page 22)
No Wake Charters, Florida (page 68)
Paya Bay's Lil' Beach, Honduras (p 40)
Playa de las Suecas, Panama (page 40)
Playa Sonrisa, Mexico (page 37)
Praia do Pinho, Brazil (page 44)
Sorobon Beach, Bonaire (page 18)
Sunset Waters, Curaçao (page 19)
Wailea Bay, Hawaii (page 72)

About the authors

Introducing the US and UK organisations that combined to publish a truly international guide

The World's Best Nude Beaches and Resorts is the latest in a long line of publications produced by The Naturist Society LLC, a US membership organisation that promotes nude recreation, and Lifestyle Press, a UK travel publisher.

The Naturist Society LLC is the frontrunner in the promotion of family-friendly nude recreation in North America. Nude swimming, boating, hiking, camping or even naked gardening… TNS promotes all aspects of rich, healthy, naturist living, believing that "Body Acceptance is the Idea, and Nude Recreation is the Way."

In partnership with the Naturist Action Committee, the Naturist Education Foundation, and local skinny-dipping groups across the continent, TNS continues to expand and defend naturist freedoms at beaches, riversides, hot springs and campgrounds. From naked free-range hiking in the wild to a relaxing week at a clothing-optional resort, TNS encourages everyone to experience the freedom of naturism! For more info see www.naturistsociety.com.

Lifestyle Press is a UK-based book publisher that specialises in naturist travel guides. It has produced two titles aimed at a UK audience, Bare Beaches and Bare Britain.

This guide is the first collaborative venture to join the naturist communities of North America and Europe in a single publication. Like naturism itself, we aim to break down international barriers and encourage respect between all those who simply prefer to bathe as nature intended.

Pictures in this book

We have included photographs of as many nude beaches as possible in this book. Although the images accurately portray both the beaches and the mix of visitors who enjoy them, note that all general beach pictures have been carefully edited to ensure no individual is identifiable, other than those who have given explicit permission.

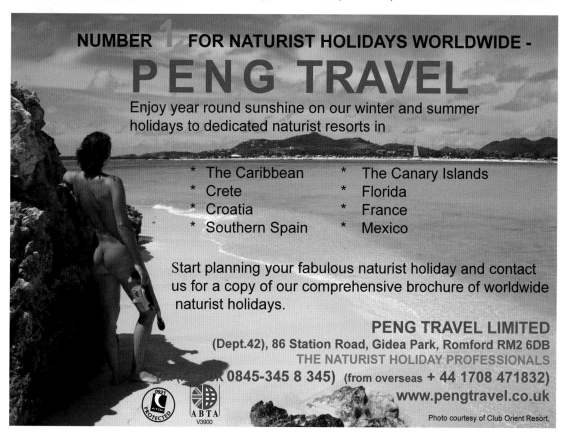

Caribbean and Bahamas

Renowned for their gorgeous tropical shores and glamorous lifestyle, the Caribbean and Bahamas have so many nude beaches it's hard to know where to start. For the pale-skinned, sun-starved denizens of Europe and North America, this part of the world beckons like a paradise. Year-round warmth, palms, white sand, exotic food and drink, and lilting rhythms spell relief from rules, stress and schedules.

Jamaica reigns supreme as having the most opportunities to shuck one's duds. 'No problem,' seems to be the ubiquitous reply to whether one can jump in the warm surf naked. Resorts range from small beachfront properties to mega-destinations with high-octane party atmospheres. Elsewhere in the Caribbean some of the world's best nude beaches invite skin and scuba diving, windsurfing, sailing, island hopping, and the simplest of life's pleasures: just laying out on the sand. Many of the high-end resorts have nude beaches on hand, and we've listed most of the better and more accessible ones in our guide.

Antigua

Hawksbill Hotel nude beach, Hawksbill Bay

A gorgeous hidden bare beach with that wonderful "away from it all" feeling for au naturel sunbathing and great snorkeling. The hotel has no less than four beaches and the bare one is a short walk from the accommodation. You do not need to stay at the hotel to use the beach.

Aruba

Renaissance Aruba, Seaport Village

A 40-acre private island owned by this otherwise textile resort has two beaches.
Practical info
The nude area is at the west end of the island, and the journey from the mainland takes five minutes in the courtesy launch. The modern Dutch hotel is close to the town center.

Bahamas

Eleuthera bare beaches, Eleuthera Island

Two deserted beaches to die for, with soft pink sand and translucent sea, must make this pair high-ranking on any 'world's best' listing – and they are perfect for indulging yourself as nature intended. Add to that just one luxury holiday house on each beach and you know you're on to something special.

Practical info
Aarons Beachhouse, seven miles north of the island capital, Governor's Harbour, is built in a contemporary style and has two bedrooms and two bathrooms, while Sable Rose located near North Palmetto Point sleeps just two people.

▲ On a cruise in the Bahamas, you can pick your own deserted island. Picture by Michael Cooney

Hawksbill Hotel

Tel: +1 268 462 0301
www.hawksbill.com

Renaissance Aruba

Tel: +2978 36000
www.renaissancehotels.com

Aarons Beachhouse and Sable Rose

www.bahamas-beach-rental.com

▼ The average temperature in the Caribbean area changes surprisingly little from one season to the next, which helps encourage visitors out of their clothes all year round. Picture below shows a secluded beach in the Bahamas, picture opposite shows the nude beach on Aruba, by Michael Cooney

The Caribbean

Bonaire

Sorobon Beach Resort

This is a delightful shallow bay protected by a barrier reef, ideal for swimming, snorkeling, sailing and windsurfing. The dazzling white sands are part of the clothing-optional resort, a relaxed haven on this tiny Caribbean island. Sun shelters built from palm trees and gentle trade winds ensure there is always a cool spot in the heat of the day. Wildlife abounds on land, in the air, and underwater. Tour the large island park at the north end of the island to find multiple secluded coves for additional skinny-dipping, or step into the water anywhere for world-class scuba diving.

British Virgin Islands

Havers Villa, south coast of Tortola

Not a beach but somewhere special to relax au naturel or to arrange some clothes-optional sailing. A large private family villa which guests share with the owners. It is located 500 feet above the sea. There is a swimming pool and costumes are optional at all times. The owners, Barry and Roz Rice, operate a yacht charter business and can offer bare cruising.

▲▼ Naturists love Sorobon's relaxed beach and comfortable resort. Pictures top left and right, and below, from Donald Stewart

Sorobon Beach Resort
Tel: +599 717 8080
www.sorobon.com

Havers Villa
Tel: +1 284 494 3656
www.endlesssummer.com

US Virgin Islands

Flamboyance Yacht Charters, St Thomas

Little beats spending days on end naked under the sun, in crystal clear water, or relaxing on isolated beaches found only by boat. Add luxury dining to the mix, and a private nude vacation orchestrated by naturists experienced at sea may be more than you could have dreamed of.

Curaçao

Sunset Waters Beach Resort

A private area of the beach at this all-inclusive textile resort is reserved for au naturel bathing. Sparkling clear sea makes swimming, snorkeling, and diving particularly popular.
Practical info
The resort is on the north-west coast of the island, 25 miles from the airport.

▲ Warm seas as nature intended. Top pic Charlie Simonds, above Donald Stewart, above right Cayo Largo pic from www.cayolargo.net

Flamboyance Yacht Charters

www.boatinthebuff.com

Sunset Waters Beach Resort

Tel: +5999 864 1233
www.sunsetwaters.com

Cayo Largo Holidays

Tel: +537 204 6366
www.grancaribe.cu
www.cayolargodelsur.cu
www.captivating-holidays.com/cuba

Cuba

Cayo Largo beaches, Los Canarreos islands

Here you will find all the ingredients of a tropical garden of Eden – great expanses of white sand as fine as talcum powder, warm clear turquoise sea, and almost permanent sunshine. Just 25 miles long, the island has lots of completely undeveloped beaches. Bare bathing, which has a long tradition here, is widely practised and accepted, if not immediately in front of the beachside hotels. There is a cluster of all-inclusive properties forming the Gran Caribe Resort. A favorite with cabana style rooms, close to a pleasant nude beach, is Hotel Villa Lindamar.
Practical info
A Canadian couple have developed an excellent website about the island and its au naturel opportunities at www.cayolargo.net

The Caribbean

Dominican Republic

Eden Bay

Tel: +1 809 589 7750
www.edenbay.com

Eden Bay, Playa Grande, Abreu, Cabrera

A dedicated all-inclusive nude resort set on the edge of the Caribbean. A beautiful natural bay with the Atlantic Ocean lapping on the bare beach is just a few steps from a large bar, two swimming pools, and spa. There is a restaurant and third larger pool with swim-up bar up the hill. White sand, palm trees and lush vegetation all conspire to make this tropical holiday resort a must for all-over tan enthusiasts.

Guadeloupe

Plage Tarare, Grande Terre

Eight kilometers east of Saint-François on the north shore of Pointe-des-Châteaux, at the eastern tip of Grande-Terre, is Pointe Tarare, site of the first legally designated nude beach in the western hemisphere.

The picturesque Plage Tarare often has wild surf breaking on its protective reef, but has firm sand for wading. Palms provide shade from the sun. On weekdays there are few people on the beach but they are often clothed. At weekends the beach is more commonly nude with 50 or 60 users.

You also may climb the bluff of Plage Tarare to enjoy a great view down to the Pointe-des-Châteaux, itself a mandatory visit.

Practical info
Drive east from Grande Anse to La Plage de Clugny, identified by a sign on the road. Then turn around and drive back uphill to the west. Part way up the hill is an indistinct turnoff on the right. Drive along this dirt track, park, and walk the trail downhill to the left to the beach.

Don't want to get dressed after spending the day at Plage Tarare? Two small naturist resorts are located in the hills nearby and offer bungalows for two to four people: Eden Nat and Résidence Club Caraïbes.

Eden Nat

Tel: +590 83 45 71
www.eden-nat.com

Residence Club Caraïbes

Tel: +33 6 90 44 11 54
www.caraibesnat.fr.fm

Jamaica

Grand Lido Negril, Bloody Bay, Negril

An ultra modern resort with a country club feel, Grand Lido Negril has eight restaurants and fine accommodation. The rooms offer a sunken living area and double doors to either a deck or directly to the lawn and beach.

The resort has a huge beachfront with fine sand and multiple water sports. A delightfully secluded white sand cove at this all-inclusive resort is reserved for bare bathers. Another beach is available for those who prefer to wear clothes to go swimming. And it's the same for the two pools – one with swimsuits and one without. The club is operated by SuperClubs (see page 22 for all SuperClubs contact details), and a recent winner of the Conde Nast readers' choice 'Best Resort' award.

▲ Whether you're underwater in the reefs or exploring the tropical landscape, there's no hiding the natural beauty of the Caribbean's wildlife. Picture by Rod Burkey
▥ Opposite top: the unspoilt sands of Aruba: snorkeling and diving are superb all around the Caribbean. Picture by Michael Cooney
▥ Opposite bottom: Riding the waves, at Eden Bay, Dominican Republic. Picture by Michael Cooney

All SuperClubs resorts

Tel: +44 20 8290 3600 (UK)
Tel: +1 800 330 8272 (US)
www.super-clubs.com

▲ It may be popular but the Caribbean still has dozens of quiet beaches suitable for nude bathing. Bottom picture Kevin & Debbie Rudd ▼ Grand Lido Braco would keep any nude beach lover happy for days on end. Picture by Michael Cooney

Hedonism II, Bloody Bay, Negril

Two lovely tropical beaches at this SuperClubs all-inclusive resort, one for nudes and the other for 'prudes'. There is also a spa pool for bare bathers. You can even take a nude cruise on the resort's yacht. This resort and its sister, Hedonism III, have a reputation for an adult orientation and are popular with swinging couples. However, it's not that over the top, especially in public, and many other holidaymakers simply enjoy the lively party atmosphere.

Hedonism III, Runaway Bay

A moderately sized nude beach on a walled lagoon with gleaming white sand and turquoise sea is just waiting for buff bathers at this all-inclusive adult resort. There is a better beach at the resort, but it's for those who prefer to wear a bathing suit. Hedonism is designed for party-spirited "social interaction" but is still enjoyed by many naturists.

Grand Lido Braco, Trelawny Bay

Grand Lido Braco is considered by many to be the best nude recreation facility in the Caribbean. Nearly half the resort has been designed for relaxation in the buff, including a beautiful reef-protected nude beach. Accommodations, a swimming pool, two spa pools, a bar and a clubhouse diner open 24 hours are available on the bare side. The enormous nude pool is the biggest for skinny-dipping in the Caribbean. The whole resort is styled like a traditional Jamaican village. This site is operated by SuperClubs.

Breezes Golf and Beach Resort, Runaway Bay

Two beautiful soft sand beaches, gleaming white in the sun – the small one is clothing-optional but encroached upon by textiles on all sides. A nude spa pool sits by the bare beach at this SuperClubs resort.

▲ All-over bliss at Grand Lido Braco. Top picture by Kevin and Debbie Rudd. Bottom picture by Michael Cooney

Sans Souci Resort and Spa, Ocho Rios

A lovely clothes-optional beach where nude and clothed bathers can relax on tropical white sand. It's within an all-inclusive Mediterranean-style resort. This hillside botanical garden offers romantic views over several blue water bays. Walking around this cliff side property is a treat.

Practical info

The au naturel facilities are separate from the main lodging, where clothing is required, but can be accessed via a short walk down the lush tropical path to a bay where the White River flows into the sea. The nude area has a freshwater swimming pool with swim-up bar and waterfall grotto. A hot tub is available on the deck along with showers and a snack bar providing lunch and drinks throughout the day.

Sans Souci Resort and Spa

Tel: +1 876 994 1206 / 1353
www.sanssoucijamaica.com

Couples Tower Island

Tel: +1 888 403 2822
www.couplesochorios.com

Couples

Tel: +1 876 957 5960
www.couplesnegril.com

Couples Tower Island, Ocho Rios

A well-known bare island, which is featured in the Travel Channel's list of top nude beaches worldwide. In this guide there's too much competition to award that accolade, but it is indeed a wonderful spot. There is a pool with swim-up bar, double hammocks for romantics, and lots of loungers. The island is owned by the hotel and is 200 yards offshore, with plenty of seclusion for all-over tanning. The resort's courtesy launch ferries you on request.

Couples, Negril

On one side of this lovely destination is a super tropical nude beach for relaxing and swimming in aquamarine sea. The all-inclusive luxury resort is relatively new, but has already won a major award for the quality of its facilities and service, among them of course the choice to sunbathe and swim naked.

▼ Some of the world's most highly rated nude facilities are located on Jamaica, including Couples, below, and opposite page at the bottom, and Sans Souci, opposite top. All pictures by Michael Cooney

Sunset Beach Resort and Spa, Montego Bay

A private bare cove is one of three beaches at this big holiday center; the other two are for swimsuit wearers. This is a good value, all-inclusive 420-room high-rise resort, which has recently been refurbished. Rooms at the Beach Inn are the closest to the nudist area.

Decameron Club Caribbean, Runaway Bay

A clothing-optional area has been set-aside for true sun lovers on the pretty white sand beach at this popular all-inclusive holiday resort.

Starfish Trelawny Resort, near Montego Bay

There is a clothes-optional beach at this moderately priced all-inclusive family-style resort (owned by SuperClubs). The bare beach here is for adults only.

Point Village Resort, Bloody Bay, Negril

There is a secluded nude cove at this all-inclusive condominium complex (room-only accommodation also available). It lies between Hedonism II and SuperClub's Grand Lido, but under separate management.

Carib Beach Apartments, Rutland Point, Negril

A sandy cove is available for nude sunbathing at this small group of apartments, next to Point Village Resort. The apartments are set in pretty subtropical gardens on the beachfront.

Sunset Beach Resort and Spa

Tel: +1 800 330 8272
www.sunsetbeachjamaica.com

Decameron Club Caribbean

Tel: +1 876 973 4802
www.decameron.com

Starfish Trelawny Resort

Tel: +1 876 954 2450 or
+1 800 659 5436
www.starfishresorts.com

Point Village Resort

Tel: +1 876 957 5170
www.pointvillage.com

Carib Beach Apartments

Tel: +1 876 957 4358
www.jamaicalink.com/carib/

▼ If you feel life's getting a bit dull, a couple of minutes on a Jamaican nude beach will soon snap you out of it. Picture by Michael Cooney

Firefly Cottages, Negril

This lovely clothes-optional beach is open to the public and is directly in front of the family-run holiday cottage resort, which has 20 air-conditioned rooms. To quote from the website: "Whether you call it au naturel, skinny dipping, topfree, nude or naturist, you can enjoy it here quietly on the beach, in the Jacuzzi or veranda, but best of all in the Caribbean Sea. We don't make a big thing out of being privileged to offer you a clothes-optional beach."

On the same bare beach, next door to Firefly, Secret Cabins offers bargain low-price rooms for the budget traveler. Access to some of the Firefly facilities is available.

> **Firefly Cottages**
> Tel: +1 876 957 4358
> www.jamaicalink.com
>
> **Secret Cabins**
> Tel: +1 876 957 9325 or
> +1 876 957 4358
> www.jamaicalink.com/secrets

▲ Naturist sailing trip off St Martin. Picture by Donald Stewart

Drumville Cove, Negril

There is no nude beach here, but there is at least a secluded nude lounging area on the cliffs above the sea, at this cozy all-inclusive resort.

Home Sweet Home, Negril

Clothes-optional sunbathing is available on terraces built in the cliffs, with chairs and sunbeds provided. A serviced seaside resort where all 14 rooms have private verandas overlooking the Caribbean. Two accommodation units have large private balconies suitable for nude sunning, available on request.

> **Drumville Cove**
> Tel: +1 876 957 4369
> www.negril.com/dcmain.htm
>
> **Home Sweet Home**
> Tel: +1 876 957 4478
> www.homesweethomeresort.net
>
> **Catcha Falling Star Resort**
> www.catchajamaica.com

Catcha Falling Star Resort, Negril

A private cove for naturist bathing has been set aside at this laid-back 3-star resort. There are several villas and private suites available.

Puerto Rico

Palomino Island, Fajardo, Las Croabas

This private offshore island is owned by the El Conquistador Resort and has a clothes-optional area on the far side. The hotel operates a water taxi service.

> **El Conquistador Resort**
> Tel: +1 787 863 1000
> www.elconresort.com

St Barthelemy

Gouverneur Beach, south coast

Anse du Gouverneur attracts some nude bathers. Secluded and beautiful, this beach has a sharp drop-off near the shore. It can be very wind-blown. It is reached by 10 minutes of driving a very steep, winding road beginning in the back street of Gustavia via Lurin. A regular vacationer to St Barths says the biggest change regarding nudity is that the local residents who strip off here now outnumber the tourists.

▲ St Barthelemy's beaches attract a number of nudists, both from overseas and living locally

▲ Saline Beach, St Barthelemy, has a long tradition of nude use and is just minutes from the airport

▲ Cupecoy Beach on St Martin

Saline Beach, south coast

Anse de Grande Saline is a delightful and safe beach, only a 10-minute drive from Gustavia and the airport. The turnoff is near the far (east) end of St Jean Bay. Every cab driver knows the way. Well accepted as a nude haven, its long crescent is never crowded. The bodysurfing can be great. There is now a pleasant cafe and snack bar on the trail to the beach.

St Martin/Sint Maarten

Cupecoy Beach, on the Dutch west coast

Backed by low sandstone cliffs, the secluded string of beaches known as Cupecoy Beach is almost always nude, especially at the western end. Cupecoy Bay is on the Dutch western coast of the far-flung west peninsula of Sint Maarten, known by locals as the lowlands or terres basses. Cupecoy is a mile west of Sheraton's huge Mullet Bay Hotel. Sand comes and goes with the season, so there may be room for hundreds or only dozens. Peaceful, beautiful, and no hassles.

Practical info

Park near the blue and white 'Cupecoy Beach' sign about 200 meters from the French border. Follow the well-worn path through the wall to the beach.

Baie Rouge Beach, on the French west coast

At Pointe du Bluff, Red Bay is a great beach for those staying in Marigot: They drive five minutes west instead of 25 minutes to Orient Bay. Breathtaking rock formations, lively beach scene. Ample parking. Bar and snacks.

Practical info

Starting westward from Philipsburg on the circle road, at 4km beyond the French border – between la Samanna and the PLM St Tropez Beach hotels – find the sign for Baie Rouge. Turn left and follow the dirt road to parking. The beach area to the right (east) is topfree; while the *plage naturiste* itself is 100 yards to the left (west).

Orient Bay, on the French north-east coast

This breathtaking mile-long sweep of white sand lapped by an aquamarine and turquoise sea is famed for its nudist credentials. White sand, clear water, and three uninhabited islands in close vicinity make Orient Bay the ideal tropical setting for a most relaxing naturist family vacation paradise. Club Orient naturist resort is right on the beach at the southern end of the bay and has been accommodating sunseekers for over 20 years – and it's now more popular than ever.

The resort offers 137 spacious oceanfront or garden units, which accommodate 3-7 persons each. Every unit is equipped with full kitchen, dining area, air conditioning, phone and internet service, a safe for your valuables, full bathroom with tub or shower, picnic table, beach chairs, front and back patio, an outdoor shower and a specially chosen bottle of Bordeaux wine, compliments of the resort.

You'll never have to get dressed to leave the site, as Club Orient has

thought of everything for you: a fully stocked grocery store, boutique, two tennis courts, a water sports facility, a spa and wellness center, Papagayo Restaurant with daily happy hour, live entertainment, and a weekly manager's cocktail party.

As other developments have sprung up in this lovely area, only the generous section of sand in front of the resort is fully nude throughout the day. However, first thing in the morning, residents and early birds often start the day by enjoying a naked stroll from one end of the bay to the other. Braver souls find "no problem" the usual response when they ask beach entrepreneurs if they can go parasailing naked over the bay.

Lots of water sports, bars and restaurants are available all the way along the beach. It gets very busy when guests from cruise ships calling at St Martin make a beeline for Orient Bay. If it gets a bit hectic, take a picnic and discover the tranquility of the nearby uninhabited and clothing-optional Tintamarre Island by sailing

▲▼ Beautiful nude beaches and the naturist resort of Club Orient make St Martin a top destination. Picture top left Michael Cooney; top right Ross Stevenson; bottom left Rod Burkey; below Michael Cooney

Orient Bay accommodation
Full details are listed overleaf.

La Villa

Restaurant • Two Bars • Spa • Tennis • Watersports • Boutique • Beach Chairs • Umbrellas

Leave it all behind

The Caribbean

Club Orient

Your Natural Choice!

1-800-690-0199
www.cluborient.com

Tel ++(590) 590 87 33 85
Fax ++(590) 590 87 33 76
clubo@cluborient.com
1 Baie Orientale
97150 St. Martin, FWI

Escape to a paradise with white sand shores and crystal clear waters. Enjoy the serenity of our Island and the freedom of our naturist resort, where clothing is optional throughout the entire property.

Accommodations provide a blend of traditional Caribbean simplicity and European luxury. We offer 137 spacious ocean front or garden units accommodating 3 to 7 persons each. Each is equipped with a full kitchen, dining area, air-conditioning, phone and internet service, full bathroom with tub or shower, picnic table, beach chairs, front and back patio and an outdoor shower.

naked – and thoroughly escape from the 21st century.

In the hills overlooking Orient Bay, and well within walking distance of the clothing-optional Orient Beach is Club Fantastico, a new naturist resort with swimming pool, large Jacuzzi, two bars and a restaurant.

There are a number of other places to stay in the Orient Bay area. The intimate 3-star Hotel L'Hoste is on the beach not far from the bare area. The hotel is not naturist but has a relaxed approach to clothes-optional dress in the grounds and by the pool.

Green Cay Village has 16 luxury villas overlooking the beach. It is five minutes' drive to the nude section, but several of the villas with pools

have sufficient privacy for bare sunning and swimming.

Hotel La Plantation has 17 villas set in five acres of tropical gardens on Orient Bay. Its Coco restaurant on the beach has lounge chairs for clothes-optional sunbathing and the main bare beach is one kilometer further along the shore.

A very short drive south of Orient Bay, Caribbean Nature by Oyster Pond Lagoon and Marina is an informal naturist property. Accommodation is in garden bungalows around a swimming pool. The site is French owned and operated. Fine views over the bay and marina. The nearest clothed beach and shops are 150 meters.

▲ **Exploring around the island, left, and two naturists take an early morning stroll the full length of Orient Bay. Picture on left by Paul Carlson, picture on right Rod Burkey**

Club Orient

1 Baie Orientale
Saint Martin, French West Indies
Tel: 800 690 0199 (toll free from US)
Tel: +590 87 33 85
www.cluborient.com

Club Fantastico

96 Baie Orientale
Saint Martin, French West Indies
Tel: +590 87 69 82
Tel: 973 575 1706 (from US)
www.clubfantastico.net

Hotel L'Hoste

Tel: +590 87 42 08
www.hostehotel.com

Green Cay Village

Tel: +590 29 48 72
www.greencay.com

Hotel La Plantation

Tel: +590 29 58 00
www.la-plantation.com

Caribbean Nature

membres.lycos.fr/naturissimo/
membres.lycos.fr/legalion/

St Vincent

Petit St Vincent Island, south of St Vincent

A beautiful "Robinson Crusoe" island, two-thirds of which is beach. The owners say about nude sunbathing: "While we are not a clothing-optional resort, the privacy on the patio of the cottages would allow this, and the

staff can provide directions to suitable areas of beach." This is an exclusive private estate with 22 luxury cottages on the tiny 113-acre tropical islet. This little island is 40 miles south of St Vincent.

Hope Bay, Bequia Island, south of St Vincent

The archetypal deserted tropical beach, palm trees swaying in the breeze and white sand gleaming in the Caribbean sun. The beach is a little off the beaten track and requires a pleasant walk along the coastal path to get there. You will probably have the bay to yourself and can then enjoy the freedom of relaxing au naturel. Bequia Island is

9 miles south of St Vincent.

The nearest place to stay is the Old Fort, a laid-back hilltop country inn which was formerly a plantation house dating back to the early 1700s. It has six suites, a swimming pool and fabulous views all set in 30 acres of lush gardens and just 25-30 minutes' walk from Hope Bay.

Petit St Vincent Island

Tel: +1 513 242 1333
www.psvresort.com

Old Fort

Tel: +1 784 458 3440
www.oldfortbequia.com

Latin America & Mexico

Mexico has discovered that people from around the world want to enjoy the country's crystal clear waters, magnificent beaches, and amazing cuisine... and many want to do so naked. Resorts along Mexico's 'Riviera' on the Quintana Roo coastline south of Cancun are beginning to open and advertise clothing-optional beaches.

Naturism in Central America has yet to take off, although a small selection of beaches are tacitly recognized as places that international visitors can go for sunbathing and skinny-dipping.

Brazil tops the charts in South America when it comes to developing naturist vacation opportunities. Nearly a dozen nude beaches string the coastline like jewels. Clubs range from small and primitive to fully developed vacation destinations. Note that many Brazilian beaches and resorts discourage or even bar single men – and rather than the 'clothing-optional' approach, nudity is often obligatory or expected.

Mexico

1. Soliman Bay
2. Playa Sonrisa
3. Punta Serena
4. Playa Zipolite
5. Kantenah Bay

Playa Sonrisa

Tel: +1 983 838 1872 (US number for reservations)
www.playasonrisa.com

■ Fashion on the beaches of South America is turning to the nude look. Picture opposite shows Brazil's new naturist beach in Rio de Janeiro, taken by Jorge Barreto of www.abrico.com.br
▼ Enjoying a secluded beach the Mexican way, at clothing-optional Villa Dolce Vita on Soliman Bay. Picture by Michael Cooney

Villa Dolce Vita, Soliman Bay, Quintana Roo

A luxury beachfront villa that is naturist-friendly. The only B&B in the area, Villa Dolce Vita offers two bedrooms, each with a private bath, in a separate casita located directly on the beach. The beachfront pool is private and ocean kayaks are available. The beach is secluded enough for nude sunbathing and skinny-dipping, so you can return home with a full tropical tan.

Villa Dolce Vita

Tel: +52 984 128 5283
www.villadolcevita.com

Playa Sonrisa, Xcalak, Quintana Roo

A small naturist seaside resort far from anything, except quiet, good food, and some of Mexico's best skin and scuba diving. Fishing and kayaking can keep you at the water, or you can just relax in a hammock.

Punta Serena Villas and Spa, Jalisco

Overlooking the beautiful Tenacatita Bay is a small adults-only, all-inclusive resort where clothing is optional at the swimming pool, in the two hot tubs and on the beach. The private 400m long beach is accessible only by the hotel and sea, with most guests going nude. Lodging includes two- or three-bedroom villas or spacious rooms. Only 45 minutes from Manzanillo.

Punta Serena Villas & Spa

www.puntaserena.com

Playa Zipolite, Zipolite, Oaxaca

The only public beach in Mexico where the town's mayor and local business leaders will be happy to see you nude. Hand painted signs around this small village point visitors to the nude beach – and the whole beach is indeed clothing-optional. There's not much else driving the local economy here, so locals know that Mexican and international visitors wanting to walk a mile of sandy beach naked will keep everyone happy.

Room reservations are difficult to obtain ahead of time, it seems no one has a phone, and even getting to this coastal village can be a challenge. Just show up sometime other than Easter or Christmas and you'll find a low-price, ultra-rustic room within a few yards of a great beach with dangerous surf. Come to Oaxaca to taste the real Mexico; head to Quintana Roo and its coastal resorts if you want upscale amenities.

Other nudist beaches in Mexico

There are many other informal places to stay on Mexico's Caribbean coast where nude bathing is possible. All the resorts and accommodations listed here are handy for naked sunseekers. Clothing-optional lodging is still rare in Mexico, but along the Mayan Gold Coast, near Tulum, it's not difficult to find your place fully in the sun.

For instance, Azulik Villas, Cabañas Copal, and Papaya Playa Resort are each small textile holistic resorts near

Tulum with access to the same coastline, one small part of which is clothing-optional.

Azulik Villas
www.azulik.com

Cabañas Copal Hotel
www.cabanascopal.com

Papaya Playa Resort
www.papayaplaya.com

▲ Top: the Mayan Gold Coast has plenty of places suitable for nude bathing; picture by Michael Cooney. Above and opposite: Playa Zipolite, Mexico's only public beach where nude bathing is actively welcomed. Pictures by Mark Storey

Latin America

■ Enjoying a prime location on Mexico's Caribbean coast, Hidden Beach Resort is a modern, luxury development where you can wander at will without ever needing to dress. Pictures of the resort opposite by Michael Cooney

Hidden Beach Resort, Kantenah Bay

Mexico's only luxury, all-inclusive naturist resort for adults only is situated on Kantenah Bay, Quintana Roo. With its own stretch of white sandy beach, it boasts 42 beachfront suites overlooking the Caribbean. There is an artificial river flowing through the resort grounds into and beyond a huge swimming pool. This resort is where you go in Mexico when you want to effortlessly say 'yes' to everything.

Hidden Beach Resort

Tel: +1 888 754 3907 (US number)
www.hiddenbeachresort.com

COSTA RICA

• San Jose

Playita

▼ Costa Rica's Pacific coast has a lovely clothing-optional cove at Playita, backed by trees and with pretty views over neighbouring islands. Picture by Michael Cooney

Costa Rica

Playita, Manuel Antonio National Park

On the Pacific coast, 130km south from San Jose and on the south-eastern outskirts of Quepos, is the 683-hectare Manuel Antonio National Park and its clothes-optional beach Playita (Little Beach). It's an amazing jungle coast with army ants, sloths, monkeys, and astounding flora.

Playita is 500 yards of calm warm water in a half-moon cove, with clean white sand shaded by palm trees.
Practical info
Drive into the park at the first entrance past the Hotel Karahe. Proceed to the two-kilometer-long Playa Espadilla, the main beach, where you will walk north-west, wade a small estuary, cross a small cove then clamber over a rock barrier at its north end to the smaller but equally beautiful Playita. Plan your time: there is no access in or out of Playita at high tide!

On the southern end of Playa Espadilla there's a Bar del Mar with drinks, snacks, snorkel and flippers, lounge chair and umbrella rental.

Honduras

Paya Bay

HONDURAS

Paya Bay's Lil' Beach, Roátan, Bay Islands

There are two lovely beaches at the textile Paya Bay Resort, the smaller of which is open for bare bathing and awesome snorkeling. According to the management: "It is clothes-optional for the use of our guests, very secluded, and private."

The resort's dive center can take you by skiff to the world's second longest barrier reef, just 500m offshore – an obvious choice for divers. Paya Bay has attractive cabins overlooking the Caribbean, and offers all-inclusive meal plans.

Paya Bay Resort

Tel: +504 435 2139 or
+1 936 628 2204 (US office)
Fax: +504 435 2149 or
+1 936 628 6081 (US office)
www.payabay.com

Panama

Panama City

PANAMA

Playa de las Suecas

Playa de las Suecas, Contadora Island

Non-naturist Contadora Island Resort is on the 11th largest of the Pearl Islands off the Panama Pacific Coast. It is accessible by a 16-minute plane ride from Panama City and offers an all-inclusive package, passable international cuisine, pool with swim-up bar, golf and tennis courts, and a small casino. It's not the fanciest hotel, but the diving is good and Panama's only public nude beach is nearby.

Practical info

From the right end of the main beach, a path leads through a wooded area up a small hill for about five minutes to a lovely white-sand beach used topfree. Just past this area and over some rocks (impassible at high tide) is Playa de las Suecas (Swedish Beach), accepted for nude use. It's about 400 meters long, pleasant, clean, and great for skin diving at low tide.

The best time to visit is from mid-December through to mid-April. The beach is particularly popular with Canadians and Germans.

Contadora Island Resort

www.hotelcontadora.com

▼ **Chilling out the natural way in Panama. Picture by Michael Cooney**

▲ The nude cove of Paya Bay's Lil'
Beach in Honduras. The resort is
500m from a huge coral reef, with
superb snorkeling just offshore.
Pictures by Mark Storey

Argentina

ARGENTINA

Buenos Aires •

Mar del Plata •

Playa Escondida

Playa Escondida, Buenos Aires

'Hidden Beach' is the first and only naturist beach in Argentina. Established as clothing-optional in 2000 by the local municipality, due in large part to the urging of local naturists, this public beach has a rustic atmosphere coupled with services provided by two naturist cousins who maintain the beach. They offer basic food and drink, showers, massage, and a small boutique. The beach stretches for 200m, and is set amid cliffs, dunes and open grasslands. Escondida is popular with naturists wanting escape from Buenos Aires to the north, and from Brazilian and Uruguayan vacationers seeking international fun in the sun.

Practical info

Playa Escondida is 25km south of Mar del Plata on Route 11, and about 2.5km south of the hotel complex of Chapadmalal. A road sign lets you know you are there.

Eden, Buenos Aires

An hour from the city of Buenos Aires is Eden, a small family-friendly naturist club open to folks with a clothes-free state of mind. They offer simple weekend lodging, a pool, garden, and restaurant.

Yatan Rumi, Córdoba

'Naked Rock' is a rustic naturist club, high in the mountains, and sitting amidst 1,200 hectares of wildlife, farmland, waterfalls, and rivers. Don't look here for posh amenities, but if you like the idea of hiking nude for kilometers, sliding naked down granite waterfall shoots, or skinny-dipping the day away, drive the rough road here for a rugged experience of a lifetime.

Eden

www.eden.org.ar

Yatan Rumi

www.yatanrumi.com.ar/web/home.htm

41

Brazil

Praia Tambaba, Paraíba

Conde had a naturist prefect called Aluisio Régis who designated Tambaba as the first Paraíba state official nude beach. The beach has been described as one of the 10 most beautiful on Brazil's Atlantic coast.
Practical info
Conde city lies 98km north of Recife or 118km south of Natal, in the north-east of the country. The city is on the Brazilian highway BR-101. The nude beach extends for 15km south from Jacumã. Men are not allowed on Tambaba beach unless accompanied by a woman. For more information see www.tambaba.com.br.

Massarandupió Beach, Bahia

A long, open and clothes-free beach near Salvador with kiosks selling food and drink. Mandatory nudity at Massarandupió helps deter gawkers and entices naturist families to stay for the day or longer.

Barra Seca Beach, Espírito Santo

This is a pristine official naturist beach near Linhares, on the coastal road halfway between São Paulo and Bahia. For more information see www.sampanat.com.br/barraseca/barraseca.htm.

Rama Nat, Minas Gerais

More a resort than a club, Rama Nat caters to those wanting beautifully manicured surroundings, an atmosphere ready for a party, and drinks served poolside with a smile. Popular with naturists wishing to leave the hubbub of São Paulo, two hours away. See www.ramanat.com.br

Praia do Olho de Boi, Rio de Janeiro

Just 125 miles north-east from Rio de Janeiro, Búzios – the fishing village that became an international symbol of chic – once had local nude beaches. Now, like St Tropez, Búzios' nude beaches have shifted to more acknowledged and durable locations, where no one need claim that they are offended.
Practical info
Drive north from Búzios on the Estrada de Usina to Ponta Olho de Boi. The semi-sheltered ocean beach here is officially clothes-optional. See www.buziosturismo.com/mapas/ab.html.

Praia Brava, Rio de Janeiro

Praia Brava, 'wild beach', is closer to the city of Rio than Búzios and is reached by the same highway.
Practical info
From Rio, Praia Brava is 191km or a 2.5 hour drive to Cabo Frio. From the center of Cabo Frio, drive north 6km. Cross the bridge over a canal at Itajuro and guide yourself oceanward, toward the vicinity of Praia de Peró along a badly marked dirt road. Your next landmark will be the Canal das Ostras on your right as you drive on Avenue do Espadarte to Porto Veliero. Encountering the inlet, angle left along it until opposite Japanese Island. You'll have passed the windmills of a saline (salt evaporation yard) on your left. Park and walk the final 300 yards. The fine beach here is free of pollution and open to the sea. For more information see the website br.groups.yahoo.com/group/natlagos/.

While in the area visit Racanto Paraíso, a naturist club with pool and small fishing lake (see box on right).

1. Praia Tambaba
2. Massarandupió Beach
3. Barra Seca Beach
4. Praia do Olho de Boi
5. Praia Brava
6. Abricó Beach
7. Praia do Pinho
8. Praia da Galheta
9. Pedras Altas

Racanto Paraíso
www.paraisonaturista.com.br

▲ A true community of naturist regulars has grown up around Abricó Beach in Rio since it gained official nude status in 2004. The beach users have set up a website at www.anabrico.com. Pictures on this page and opposite by Jorge Barreto of www.abrico.com.br

Abricó Beach, Rio de Janeiro

A gorgeous, secluded white sand bare beach on the outskirts of this exciting city. After many requests from locals, the authorities recently agreed to grant official nude status to this idyllic little bay, which has an unspoiled backdrop of natural green vegetation.

As an alternative to the sand, smooth rocks at the side of the beach provide a sunbathing platform just above the ocean. There is already a thriving beach community and the local support group – Associação Naturista de Abricó – continues to work with officials to keep Abricó a Brazilian centerpiece for naturism. See the beach group's website at www.anabrico.com.

Latin America

▲ The happy face of Brazilian naturism. Pictures by Jorge Barreto of www.abrico.com.br

Mirante do Paraíso, São Paulo

This is an excellent resort sitting in a stunning location – at the top of a hill beside a winding river valley, 50 miles from the state capital. The swimming pool, with its view overlooking the river, is incredible.

Rincão Naturista, São Paulo

This naturist club is set in a simple, farm-like atmosphere near the town of Cunha, to the east of the capital. Rincao Naturista will give international travelers a true taste of local Brazilian club naturism.

Mirante do Paraíso
www.mirantedoparaiso.com.br

Rincão Naturista
www.rincao.com.br

Colina do Sol
www.colinadosol.com.br

Praia do Pinho, Santa Catarina

Brazil's most famous – and first officially sanctioned – naturist beach ranks near the top of the world's best nude beaches. You can even stay here: the Praia do Pinho beachside complex provides a choice of lodging, from campsites to individual bungalows. Clean sand, great snorkeling and lusciously green surroundings make 'Pine Beach' an international favorite.
Practical info
From Florianópolis, take a bus or rental car for 70km north almost to Camboriú. Turn off coastal route 101 at kilometer marker 140. Go 8km to the beach on a dirt road. More info at www.praiadopinho.com.br.

Praia da Galheta, Ilha de Santa Catarina

On Ilha de Santa Catarina, 30km east of Florianópolis, Praia da Galheta nude beach lies to the south of Barra da Lagoa town. The town and beach are near Lagoa da Conceição lagoon.
Practical info
The beach is reached by a trail through the rocks which starts at the bridge at the north end of Praia Mole. For more information see www.galheta.cjb.net.

Pedras Altas, Santa Catarina

Official small nude beach on highway BR-101, 30km south of Florianópolis in Palhoça county. Calm, clear water, with rustic motel, bar and restaurant. For more information check out www.pedrasaltas-naturismo.com.br.

Colina do Sol, Rio Grande do Sul

More than a resort, Colina do Sol is a naturist town resting on a small hill in the Southern Mountains, about 50km from Porto Alegre International Airport. The entire site is either clothing-optional or nudity-required. A large lake for swimming, nature trails, several pools and full service amenities make this a destination of choice for many international travelers.

▲ Off for a swim, by Michael Cooney

Chile

Playa Luna, Valparaiso

Chile's only officially sanctioned nude beach requires a 20-minute walk 6km from Horcón Creek in the town of Puchuncaví, but its 500 meters of open sand and its attraction to scores of naturists on sunny weekends make it South America's best Pacific Coast clothes-free site. The beauty of this coastal region regularly draws visitors from Santiago: the beach is about 150km away, to the north-west of the city.

Uruguay

Playa Chihuahua, Punta del Este

Playa Chihuahua is a broad white sand playground on the Atlantic Ocean in Portezuelo, backed by woods, and accepted for full nudity. Even though the town of Punta del Este is only 40 minutes by air from Argentina, the vast majority of the users are nonetheless Uruguayan or Brazilian. Rare on naturist beaches, this one has lifeguards and a restaurant. Punta del Este is an international resort and hotel guests often go topfree.
Practical info
At kilometer 124 on the Montevideo-Punta del Este highway, turn on a dirt road towards the ocean. Park, and wade the lagoon to the beach. Or exit at marker 125, park at hotel Cabaña del Tío Tom, and walk back along the beach to the clothing-optional zone. See playachihuahua.com.

The USA

The US has delights for every naturist traveler, from rustic nudist campgrounds appealing to families on a budget, to upscale resorts with fine dining and dancing. Or set off into the continent's pristine wilderness areas to find isolated shores of alpine lakes and trails, particularly in places such as California, Colorado, Nevada and Utah. There are also many hot springs around the country – ideal relaxation after a day of 'free range' hiking (see pages 102-103).

The choice by the sea is just as huge: nude bathers can pick from remote stretches of sand in the west, tropical and subtropical bays in the south, and urban seascapes that attract thousands of skinny-dippers each weekend. All the beaches listed here are well-established as clothing-optional, and without known legal hassle at the time of publication. But remember that local situations and laws do change: the Naturist Action Committee (www.naturistaction.org) has up-to-date information on all the areas covered in this guide.

The USA

El Dorado Hot Springs

PO Box 39
Tonopah, AZ 85354
Tel: 623 386 5412
www.el-dorado.com

Other Arizona naturist contacts

Shangri La Ranch
44444 N. Shangri La Lane
New River, AZ 85087
www.shangrilaranch.com

Arizona Wildflowers
PO Box 26465
Phoenix, AZ 85068
www.azwildflower.com

Canyon State Naturists
PO Box 54756
Phoenix, AZ 85078
www.canyonstatenaturists.org

US phone numbers

All phone numbers in the US section
are correct for dialing within the States.
If dialing from abroad remember to add
the US international dialing code +1

Arizona

El Dorado Hot Springs, Tonopah

El Dorado has clothes-free soaking
hot pools and rustic RV/tent camping
on 6.7 acres of desert with mountain
views. Biking, hiking, and petroglyph
and wildlife viewing nearby.
Practical info
The springs are only 40 miles west of
Phoenix, on I-10.

Mira Vista Resort, Tucson

The Butterfield stagecoach stopped
here in the 1850s; now its owners
hope to make it one of the premier
US naturist resorts. The lodging
retains a feel of the old Wild West,
with its western-style furniture,
architecture and landscaping. Views
of the Tucson and Santa Catalina
mountains delight poolside visitors;
desert walks into the Saguaro
National Park enchant those wishing
to see more of the countryside.

Practical info
After enjoying the pool, spa, tennis
court and fitness center, the full-
service restaurant will serve a variety
of fine meals to satisfy every appetite.

Mira Vista Resort

7501 North Wade Road
Tucson, AZ 85748
Tel: 520 744 2355
www.miravistaresort.com

1. Angel Falls
2. College Cove & Baker's beach
3. Red Rock Beach
4. Muir Beach
5. Black Sands Beach
6. Perles Beach
7. Baker Beach
8. Gray Whale Cove
9. San Gregorio Beach
10. Bonny Doon Beach
11. Red, White & Blue Beach
12. Pfeiffer Beach
13. More Mesa Beach
14. San Onofre Beach
15. Black's Beach

California

Wilbur Hot Springs, Colusa County

A spacious former stagecoach hotel north of Sacramento with a clientele who return for the relaxation, yoga, massage, community kitchen and outdoor clothing-optional area featuring soaking pools, a swimming pool, sauna and sun deck. The 240 acres in open hilly terrain are great for hiking.

Laguna del Sol, Wilton, near Sacramento

A 238-acre nudist resort with grassy camping areas, RV hookups, motel, restaurant, entertainment center for dancing, full bar, lake with fishing and boating, fitness center, two spas, tennis, volleyball, two outdoor swimming pools and indoor pool with spa. Ask about the stream with the swimming hole that you can walk to nude.

Angel Falls, Madera County

Over two decades of nude use at this beautiful area of Bass Lake north of Fresno, with easy access. Large, smooth rocks for sunning and numerous whirlpools perfect for swimming.
Practical info
From Fresno, take Route 41 north, turn right on Highway 274, the Bass Lake turnoff. Go about 4 miles to two forks in the road. Keep to the left both times, staying on Highway 274. Go about a half-mile, turn left on to a small driveway and go to the right through a steel green gate. Parking is along the stream (if you cross over a bridge you have gone about 200 feet too far). Hike 10 minutes up along this stream to Angel Falls. If you cross the stream and hike another 10 minutes along the right side of the stream you will reach Devil's Slide with more pools in the rocks. Clothing-optional use is from the parking area up to Devil's Slide (Angel Falls is halfway in between).

▲ Golden sand, warm sunshine and a long stretch of coast: three reasons why California is such a popular destination among naturist travelers. Picture by Michael Cooney

Wilbur Hot Springs

Tel: 530 473 2306
www.wilburhotsprings.com

Laguna del Sol

8683 Rawhide Lane
Wilton, CA 95693
Tel: 916 687 6550
www.lagunadelsol.com

The USA

▲ Naturists gather to enjoy one of California's many popular nude beaches. Pictures by Michael Cooney

College Cove & Baker's Beach, Humboldt

Part of Trinidad State Beach, College Cove is popular on the relatively few sunny days that the region enjoys. Nude use is south of the big rock; the water is icy.

Practical info

From Eureka, drive north on Highway 101 about 25 miles to Trinidad. Follow signs to Trinidad State Beach parking area, but continue on the old highway about three quarters of a mile more and over a ravine, and look for the dirt parking lot on the left (if you reach Abalone Beach, you've gone too far). Park and follow trails that begin on the left side of the parking lot. A trail on the north side

of the lot leads to College Cove North which sees marginal nude use. Expect more nudes at College Cove South in part due to the more difficult trail.

Baker's Beach

If College Cove is too crowded, turn around and head for Baker's Beach, which is 12 miles north of Arcata on Highway 101. Take the Westhaven exit to Scenic Drive and head north. Stop at parked cars and a large, vine-covered residence and its rusted metal 'Private Property' sign on right. Parking on Scenic Drive has caused some problems for residents; be sure to leave enough road clearance for passing traffic.

Orr Hot Springs, Mendocino County

Splendid individual and group hot tubs, warm creek-flow pool, sauna, flower and vegetable gardens, lodge and community kitchen; massage available. No visit is complete

without a half day, perhaps picnicking, two miles west by a stream in primeval Montgomery Redwoods – many trees 300 feet tall and 1,000 years old.

Meadowlark Country House, Sonoma County

Located one mile from Calistoga in the heart of the Napa and Sonoma Valley wine country, Meadowlark's amenities include spacious gardens, a clothing-optional mineral pool with a

sundeck, hot tub, sauna and in-house massage complete with a magnificent view of the mountains. Bringing young children is not recommended, for safety and privacy reasons.

Sierra Hot Springs, Sierra County

A rustic spiritual retreat, with a renovating 'gold-rush' era hotel, offers

clothing-optional indoor and outdoor soaking pools. Call for reservations.

Orr Hot Springs

13201 Orr Springs Road
Ukiah, CA 95482
Tel: 707 462 6277

Meadowlark Country House

Tel: 800 942 5651
www.meadowlarkinn.com

Sierra Hot Springs

Tel: 530 994 3773
www.sierrahotsprings.org

Harbin Hot Springs, Lake County

Formerly a major society spa, now Harbin's unceasing waters, clear air and skein of hillside trails lead to new-age renewal. Clothing-optional cold and hot pools, sun deck, massage and vegetarian restaurant. The center offers day visits, camping, cabin rental and conferences.

> **Harbin Hot Springs**
> 18424 Harbin Springs
> Middletown, CA 95461
> Tel: 707 987 2477
> www.harbin.org

Muir Beach, Marin County

This beach is popular and relatively hassle-free. The unclad part is, in fact, located in front of private property. An excellent site for swimming, since the waves are small and the cove has a sandy bottom. Arrive before 10:30am on weekends to get a parking spot.

Practical info
From Highway 101 north of San Francisco, drive 5.6 miles along Highway 1 to Muir Beach State Park's entrance on the left. Park for free, walk out to the beach, and head north across a set of rocks to the smaller nude section.

Red Rock Beach, Marin County

This is one of northern California's most popular nude beaches. With merely 100 yards of sand between two rocky points, Red Rock has a lot going for it: Frisbee, body-surfing in chilly water, sun, and conversation. Tides and weather patterns can increase the size of the beach, or make it all but disappear overnight. Arrive early to find a good place to set out your towel. Fans have created the beach's very own website at www.redrockbeach.com.

Practical info
A half-mile south of Stinson Beach on Highway 1 and at a dip in the curvy road, find a large dirt parking area to the west. Walk the steep and sometimes weathered trail to the rocks below, and clamber across them to Red Rock Beach, which lies immediately to the north.

▼ **The rocks are certainly in evidence at California's aptly named Red Rock Beach, but there's also 100 yards of sand to enjoy. Picture by Michael Cooney**

▲ Surfing and an all-over tan, two of the ultimate Californian experiences. Picture above at Red Rock Beach by Michael Cooney, picture on right by Juan Picca

Black Sands Beach, Marin County

A stunningly beautiful beach looking out to San Francisco. Black basalt sand keeps you warm as you lie down, even if the day is cool.
Practical info
Drive from San Francisco north on Highway 101 across the Golden Gate Bridge. Take the second turnoff at Alexander Avenue, go under the freeway and follow signs to the Marin Headlands. In less than a quarter mile you'll be on Conzelman Rd. From here, drive 2.6 miles – partly on a one-way road – to a dirt parking lot on the left, big enough for about 20 cars. The half-mile trail goes straight to the beach.

Perles Beach, Angel Island, San Francisco Bay

The Bay and Golden Gate bridges, Alcatraz Island and the San Francisco skyline add up to a world-class view from this gem of an island beach.
Practical info
Take the morning Angel Island-Tiburon Ferry (timetables online at www.angelislandferry.com), and walk an easy 1.5 miles to Perles Beach. The beach is not officially sanctioned as clothing-optional, but used as such by locals for years.

Baker Beach, San Francisco, near the Presidio

San Francisco's best known beach for getting an all-over tan also has a view of the Golden Gate Bridge to the north. Wide open sand offers room for ultimate Frisbee or relaxing by yourself. Ease of access attracts the curious clothed as well as the free-spirited nude, but everyone gets along. The well-established tradition of nude use and freedom from legal hassle makes Baker Beach one of California's best bets, even though the water is cold and often rough.
Practical info
From downtown go west on Geary; turn north on to 25th Avenue to Lincoln Boulevard; turn right and take the second left on to Bowley Street. Turn right on to Gibson Road to the east parking lot. Walk north up the beach to the nude area north of the brown and yellow Hazardous Surf sign.

Gray Whale Cove, San Mateo County

California State Parks officials will rarely say so publicly, and they've done their best to not let anyone know about it, but Gray Whale Cove is as clothing-optional as you can get without being officially designated as such. You'll not find a sign telling you so, but the entire beach has clothed and unclothed mingling amicably.

There has been a tendency for nude sunbathers to keep to the northern and southern ends of the beach, but be confident in using the entire stretch of clean, soft sand naked as you wish. As with all nude beaches on public lands on the California coast, there are no amenities other than an outhouse at the top of the trail to the beach, so bring what you'll need for the day.
Practical info
Drive Highway 1 approximately seven miles south of Pacifica or 1.3 miles north of Montara State Beach, and find a large no-fee gravel parking lot east of the road. The only sign you are likely to see will say 'Beach Parking, 8am-Sunset.' Cross the highway and walk down the trail to the beach.

The USA

San Gregorio Beach, San Mateo County

The historic 'first' among recognized nude saltwater beaches in North America. In the 1960s, San Gregorio was witness to the emergence of the free-beach movement in the US. Hundreds of college students from San Francisco and surrounding environs made their way to the two-mile-long beach to dance, play music, and drive more conservative minded busy-bodies to distraction. Today, the open beach still beckons naked sunbathers. While beach-goers at the state park of the same name immediately to the south wear baggy swim trunks and oversized T-shirts, far happier men, women and children take the private road to the top of the cliff overlooking the beach to the north, pay the modest sum to park, and walk down to a legal, hassle-free day of naturist recreation.

Practical info
Drive Highway 1 south approximately one mile to where Highway 84 intersects from the east. A mere 100 yards to the north take a dirt road west past a white gate, and drive to the parking area at the road's end.

Bonny Doon Beach, Santa Cruz County

One of a string of gorgeous, cliff-backed beaches along the coastal route between San Francisco and Santa Cruz, Bonny Doon is a gem along California's 'Naturist Highway.' There are no facilities, but routine nude use guarantees naked company each sunny weekend at this out-of-the-way, crescent-shaped beach.

Practical info
Drive Highway 1 one mile south of Davenport to a gravel parking area on the west side of the road. Park, and walk over the dune and down a path to the beach. On windy days regulars stay close to the cliffs at the north end, although the entire beach is clothing-optional. Davenport is a small town with only the Davenport Inn for lodging. Additional motels can be found in Santa Cruz to the south.

A long-standing user group is the Bay Area Naturists. See their website for information on this and many other beaches along California's 'Naturist Highway' at www.bayareanaturists.org.

Red, White & Blue Beach, Santa Cruz County

Only two and a half miles away from Bonny Doon is the more private and equally attractive Red, White & Blue, so named because of the colored mailbox along the highway. California seashore at the water line is not privately owned, but much of the access to the shore is. The naturist-friendly owner of the property leading to this beach has made a commitment over the years to keeping the site clothing-optional.

For a reasonable price, folks can pay to use primitive campsites, water, restrooms, barbecue pits and showers, as well as the 200-yard-long beach. The caretaker and entrance fees keep the gawkers out, and the legality of nude use of the campground and beach is never in question. So for more timid visitors who balk at even the potential for such problems, Red, White & Blue is well worth the small cost.

Practical info
Drive 3.6 miles south of Davenport on Highway 1 and turn right on to Scaroni Road with its red, white and blue mailbox. Continue on the dirt road to the entrance gate and beach.

Other local nude beaches
Nearby are Panther Beach and its beautiful neighbor to the south, Hole in the Wall Beach. The latter is accessed by a tunnel in the cliff jutting into the ocean. Both beaches have been used nude for years, but rowdy drinking parties at night and bored farm laborers sitting atop cliffs looking for an eyeful make these secluded sites a hit-or-miss proposition. The rough, paved parking area is one mile south of Davenport on the west side of Highway 1.

Not quite as pretty but seeing fewer gawkers is Laguna Creek Beach, found 2.7 miles south of Davenport. The trail to the beach is opposite Laguna Road, entering Highway 1 from the east. Once you reach the beach, turn north and find your place in the sun. In the last few years there are more clothed people than nude, but the local word is still out that naturists are generally welcome here.

Other California naturist contacts

Beachfront USA
PO Box 328
Moreno Valley, CA 92556
www.bfusa.org

Camping Bares
PO Box 81589
San Diego, CA 92138
www.campingbares.org

River Dippers
PO Box 188366
Sacramento, CA 95818
www.riverdippers.org

Sonoma County Naturists
PO Box 237
Healdsburg, CA 95448
www.scnaturist.org

Southern California Naturist Assn.
23679 Calabasas Road, Suite #160
Calabasas, CA 91302
www.socalnaturist.org

Whales Cave Conservancy
PO Box 12814
San Luis Obispo, CA 93406

Glen Eden Sun Club
25999 Glen Eden Road
Corona, CA 92883
www.gleneden.com

Silver Valley Sun Club
48382 Silver Valley Road
Newberry Springs, CA 92365
www.silvervalleysunclub.com

The Sequoians
PO Box 2095
Castro Valley, CA 94546
Tel: 800 404 6833
www.sequoians.com

■ **Admiring the sea spray on the rocks at the end of Bonny Doon Beach, which has long been used by naturists. Picture by Michael Cooney**

Lupin Lodge, Santa Clara County

The naturist lodging of choice when touring the many beaches in Santa Cruz County. It is also near San Francisco and Monterey nude beaches.

A frequent host to Naturist Society Gatherings, Lupin offers a full-service restaurant with scenic terrace, cabins, yurts, tent sites, pool, hot tub, sauna, tennis, volleyball, massage, children's playground, hiking and more on 110 wooded acres in the Santa Cruz mountains. Lupin has long been on the cutting edge of North American naturism in offering seminars, workshops, and lectures on personal enrichment and expression. Their interest in the arts attracts artists and their work from the San Francisco Bay area.

| **Lupin Lodge** |
| 20600 Aldercroft Heights Road |
| Los Gatos, CA 95033 |
| Tel: 408 353 9200 |
| www.lupinlodge.org |
| **Kiva Retreat** |
| 702 Water Street |
| Santa Cruz, CA 95060 |
| Tel: 831 429 1142 |
| www.kivaretreat.com |

Kiva Retreat, Santa Cruz

Hot tubs (community and individual), cold plunge, showers, sauna, social room, sunning lawns, library/reading room with fireplace are all available at this entirely clothes-optional retreat named after a Hopi Indian word meaning 'sacred circle.' Built in 1980, Kiva Retreat was modeled after a Japanese bath house, offering a peaceful respite from hectic life.

Pirate's Cove, San Luis Obispo County

Pelicans dive and seals frolic at this long-established nude beach just north of Pismo Beach and south of Avila Beach. More recently, farm workers with the day off vie for space on the clifftop with developers building homes with a view. Still a favorite with naturist locals.
Practical info
Take the Avila Beach exit from Route 101, six miles south of San Luis Obispo. Drive west for two miles on Avila Road. Take the blacktop spur cutting up to the left, which is marked by a sign saying 'Not a Through Road – No Overnight Camping.' Follow this road over the sea ridge, about 0.5 miles to the parking area. After a rather steep descent, you'll be on the beach itself.

▲ Stretching out at a gathering organized by The Naturist Society LLC. The gatherings are held across the country, including Lupin Lodge in California. Picture by Michael Cooney

More Mesa Beach, Santa Barbara County

Santa Barbarans swear by More Mesa's white sand, sheltered location, and broad prospects. Horseback riders, surfers, volleyball zealots, Frisbee hurlers, the elderly, and infants share the beach, naked and clothed.

On the mesa top the sandy soil supports one of the few remaining natural ecologies in greater Santa Barbara. That, plus the view, inspired environmentalists to preserve the large tract.

The blobs of oil found on the beach are supposedly from natural seepage out at sea. Locals keep bottles of baby oil on hand to rub off the black goo. Don't let this put you off; More Mesa is one of California's naked treasures.
Practical info
From Highway 101, exit on Turnpike Road to the south, then turn left on Hollister, going two blocks and turning right on Puente Drive. Follow Puente for about 3/4 mile – its name changes to Vieja Drive. Park your car near the entrance to Mockingbird Lane. Mockingbird Lane is not open to vehicles, so walk to the end and take the established descent at the terminus of the ruts in a stand of eucalyptus trees.

Benton Hot Springs, Mono County

Clothing is optional in tubs at Benton Hot Springs, the only business in the town of the same name. A naturally vegetated setting and individually sited facilities for privacy. Groups/ private parties can be arranged.

| **Benton Hot Springs** |
| Route 4, Box 58 |
| Benton, CA 93512 |
| Tel: 760 933 2507 |
| www.395.com/oldhouse |

Pfeiffer Beach, Monterey County

The wild and rugged Big Sur coast offers many opportunities for solitary clothes-optional activities. Pfeiffer Beach (not to be confused with Pfeiffer Big Sur State Park, which is wholly textile) provides, quite simply, a social occasion with a fine breeze and a view of offshore rock formations and huge floating kelp.

Practical info

Pfeiffer Beach is in Los Padres National Forest. South of (textile-only) Pfeiffer Big Sur State Park on Highway 1 and across from the US Forest Service office is unmarked Sycamore Canyon Road, the only oceanside road of significance in the area. At the end of the 3-mile long road is the federal beach parking lot; park and take the path to the beach. Walk north along the sand about 1/4 mile to the nude haven, well out of view of the casual beach tourists.

▲ Soaking up the sun amid the rugged setting of Pfeiffer Beach
▼ Space and freedom to be yourself at one of the wilderness springs in the Tecopa area. Pictures this page by Michael Cooney

Tecopa Hot Springs, Inyo County

A nice but very rustic idyll near Death Valley (itself offering miles of fabulous nude hiking for free-range naturists). Nudity at the Tecopa Springs is required, according to terms of an Inyo County treaty with the local Indian tribe. Separate bathhouses make mixed-bathing impossible. Open 24 hours.

Practical info

The springs are located between Baker and Death Valley; lodging can be found at the Tecopa Hot Springs Resort, off Highway 127. From Shoshone, take Highway 127 south toward Tecopa. About five miles down the road there is a sign for Tecopa Hot Springs. Turn left and follow signs for three miles. The springs are directly across the street from an RV park.

Tecopa Hot Springs

Tel: 619 852 4373
tecopa-hot-springs.beach-cities.com

The USA

Terra Cotta Inn, Palm Springs

A classic hotel from the 1950s, this renovated and fully clothing-optional inn features a heated garden pool and Jacuzzi spa, barbecue facilities, 17 guest rooms with private baths, cable TV, VCR and air conditioning. Kitchens and private patios are also available.

Living Waters Spa, Palm Springs

This European style clothing-optional resort spa has two natural hot mineral water pools, non-smoking rooms, massage, king-size beds, free wireless LAN internet connection, couples massage workshops, morning breakfast and afternoon hors d'oeuvres, complete privacy, and a relaxing, romantic and de-stressing environment.

Morningside Inn, Palm Springs

Morningside Inn is a fully clothing-optional hotel with rooms that have VCRs and kitchens; some have private patios; three cabanas with microwave/fridge. Heated pool and spa, exercise area.

Desert Shadows Inn Resort & Villas

This premiere naturist resort in Palm Springs on the Pacific Coast brings a European standard to California. There are acres of meticulously landscaped grounds and Mediterranean-style villas behind secluded gates, and the site offers panoramic mountain views and sunshine year round.

Amenities include the Sunset Cafe restaurant and bar, a spa, tennis courts, a putting green, three swimming pools, water volleyball, two Jacuzzis, an exercise room, and excellent service.

The USA

▲ A jewel among California's nude beaches, San Onofre has a great user group that looks after the beach. Picture by Michael Cooney

Turtle Back Mesa

PO Box 8038
Palm Springs, CA 92263
Tel: 760 347 5358
trtlbkmesa@aol.com

Turtle Back Mesa, Palm Springs

Soak in naturally hot water from a well on the property. This quiet two-bedroom naturist B&B provides desert solitude within minutes of Palm Springs. Also features an enclosed patio with swimming pool.

San Onofre Beach, San Diego County

A southern California jewel not to be missed is San Onofre State Beach. Outdoor showers and toilets are located at the parking lot. Lifeguards are on duty during the summer months, and trash cans are located along the beach. The beach itself is soft, warm sand, but depending on the season the shoreline can be a mix of sand, pebbles, and cobbles. Any time spring through fall, however, will offer a safe, relaxing day here. The model user group, Friends of San Onofre Beach, helps keep the environment pleasant and safe for all visitors (see www.friendsofsanonofre.org).

To the north you will see the twin globes – 'Les Boobs' – of the San Onofre nuclear plant. On a clear day to the south you may view the headland of Torrey Pines State Beach, just beyond

which lies Black's Beach. San Onofre's own sandstone cliffs are more sculptured (if not as high or dangerous) as those of Black's Beach, with lizards, swallows, and squirrels.

Practical info
On Interstate 5 a few miles south of San Clemente, take the San Onofre Park/Basilone exit. Go south on the oceanside frontage road to the entrance to San Onofre State Park. Pay the entry fee, go 3.5 miles to the end of the road passing numerous parking lots, and park near the last restroom. Trail 6 starts here. Go down to the beach, turn left (south) for about 0.6 mile past the last lifeguard station for the clothing-optional section at the far southern end of the park. Do not disrobe until you pass the wash after that station. Stay north of the Camp Pendleton fence.

Black's Beach, La Jolla, San Diego County

▲ Striding the sands at Black's Beach, the most famous of America's Pacific coast nude beaches. Picture by Michael Cooney

On the Pacific coast's most famous clothing-optional beach, nudity has been legal, then banned, and is now informally tolerated on the section overseen by Torrey Pines State Park. A long and challenging trail leads down to nearly two miles of open, clothes-free beach. The hike is well worth it.

Surfers in wetsuits share waves with naked body-surfers; skinny-dippers dry out under the sun, play volleyball, and munch on grilled food cooked by regulars who carry grills from the parking lot above. Hang gliders soar overhead after launching themselves off the 300-foot cliff behind the beach. There's always something to do at Black's, and that makes it one of the premier nude beaches in North America. If you are in the San Diego area, you must not miss it.

Black's has one of the country's most active support groups, the Black's Beach Bares. See their website for weather conditions, reports on relations with rangers, and a calendar of activities at www.blacksbeach.org.

Three naturist clubs are nearby: Sun Island Resort, De Anza Springs Resort and San Diego Naturist Club.

Sun Island Resort, near San Diego

Sun Island Resort (formerly Swallows Sun Island) is located in the hills of El Cajon near San Diego. They offer motel rooms, swimming, Jacuzzi, tent and RV camping. There are weekend dances and also karaoke for entertainment. There is a cafe on the grounds.

De Anza Springs Resort, east of San Diego

De Anza Springs Resort is situated on 500 acres and surrounded on three sides by the rugged hills of the Anza-Borrega State Park. It offers a lovely desert oasis with trees, lawns and a sparkling swimming pool. There are more than 300 RV and tent sites, most of which offer full hook-ups. There are also travel trailers and park model villas for rent.

Sun Island Resort

1631 Harbison Canyon Road
El Cajon, CA 92019
Tel: 619 445 3754
www.sunislandresort.com

De Anza Springs Resort

1951 Carrizo Gorge Road
Jacumba, CA 91934
Tel: 619 766 4301
www.deanzasprings.com

San Diego Naturist club

www.sandiegonaturistclub.com

■ Picture opposite: the wide open spaces of Colorado look even better when you're soaking naked at Orient Land Trust. Picture by Michael Cooney

Colorado

Orient Land Trust/Valley View Hot Springs

On the west slope of the Sangre de Cristo Mountains at 8,700 feet, an hour from the Monarch and Wolf Creek ski areas, OLT overlooks San Luis Valley. Entirely clothes-optional. Hiking and music-making, four natural hot spring pools and an 80-foot swimming pool.

Rustic cabins and rooms available (make reservations!) or camp out. Nearest food service/shop is 13 miles away. Kitchen facilities and sauna, firewood provided. Children free. Weekdays open to the public, weekends and holidays for members and guests.

Dakota Hot Springs, near Colorado Springs

A hot clothing-optional pool with food and drink services, located in a desert valley surrounded by majestic mountains, south-east of Colorado

Springs. RV and tent sites (no hookups). Open year round. Clothing-optional Wednesdays through Mondays (clothing required on Tuesdays).

Orvis Hot Springs, south-west of Montrose

Less than an hour from the ski resort of Telluride, 1.3 miles south of Ridgway from Route 550 in the direction of Ouray, this rustic lodge with a scenic view of the Mt Sneffels

Range rents tent sites and six guest rooms, bicycles, cross-country skis, and access to four indoor tiled soaking pools and several outdoor clothing-optional hot ponds.

Orient Land Trust/Valley View Hot Springs

PO Box 65
Villa Grove, CO 81155
Tel: 719 256 4315
www.olt.org

Dakota Hot Springs

1 Malibu Boulevard, US Highway 50
Penrose, CO 81240
Tel: 866 882 1010
www.dakotahotsprings.com

Orvis Hot Springs

1585 County Road 3
Ridgway, CO 81432
Tel: 970 626 5324
www.orvishotsprings.com

The USA

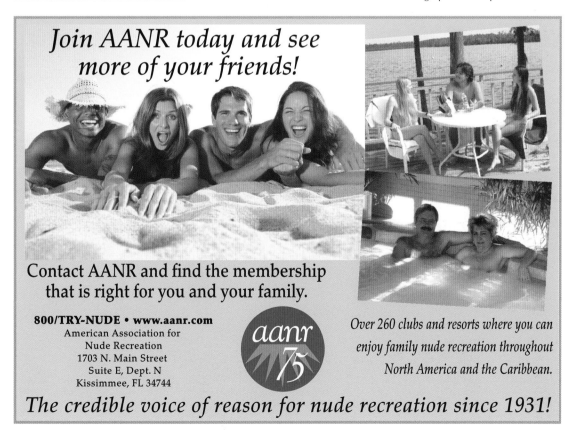

Connecticut

Solair Recreation League, North Woodstock

A family nudist resort on 400 acres in a peaceful valley in North Woodstock. The resort offers cabin rentals, tent and RV sites for overnight stays. There are miles of hiking trails, a lake for swimming, boating and fishing, a sand volleyball court, shuffleboard, two tennis courts and a large, heated pool. For full details see the resort's website at www.solairrl.com.

Florida

1. Apollo/Playalinda beaches
2. Haulover Beach

Apollo/Playalinda beaches, Cape Canaveral

A terrific pair of beaches with open sand, warm water for swimming and a long tradition of nude use. Both Playalinda Beach and Apollo Beach are part of the Cape Canaveral National Seashore, with distant views of NASA's space shuttle launch area across the water. Playalinda has more parking and is the favorite haunt of the Central Florida Naturists (www.central-fla-naturists.org), but both beaches offer the purest of Florida sun and enjoy the raves of naturists in the region.

Although separated by just a few miles of textile Klondike Beach, Playalinda and Apollo receive different visitors, as the approach to each is far to the south and north respectively.

Practical info

For Playalinda, take Highway 1 or 95, Route 406 east through Titusville. Cut on to Route 402, pass the Seashore headquarters, and continue to the beach. Turn left (north) through the gates and for five miles follow the paved road behind Playalinda Beach. Get as close to the dead-end as possible and park. Parking is limited; arrive early. Continue north on foot to where you find others are clothes-free before getting natural. Stay out of the dunes, as delicate wildlife greatly admired by park authorities nest there.

For Apollo Beach, from I-95 take Exit #249. Drive east on State Road 44 into New Smyrna Beach. SR 44 becomes A1A and Turtle Mound, and turns south. Proceed approximately 9 miles to the end of the road to parking lot #5. The nude section of the beach is just south of the crossover. Parking is limited, so arrive early.

▼ **Enjoying the simple delights of Florida's Apollo/Playalinda beaches. Picture by Michael Cooney**

Haulover Beach, north Miami

Just north of Miami is a model clothing-optional urban beach attracting visitors from the world over. Haulover Beach offers more than a half-mile of pure white sand and seashore, with parking, trash cans, concessions, restrooms, lifeguards, and signage for the clothing-optional section. This may be the most popular nude beach in North America, and much of that is due to the efforts of the primary user group, South Florida Free Beaches (www.sffb.com).

Since being established in the early 1990s, nude beach use has gone from a few hundred to several thousand people a day during the peak months of April through October. The economic impact on South Florida has been tremendous. The parking lot has become a welcome source of revenue for Miami-Dade County. Nearby hotels enjoy an 85 per cent occupancy rate year-round; the entire community has benefited. Haulover is a prime example of what is possible when a dedicated group of naturists work together to create a resource for its community.

Practical info

From Interstate 95, exit at Golden Glades Interchange on to State Road 826 east or go east on 125th Street. Find Haulover County Park at about 150th St on Collins Avenue (Route A1A) and park in the northernmost fee parking lot. Arrive before 11am on sunny mornings because the lot can fill up. Walk to the beach through the tunnel underpass.

▲ Haulover Beach is one of the world's most successful urban nude beaches. Easy access can work both ways for naturism in city areas, but Haulover's diligent user group has helped keep this beach safe, well managed and extremely popular. Picture by Michael Cooney

Sunsport Gardens, near West Palm Beach

Sunsport Gardens is a subtropical family naturist resort 20 minutes west of West Palm Beach. They feature rental accommodations, full RV hookup sites and campsites for tenting. Sunsport Gardens is the annual host site for the Midwinter Naturist Festival every February.

Included in amenities are: volleyball, tennis, horseshoes, petanque, a heated swimming pool, hot tub, spa, sauna, fishing and kayaking ponds, children's playground, jungle nature trail on 40 acres of lush, tropical vegetation, and a full-service restaurant with nightly specials.

Sunsport Gardens

14125 North Road.
Loxahatchee, FL 33470
www.sunsportgarden.com

Sunnier Palms Members Lodge

8800 Okeechobee Rd.
Ft. Pierce, FL 34945
www.sunnier.com

Sunnier Palms Members Lodge

Sunnier Palms is a volunteer-oriented nudist park. Situated on 23 acres, the resort has a 12-acre pine forest with nature trails, gardening area, tenting and 50 park sites with full hook-ups. There is also a heated swimming pool, hot tub, and pavilion with complete kitchen and TV access.

Cypress Cove Nudist Resort, Kissimmee

Experience Florida as nature intended. Cypress Cove has all the amenities travelers could want in a clothes-free setting. There is a hotel, full-service restaurant, bar and grill.

The resort also offers two pool complexes, hot tub, massage and fitness centers, tennis courts, a 50-acre lake, chip-and-putt golf and more.

Cypress Cove Nudist Resort

4425 Pleasant Hill Road
Kissimmee, FL 34746
Tel: 407 933 5870
www.cypresscoveresort.com

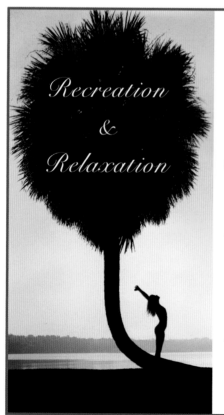

The USA

Sunsport Gardens
Family Naturist Resort

An ecological and health conscience club welcoming ALL naturists since 1965.

There's always something fun happening at Sunsport Gardens!

Home of the MidWinter Naturist Festival

Children and Family Friendly

Host to the Summer's Annual Youth Camps—Scholarships Available.

A natural, tropical setting in Florida.

Affiliated with TNS

Spend a day, a week, or an eternity!

Amenities include: an 88 degree swimming pool, spa, sauna, volleyball, tennis, fitness center, petanque, horseshoes, full service restaurant, RV hookups, camping, cabin rentals, children's playground, fishing, Wi-Fi, boating, jungle nature trail, and Saturday night dances.

Sunsport Gardens • 14125 North Road • Loxahatchee, FL 33470

(800) 551-7217 • manager@sunsportgardens.com
www.sunsportgardens.com

An Easy Drive To Haulover Beach!

Caliente Resort, Land O'Lakes

This luxury resort, club and residential community is one of the top-end clothing-optional vacation destinations on the East Coast. Caliente has hotel rooms, rental cottages and apartments. Come to relax or party it up with dancing at night, a professional-caliber tennis club, a beautiful resort spa, five swimming pools, fine or informal dining, and a program of entertainment and events for members and guests.

> **Caliente Resort**
>
> 21240 Gran Via Boulevard
> Land O'Lakes, FL 34637
> Tel: 800 326 7731
> www.calienteresort.com

Paradise Lakes Resort, Lutz, north of Tampa

Paradise Lakes has 80,000 annual visitors and 5,700 members. An upscale vacation resort with over 100 rental condos and hotel rooms, 70 RV spaces, retail stores, restaurant, nightclub, poolside bar and grill, spas, sports courts and, oh yes, a cypress-bordered lake where ospreys fish; all on 73 acres. Nightly entertainment, supervised children's activities.

> **Paradise Lakes Resort**
>
> 2001 Brinson Road
> Lutz, FL 33558
> Tel: 813 949 9327
> www.paradiseclubs.com

▲ Cooling down in one of the five swimming pools at Caliente Resort. Opposite: freelance nude bathing on North Captiva Island, Florida. Pictures by Michael Cooney

Lake Como Family Nudist Resort, Lutz

Covering some 200 acres, Lake Como offers visitors five lakes, sandy beaches, and complimentary use of kayaks, paddleboats, and canoes. In addition the resort offers three clay tennis courts, volleyball, basketball, petanque, shuffleboard and horseshoe courts, a driving range, billiard tables, darts, and a beautiful nature trail for hiking. Amenities abound with a heated pool, recreation hall, whirlpool/spa, sauna, and the ultimate in relaxation – professional massage services. The sand-floor 'Butt Hutt' is open every day, as well as a full-service restaurant. Lodging includes motel rooms, RV sites with hookups, and tenting.

> **Lake Como Family Nudist Resort**
>
> 20500 Cot Road
> Lutz, FL 33558
> www.lakecomoresort.com

Naturist options in Florida Keys

There are a number of naturist places to stay and things to do in Florida Keys, as outlined below.

Marreros Guest Mansion
Marreros Guest Mansion in Key West is a splendid old house within short walking distance of downtown Key West. This textile B&B has a clothing-optional pool and hot tub. An excellent base from which to explore what the outer Florida Keys have to offer.

The Pilot House
The Pilot House is situated in historic Old Town Key West. This is a delightful Victorian-style B&B which offers guests a clothing-optional backyard pool and spa.

No Wake Charters
While you're in Key West, drive toward the mainland, to Marathon in the Keys, and sign up with Captain Ran Baird's No Wake Charters for a half- or full-day sail to glorious skin-diving sites… and all clothes-free.

> **Marreros Guest Mansion**
>
> 410 Fleming Street
> Key West, FL 33040
> Tel: 800 459 6212
> www.marreros.com

> **Pilot House**
>
> 414 Simonton Street
> Key West, FL 33040
> Tel: 800 648 3780
> www.pilothousekeywest.com

> **No Wake Charters**
>
> www.nowakecharters.com

> **Other Florida naturist contacts**
>
> **Sanibel Naturists**
> PO Box 6789
> Ft. Myers, FL 33911
> www.sanibelnaturists.com
>
> **SunCoast Naturists**
> 2030 Leryl Avenue
> North Port, FL 34286
>
> **Tallahassee Naturally**
> PO Box 6866
> Tallahassee, FL 32314
> www.tallahasseenaturally.org
>
> **Tampa Area Naturists**
> PO Box 923
> Lutz, FL 33548
> www.tanfl.com

■ Some states may lack formal naturist places, but they make up for it with plenty of open space. Pictured opposite: two adventurous spirits explore the Arches National Park in Utah. Picture by Michael Cooney

Georgia

Bell Acres Resort, north-east Georgia

Bell Acres is located on 70 acres of hilly woodlands in north-east Georgia. Amenities include a swimming pool, hot tub, clubhouse, volleyball court, hiking trail and camping from tent sites to full hookup sites. Four rental cabins are also available.

Bell Acres Resort

www.bellacres.com

Paradise Valley Resort, north of Atlanta

Paradise Valley Resort, located in Dawsonville, is situated in a beautiful mountain valley about an hour north of Atlanta. This breathtaking property features brand new condominium rentals, a 70-foot conversation pool, both indoor and outdoor swimming pools and an indoor and outdoor hot tub, challenging and engaging hiking trails, and an active social schedule.

Paradise Valley Resort

www.paradisevalleyclub.com

Serendipity Park, North Georgia Pines

Serendipity Park

www.serendipity-park.com

A full-service family-oriented nudist facility with a large clubhouse, pool, spa, sauna, gym, cafe and hiking along beautiful Blue Creek.

The USA

The USA

Hawaii

▲ The volcanic origins of Hawaii are starkly evident on stunning Kehena Black Sand Beach, where a long tradition of nude bathing continues. Picture by Michael Cooney. Pictured opposite: naturists mark another perfect day at Little Beach on Maui. Pictures by Michael Cooney

Kehena Black Sand Beach, Hawaii

Visually stunning, this laid back beach has been traditionally nude as long as anyone can remember. Getting to the beach from the roadside parking area requires care in navigating the trail through the rugged lava rock that drops more than 50 feet to the beach. Depending on the time of year and condition of the surf, getting in and out of the ocean takes some very careful timing.

The beach is less than 200 yards long, with the area covered in sand varying with the seasons. A 50-foot cliff forms the back of the beach, making the trail the only way in and out.

Practical info
From Hilo, take Highway 11 to Keaau then go left (south) on Highway 130. Continue south for about 20 miles to the intersection with Highway 137 at the coast. Make a sharp left turn on to 137 and head north-east for about four miles, and watch for the scenic viewpoint near Mile Marker 19. Park along the road here and follow the trail that goes from the turnout to the beach.

Wailea Bay 'Beach 67,' Hawaii

Wailea Bay Marine Preserve's two beaches are nicknamed 69 and 67. Beach 69 is the larger and is great for snorkeling and diving. Beach 67, on the north side of the bay, is smaller and frequented by naturists. Authorities occasionally patrol the area and request visitors to dress.

Practical info
On Highway 19 at mile marker 71, turn into Puako Village, then turn right on to Old Puako Road. Access Beach 67 by taking the gravel road at telephone pole #67. Drive from here to the bluff, park, and then hike down to the beach.

MAUI — Blue Pool
Little Beach — Hana • — Red Sands
Alelele Bridge Falls

Wailea Bay

Hilo •

HAWAII

Kehena Black Sand Beach

Banana Patch retreat, Hawaii

Near some of the world's best snorkeling on Hawaii's southern Kona Coast, the Banana Patch is a clothing-optional retreat with two bungalows and a fully furnished tree house, each with private Jacuzzi and sunning areas.

Hangin' Loose retreat, Hawaii

A naturist hideaway near Hilo, its luxuriant six acres feature a myriad of vibrant tropical flowers and plants, along with the night sounds of coqui frogs. A swimming pool, two yurts, and cottage – each with its own hot tub – make this a perfect naked base for visits to nearby Kehena Beach.

Little Beach, Maui

This could be the best nude beach ever. Fine sand on a gentle slope, beautiful water, a great view, wonderful people – what more could you want? This side of the island has very little rain, averaging only seven inches a year.

Each Sunday evening young people from all over the island gather for the traditional sunset drumming. This is a must-attend experience that will defy description back home. The beach user group Friends of Little Beach (www.littlebeachmaui.com) has worked for years to keep this famous naturist site open to clothes-free use.

Practical info

Located on the sunny and dry south side of the island just north of Big Makena Beach, reach Little Beach by heading to the right to Red Hill, a rugged lava outcropping. The climate is perfect and permits visitors to be comfortably nude all year.

Banana Patch

PO Box 1107
Kealakekua, HI 96750
Tel: 800 988 2246
www.bananabanana.com

Hangin' Loose

PO Box 1863
Keaau, HI 96749
Tel: 866 543 6324
www.hanginloose.com

▼ A Pacific island setting plus friendly naturists add up to one of the world's best nude beaches: Little Beach. Pictures by Michael Cooney

▲ Tropical waterfalls on Hawaii are popular with all tourists: you might have to get up early to enjoy an undisturbed skinny-dip. Picture top right Blue Pool, others Alelele Bridge Falls, all by Michael Cooney

Alelele Bridge Falls, Maui

A tall jungle waterfall with a sparkling clean pool below, Alelele Bridge Falls is just the kind of place that Hawaii travelers dream of. With several small caves to explore, everything you need to enjoy the morning sun is here in this tropical oasis.

Practical info

Located just a quarter mile off the Hana Highway, access is on a well-used trail through the remains of an ancient Hawaiian village. These falls are accessible yet uncrowded. The Hana Highway offers so many waterfalls that most tourists drive straight past this one, which is not visible from the road.

Take the highway beyond Hana to the backside of the island. Alelele Bridge is located just past mile maker 39; park at the bridge and follow the trail upstream.

Blue Pool & Water Fall, Maui

A beautiful tropical waterfall located on the shore, with fern- and moss-covered walls dripping water. This is what you come to Maui to see. Now popular with tourists, naturists should visit in the early morning, when the sun warms the area and there is privacy to swim in the clear pool.

Practical info

Take Ulaino Road off the Hana Highway just after mile marker 31 towards Ka 'Eleku Caverns and Kahanu Gardens. Keep going to the end of the road, parking in one of the front yard fee lots. Ignore the various 'No Trespassing' signs and proceed to the fresh water stream. Head to the left along the beach and you will see the pool just past the cliff. Use great care and wear good shoes to navigate these unusually challenging and potentially dangerous rocks.

The USA

Red Sands Beach, Maui

Visually stunning and physically challenging to reach, Red Sands Beach is made up of crumbling red and black volcanic cinders that can be rough on the feet. A strip of jagged lava forms a breakwater that in heavy surf causes increased turbulence in the pool at the head of the beach. Some beach users enjoy the foam and rushing water while others find the effect overwhelming. Nude and textile use continues side by side, but with the increased number of tourists visiting the Hana area, both groups may feel a bit self-conscious. Still, this is a beach well worth visiting.
Practical info
From the Hana Community Center, park on the side of the road and proceed across the grassy area. About half way you will see where the trail begins towards the ocean. Go left along the coastline past the warning sign up and around the point to where you will see the beach down the trail.

Venus Pool, Maui

A black sand beach, a large fresh water pool, flat rocks for sunning, and unlike many other Hana locations, afternoon sun. Not on any tourist's agenda, you may well have the place to yourself.
Practical info
Take the Hana Highway out of Hana towards Seven Pools. Once you pass Homea Beach Road look for mailbox 27 on your right. Park off the road across from the mailbox. The trail begins on the other side of the fence through a cow pasture. When you see the remains of the old Portuguese stone oven to your left, take the trail to your right all the way to the beach and pool.

▲ Difficult access is a blessing in disguise for Red Sands Beach: it keeps away clothed tourists and leaves the sands and foaming surf for free spirits to enjoy as nature intended. Pictures by Michael Cooney

Makahiku Water Falls & Pools, Maui

Located above the famed Oheo Gulch, the further you go up the trail the more privacy you get. The pools above Makahiku Falls are good, and so are the second set of falls further up the mountain.

Practical info
Take the Hana Highway to the Haleakala National Park, home of the Seven Sacred Pools. Check out the pools and then proceed across the road to the trail up to the waterfalls.

Twin Springs Resort
HCR 35
Boise, ID 83716
Tel: 208 861 1226
www.twinspringsidaho.com

Sun Meadow Resort
www.sunmeadow.org

Idaho

Twin Springs Resort, Boise County

An hour from the town of Boise along the Middle Fork of the Boise River. The clothing-optional springs are some of the few in the state that are sulphur-free. The thermal springs heat the hot tubs, communal pool, rental cabins and steam sauna. It makes these mineral waters perfect for a long soak after a relaxing day exploring the surrounding area. Reservations mandatory.

Sun Meadow Resort, Kootenai County

With 75 acres of meadow and timber there are miles of trails for walking, biking or cross-country skiing. It is equidistant to Spokane, Washington, and Coeur d'Alene, Idaho. Hotel rooms, indoor pool, library, exercise area and stage. The patio borders the lodge, spa, outdoor pool and children's play area.

▲ Freestyle skinny-dipping in the wilderness Moab area of Utah. Picture by Michael Cooney

Chicago Sun Club
www.aanrmidwestsun.com/csc

Blue Lake Club
www.bluelakeresort.org

Drakes Ridge Rustic Nudist Retreat
www.drakesridge.com

Lake O' the Woods Club
www.lowc.org

Sunny Haven Recreation Park
www.sunnyhaven.com

Illinois and Indiana

Chicago Sun Club, Kane County, NE IL

This non-landed group in the Chicago area has activities year round. In the winter they have bi-monthly get-togethers while during the summer they visit area landed clubs, attend nude car shows and other events.

Blue Lake Club, Whiteside Co, western IL

Located in north-western Illinois on about 20 acres. The pond is chlorinated and has a nice sand beach. There are spaces for RV hookups and several small motel rooms. You can enjoy volleyball, horseshoes, shuffleboard, children's playground and a snack bar (on weekends).

Drakes Ridge Rustic Nudist Retreat

This club has a quiet, back-to-nature atmosphere. There is camping and cabins, hiking, fishing, sports facilities, pool, children's play area and clubhouse. The season is Memorial Day weekend through Labor Day.

Lake O' the Woods Club

Located on a 130-acre wooded tract in Valparaiso, Ind., just an hour from Chicago. The clubhouse has a guest kitchen, co-ed showers, sauna, and meeting room. There is a heated swimming pool, hot tub, tennis courts, sand volleyball court and a play area for children. The scenic 20-acre lake has two sand beaches and great fishing; rowboats, canoes and paddleboats are available for guests. Don't miss the wonderful hiking trail around the lake.

Sunny Haven Recreation Park

A small member-owned club on 20 acres in the South Bend, Ind. area. Amenities include a heated pool, sauna, hot tub, volleyball, petanque, miniten, shuffleboard and a restaurant. There are RV and tent sites available.

The USA

77

Maine

Richmond Sauna Bed & Breakfast

A clothing-optional B&B with large outdoor hot tub, heated swimming pool, and private Finnish style sauna rooms. Open year round. Adults only.

Massachusetts

Truro Beach, Cape Cod National Seashore

The National Park Service banned nudity at Cape Cod National Seashore in the 1970s; but naturists have generally good relations with rangers there, and one stretch of beach still sees a great deal of quiet nude use. Locals suggest covering up when approached by a ranger.

Practical info

Go to the ocean beach of Truro, nearly at the tip of the Cape off Route 6, between Ballston Beach and Longnook Beach; or for solitude, walk north from Longnook Beach. Parking permits are required and available only to residents and those staying at local hotels. Herring Cove Beach just outside Provincetown also has nude use, much of it gay, and can be reached by foot, bike, or paying NPS' daily parking fee.

Richmond Sauna Bed & Breakfast

81 Dingley Road, Richmond, ME 04357
Tel: 800 400 5751
www.richmondsauna.com

Other Maine naturist contacts

Maine Coast Solar Bares
PO Box 1464
Auburn, ME 04211
www.mcsb.ws

Other Massachusetts naturist contacts

Pilgrim Naturists of New England

PO Box 320273
Boston, MA 02132
www.sunclad.com/pilgrim

Sandy Terraces

PO Box 98
Marstons Mills, MA 02648
www.members.aol.com/ftnancy/STA.html

▼ **Freestyle nude bathing in Massachusetts, below. At Lake Mead in Nevada (opposite) naturists enjoy discreet use of deserted shores. Pictures by Michael Cooney**

Michigan

Otter Creek, Sleeping Bear Dunes Lakeshore

Otter Creek is a sand beach with clean water and a great view of Lake Michigan, 22 miles west of Traverse City. Naturists aren't bothered when no one complains. They're discreet and help to keep the seashore clean.

Practical info
Find Empire 22 miles west of Traverse City. Drive south 4 miles on Route 22 to Esch Road, turn right, go to the beach and park. Walk north on the beach for at least a mile to the area used nude.

Turtle Lake Resort, Union City

A 160-acre, year-round naturist facility situated between Detroit and Chicago. Winter events are held almost weekly in the 10,000 square foot clubhouse with heated pool and hot tub.

Miniature golf, fishing, boating and canoeing, horseshoes, shuffleboard, volleyball (sand and mud), water slide, and five playgrounds for the kids. Rental units, 200+ full hookup RV sites.

Forest Hills Club, central Michigan

Forest Hills Club is a co-operatively owned nudist facility located on 45 acres in central Michigan. It is open to visitors May 1 through October 31.

Spruce Hollow, south-west of Traverse City

Enjoy the charming natural beauty of an evergreen forest in northern Michigan. Open June to September. 25 miles south-west of Traverse City.

Turtle Lake Resort

2101 Nine Mile Road
Union City, MI 49094
Tel: 866 321 4710
www.turtle-lake.com

Forest Hills Club

PO Box 105
Saranac, MI 48881
www.foresthillsclub.com

Spruce Hollow Campground

8700 W. 6 1/2 Road
Mesick, MI 49668
www.sprucehollow.org

Other Michigan naturist contacts

Michigan Nude Beach Advocates

1801 S. Fletcher Rd
Chelsea, MI 48118
www.michigannudebeachadvocates.org

Southeast Michigan Naturists

PO Box 8127
Ann Arbor, MI 48107
www.smnaturists.org

The USA

Missouri and Montana

Naturist places and organizations

Two places of interest to naturists in the state of Missouri are Show-Me Naturists and the Show-Me Acres

Nudist Campground & Resort. Naturists in Montana should contact the Montana Naturist Organization.

Nevada

Lake Tahoe, north-east shoreline

Close to the neon-rich nightlife of Reno and South Lake Tahoe, these crystal-clear coves offer the most scenic inland skinny-dipping in North America. Cove after cove, some with a sandy beach, others with large rocks for sunning, present themselves like precious pearls on a string. The water here is warmer than in most of the icy cold lake, so swim out to the huge granite boulders and bask in the mountain air.

Clothing-optional areas include Secret Cove Beach, Secret Creek Beach, and Whale Beach. Few are signed, so just be on the lookout for naked folk, and join in.

The US Forest Service has

jurisdiction of the Nevada shore from Incline Village to Cave Rock. Its rangers are unconcerned about discreet sunbathing, and they've occasionally posted advisory signs to alert the unwitting clothes-minded public that skinny-dippers may be encountered.

Practical info

From Spooner Summit on US 50, drive approximately 5 miles north on Highway 28. In the lot marked 'National Forest Parking Area' on the left, find the main path leading south half a mile and beyond to the beaches. Moderately priced motels, restaurants, and casinos are nearby to the north in Incline Village.

▲ Highly valued by naturists, Lake Tahoe is a beautiful place to skinny dip. Picture by Michael Cooney

Missouri naturist contacts

Show-Me Naturists, Missouri

7201 N Route E
Columbia, MO 65202
www.show-me-naturist.tripod.com

Show-Me Acres Nudist Campground & Resort, Missouri

5492 Black Elk Lane
Stover, MO 65078
www.midwestsun.com/showme

Montana naturist contacts

Montana Naturist Organization

PO Box 192
Corvallis, MT 59828
www.montananaturist.org

Other Nevada naturist contacts

Las Vegas Bares

PO Box 231118
Las Vegas, NV 89105
www.lasvegasbares.com

Tahoe Area Naturists

PO Box 975
Zephyr Cove, NV 89448

New Jersey

Gunnison Beach, Sandy Hook

Located on the edge of New York Harbor, Gunnison Beach is part of the Sandy Hook unit of the Gateway National Recreation Area. Sandy Hook is a 6-mile long peninsula known for exceptional beaches, wildlife, fishing, and historic sites. Used nude by soldiers when the US Army had a base nearby, today Gunnison Beach hosts thousands of naked people on sunny weekends and is the most popular portion of the Gateway National Recreation Area.

Gunnison is overlooked by the historic Sandy Hook lighthouse, which offers dramatic views of lower Manhattan and the Verrazano Narrows Bridge. This long, beautiful beach is recognized as clothing-optional, with official signs and full lifeguard and police protection.

It is also one of the largest clothing-optional beaches on the Atlantic Coast, drawing more than 5,000 visitors a day on most sunny summer weekends during its peak season from May to September. Parking lots fill quickly, so arrive early in the day.

Unlike many nude beaches, it offers changing areas, bathrooms, a snack bar and showers at the entrance to the beach. There is also a snack trailer on the beach. The nearby New Jersey beach towns offer great restaurants and a wide variety of accommodations. All of this helps makes Gunnison Beach on Sandy Hook a great naturist destination. For more information contact the primary naturist user group, Friends of Gunnison (www.gunnisonbeach.org).

Practical info

From the north, take the Garden State Parkway to Exit 117. Follow the signs to Sandy Hook. From the south, take the Garden State Parkway and watch for signs to Route 36E (Exit 105). Follow this to the ocean and continue on Route 36 to Sandy Hook. From the fee station, continue to Gunnison Beach at Parking Lot G. Walk the boardwalk to the clothing-optional beach marked by signs.

▼ **One of the most popular nude beaches in the US – and the world for that matter – Gunnison Beach in New Jersey can attract up to 5,000 bare bathers on a hot weekend. Picture by Michael Cooney**

The USA

Rock Lodge Club, near New York City

Rock Lodge Club is located near New York City and offers a spring-fed lake with two beaches, tennis courts, hiking trails, volleyball, hot tub and sauna.

Goodland Country Club, west of New York

Goodland Country Club is one of the country's oldest nudist resorts, in operation for over 75 years. It is located in a rural setting approximately 50 miles west of New York City. Amenities include swimming pool, hot tub, sauna, massage, volleyball, cabins, trailer and campsites.

New Mexico

Ten Thousand Waves, Santa Fe

Don't miss it! Like the great hot springs of Japan, Ten Thousand Waves has hot tubs, saunas, massage, acupuncture, yoga, and facials; just 3.5 miles from downtown Santa Fe. Kimonos, towels, and sandals are provided, but the facility is largely clothing-optional until 8:15pm. Light food and drinks in lobby.

Naturist bed and breakfasts, Albuquerque

Mi Casa B&B is a private naturist home offering guests a king-size bed, TV, private bath and backyard pool and hot tub. Nearby in the mountains east of Albuquerque is naturist-friendly Sandia's Secrets B&B with gardens, hot tub, sundeck, and the quiet of the country. Both B&Bs often host social events organised by local nudist travel club Roadrunner Naturists.

New York

Chautauqua Gorge, western New York

Local residents posted a 2-mile stretch of the gorge for clothes-optional use. Skinny Dip Falls is especially popular with young hikers and campers.
Practical info
From Buffalo follow I-90 south to Westfield (Exit 60). Follow Route 394 a short distance south to the center of Westfield and turn right on to Route 20. After crossing a bridge, turn left on Chestnut Street and follow it uphill (away from Lake Erie) for 3.4 miles to Ogden Road. Turn left on Ogden and go 1.5 miles to a dirt road marked only by a snowmobile trail sign. Turn left, go 0.6 miles to the end. Park off-road or in the parking area at the top of the trail. Take the trail down to the streambed, then follow the gorge downstream one mile to Skinny Dip Falls.

Southwick Beach, Lake Ontario

Known even by rangers as the 'natural beach' section of Southwick Beach State Park, this is a secluded nude area on Lake Ontario that delights its users.
Practical info
From Syracuse take Route 81 north to exit 40 (Mannsville/Pierpont Manor). Go left at the end of the exit ramp and find the sign for Southwick Beach State Park. Follow Route 193 west about 5 miles to the intersection of Route 3 and the park entrance. Drive to the beach and clubhouse, park, walk left (south) about a mile to this 'natural beach.'

Rock Lodge Club

PO Box 86
Stockholm, NJ 07460
www.rocklodge.com

Goodland Country Club & Spa

PO Box 575
Hackettstown, NJ 07840
www.goodlandcc.com

Ten Thousand Waves

3451 Hyde Park Road
Santa Fe, NM 87501
Tel: 505 992 5025
www.tenthousandwaves.com

Mi Casa B&B

Tel: 505 293 8804
Yvonne125@earthlink.net

Sandia's Secrets B&B

Tel: 505 286 0221
awnre@juno.com

Other New Mexico naturist contacts

Roadrunner Naturists

PO Box 25732
Albuquerque, NM 87125
www.roadrunnernaturists.com

Club Nude & Natural

1327 Barelas Rd. SW
Albuquerque, NM 87102

SunTree Travel Club

www.suntree.net

1. Chautauqua Gorge
2. Southwick Beach
3. Potter's Falls
4. Lighthouse Beach
5. Smith Point

Juniper Woods

1226 Schoharie Tpke.
Catskill, NY 12414
www.juniperwoods.com

Empire Haven Nudist Park

5947 Sun Lane
Moravia, NY 13118
www.homestead.com/empirehaven

Other New York naturist contacts

Bonita Nudist Park

215 Tuttle Hill Road
Candor, NY 13743
www.bonitanudistresort.com

Long Island Travasuns

www.travasuns.org

Naturist Rochester

PO Box 283
Penfield, NY 14526
www.naturistrochester.org

Potter's Falls, Ithaca

Secreted away in a liberal college town among many other creeks, waterfalls, gorges and small ponds that can be used nude, Potter's Falls is the favored skinny-dipping spot. Strong swimmers can swim underneath the falls, and there are large flat rocks for sunning.

Practical info

From Ithaca take Route 79 out State Street south-east. Shortly beyond the intersection of Pine Tree Road, watch for a gate with a sign stating, 'Watershed, City of Ithaca, No Visitors.' Park on the edge of the road and walk past the gate down the service road until you reach the dam at the end of the reservoir. Turn right just before the dam and walk on the path about seven minutes to reach Potter's Falls.

Empire Haven Nudist Park, Finger Lakes

Empire Haven Nudist Park is located in the beautiful Finger Lakes Region of upstate New York. Fresh mountain air provides for warm days and cool nights, a refreshing setting for a full range of activities from May through to September. The park offers a heated swimming pool, hot tub and sauna. Hiking trails are available on nearby state-owned land.

Juniper Woods, Greene Co, near Catskill Mts

Juniper Woods is a family-oriented clothing-optional campground in upstate New York. It offers 50 campsites with water and electricity, a modern bathhouse, pavilion, clubhouse, swimming pool and conversation pool. The campground also offers walking trails, lakes for fishing, and a range of other outdoor activities.

The USA

Full Tan Sun Club, Sprakers

Full Tan Sun Club is a family-oriented, singles-friendly nudist campground.

Rentals are available at the site and the clubhouse has a small snack bar.

Full-Tan Sun Club

1350 Carlisle Rd.
Sprakers, NY 12166
www.fulltansunclubofny.com

Lighthouse Beach, Fire Island

Numerous opportunities present themselves on Fire Island for quiet nude use of lonely stretches of open sand, but Lighthouse Beach is the hands-down favorite of naturists in this region.

Located just an hour from New York City off the southern shore of Long Island, Lighthouse Beach is pristine and protected. Clothing-optional use of Lighthouse Beach is recognized by the National Park Service with signs, ranger patrols, and an understanding that naturists are an important and vital user group. Hundreds of naked singles, couples, and families enjoy the safe and socially healthy atmosphere at Lighthouse, with much of the good atmosphere due to the family-friendly work of the key user group, Friends of Lighthouse Beach (www.friendsoflighthousebeach.com).

Practical info

Drive east on Long Island by Southern State Parkway to the Robert Moses Causeway south to Robert Moses State Park. At the traffic circle around a large water tower head east and park in Field #5. Walk toward the 168-foot, gray and white lighthouse, and at a gravel road turn right, and find a boardwalk trail over the dunes to the western section of the clothing-optional beach.

There are two clothing-optional sections to this beach. Split by a 300-yard 'no-nudity' zone where a path from the lighthouse drops people on to the beach, the western portion is approximately one quarter mile long, and the eastern portion is approximately two thirds of a mile long. The textile-only section gives visitors to the lighthouse the chance to walk to the beach without bumping into naked sunbathers. It's a unique setup, but it seems to keep everyone happy.

▼ Nearly a mile of nude beach, divided into two sections, make Lighthouse Beach a hugely popular spot to escape the city heat in summer. Picture by Michael Cooney

▲ Freedom... New York style. A skinny dipper on the sands at Fire Island. Picture by Barnaby Hall

The USA

Smith Point, Fire Island

This remains a delightful haven for nude recreation – accepted alike by federal rangers and Suffolk County deputies. Far less crowded than Lighthouse Beach, Smith Point offers long quiet walks on lonely stretches of sand.

Practical info

Take the Sunrise Expressway to Exit #58 at Shirley. Turn south on to William Floyd Parkway and drive 5 miles to Smith Point. Just before turning left to go to Smith Point County Park, you will pass an octagonal-shaped visitor center on the right for Fire Island National Seashore. Continue to the vast county parking area, and walk back to the visitor center.

From this building, find the boardwalk heading west, parallel to the shore. Follow it for five minutes and turn left at a fork, heading to the Atlantic. Once on the beach, walk 200 yards west to find near the dunes two white 4x4 posts, each with a green stripe at the top. According to rangers, you may go nude for a mile west of here.

North Carolina

Other North Carolina naturist contacts

North Carolina Naturists

PO Box 49108,
Charlotte, NC 28277
www.ncnaturists.com

Triangle Area Naturists

PO Box 12011
Research Triangle Park, NC 27709
www.trianglenaturists.com

Coventry Club & Resort

65 Harbour Drive
Tabor City, NC 28463
www.coventryresort.com

Ocracoke Beach, Cape Hatteras Seashore

Ocracoke Beach is an unofficial but well-established clothing-optional site on the Atlantic side of Ocracoke Island, which is one of the barrier islands that make up the Outer Banks of North Carolina. It used to be the domain of Edward Teach, otherwise known as Blackbeard the Pirate. Most of the island is now part of Cape Hatteras National Seashore, which is a unit of the National Park Service.

Practical info

Ocracoke Island is accessible only by ferry or by small aircraft. From the village of Ocracoke, take Highway 12 north-east for about 5 miles and turn right at Ramp 67. Four-wheel drive vehicles are recommended. Partially deflate tires for better traction on the sand. Open sunrise to sunset.

The USA

Ohio

Bare Valley Family Nudist Camp

Almost totally surrounded by Wayne National Forest, this club is only a short 45 minute drive from Columbus. Plenty of hiking trails, a heated swimming pool, volleyball, petanque and horseshoes are available here.

Paradise Gardens Family Nudist Resort

This resort is situated on 35 acres and boasts a 2-acre pond with great fishing. Olympic size swimming pool, hot tub and sauna. Open year round.

Sunn Jammers Recreational Park

Sun Jammers Recreational Park is located in central Ohio on 62 acres of rolling hills. Enjoy the 4-acre lake, which has been stocked with game fish, or simply relax on the beach area, complete with rafts and paddleboat. Sunn Jammers offers 96 campsites with full hook-ups.

Bare Valley Family Nudist Camp

PO Box 934
Logan, OH 43138
www.barevalley.com

Paradise Gardens Family Nudist Resort

6100 Blue Rock Road
Cincinnati, OH 45247
www.nudelife.com

Sunn Jammers Recreational Park

PO Box 70
Newark, OH 43058
sunnjammer@alltel.net
www.sunnjammers.com

Other Ohio naturist contacts

Northcoast Naturists

PO Box 33673
Cleveland, OH 44133
www.northcoast-naturists.org

Oklahoma

Oaklake Trails Naturist Park

This club is located on 400 acres and has miles of hiking trails. The facilities at Oaklake Trails include clubhouse, pool, playground, volleyball court, petanque court, shuffleboard and campsites.

Oaklake Trails Naturist Park

24601 Milfay Rd
Depew, OK 74028
www.oaklaketrails.com

Other Oklahoma naturist contacts

River Valley Naturists

PO Box 72
Shady Point, OK 74956
www.rivervalleynaturist.homestead.com

Oregon

Breitenbush Hot Springs, east of Salem

Clothing is optional·anywhere there's water in this eco-friendly, rustic resort. The atmosphere is environmentally aware, the hearty food served is vegetarian, and the attitude generally favors those who like their trees up and their pants down.

Sign up for workshops on holistic health and alternative medicine. Nude hiking and cross-country skiing will tempt the freest of spirits. The hot pools, steam sauna, river-dipping, massage, yoga, aerobics, aromatherapy, hydrotherapy and herbal wraps allow others the quiet and relaxation they seek.

Practical info
From Salem, take Highway 22 to Detroit, turn left (north) on Route 46 at the one gas station, and continue 10 miles to Cleator Campground. Just 100 feet past it, take a right over the bridge across the Breitenbush River. Follow signs, taking every left turn after the bridge, to Breitenbush parking. Phone first for reservations.

Breitenbush Hot Springs Retreat

P.O. Box 578
Detroit, OR 97342
Tel: 503 854 3320
www.breitenbush.com

1. **Collins Beach**
2. **Rooster Rock State Park**
3. **Keno Road Quarry**

■ Perhaps the most complete way of getting some sea air on your skin, nude cruises have become a regular part of the naturist travel market. Pictures on right by Michael Cooney show a cruise organised by Bare Necessities, a naturist travel firm

Collins Beach, Sauvie Island, north of Portland

Sauvie Island's north end on the Columbia River is a large, popular family recreation site managed by the state Dept of Fish and Wildlife. Signs acknowledge the legal status of nude use here. People fish, wade, swim, kayak, play volleyball and sunbathe on Collins Beach – nearly all, au naturel.

There are porta-potties in the parking lot, but no other amenities. You can buy food and drink at the small store near the bridge you cross driving on to the island. A 10pm curfew keeps use of the beach to the day. A model local user group, the Oregon Clothing-Optional Beach Alliance (www.orcoba.org),

works with site officials in hosting beach cleanups and social gatherings.

Practical info

From Portland, go 10 miles north-west on US 30. Turn right over Sauvie Island Bridge. Buy a parking pass at the store near the island side of the bridge, then continue north beyond the store for 1.8 miles. Turn right on Reeder Road and go 10.7 miles until it becomes gravel (passing Reeder Beach and Walton Beach, both clothing-required). Shortly after the road becomes gravel, find parking on the left and signs on the right saying, 'Collins Beach, Clothing Optional Area, Nudity on Beach Only.'

Rooster Rock State Park, east of Portland

At the south end of the majestic Columbia River Gorge, Rooster Rock has seen legally sanctioned nude use longer than any public lands site in North America. Clothes-mandatory and clothes-optional beaches are side-by-side, but separated by acres of river brush. Boaters gather and party on weekends. The nude area includes open stretches and small pockets of sand on the mainland shore, as well as on Sand Island, usually accessible by wading 100 meters of waist-deep water. Toilets are at the clothes-mandatory parking lot above the beach.

Rooster Rock can be one of the best

nude beaches in North America, or one hardly worth going to. If the river level is high, much of the nude beach is underwater or inaccessible without a boat. Later in the summer, the dry, clean sand emerges and people arrive with kites, games and barbecues.

Practical info

Drive 25 miles east from Portland on I-84, turn off at Rooster Rock State Park (Exit 25), pay a modest day-use fee to enter the park, proceed to the far east end of the parking lot, and walk eastward down to the river. The beach is also looked after by ORCOBA (see listing above).

Keno Road Quarry, Ashland

This old rock quarry is used regularly by local sunbathers and skinny-dippers. Keno's flat spots on which to lay out comfortably are few. Folks in the know bring an air mattress to float on.

Practical info

Exit I-15 at the south end of Ashland. Take Highway 66 south a little way to Dead Indian Road. Go left (east) about

15-20 miles. Approximately 1.5 miles after passing the Howard Prairie Reservoir turnoff, watch for a turn to the right. The Keno Road name appears after the turn. Go 0.75 miles to the top of the hill. Turn right at the gravel piles. Follow the gravel road around to Bare Lake; the beach is at the north-east end.

Squaw Mountain Ranch, Estacada

This year-round facility is in the foothills of the Cascade Mountains and is one of the oldest US nudist resorts. You'll find

a wood-fired sauna, private lake, shared kitchen, swimming pool, club house, lodge and acres of hiking trails.

Willamettans, near Eugene

This member-owned nudist club is the largest in the Pacific Northwest, and

is just 30 minutes' drive away from Eugene, Oregon.

Bare Necessities Tour & Travel
would like to welcome you aboard!

Since 1991, Bare Necessities Tour & Travel has been America's premiere clothing-optional tour production company. With cruise charters aboard ships as elegant as Holland America's Maasdam and as regal as the Star Flyer to destinations as Exotic as Thailand; as pristine as the South Pacific; as perfect as the Caribbean and as unexpected as Alaska, it is easy to understand why Bare Necessities is the undisputed leader in Naturist Travel.

find out more:
www.cruisenude.com

Pennsylvania

Sunny Rest Resort, Poconos

This clothing-optional club is located in the Pocono Mountains just north of Philadelphia. There are motel rooms, camping with hookups, heated pool, volleyball courts, fitness center, sauna and hot tub.

PSHS Inc, near Reading

This resort has over 130 acres where you can enjoy nature walks, games or just lounging by one of the two pools (one indoor, one outdoor). In addition there is a hot tub, tennis and volleyball courts, petanque and shuffleboard.

Sunny Rest Resort

425 Sunny Rest Drive
Palmerton, PA 18071
www.sunnyrest.com

PSHS Inc

5028 Camp Road
Mohnton, PA 19540
www.pennsylvan.net

Other Pennsylvania naturist contacts

West Penn Naturist

PO Box 4528
Pittsburgh, PA 15205
www.westpennnaturist.com

South Carolina

Cedar Creek Family Nudist Park, Lexington Cty

Cedar Creek is the home of the southeast's largest music festival for nudists, NudeStock, held each year in September. Amenities include swimming pool, hot tub, nature trails, sand and water volleyball, RV sites with hook-ups, clubhouse and year-round social events.

Cedar Creek Park

260 Gantt Mill Road
Leesville, SC 29070
www.cedarcreekpark.com

Other South Carolina naturist groups

Travelites

PO Box 90836
Columbia, SC 29290
www.travelites.info

Tennessee

Cherokee Lodge & Resort, near Crossville

Cherokee Lodge near Crossville is open year round. Plenty of cabins, rooms and camping sites are available. There are hiking trails through the scenic woods, pool and even an authentic teepee.

Cherokee Lodge & Resort

324 Trails End Road
Crossville, TN 38571
www.cherokee-lodge.com

Texas

Emerald Lake Nudist Resort, Houston area

Emerald Lake Resort is located on a private 12-acre lake with great fishing. Rental rooms in addition to RV and tent sites available. Open year round.

Lone Star Resort, Navasota

Lone Star Resort is nestled in the heart of Texas ranch country, on 45 acres complete with towering pine and majestic oaks. Nightly rental of RV and tent spaces is available. Lone Star Resort also rents long-term RV sites and mobile home sites for snowbirds.

Emerald Lake Nudist Resort

23198 Loop 494
Porter, TX 77365
www.vealj.com/nudist

Lone Star Resort

18198 FM 362
Navasota, TX 77868
www.lonestarresort.com

▲ Hippie Hollow is one of America's most famous nude beaches. Although adults-only it has a true naturist atmosphere and is highly popular. Pictures by Michael Cooney

TEXAS

Dallas

Hippie Hollow Austin

Houston

South Padre Island

Hippie Hollow, Austin

A county park on sparkling Lake Travis, north-west of Austin. Known to only a few as McGregor Park; even official county documents and signs use the name Hippie Hollow. A rocky shoreline and gravel parking, not much more – except one of the country's most famous skinny-dipping locations, officially clothing-optional and loved by thousands. Open year-round during daylight hours, with children excluded by order of a prudish county commissioners' court, Hippie Hollow attracts those wanting to float, swim and sun in the nude.

Lake Travis is used for regional flood control, so its level and temperature vary considerably throughout the year. A generous swimming area is marked by buoys, and many visitors bring inflatable rafts for floating. In the late summer and fall, the water is typically low and warm. The large rock slabs found along the shore extend under water,

so do not dive recklessly from the limestone ledges.

Practical info

Drive north-west from Austin on RM 2222, then west on Highway 620. Turn right on Comanche Trail, which skirts the lake, and travel 2.2 miles. Look for the Hippie Hollow sign, and turn left into the parking lot. A parking fee is charged. Walk down to the paved trail from the south-west corner of the lot, and from there to any of the several rocky paths that lead to the water. A couple of chemical toilets serve the area. No open fires, no glass, no pets. Park closes at dusk; no overnight camping. The Hill Country Nudists are frequent visitors to Hippie Hollow.

> **Hill Country Nudists**
>
> PO Box 91802
> Austin, TX 78709
> www.hillcountrynudists.com

▲ Lake life, at The Ledges in Vermont. Picture by Michael Cooney

South Padre Island, Cameron County

The south Gulf Coast of Texas is known to students on spring break and to more mature snowbirds for gentle breezes, sunny skies, abundant shells and fishing.

Practical info

From Port Isabel, take Highway 100 across the causeway to South Padre Island. Turn left at Padre Boulevard and follow signs to the Convention Center, 4 miles from the end of the causeway. Continue north another 4.5 miles on this road, which becomes known as Ocean Boulevard. At Beach Access Point #6, drive on to the beach and turn left (north). From the beach access sign, travel about 8.5 miles along the beach. The unofficial nude beach is marked by a log with the word 'nude' painted on one end. Four-wheel drive vehicles are recommended, though many 2WD vehicles can make it. If driving on the beach, stay on the dark, wet packed sand; low tide is best.

BB's Hideaway, east Texas

BB's Hideaway is between Dallas and Shreveport in East Texas on 40 acres. Walking trails, pool, hot tub and plenty of RV and tenting sites available.

Bluebonnet, central Texas

Located on 55 acres with rolling hills, oak trees and beautiful meadows, with plenty of space for nature walks or jogging. The site is open year round.

Natural Horisun, Houston

Natural Horisun is located on 32 acres of pecan trees just outside of Houston. Plenty of RV and tent sites are available to rent.

Natures Resort, Rio Grande Valley

Natures Resort is located in the Rio Grande Valley of south Texas. Warm winters make Natures Resort a great place to spend the winter months. South Padre Island and Mexico are both close by.

Riverside Ranch, San Antonio

Riverside Ranch is located on 22 acres and is just 25 minutes' drive from San Antonio. The resort is open all year round.

Wildwood Naturist's Resort, Decatur

The resort is located on 118 beautiful acres. Nearby attractions include Texas Motor Speedway, Six Flags Over Texas, Vineyards, Wise County Antique Auto Show and much more. Open year round.

BB's Hideaway

PO Box 966
Canton, TX 75103
www.bbshideaway.com

Bluebonnet

699 CR 1180
Alvord, TX 76225
www.bluebonnetnudistpark.com

Natural Horisun

11715 FM 442
Boling, TX 77420
www.naturalhorisun.com

Natures Resort

10201 Monte Cristo Road
Edcouch, TX 78538
www.naturesresort.net

Riverside Ranch

1238 County Road 125
Elmendorf, TX 78112
www.riversideranch.net

Wildwood Naturist's Resort

241 Private Road 1179
Decatur, TX 76234
www.wildwoodnaturist.com

Other Texas naturist contacts

Sunbirds Sun Club

PO Box 111524
Carrollton, TX 75007

Roamin' Bares

PO Box 61
Gorman, TX 76454
roaminbares@yahoo.com

Sandpipers Resort

9504 North Seminary Road
Edinburg, TX 78541
www.sandpiperresort.com

Want to see more?

Fabulous sights on our
exclusive naturist tours.
The world's largest
naturist catalog.
Great stories and pictures
in *Travel Naturally*.

It's all here, and more...
CALL AND SEE!

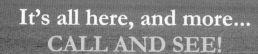

Inter naturally INC.

MAGAZINES   TRAVEL   BOOKS/DVDs

SUBSCRIPTION AND FREE CATALOG: (973) 697-3552 — TRAVEL SERVICE: (973) 697-8099
www.Internaturally.com

Vermont

The Ledges, southern Vermont

Close to Massachusetts and cherished by many skinny-dippers as the premier site of Vermont as well as exemplary of what a more body-tolerant corporate America should support and enjoy in its natural preserves.

Located a short distance from one of PG&E's clothed picnic grounds and in a portion of the Green Mountain National Forest, large flat rocks offer naked sunbathing and diving platforms. The water level of Harriman Reservoir is lower later in the season and thus opens more places to enjoy the sun. Supported and frequented by the local naturist group, Friends of the Ledges (see ledges.dimentech.com).

Practical info

From Brattleboro take Route 9 west toward Wilmington, and bear left on to Route 100 south. Watch for the 'Flame Stables' sign and bear right up the dirt access road, passing a few homes and continuing almost a mile to the picnic grounds. Once there, park as close to the lower right parking and picnic area as possible. Continue to the right along the shore until a well-trod path becomes evident, and follow it five minutes to The Ledges.

▼ Innocent pleasures at The Ledges, commonly regarded as the best nude bathing site in Vermont – although other lakes are enjoyed here too (picture opposite). All pictures by Michael Cooney

The USA

96

Cunningham Cove, Lake Willoughby Park

Hassle-free, sandy wading beach for children and water sports. There is clean but chilly water with fine trout fishing and water-skiing.

Practical info

Drive north on I-93 or I-91 and exit from I-91 at Lyndon. Then take Route 5 north to West Burke, bearing right on to Route 5A to south end of Lake Willoughby. Park either at the clothed beach by the road, or about 200 feet south of this on the left. A trail from this second parking area leads down to the lake at Cunningham Cove, which lies around a small point from the clothed beach.

Abbott's Glen Inn

Located in southern Vermont, and the ideal place to stay after a day at The Ledges. There are 55 acres with a pond, meadows, hiking trails, and over 1,500 feet of gentle stream frontage, some of which invites cooling dips on hot days.

Lodging includes daily breakfasts featuring local foods, five lovely guest rooms, comfortable sitting areas, wood stove, indoor hot tub and Finnish sauna. Tent camping available. Trails for hiking in the summer and cross-country skiing in the winter. Massage and dinners available on weekends for a fee.

Punch Bowl, Mad River, Warren

Privately owned and supervised, the Punch Bowl is open to the public and offers a litter-free beach, sunning rocks, no gawkers, good diving, a small waterfall and an island.

Practical info

Take I-89 to Waterbury and go south on Route 100 to Irasville. From routes 100 and 17 in Irasville, take 100 south for 2.7 miles. On the right is a private driveway, then an open field. Park at the north end of the field, go 0.3 miles north of the steel bridge over Mad River, and follow the tracks through the field to the end. Walk left down to the river.

Rock River, North of Brattleboro

Widely recognized as a skinny-dipping hole by locals, Rock River has low cliffs suitable for diving and a sandy beach for picnicking. The first large pool is used mainly by clothed swimmers, pools upstream by skinny-dippers.

Practical info

From the Route 5 and Route 30 interchange in Brattleboro, drive Route 30 north for nearly 19 miles to Williamsville Road, just before crossing a bridge over Rock River. Find a large, off-pavement, roadside parking area on the right side of Route 30.

Walk along Williamsville Road – which becomes Depot Road – for 150 yards, and turn down the first right at Station Road. Walk the unpaved road for another 150 yards, which curves to the left and becomes a trail past a dilapidated cabin. Walk the often slippery riverside trail past one swimming hole (usually textile) a quarter mile to the next, where the path crosses a creek and dips down to the second large swimming area with sandy beach. Additional swimming holes upstream.

Virginia

White Tail Park

This family-oriented nudist resort is located on 45 acres about 50 minutes from Norfolk, Richmond, Virginia Beach and Colonial Williamsburg. RV and tent sites available as well as other indoor lodging, indoor and outdoor pools, hot tub, playground and many planned activities.

Abbott's Glen Inn

3542 Vt. Route 112
Halifax, VT 05358
Tel: 802 368 2525
www.abbottsglen.com

Other Vermont naturist contacts

Coventry Club & Resort

468 Beebe Hill Road
Milton, VT 05468
www.coventryresort.com

▲ **A skinny-dipper cools off in Vermont. Picture by Michael Cooney**

White Tail Park

39033 White Tail Drive
Ivor, VA 23866
www.whitetailpark.org

Other Virginia naturist contacts

Capital Area Family Naturists

PO Box 3413
Merrifield, VA 22116
www.cafnat.org

Potomac Rambling Bares

PO Box 515
Oakton, VA 22124
www.prbares.org

▲ **Enjoying rural Vermont as nature intended. Picture by Michael Cooney**

The USA

Washington

Doe Bay Resort, Orcas Island

Often called the best of the San Juan Islands, Orcas Island is a nature-lover's dream. Island forests, deer, and sea life coexist with small restaurants and art galleries. Doe Bay Resort is an eco-friendly retreat from high-tech madness.

Vegetarians will appreciate the cafe menu, while naturists will be eager to visit the resort's small, pebbly, but delightfully clothing-optional beach, with views of the beautiful San Juan Island seascape.

Then you can soak in any of the three clothing-optional tubs – warm, hot, and hottest – above the nude beach, or steam away your cares in the sauna. Overnight lodging ranges

from bare rooms, rustic cabins and beach-side yurts, to entire apartments.

Practical info

Drive north from Seattle for one hour to Anacortes, and then take the Washington State Ferry to Orcas Island. Once on Orcas, drive north on Horseshoe Highway through Eastsound and follow the signs from here to Doe Bay.

Doe Bay Resort

PO Box 437
Olga, WA 98279
Tel: 360 376 2291
www.doebay.com

Dressed in nature's garb at leafy Avalon. Picture by Michael Cooney

The USA

West Virginia

Avalon, Paw Paw

Nestled in the hills of West Virginia, Avalon is the perfect retreat for naturist activities or just relaxing. A four-season resort and community with a casual atmosphere, offering a fine restaurant and bar, casino lounge, weekend entertainment and dancing on Saturday night. Recreation abounds with tennis and volleyball, indoor and outdoor pools, hot tubs and sauna, plus hiking on nature's lovely trails. Workshops, special activities, massage and holiday events are always on the calendar. Enjoy a weekend, week, or day visit and stay in modern hotel rooms, rental condos, or campsites. Just two hours from Washington, DC and Baltimore, Md, and three hours from Pittsburgh, Pa.

Avalon

PO Box 369
Paw Paw, WV 25434
Tel: 304 947 5600
www.avalon-resort.com

▼ Who needs the sea with a naturist beach this good? Wisconsin's Mazo beach is a jewel in the American Midwest, much appreciated by the skinny-dippers who gather here in large numbers. Pictures by Michael Cooney

Wisconsin

Mazo Beach, Mazomanie State Wildlife Refuge

Popular, secluded and scenic, this clothing-optional site along the Wisconsin River ranks at the top of the list for Midwest public lands skinny-dipping. A wide open sandy beach, warm water, and a strong presence by friendly naturists keep Mazo a favorite of Wisconsin and Midwest naturists.

Friends of Mazo Beach sponsor weekend activities such as clothing drives, corn roasts, Christmas in July, a Nude Olympics and volleyball tournaments. Visitors are welcome to participate.

Practical info

From the north-west, take I-94 E to US-12 (exit 92). Go 23.6 miles (through Sauk City) and turn right on WI-78. Go 4.1 miles and turn right on (second) Laws Drive. Or from the north-east, take US-151 south to Sun Prairie and turn on WI-19 going west. Go 16.5 miles and turn right on US-12. Go 9 miles and turn left on County Y. Go 5.2 miles and turn right on (second) Laws Drive. Or from Madison, take US-12 north toward Sauk City for 16 miles. Turn left on County Y. Go 5.2 miles and turn right on (second) Laws Drive.

Once you are on Laws Drive, continue for 0.2 miles and turn left on the first gravel road. Proceed 0.2 miles to a parking lot on the left. Walk the one-mile gravel road to the clothing-optional section of the beach.

The USA

▲ Hot springs and no costumes in the great outdoors. Opposite page: Orient Land Trust in Colorado. Above left: a wilderness hot spring in the Tecopa area, California. Above right: Tanque Verde Falls in Arizona. Pictures by Michael Cooney

Hot springs

North America still has an astounding amount of wild lands, and many of them may easily be explored nude. Just hike, bike, paddle, ski, or snowshoe a distance from the trailhead, parking lot, or boat ramp, and you will have multiple lifetimes' worth of naked exploration before you. Laws differ from region to region, and may depend on which government agency is in charge of the particular tract of public land, but get away from the crowds and you'll have ample opportunity for some of the best nude recreation this continent has to offer.

For many Americans, it doesn't get any better than a long, soothing soak in a natural hot spring. Surrounded by gentle steam rising from the water, the only sounds heard are from birds or a nearby stream, far away from cars, crowds, and concrete. Hot springs are a mini vacation all to themselves.

There are hot springs found from

the Atlantic to the Pacific, but most are found in the Southwest, the Pacific Northwest, and in Southern California along the south-eastern slopes of the Sierra Nevada. Entrepreneurs have turned many into commercial establishments, and some open them to nude use. The best of these have already been listed in this guide.

Equally popular – although with those wishing to work a bit for their soaks – are the undeveloped hot springs in more primitive areas. Some of these are only a few meters from the road, while others require a day's hike through stunning wilderness territory. In the panel on the left are some of the best natural, non-commercialized, and easily accessible hot springs that see regular nude use. For directions and more information, see the excellent hot spring guides by Marjorie Gersh-Young, available at Aqua Thermal Access (831) 426-2956.

Some of the best US hot springs

Buckeye Hot Spring, CA
Travertine Hot Springs, CA
Hot Creek Area, CA with
L'il Hot Creek, CA
Pulky's Pool, CA
Crowley Hot Spring, CA
Jerry Johnson Hot Springs, ID
Spencer Hot Springs, NV
Three Forks, OR
McCredie Hot Springs, OR
Meditation Pool Warm Spring, OR
Cougar Hot Springs, OR
Bagby Hot Springs, OR

Canada

Canada generally has a more relaxed attitude than the US to bare bodies, and there are some hugely popular, world-class beaches and resorts here to satisfy local and international demand. Indeed Wreck Beach in Vancouver is one of the world's most popular nude beaches, attracting up to 14,000 naked souls on a hot weekend.

Canadian nudist clubs and resorts go out of their way to make overseas visitors feel particularly welcome – but do get in touch first to arrange your visit. Prices at clubs tend to be a little lower in Canada than in the US for comparable facilities. And there also tend to be more young families; all of the Canadian clubs listed in this guide are open to children and their parents.

The Naturist Action Committee (www.naturistaction.org) and Federation of Canadian Naturists (www.fcn.ca) provide online information about Canadian laws and issues pertaining to nudity.

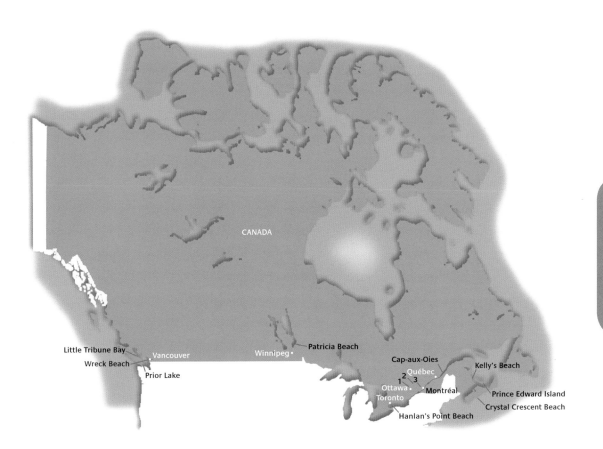

CANADA

Little Tribune Bay
Wreck Beach
Vancouver
Prior Lake
Winnipeg
Patricia Beach
Cap-aux-Oies
Québec
1 2 3
Ottawa
Montréal
Toronto
Hanlan's Point Beach
Kelly's Beach
Prince Edward Island
Crystal Crescent Beach

Québec beaches
1. Meech Lake
2. Lac Simon
3. Oka Park

Canada

British Columbia

Prior Lake, Victoria, Vancouver Island

Victoria, the capital of British Columbia, is a charming city on the southern tip of Vancouver Island. Victorians (at least those who do not live up to their name) established a nudist beach at Prior Lake within Thetis Lake Park. In July 1978 city officials conceded that it would be pointless to enforce laws against nude bathing.

Prior Lake doesn't have a beach – rather, it has a pier on which to sunbathe. The pier is small but popular; the lake offers a refreshing swim on a hot day. There are no nearby amenities.

Practical info
From central Victoria drive north on Highway 1 to Exit 8 (Helmcken Road). Head north on Helmcken Road, turning at the first left on to Watkiss Way. Drive 1.5km to the intersection with Burnside Road West. Continue on Watkiss for 2.8km to a locked gate and the Prior Lake trailhead on the left. Follow the trail 100m down to the clothing-optional area and pier.

■ It's the people who make nude beaches such nice places to be – as a trip to Wreck Beach in Vancouver will prove to anyone. Picture opposite by James Loewen

Wreck Beach, Vancouver

Wreck Beach is a naturist success story and home to up to 14,000 laid-back nude bathers on a hot weekend. No beach in North America compares to Wreck in terms of the quirky and quixotic community that thrives there. Sun-worshippers, drummers, jammers, food vendors, Frisbee-tossers, and kayakers all blend, mingle, and merge into a naturist calliope of free-spirited joie de vivre.

Practical info

From Route 99 south of Vancouver, drive north, past the airport, and immediately exit at the river's far side on to Marine Drive. You'll exit going east and double back, passing under Route 99 and threading through some small streets until you're on Southwest Marine Drive going west. Continue for several kilometres until you reach the UBC campus.

Extending from the Musqueam

Indian reserve to West Spanish Banks is 7.8km of clothing-optional beach at the mouth of the north arm of the Fraser River. The Greater Vancouver Regional District has extended legal status but allocated no support to Wreck. So entrepreneurs have packed in food and drink. Police and rescue, when required, have come by hovercraft over the waves.

The main beach is at trail/gate 6 (near the intersection of Northwest Marine Drive and University Boulevard, directly opposite Place Vanier Residence). Park in the visitor (pay) lot. On weekends, some staff parking lots are available to the public. Go down the long, steep set of steps to the beach.

Additional information and effective support of clothes-free use of the beach is provided by the Wreck Beach Preservation Society, whose website is www.wreckbeach.org.

▲ A wild beach, yet right on a city's doorstep – Wreck Beach is as full of variety as the many people who come to enjoy its unique atmosphere. Pictures by James Loewen

Little Tribune Bay, Hornby Island

Set off the eastern shore of Vancouver Island amid dozens of equally pristine rocky isles, Little Tribune Bay and the eco-friendly surrounding community recall the best of the late 1960s. Don't expect lush accommodation, but comfortable textile B&Bs and campgrounds are available nearby, along with small farms and co-op grocery stores. Little Tribune is the smaller of two bays, and even with home construction nearby remains a favourite with a younger crowd more inclined to wear organic cotton or hemp than the latest fashion designs. The beach is wide and the walk to the water shallow.

Practical info

Travel from the Canadian mainland to Hornby Island is time-consuming and requires three ferry crossings, but Little Tribune is worth it, especially if you bring a kayak and enjoy some naked paddling here and elsewhere along the rugged coastline.

On Vancouver Island, drive Highway 19 north of Fanny Bay to the Denman Island Ferry. From Denman Island take another ferry to Hornby Island. From there, follow the island road clockwise to the north end of Hornby at the intersection of Shields and Central Roads. Drive Central Road 200m to the dirt Tribune Bay

Road on the left, and follow it 200m more to the beach.

Once out on the North Gulf Islands, another established skinny-dipping site is on Cortes Island. A small portion of Hague Lake has been used naked by locals for years. Drive Highway 19 on Vancouver Island to the town of Campbell River; take the ferry to Quadra Island, and another to Cortes Island. From there, drive Harbour Road; go right on to Carrington Bay Road; left on to Whaletown Road; right on to Gorge Harbour Road; right on to Seaford Road and past Gunflint Lake to Hague Lake on the left. The main parking lot is on the right across the road. The nude section of the lake is beyond the developed clothed section, along the rocks approximately 10m from where you first find the lake.

Cufra Cliffs B&B is on Thetis Island to the south. This clothing-optional B&B offers a quiet, even serene getaway with an outdoor hot tub and a view of Cufra Inlet.

▲ Hornby Island's nude beach at Little Tribune Bay offers a true back-to-nature experience in keeping with the rest of this unspoilt island. Picture by Loretta Prosser

Little Tribune Bay accommodation
Cufra Cliffs
Tel: +1 250 246 1509
www.cufracliffs.com

Manitoba

Patricia Beach, Lake Winnipeg

Patricia Beach Provincial Park at the south end of Lake Winnipeg is an hour's drive north of Winnipeg on Highway 59. The sandy, naturally pristine beach sits on a peninsula jutting into the lake. The natural beauty and naturist camaraderie draw dozens of naturists on hot summer days.

Practical info

Pay the entrance fee and park in the northernmost lot behind the beach. Walk less than 1km north and ford the wide creek to enjoy a kilometre of fine, white sand, which has over 30 years' tradition of nude use.

Another option is head to the more secluded Beaconia Beach, situated on an island in the same lake. Continue north on Highway 59 beyond the turnoff for Patricia Beach a few kilometres to Provincial Road 500; turn left and go 2km to the small town of Beaconia. Continue until the road turns to the right, but take the gravel road leading straight ahead instead for approximately 2km more to a parking area. Walk beyond the dunes to the beach, turn left, and continue 1km to the clothing-optional section of Beaconia Beach.

▼ A city success story to cheer any free-minded Canadian: Hanlan's Point Beach has official status as a clothing-optional beach. Middle and bottom pictures by Paul Rapoport

Ontario

Hanlan's Point Beach, Toronto

One of North America's best free beach success stories, Hanlan's Point was used nude quietly for years. It came under attack by anti-nudity forces in the 1990s, until naturists convinced the Toronto City Council to engage in a pilot project to see how officially sanctioned clothing-optional use would work in an urban environment. In 1999 the city voted 41 to 9 to officially designate the beach clothing-optional.

Practical info

A small ferry takes you on a short ride

to an island near Toronto's bustling downtown. A leisurely walk through the island park brings you to the clothing-optional beach, which faces away from the city and out across Lake Ontario. Avoid going nude in any area that is visible from the walkways.

Take the Hanlan's ferry at the dock on Bay Street in Toronto city centre. Off the ferry, follow the fencing south until it ends at a changing building, where there is access to the beach. Signs direct visitors to the clothing-optional area.

Canada

Canada

Bare Oaks Family Naturist Park, Sharon

Bare Oaks is a year-round park with traditional naturist values. It is a place where the entire family can experience naturism. The varied modern facilities are nestled in the natural wilderness of the Ontario greenbelt and Oak Ridges Moraine. It offers day-use membership and seasonal campsites but also welcomes visitors and travelers.
Practical info
Located between Toronto and the gateway to Ontario's cottage country, it is the perfect location to stay while visiting Toronto. A short drive south on Highway 404 gets you into Toronto in about 30 minutes.

Club Naturiste Richard Brunet, St-Eugène

A primarily French-speaking club of 24 wooded hectares, 50 minutes' drive away from Montréal. Pool, sauna, hot tub, children's playground, bar, simple restaurant and (clothed-only) dancing.
Practical info
For more information and to arrange a visit, contact the club first.

Sunny Glades Nature Park, Bothwell

This 38-hectare rustic naturist park features swimming pool, pond, spa, hiking trails and a lovely restored barn that serves as a recreation hall. Lodging includes rental rooms, camping, trailers and a modern cottage.
Practical info
For more information and to arrange a visit, contact the club first.

■ Family naturism from start to finish at Bare Oaks near Toronto. Picture supplied by the park

Bare Oaks Family Naturist Park

20237 Kennedy Road
Sharon, ON L0G 1V0
Tel: +1 905 473 6060
www.bareoaks.ca

Club Naturiste Richard Brunet

400 Domaine Road
St-Eugène, ON K0B 1P0
Tel: +1 613 674 5277
www.cnrb.ca

Sunny Glades Nature Park

PO Box 309
Bothwell, ON N0P 1C0
Tel: +1 519 695 3619
www.sunnyglades.com

Québec

Meech Lake, Gatineau Park, Gatineau

A sandy beach on a north-east section of Meech Lake, surrounded by superb scenery and shaded by majestic pine trees. Ideal for swimming. Naturists and textiles mix with full tolerance.
Practical info
From Ottawa, take Highway 5 north through Hull, as far as Exit 12 for Gatineau Park. Turn left towards the park and continue 6km further to the parking lot for O'Brien Beach on Meech Lake. This beach is textile only. From the parking lot, find the path (No. 36) which heads north towards the wooded area at the right of the changing cabins. After a 10-minute walk you will cross a small bridge over a narrow part of the lake. Textiles and naturists sometimes bathe upstream from this bridge. Continue past the bridge, to where the path divides, and take the left fork to the sandy beach.

For more information on Meech Lake, contact the Federation of Québec Naturists (www.fqn.qc.ca).

▲ Not only is there a tree-lined oasis for nude swimming, but even a sandy beach at Meech Lake near Ottawa. The textiles who come here aren't fussed by nude bathers either, making for a happy coexistence. Pictures by Luís Barrantes

Canada

▲ With a long sandy shore more like an ocean beach than an inland lake beach, Lac Simon's nude bathers take full advantage of the chance to enjoy the outdoors as nature intended – and are campaigning to keep things that way. Picture by Marc A. Boileau

Lac Simon, Duhamel, north-west of Montréal

Halfway between Montréal and Hull on Route 148, take Route 321 north to Duhamel, which has a deli and a hotel.

Practical info
Park at the SÉPAQ-operated public beach and walk east along Lac Simon. Reaching the shallow Nation Nord River, ford it and you're there!

Lac Simon has been used nude for many years, but as of this publication, the municipality of Duhamel is trying to ban nudity on even this one isolated portion of lakeshore. Naturists there have ridden out such nonsense before, and may be expected to once again.

Canada

Oka Park, west of Montréal

Located within Oka Park with its cycle trails, forest and water sports, the long beach attracts a mixture of textiles and nudes, singles and families – and unfortunately some voyeurs. A few hundred metres of clean sandy beach along the refreshing Ottawa River and the comfort in knowing this beach is well-established as clothing-optional make it one of Canada's best bets for public lands skinny-dipping.
Practical info
Route 640, Montréal's beltline on the north, will take you 35km south-west, through St Eustache, becoming Route 344, ending at Oka Park on the Ottawa River. Many nudists arrive by boat. The sandy beach is on the north shore of Lac des Deux Montanges. Nude bathers go to the east end of the 2.5km strand, past the end of the lifeguarded beach.

Across the Ottawa River and in the country's capital bearing the same name, you can stay at either of two clothing-optional B&Bs. Both the Sunshine Manor B&B and the TLC B&B are located in quiet neighbourhoods and provide central locations for naturist explorations including Oka Beach.

▲ Two of Canada's best river nude beaches are handy for nearby urban areas. Oka Park, on the left, is near Montréal; picture by Richard West. Cap-aux-Oies is handy for Québec City and offers a huge expanse of firm sand when the tide is out

Cap-aux-Oies, north-east of Québec City

A delightful, quiet beach along the St Lawrence River. When the tide is out, acres of firm sand open up for tidal exploration.
Practical info
Drive Highway 138 north-east of Québec City to Baie-St-Paul. Turn right on to Route 362, drive 25.3km and turn right on to Rang Cap-aux-Oies. Drive down a steep road toward the river, turn left at the sign directing you to the plage (beach) and continue to the end of the road and a small dirt parking area. Park and walk left up the beach beyond the large rocks piled against the railroad embankment to what is accepted as the clothing-optional area.

Centre Naturiste la Pommerie, St-Antoine-Abbé

Just about the prettiest naturist park in North America, La Pommerie is as close to France as many North Americans may get.

Open fields, extensive apple orchards, vineyards tended by naturists who make their own wine, a love for good cooking, church bells tolling in the small town nearby, and nary an English word to be heard. Whatever language you speak, however, folks at La Pommerie welcome naturists from all over.
Practical info
Life is quiet here, as club members and visitors are asked not to drive their cars on the grounds once they've settled in. Men, women and children walk or ride bikes – some even ride small ponies – to and from the two swimming pools, the pond, and the cafe. Petanque and horseshoes are popular, as they are at many eastern Canadian clubs.

Oka Park accommodation

Sunshine Manor B&B
Tel: +1 613 591 6317
www.sunshinemanor.net

TLC B&B
Tel: +1 613 838 5890
www.tlc-bandb.ca/naturists

Centre Naturiste la Pommerie

2914 Route 209
St-Antoine-Abbé, QC J0S 1N0
Tel: +1 450 826 4723
www.pommerie.com

Domaine le Cyprès, Montauban

Domaine le Cyprès

708 Route de la Chute du Huit
Montauban, QC G0X 1W0
Tel: +1 888 399 2573
www.domainelecypres.qc.ca

The largest naturist centre in Québec, this 226-hectare club sits beside the refreshing Batiscan River, two and a half hours' drive north-east of Montréal. A brief naked walk takes you upstream to a short but dramatic waterfall.

Nude canoeing is available on quieter waters downstream, along with volleyball, petanque, and the requisite lounging by the pool.

Practical info
Le Cyprès is clothes-free, and all are expected to be nude as weather permits. The restaurant serves reasonably priced food to the nude and clothed both indoors and outside at the poolside patio.

New Brunswick

Kelly's Beach, Kouchibouguac National Park

Kouchibouguac National Park offers 40km of sandy shore on the Northumberland Strait. Of the four areas of dunes, only two are accessible by car. The main dune, South Kouchibouguac, is 7km long, ample to accommodate the clothed and the nude sunbather. The best weather is from mid-June to the end of August, with the water reaching its warmest temperatures (58° to 60°F) at the end of the season.

Practical info
Take Route 11 from Moncton to Kouchibouguac Park. Park at Kelly's Beach; walk along the boardwalk to the dune, about 15 minutes. The main bathing area is at the end of the boardwalk; go about 1.5km further south before stripping down.

▼ With 7km of sand, there is plenty of space to find a private nude area at Kelly's Beach. Picture by Neil Hicks

Canada

Nova Scotia

▲ Pretty, popular and firmly on the tourist map: Crystal Crescent Beach is looked after by a friendly community of naturists. Picture by Neil Hicks of the beach's Bluenose Naturist Club. Visit their website at www.bluenosenaturists.com

Crystal Crescent Beach, south of Halifax

The capital of this eastern maritime province, Halifax has its own tolerated nude ocean beach – recommended to visitors who ask the tourist bureau. Great scenery, up to 300 friendly people on a weekend. Rocks to either side protect this sandy beach, but little will protect you from the chill of the Atlantic. Only the heartiest naturist is likely to want more than a quick skinny-dip. A fabulous beach nonetheless.

The Bluenose Naturist Club (see box for website details) was formed after arrests were made at Crystal Crescent Beach on a weekend over 15 years ago. Today they still enjoy the beach and organize swims and house parties in the winter.

Practical info

Drive south from Halifax on Route 349 for 2.6km and turn right, following the Old Sambro Road for 18.1km via Harrietsfield. In Sambro at the stop sign, turn right and drive 2.4km, following the signs to Crystal Crescent Beach.

From the parking lot here, to the right you can see the first two beaches which are clothes-required. Walk for about 20 minutes south, either along the shore or along the overland path, past the second beach to the third. Starting with this third beach and south along the rocks, the entire coast and peninsula are openly clothes-optional.

> **Bluenose Naturist Club**
>
> www.bluenosenaturists.com

▲ A new resort that is already proving popular among Canada's naturists, The Oasis offers a heated pool and secluded woodland setting on Prince Edward Island. Pictures by Bruce Bishop

Prince Edward Island

The Oasis Resort, Cavendish

One of Canada's newer naturist clubs, The Oasis lays claim to a warmer climate than much of the surrounding area, giving naturists a bit more of that highly valued warm sunshine in spring and fall. It's a small club, with a handful of camping sites and efficiency studio units, but a favourite among Canadians who travel the country looking for clothes-free recreation.
Practical info
Canada Select – the nation's accommodations rating program – gave The Oasis a four out of five star rating for its charm. High praise indeed!

Spain: mainland beaches

The popularity of nude beaches has taken off in Spain in just a single generation. Although something of a late starter compared to other European countries, it has been making up for lost time since it gained its first official nude beach in 1979. The Spanish, especially the younger generation, are now among the most enthusiastic advocates of naturist beaches, and there are reckoned to be more than 700 beaches which see some form of nude use.

It is good news for holidaymakers – and of course for the tourist industry which has picked up on the trend in a big way. Spain has expanded its naturist bathing facilities on a breathtaking scale, and continues to develop apace. There is a huge choice of places to stay near many of the nudist beaches, including some hotels with au naturel terraces. There are also some lovely naturist resorts, particularly in the hot and sunny south of the country. With attitudes so relaxed in Spain these days you might discover naked bathers on almost any rural or undeveloped beach.

Spain : mainland

Costa de la Luz
1. Playa Nueva Umbria
2. Playa de Castilla South
3. Playa Camarón-Tres Piedras
4. Playa de la Cortadura
5. Calas de Poniente
6. Cabo de Trafalgar North
7. Canos de Meca
8. Playa de Bolonia
9. Playa Alcaidesa

Costa del Sol
10. Costa Natura
11. Cabopino Playa
12. Benalnatura beach
13. Almanat Beach

Costa Tropical
14. Cantarrijan Playa
15. Playa del Muerto
16. La Joya

Costa Almeria
17. Playa Cerrillos
18. Playa Cabo de Gata
19. Playa de Monsul
20. Cala de San Pedro
21. Playa Los Muertos
22. Cala del Bordenares and
      Cala del Sombrerico
23. Vera Playa

Costa Calida
24. Bolnuevo beaches
25. El Portus
26. Playa Negrete and Playa Parreno

Costa Blanca
27. Playa los Tusales
28. Playa El Carabassi
29. Platja Esparrello
30. Cumbre del Sol
31. Playa de Sant Llorenc

Costa Dorada
32. Playa El Torn
33. Platja Savinosa
34. Cala Fonda
35. El Fonoll Poble Naturista

Costa Brava
36. Mar Bella
37. Playa de la Musclera
38. Playa de Vallpresona
39. Playa de Pals
40. Platja Sant Pere Pescador

Costa Verde
41. Playa de los Nudistas
42. Playa de Valdearenas
43. Playa de Ballota
44. Playa de Torimbia
45. Playa de l'Arena de Vega
46. Playa Conbouzas
47. Playa de Castro de Baroña

▥ Picture on opposite page shows the
beach at Cumbre del Sol on the Costa
Blanca. Picture by Charlie Simonds

Costa de la Luz

Playa Nueva Umbria, La Antilla, Huelva

This is a beautifully unspoilt, official nudist beach near the Portuguese border. Backed by pinewoods, fine golden sand and dunes stretch for more than 10 kilometres. It is reputed to be the best beach on the coast and part of it is specifically set aside for nude use.

The sea and sands are so beautiful they are often compared to the Caribbean and as a consequence there are lots of swimsuited holidaymakers near the popular resort of La Antilla. But with so much space it's easy to escape the crowds on the peninsula of the protected natural park at the mouth of the Rio Piedras.

Practical info
Travel west from Huelva on the N431

to Lepe and take the HV4116 south to La Antilla. Go through the village heading east towards El Terron and fork right at the signpost to Nueva Umbria.

The nearby 4-star Hotel Spa Playacartaya at Nuevo Portil, El Rompido, has a dedicated naturist terrace for guests to sunbathe au naturel. It also runs a boat service for the 1km trip along the coast and across the estuary to the naturist beach on the spit (La Fletcha).

> **Playa Nueva Umbria accommodation**
> Hotel Spa Playacartaya
> Tel: +34 959 62 53 00
> www.playasenator.com

▲ If you ever feel like getting some beach to yourself, the Costa de la Luz has some wonderfully wide open spaces to enjoy

Playa de Castilla South, Matalascanas, Huelva

This is probably the longest and most solitary sandy beach in southern Spain. The 20km of shoreline is part of the Donana National Park, which is famous for its flamingos. There are no proper roads behind the coast so by walking a short distance you can

have as much beach to yourself as you want in this nudist haven.

Practical info
Drive 40km south-east from Huelva on the C442 coast road to the resort towns of Torre de la Higuera and then Matalascanas. Walk south down the beach.

Playa Camarón-Tres Piedras, Chipiona, Cadiz

A long mostly undeveloped sandy shore popular with surfers. There are plenty of spots away from the beach car parks used for informal nude bathing. Also further south down the coast towards Rota naturists use Playa de Punta Candor.

Practical info
From the lively tourist town of Chipiona take the CA604 coast road south past the Sanctuary of the Virgin de La Regla and Playa de Regla, to the quiet areas of beach near the small village of Tres Piedras.

Playa de la Cortadura, City of Cadiz

This urban beach on the outskirts of historic Cadiz has easy access from the main highway running along its length. Firm golden sand stretches for 2.5km.

In 2004 local naturists requested that a section be designated for nude bathing, but the City's mayoress (Teófila Martinez) declared it was not necessary: "Beach users can wear as much or as little as they like

anywhere on the shore," she declared. Expect a mix of swimsuited and some nude bathers. Beach bars operate in summer.

Practical info
Playa de la Cortadura is located along the isthmus immediately south of the city, adjacent to the N IV highway. Being a city beach, facilities include parking, toilets, a first aid post and provision for disabled access.

▲ Spain's long Atlantic coastline is less crowded than the Mediterranean so you're never too far from a secluded stretch of sands

Spain: mainland

Calas de Poniente and others, Cabo Roche

This part of the coast has several attractive coves, with course golden sand backed by low rugged cliffs, all of which are used by nudists and promoted as such by the local tourist office. Cala Tío Juan de Medina is particularly popular and has wooden stairs down the cliff, although some of the other coves require a moderate scramble to reach them. And a short distance south down the coast, the beach at Cala de Camacho is also designated for nude bathing. The nearby Camping Cala del Aceite has some excellent naturist facilities.

Practical info
From the N340 coastal highway north-west of Vejer de la Frontera and Conil de la Frontera take the CA2135 minor road to Cabo Roche (& Puerto Conil). Turn right (north) at Cabo Roche lighthouse on to the recently asphalted track along the coast to two parking areas and marked paths to the coves.

Camping Cala del Aceite is a well-equipped campsite (textile), but with a fine naturist area for those who prefer to camp or caravan in the buff. The owners have also built an impressive pool and leisure area for the nudists.

Cabo de Trafalgar North, Canos de Meca

A fantastic huge sweep of almost white sand stretches for mile after empty mile here. The Atlantic ocean rolls up on this beautifully unspoilt coastline and there is space enough for everyone. The dress code is completely relaxed and beachgoers will be a mix of those in the buff and those wearing swimsuits.

Practical info
It's very easy to find. On the coast road 1km north of Canos de Meca turn left at the sign to Cabo de Trafalgar. After 700 metres, park below the lighthouse and walk to the beach on the right (north).

The Hostal La Aceitera is a small family-run rural property approached along a short unmade track off the coast road. The clothes-optional beach is 450 metres' walk away.

The Hostal Mini Golf is a simple 1-star pension with a choice of accommodation by the turn to the lighthouse at Cabo de Trafalgar. The hostal website says: 'These beaches are considered the most virgin in the area, where nudism surprises no one.'

Canos de Meca, Barbate

This is a picturesque and popular golden sandy beach backed by natural low cliffs on the edge of the Brena Natural Park. The traditionally nude beach has a friendly atmosphere and is popular with young people.

Practical info
Drive south through the village of Canos de Meca to the end of the road by the Hostal Mar Frente. A path and steps lead down to the beach in less than two minutes. The Hostel Mar de Frente is extremely stylish, well beyond its 2-star rating, and has its own private steps to the clothes-optional beach.

Playa de Bolonia, El Lentiscal, north of Tarifa

This is a favoured Atlantic surfing location by the Straits of Gibraltar so expect breezy conditions. The picturesque 4km of sands, surrounded by pine trees and dunes, have long been used for nude bathing at either end of the bay. Although still unspoilt its popularity is growing fast. Another sport that attracts a young crowd to Bolonia is rock climbing. The San Bartolo area offers 250 different climbs of varying levels with some as high as 85m. The climbing area is approximately 500m up the mountainside.

Practical info
Travel north-west from Tarifa on the N340 for 15km. Turn left (shortly after the 71-km marker post) on to the minor road to El Lentiscal. On arrival at the beach turn left (east) towards Punta Paloma, or right (west) past the Roman ruins of Baelo Claudia, towards Punta Camarinal. Apartment accommodation is available at the Hotel Don Pedro.

Calas de Poniente accommodation

Camping Cala del Aceite
Tel: +34 956 44 29 50
www.caladelaceite.com

Cabo de Trafalgar accommodation

Hostal La Aceitera
Tel: +34 956 43 70 16
www.miraalsur.com/aceitera/hotel

Hostal Mini Golf
Tel: +34 956 43 70 83
www.hostalminigolf.com

Canos de Meca accommodation

Hostel Mar de Frente
Tel/Fax: +34 956 43 72 91
Mobile: +34 661 86 13 31
www.miraalsur.com/mardefrente

Playa de Bolonia accommodation

Hotel Don Pedro
Tel/Fax: +34 956 68 85 77
www.hoteldonpedro.com

Playa Alcaidesa, near Gibraltar

The new golfing resort of La Hacienda de la Alcaidesa, 8km north of Gibraltar, has its own recently designated nudist beach. Consisting of an undeveloped area of coarse dark sand with fine shingle, the area also has stony nooks and crannies at the end of the beach around Punta Mala. Fine views of Gibraltar.

Practical info

Leave the N340 dual carriageway at exit km-124 (Alcaidesa), taking the minor road inland and then turn immediately right. Proceed straight past the next right turn (main access to Alcaidesa) continuing to the second right turn, near the campsite La Casita entrance. The unmade track passes the golf links and heads to Punta Mala, where there is parking by the beach.

Handy accommodation is available at the new (2006) Golf & Beach Vista Real Apartments and also at Camping La Casita.

Costa del Sol

Costa Natura, Estepona

As Spain's first 'official' nude beach, authorised in 1979, Costa Natura is now well known and firmly established. It is normally busy in high season and the lively bar serves a good selection of drinks and snacks. Sunbeds and umbrellas are also available to rent. The beach is directly in front of the naturist resort of the same name.

Practical info

Head south-west out of Estepona for 3km towards Gibraltar on the N340 coast road and Costa Natura is on the left. Public access to the beach is possible either side of the resort.

Costa Natura has 200 privately owned apartments set in delightful subtropical naturist gardens next to the nude beach. The properties are white Andalusian style and enjoy super coastal and mountain views.

Costa Natura – Apartment B91 is a recommended British-owned property with a big panoramic terrace perfect for outdoor living. The accommodation is airy and light.

The new 5-star Hotel Elba and Spa next door to Costa Natura is located on the beach, and is less than 100 metres from the nudist section. For that pampered experience the spa offers a choice of health and beauty treatments.

The 4-star Hotel Paraiso at Estepona is a golfing hotel 2km inland but with views of the sea. There is a nudist solarium for sunbathing on the fourth floor. The hotel is 15 minutes' drive from Costa Natura.

▼ **Morning and evening views along the beach at Costa Natura. The holiday complex is very popular with visitors of all ages**

▲▼ **Strolling along Costa Natura's beach, and enjoying its facilities**

▼ **Cabopino, peace on the beach**

Cabopino Playa, Calahonda

A super biscuit-coloured sand beach, which is unusual on this part of the Costa del Sol. Backed by extensive dunes and pine trees, the shore is clothes-optional for up to 700 metres. One area is good for skinny-dipping, but beware – other parts have submerged rocks.

There is a beach bar, where it's normal to wear light clothing. Don't let reports of 'cruising' men and couples in the dunes put you off enjoying this place. They shouldn't interfere with your relaxation on the actual beach itself.

Practical info
Mid-way between Marbella and Fuengirola on the N340 coast road – look out for signs to Puerto Cabopino.

After half a kilometre, just before entering the port, turn right into the car park and drive along the sandy track to Las Dunas bar at the clothes-optional beach. Alternatively, stop earlier and walk through the pines and over the dunes – there are lots of paths that lead to the beach.

Cabopino Camping is a well-equipped site just 1km from the nude beach. Bungalows and cabins are available to rent as well as pitches for tents and caravans.

> **Cabopino accommodation**
>
> Cabopino Camping
> Tel: +34 952 83 43 73
> www.campingcabopino.com

Benalnatura beach, Benalmadena

A cosy little cove right in the heart of the Costa del Sol, with a sheltered aspect making it ideal for winter sunning. The beach is well cared for by the bar owner, who has provided toilets and showers. It's only 150 metres long so during

summer get there early if you want a good spot.

Practical info
The beach is on the western side of Benalmadena, 2km from the marina, towards Fuengirola on the N340 coast road. The path with easy steps

▲ Compact and well used, the beach at Benalnatura has a bar and shower facilities. Picture on right by Charlie Simonds

to the beach is signposted off the access road.

The 3-star Flatotel International apartments offer some of the nearest holiday accommodation and also provide a good landmark. Travelling from Benalmadena the apartments are 250 metres before the beach. There is a bus stop outside the Flatotel.

The 4-star Hotel Playabonita is 600 metres from Benalnatura, along the coast road in the direction of Fuengirola. Finca Los Etera at Alora, near Malaga, is a 300-year-old traditional farmhouse a 30-minute drive from the nude beaches: owners Nigel and Nikki are naturists and the pool and grounds are clothes-optional. More inland nudist accommodation nearby at Finca Rojo, Casa del Sun and Finca la Bolina.

Benalnatura accommodation

Flatotel International
Tel: +34 952 44 04 67
www.flatotelcostadelsol.com

Hotel Playabonita
Tel: +34 952 44 28 40
www.playasenator.com

Finca Los Etera
Tel: +34 952 11 26 20
www.fincalosetera.net

Finca Rojo
Tel: +34 676 41 07 01
www.fincarojo.com

Casa del Sun
Tel: +34 656 39 20 60
www.liverbared.org.uk

Finca la Bolina
Tel: +34 660 45 64 09
www.bolinatura.com

Almanat Beach, near Torre del Mar

It might not be the prettiest spot in the world with light grey shingle and sand, but it is a popular and very convenient nude beach. There's a car park next to it (small charge) and a nudist beach bar serving a good choice of food. Sunbeds and umbrellas are available to rent.

Practical info
Travelling towards Malaga on the N340, 2km west of Torre del Mar, the turn to the beach and campsite is clearly signposted. A short lane through market garden crops brings you to the

camp site and parking in 600 metres.

Camping Almanat naturist site by the beach is well equipped and has a big attractive swimming pool. Residential chalets for hire. In winter the site is popular with long-stay visitors (snowbirds) from northern Europe.

Almanat accommodation

Camping Almanat
Tel: +34 952 55 62 71
www.almanat.de

▲ Easy to reach and with a well-equipped naturist resort, Almanat's beach draws visitors all year round. Pictures by Charlie Simonds

Costa Tropical

▲ Cantarrijan's dramatic setting

▲ Uncrowded Playa del Muerto

Playa del Muerto accommodation

Eagle Peak
Tel: +34 958 63 94 92
www.eaglepeakspain.com

Hotel Spa Playacalida
Tel: +34 958 61 92 00
www.playasenator.com

Cantarrijan Playa, near Nerja and Almunecar

Not one but two delightful buff beaches, popular with locals and holidaymakers alike. You can drive right up to the first one, where there is a pair of fine restaurants as well as sunbeds, umbrellas and pedalos for hire. The second (secret) beach is a few steps away, round the corner to the left as you face the sea. Here is a totally undeveloped and much bigger stretch of sand and shingle. It feels a million miles from civilisation – most users are nude and there's nothing else besides. Sheltered from the wind, it gets really warm and is used all year.

Practical info
Travel east from Nerja on the N340, and after 10km the road crosses a viaduct marking the boundary between the provinces of Malaga and Granada. In 1km turn into the lay-by on the right signed 'Almunecar La Herradura'. From there follow the small sign down to the beach, along 1.5km of unmade road.

There is little accommodation locally because of the area's protected natural status but a good choice would be Eagle Peak clothes-optional apartments, 20 mins' drive away – see next listing.

Playa del Muerto, Almunecar

A pleasant undeveloped beach of sand and shingle, officially nudist and easy to reach. At more than 500 metres long there will be room for everyone and the beach rarely gets too busy. Take your refreshments with you, or alternatively pop back into town for a drink.

Practical info
Head west along the seafront out of Almunecar and after 2km, at Cotobro, the road turns inland. Park here and the path to the nude beach is signposted round the next headland via a level promenade, no more than 5 mins walk.

Eagle Peak clothing-optional apartments, located on high ground at Cotobro, Almunecar, overlook Playa del Muerto. There are six good quality properties, a new pool, Jacuzzi and a panoramic terrace on the roof. Owners Peter and Liz offer trips into the mountains for nude walks and skinny-dipping rock pools, plus nudist boat trips round the bay. The largest lemons you'll ever see grow in the tropical garden – help yourself. Playa del Muerto is 15 mins' walk or 5 mins in the car. Cantarrijan nude beach is 20 mins' drive. The Hotel Spa Playacalida at Almunecar has a nudist terrace.

Spain: mainland

La Joya, Torrenueva, Motril

This attractive beach requires a long climb down a well-constructed flight of steps, which feels even longer on the way back! Well sheltered by rocky cliffs, the large suntrap cove has a remote away-from-it-all ambiance. There are no facilities so take your own refreshments and shade. La Joya is 35 mins' drive from Eagle Peak clothes-optional apartments in Almunecar.

Practical info
From Almunecar travel east on the N340 past Motril to Torrenueva. Go through the village and after a further 250 metres there's a lay-by with a track to Cortijo de la Joya. A few metres along the track an electricity sub-station is located near the top of the steps to the beach. The steps are obscured by extensive sub-tropical plants.

Costa Almeria

Playa Cerrillos, Roquetas de Mar

A long sand and shingle beach that feels remote, where it's easy to find space for yourself. You might encounter the occasional fisherman, but he is unlikely to disturb you. The immediate area is low-lying and cooling breezes will be welcome in the height of summer.
Practical info
The clothes-optional area is an extension of Roquetas de Mar town beach, heading south-west past Playa Serena. You can walk along the shore or take the lane running between the sea and the salt flats.

Hotel Playacapricho is a 4-star property in Roquetas with a nude sun terrace. The 3-star Hotel Playatropical in the bay at El Palmer, 8km north of Roquetas, has a small nude cove – Enix Playa – within 250 metres.

Playa Cabo de Gata

Miles of level dark sand and shingle make up this impressive and very undeveloped clothes-optional beach, which has easy access from the road. Swimming is good and the sea can be calmer than other nearby coasts. Beach users will usually be a harmonious mix of swimsuited and nudist, and with plenty of room you will easily find your own spot.
Practical info
From Almeria City head east, past the airport along the coast to the fishing village of Cabo de Gata. Go through the village and park anywhere along the road to La Almadraba de Monteleva. The beach is accessed by one of the many short boardwalks.

▲ On the rocks at Playa Los Muertos. The beach has small pebbles with patches of sand, and a very clear sea. Take care getting into the sea by the rocks at the southern end of the beach – it's tricky but well worth it if you bring your snorkel

Playa de Monsul, Ensenada de la Media Luna

This is a lovely unspoilt area south of San Jose within the Cabo de Gata Natural Park. A huge sand dune on the north side of Playa de Monsul makes an impressive landmark. Naturists usually head for the opposite side of the bay, which is more secluded. The next beach to the south – Ensenada de la Media Luna – often has more naked bathers than Monsul. The soft golden sand makes swimming a delight, provided the sea is calm. This is protected virgin country – no beach bars, so bring your own refreshments because it can be extremely hot in mid-summer.

Practical info
From the small fishing port and resort of San Jose take the unsurfaced road south towards the Cabo de Gata lighthouse, past the attractive Playa de los Genoveses (some buff bathing towards southern end). The main track continues to Playa de Monsul and Media Luna. It is 3.5km from St Jose and there is plenty of parking. Additional secluded and highly rated nudist coves – Calas Barronal and Playa Barronal – lie between Playa de los Genoveses and Playa de Monsul, but require a good walk and some easy scrambling to access.

> **Playa Cerrillos accommodation**
>
> Hotel Playacapricho
> Tel: +34 950 33 31 00
> www.playasenator.com
>
> Hotel Playatropical
> Tel: +34 950 34 05 00
> www.playasenator.com

Spain: mainland

Cala de San Pedro, Las Negras

For adventurous naturists: a pretty cove in a tranquil location that can only be reached by a longish walk, or by boat. Backed by soaring hills, this palm-tree oasis has a 220 metre clothes-optional beach of fine sand. Once a pirate stronghold guarded by a fortress, but where mostly ruined buildings and caves remain today. Now home to a small hippy community: peace and tolerance existing far from a materialistic world.

Practical info

Access is along the coastal trail GR92 heading north from the small town of Las Negras. The undulating 5km route requires stout shoes and legs! Alternatively, a longer route can be taken south from Agua Amarga on the GR92 path. The dramatic scenery en-route is amazing and frequently resembles a lunar landscape plunging into the Mediterranean.

Playa Los Muertos, Carboneras

This stunning bay has been popular with naturists for years. The large beach – surrounded by cliffs and steep hills – consists of small pebbles with coarse sand. The transparent sea reflects a deep shade of blue and sparkles in the sunlight. There are no facilities so take refreshments and shade. Costumed bathers also use the beach, but there is complete tolerance and plenty of space for everybody – it's rarely crowded.

Practical info

Take the coast road south from Carboneras past the (unsightly) industrial cement works, in the direction of Agua Amarga. In 5km there is a large car park on the left just before the turn-off to Faro Roldan (lighthouse). From the parking area it is a 15-minute walk to the beach. The path is a little steep in places, so allow slightly longer on the way back.

Cala del Bordenares and Cala del Sombrerico

Two lovely dark sand beaches in a protected rural location near the resort town of Mojacar. These bays are officially promoted for nude bathing by the local Mojacar Tourist Office (www.mojacar.es). Backed by steep rocky slopes covered with wild plants, the beaches are a world away from civilisation. Generally quiet apart from July and August. No facilities at Cala del Bordenares, whilst at Cala del Sombrerico meals and refreshments are served from a palm-fringed beach bar overlooking the sea.

Practical info

From the Hotel Indalo at Mojacar

Playa travel south towards Carboneras and after 2km turn left on to a track at Playa de Macenas. There will be much construction work around here until 2008/9, during the development Playa Macenas Beach & Golf Resort. On approaching the fortified tower by the beach bear right (south) towards a second more elevated tower (Torre del Pirucico) along the coast in the distance. Continue for 3km on the unsurfaced track, which climbs and winds inland for a time before dropping down to Cala del Bordenares. Cala del Sombrerico is 1km further on. Plenty of parking at both locations.

▲ **Costa Almeria has many nude areas, including the beaches at Cala del Bordenares, in all pictures above on the left hand side, and Playa Los Muertos, on the top right of the page**

Spain: mainland

▲ Some of the many happy faces of Vera Playa. Picture top right by Alan Avery, others by Charlie Simonds

Vera Playa, Between Garrucha and Villaricos

This is Spain's capital of nudism. A long wide beach with a big choice of naturist accommodation next to it. Great for sunning, walking and skinny-dipping. Beach bars, sunbeds, pedalos, volleyball – it's got it all. Busy in summer but still easy to find a quieter place to yourself. Almeria has the hottest and driest climate in the country, so the beach season is long – in fact anything up to 12 months. Most European nationalities come and chill out here, giving it a truly cosmopolitan and friendly atmosphere.

Practical info

Take the coast road north from Garrucha through Puerto Rey. Vera Playa is well signposted after a further 1.5km. A whole nudist community has developed over the years offering every type of holiday from camping and caravanning, through self-catering, to a luxury nude hotel. There is much ongoing building work in the vicinity.

Hotel Vera Playa is right on the beach and probably unique not only in Spain but in the world. Although offering similar standards of service to thousands of other big 4-star holiday hotels, it's the only one that is naturist.

But it's OK to dress up smartly in the evening, because clothes are required after 8pm. It is closed in the winter.

Vera Natura and La Menara apartments provide well-equipped naturist holiday accommodation with pools in the gardens. Vera Natura is on the nude beach and the newer La Menara development is further back. Bahia de Vera apartments are spacious with large outdoor terraces. There are indoor and outdoor pools, as well as tennis, volleyball and a gym. Torremar Natura apartments are some of the newest, set back from the beach with their own pool. Natsun apartments range from original 1980s (El Cano 1) to new (El Cano 3), basic to luxury, with some right on the beach. Vera Luz apartments are also part of Natsun. Parque Vera consists of townhouses and large blocks of apartments set in gardens with swimming pools. Sunclad Homes has luxury apartments to rent. Camping Almanzora naturist site for tents and caravans is popular all year. It has a pool and is close to the shops and restaurants. Just 4km inland Casa Rio Vera offers alternative rural nudist accommodation.

Vera Playa accommodation

Hotel Vera Playa
Tel: +34 950 46 74 75
www.playasenator.com

Vera Natura and La Menara
Tel: +34 950 46 73 84
www.veranatura.com

Bahia de Vera
www.bahiadevera.com

Torremar Natura
www.veranatura.com

Natsun apartments
Tel: +34 950 46 70 27
www.natsun.com

Parque Vera
www.veraplaya.info
www.parquevera.com

Sunclad Homes
Tel: +34 950 618292
suncladhomes@spanishemail.com

Camping Almanzora
Tel: +34 950 46 74 25
www.campings.net/almanzora

Casa Rio Vera
Tel: +34 639 73 93 79
www.casariovera.net

Vera Playa general information

www.veraplaya.info
www.naturistspain.com

▲ Plenty to do in Spain's sunny naturist capital, with swimming pools, tennis courts and of course the long, sandy beach

Costa Calida

Bolnuevo beaches, near Puerto de Mazarron

A string of undeveloped sand and shingle official nude beaches, which become less inhabited the further you go from town. Set in wild countryside there is little to disturb the nude beach enthusiast on these remote shores.

Practical info

From Puerto de Mazarron head south along the coast through the suburbs towards the village of Bolnuevo. Signs for Playa Nudista can be spotted along the way. Continue through Bolnuevo to a small roundabout, where an unsurfaced road continues along the coast. After the first cove all the beaches are clothes-optional.

▲ Playa Negrete in Calblanque regional park, pictured by Peter Udris
▼ The wonderfully wild setting of Bolnuevo. Beyond the first bay it's clothes free. Pictures from Solar Sid

El Portus, Portus, near Cartagena

An idyllic official nudist bay surrounded by mountains that appear to rise straight out of the sea. The beach is a mix of dark sand and pebbles and the swimming is first class – ideal for snorkelling. Often more sheltered than other places and popular throughout the year.

Practical info

Travel south from Cartagena on the local road through Canteras. After 7km from the city take the left turn to El Portus, which is a further 4km. The nude bay is next to the smaller village beach and is easy to access through the campsite.

Camping Naturista El Portus is next to the beach, with rugged grounds extending to a million square metres up the hillside. There are super indoor and outdoor pools, a restaurant, a shop and plenty of caravan and chalet accommodation. New deluxe apartments and a spa opened 2005/6. The resort is popular with naturist families from all over Europe and the whole area is totally unspoilt. As a testimony to the fine winter weather the site is open all year. Murcia and Alicante are the nearest airports.

El Portus accommodation
Camping Naturista El Portus
Tel: +34 968 55 30 52
www.elportus.com

▲ Looking over the naturist beach at El Portus, picture by Charlie Simonds

Spain: mainland

Playa Negrete and Playa Parreno, La Manga

A series of lovely long gold and ochre coloured sandy beaches in the picturesque Calblanque regional park. Playa Negrete and Playa Parreno are the most popular with naturists, but the others, including Playa Calblanque, are generally considered clothes-optional.

Practical info
Travel east on the dual carriageway MU312 approaching La Manga, and exit at signs for Playa Calblanque and Los Balones. Turn right at the Calblanque Parque sign. It's a short drive through the park to the beaches – Playa Negrete and Playa Parreno are towards the west. The park rangers welcome nudist visitors so don't hesitate to ask for directions.

The renowned golf resort at La Manga is 10 mins' drive from the beach and has a range of places to stay. The 5-star Hotel Hyatt and Las Lomas Apartments have a health and beauty spa plus indoor and outdoor pools.

Costa Blanca

Playa los Tusales, La Marina, Guardamar

A long pale sandy nude beach backed by dunes and pinewoods near La Marina. Popular with families, this delightfully unspoilt beach has more than 2km for naked bathing – room for everybody to find their own space.

Practical info
Drive south from Alicante through Santa Pola on the N332 to La Marina. Turn left down the lane next to Camping Internacional and after 1.5km at the car park turn right. From the end of the car park, south to the river Segura, the beach is au naturel.

Camping Internacional La Marina is ideal and only 15 mins' walk from the nudist beach. It has a 5-star quality grading and offers a range of facilities including bungalows for hire. It has a good local bus service too.

Playa El Carabassi, Gran Alacant

This broad sandy beach backed by extensive dunes is near a large development of new holiday homes. Towards the southern end of the beach official signs advise 'Playa Nudista'.

Practical info
Drive south from Alicante on the N332. Then 3.5km past the airport, by the Repsol garage, take the slip road on the right and flyover for Gran Alacant. Drive through the small town and down a steep hill to the beach. At the T junction cross over the road into the car park, keep right and the nude area is to your right as you face the sea – look for the sign. Inland naturist accommodation at Casa Jarmero and Alicante Nudists (villa and cabins).

▲ Spectacular El Portus. Pictures top right and above by Charlie Simonds, top left supplied by the resort

Playa Negrete accommodation

Hotel Hyatt and Las Lomas Apartments
Tel: +34 968 33 12 34
www.lamanga.hyatt.com

Playa los Tusales accommodation

Camping Internacional La Marina
Tel: +34 965 41 92 00
www.camping-lamarina.com

Playa El Carabassi accommodation

Casa Jarmero
Tel: +34 965 97 90 23
www.casajarmero.co.uk

Alicante Nudists
Tel: +34 965 66 74 38
www.alicantenudists.com

Platja Esparrello, Montiboli, Villajoyosa

An attractive, large but fairly secluded pebble cove situated outside town. Not far from Benidorm, but it feels a million miles away. It is an official nude beach with good swimming. The edge of the next cove, La Caleta, is occasionally used for skinny-dipping.

Practical info

Travel south from Villajoyosa along the N332 and after 3km turn left at the sign for Hotel Montiboli. Then bear left into a cul de sac going down to the beach about 0.5km before the hotel.

The exclusive 5-star Montiboli Hotel is set on a low promontory between the two coves. Rooms 21-27 on the top floor directly overlook the nude beach and have large private terraces ideal for sunbathing in the buff.

The 3-star Euro Tennis Hotel and Apartments is next to Hotel Montiboli and located directly behind Playa La Caleta. It is 10-15 mins' walk or 3 mins' drive to Platja Esparrello.

Cumbre del Sol, Moraira, near Javea (Xabia)

A popular 450-metre shingle beach surrounded by dramatic cliffs. It is usually sheltered and warm, with good swimming from the steeply shelving shore. A bar serves refreshments at one end of the bay and the au naturel beach users mostly use the other end.

Practical info

From Javea use the local roads south to Benitachell village, then follow signs to Cumbre del Sol and finally down the steep hill to the car park by the beach.

Casa Natura B&B guesthouse has nudist accommodation in four rooms, about 20 mins' drive from the beach. It is set in pretty subtropical gardens, with pool, terraces and boules court. Also in the area the grandly sounding Naturist Club & Resort is a hosted 3-bedroom luxury villa.

Playa de Sant Llorenc, Cullera (Valencia)

This big nude beach, backed by low dunes, is in an agricultural area with greenhouses, orange groves and abundant crops growing almost to the shore. The fine golden sand stretches for a mile or so in either direction, with buildings only visible in the distance. Swimming is good but there are no lifeguards. Popular with Spanish naturists in summer.

Practical info

From Gandia travel north to the historic town of Cullera at the mouth of the river Júcar, famous for its castle and lighthouse. Take the minor CV502 coast road north in the direction of El Perrelo and after 4km watch for a sign on the right 'Platja Naturista 500m'. Another sign by the turn indicates 'Entra de Carbonell'. A narrow lane winds for 1km (not 500 metres!) to the beach, where there is rough parking next to derelict buildings.

Sierra Natura is an inland eco nudist resort set in the hills near Moixent, 100km south-west of Valencia.

▲ All-over happiness at the dramatic beach of Cumbre del Sol, where steep cliffs (left picture) almost guarantee sunbathing temperatures. Pictures supplied by Charlie Simonds

Platja Esparrello accommodation

Montiboli Hotel
Tel: +34 965 89 02 50
www.servigroup.es

Euro Tennis Hotel and Apartments
Tel: +34 965 89 12 50
www.hoteleurotennis.com

Cumbre del Sol accommodation

Casa Natura B&B
Tel: +44 1494 580728
www.chalfontholidays.co.uk

Naturist Club & Resort
www.naturistclubandresort.com

Playa de Sant Llorenc accommodation

Sierra Natura
Tel: +34 962 25 30 26
www.sierranatura.com

▲ The long and peaceful golden sands of Playa de Sant Llorenc

Spain: mainland

Costa Dorada

Playa El Torn, Tarragona

▲ ▼ Nude beach lovers are huge fans of Playa El Torn, partly because it's so pretty and partly because of the excellent naturist holiday campsite attached. Pic above and bottom right by Charlie Simonds

A truly beautiful and popular yellow sandy naturist beach 1.6km long, enclosed by rocky headlands at either end. There is a bar on the beach selling refreshments and snacks but little other development by this lovely pine-scented coastline. Long naked walks are certainly on the cards here. There's a lifeguard and first aid post in summer and it's great for families. According to the local tourist office guide, 'El Torn is a highly privileged nudist beach where nature can be enjoyed in all its splendour' – we wouldn't argue with that.

Practical info

Leave the A7 motorway at exit 38 for L'Hospitalet de l'Infant. From town head south along the minor coast road for 2km to Naturist Camping El Templo del Sol. Park outside the resort and take the short path along the low cliff to steps down to the north end of the beach. Alternatively, a scenic minor road from the N340 leads over the hills to parking near the southern end of the bay – access to the shore from here is through a pedestrian tunnel.

El Templo del Sol naturist camping is modern and well equipped. Mobile homes are available for hire. There is a particularly impressive infinity swimming pool overlooking the sea as well as lots of other sports and entertainment facilities. It has direct access down steps to the nude beach. Only 20 mins from Reus Airport or just 5 minutes by taxi from L'Hospitalet railway station. Finca Ninfas del Agua is a naturist holiday apartment 45 minutes' drive down the coast near the city of Tortosa.

Playa El Torn accommodation

El Templo del Sol
Tel: +34 977 82 34 34
www.eltemplodelsol.com

Finca Ninfas del Agua
Tel: +34 977 26 75 26
www.fincaninfas.org

Spain: mainland

Platja Savinosa (Sabinosa), Tarragona city

This surprisingly appealing nudist beach is just 3km from the centre of the historic city of Tarragona. You can combine a morning exploring the extensive Roman heritage and ancient city walls with an afternoon skinny-dipping. The shore is officially shared with swimsuited bathers, who use the west side, but in typically laid-back Spanish style nobody really worries. When we visited, naturists were easily in the majority. Consisting of 350 metres of flat golden sand, there are showers and two beach bars. It gets packed in mid-summer and don't be deterred by the railway line to the rear – the passengers must have one of the world's most interesting commutes.

Practical info
From the city centre travel east on the coast road along the waterfront in the direction of Barcelona. After 3km look out for the filling station on the right and next to it a small signpost to Platja Savinosa. Follow the minor road downhill, around the corner and under the railway to the parking area adjacent to the beach. There is easy, level access.

▲ One of the pretty nude coves at Cala Fonda. Pic Robert Spatchursht

Cala Fonda (Waikiki), La Mora, Tarragona

Not one but a couple of pretty naturist coves go by the names of Cala de la Roca Plana and Cala Fonda – often simply referred to as Waikiki. They are off the beaten track and attract a lively young crowd. The unspoilt little bays are backed by pinewoods and have great swimming but no lifeguard. Some buff bathers use the yellow mud on the cliffs as a skin toning treatment. Take your own refreshments and sun shade.

Practical info
The coves are between Platja Llarga and La Mora. Take the N340 east out of Tarragona, and in a short distance (near km-marker 1168) turn right for Punta de La Mora and follow the signs to Camping Torre de la Mora (www.torredelamora.com). From the approach to the campsite a footpath strikes off to the right, up into the woods and has small guiding arrows. During summer simply follow the other visitors. The walk to the first cove (Cala de la Roca Plana) is almost a mile and Cala Fonda is just beyond.

▲ Year-round nudity: top pic Costa Natura, bottom pic Cumbre del Sol

El Fonoll Poble Naturista, Conca de Barberà

This is a remarkable self-contained naturist village set in 375 acres of rural countryside, about 50km inland from Tarragona. There is holiday accommodation available in refurbished historic houses and caravans, or brings your own tent. A strong community spirit underpins this unique back-to-nature centre. The village experience is highly rated in the Parafotos naturist film 'Catalunya Naturally' (see page 135).

El Fonoll Poble accommodation

Tel: +34 977 266 138
www.kadex.com/fonoll

Spain: mainland

Costa Brava

Mar Bella, Barcelona

Spain's second city enjoys a thriving beach scene right in the heart of the metropolis and the official nudist beach of Playa de la Mar Bella is no exception. Swimming is good, but stay well clear of the breakwater. It has bars, showers, toilets, children's play areas, parking, disabled access, lifeguards and safe drinking water. It's also home to the water sports centre Base Nàutica de la Mar Bella.

Practical info
The beach is next to the well-known Mar Bella sports centre at Villa Olimpica, 1km north of the marina and 2km from the Christopher Columbus statue in the city centre. Nearest metro stations: Poblenou (line IV), or Selva de Mar (line IV). Buses 36, 71 and 141. Weekend naturist swimming sessions at Bernat Picornell Olympic pool www.picornell.com.

Playa de la Musclera, Arenys de Mar

A well managed official naturist beach of clean fine-grain sand, looked after by the local authority. Popular with families, young people and male groups. Care required when swimming – steeply shelving shore with some submerged rocks.
Practical info
The beach is between Arenys de Mar and Caldes d'Estrac and is easily reached by train from Barcelona. Rail journey 35 minutes; get off the train at Caldes and it's a 10-minute walk along the promenade towards Arenys, by the Restaurant Hispania and the sailing club. The nude beach is clearly signposted. By road, take the N11 along the coast for 37km north-east of Barcelona and turn for the beach by km-marker 655.

Playa de Vallpresona, Canyet de Mar, Girona

This pretty nude beach is completely undeveloped and backed by extensive pinewoods on the surrounding hills. The gently shelving shore of coarse yellow sand gives way to rocks and boulders at the north end of the bay. Naturists mainly use the southern end.
Practical info
From Sant Feliu travel south-west on the GI 682 coast road to km-marker 33 and park at the roadside. It is an 800-metre walk down a steep narrow path to the beach – no vehicular access. The next bay to the north – Cala del Senyor Ramon – is also naturist and accessed on foot from the road at km-marker 35.

The Hotel Golden Bahia de Tossa at nearby Tossa de Mar has a nudist terrace and Jacuzzi.

> **Playa de Vallpresona accommodation**
> Hotel Golden Bahia de Tossa
> Tel: +34 972 34 31 30
> www.goldenhotels.com

Playa de Pals, near Palafrugell

▲ Playa de Pals is a superb nude beach that attracts throngs of holiday makers. Pictures supplied by Craig

Two super, official nudist coves at the southern end of the 4km Playa de Pals. Some nude bathers use the main beach, but most head for one of the two small bays. Popular with locals and holidaymakers, there's always a lively atmosphere. Use the main beach if winter storms have removed the sand from the coves.
Practical info
Travel north from Palafrugell towards Pals and watch for the sign to Platja de Pals. Drive past the golf course and park at the southern end: walk round to the coves.

Camping Relax Nat is a lovely family orientated site for nudists with three swimming pools and bungalows to rent. Located between Palafrugell and Palamos, less than 5km from the sea and a short drive to the popular Pals beach. The small naturist coves of Cala Bona and Cala Streta are even closer to the campsite.

> **Pals accommodation**
> Camping Relax Nat
> Tel: +34 972 30 08 18
> www.campingrelaxnat.com

Spain: mainland

Platja Sant Pere Pescador, bay of Roses

The sweeping bay of Roses near Girona has many remote spots enjoyed by naturists. Local roads and campsites on the shore provide easy access to miles of sandy beach. Windsurfers are attracted by the steady breezes blowing off the sea. A short walk away from the busier areas brings peace and seclusion for baring all in this undeveloped area of the Aiguamolls Natural Park. Near the mouth of the river El Fluvia – in the middle of the bay – is a favourite.

Practical info

From the town of Figueres take the C260 east towards Castello d'Empuries. Stay on the C260 and very shortly after Castello turn right on to the GI6216 minor road to Sant Pere Pescador. Follow the signs from the village to Platja Sant Pere Pescador. There's another bay here called Platja de Can Comes which is also used as nature intended.

Costa Verde

Playa de los Nudistas (el Arenal), Cantabria

We couldn't overlook a location with the name Playa de los Nudistas – no translation required! The sandy shore stretches to almost 400 metres is on an isolated and sheltered creek on the east bank of the Rio Ajo estuary, about 40km east of Santander. Surrounded by beautiful scenery, the beach is becoming more and more popular with swimsuited bathers, so at busy times expect a mixed dress code. Camping Playa de la Arena is within reasonable walking distance, whilst the 3-star Hotel Campomar is even closer.

Practical info

Head east from Santander taking the CA141 to Arnuero. Turn left in town on to the CA448 minor road following signs to Isla and Playa la Arena. Park near the Hotel Campomar and walk 750 metres south on the coastal path to the next bay – which is Playa de los Nudistas.

▲ Friendly crowds gather from all over Europe to enjoy the sun at Playa de Pals. Bottom picture supplied by Craig

Playa de los Nudistas accommodation

Camping la Arena
Tel: +34 942 67 93 59
www.campinglaarena.com

Hotel Campomar
Tel: +34 942 67 94 32
www.hotelcampomar.com

Playa de Valdearenas, west of Santander

This vast sandy peninsula almost 3km long at the mouth of the Rio Pas is set in the picturesque Parque Natural Dunas de Liencres, 15km west of Santander. Naturists can choose the breezy seaward side of the shore – popular with windsurfers – or move to the landward side by the river. The beach attracts plenty of textile visitors too but it's not hard to find a quiet spot.

Practical info
From Santander go 13km west on the CA231 to Liencres; through the town then right by the cemetery, signposted Parque Natural Dunas de Liencres. Park by the shore near the watchtower. It's a 10-min walk to the nude area in the middle of the beach. Naturists also use Playa de Somocuevas and Playa de Portio to the north-east of Valdearenas.

Playa de Ballota, east of Llanes, Asturias

Travel writer Chloë Bryan-Brown recently described this beach in The Times newspaper (London): "We favoured the deserted Playa de Ballota, west of Santander and just over the regional border in Asturias: an arc of turquoise sea, white sand, pink rocks, green cliffs and blue sky, and no one there except a few feral goats and the nudists who, in our experience, are a sign of the best beaches. We spent a perfect day there..." What more can we say?

Practical info
Take the coast road east from Llanes through the village of Cue. Before reaching Andrin turn left, signposted Vista Panoramica and Playa de Ballota.

Playa de Torimbia accommodation

Hotel Kaype
Tel: +34 985 40 09 00
www.hotelkaype.com

▼ Playa de Torimbia, a nude beach that is highly rated by many European naturists. Pictures supplied by Anne and David

Playa de Torimbia, Niembro, west of Llanes

Anne and David wrote to us to say this is one of their favourite nude beaches: "As you come round the corner there is the most perfect horseshoe-shaped bay of pristine white sand and warm, shallow water: about a kilometre of tranquillity". Access is on foot downhill, but well worth the walk.

Practical info
West from Llanes on the AS263 coast road past Celorio, bear right on the LLN11 minor road for Barro and Niembro. Between the two villages park at the busy and textile Playa Toranda and take the path over the headland to Playa de Torimbia. Or use the car park above Playa Torimbia and walk 900 metres down the steep but safe track to the beach. The 3-star Hotel Kaype is nearby at Playa de Barro.

Spain: mainland

Playa de l'Arena de Vega, Berbes

A stunning wide open sandy beach surrounded by low hills and stretching for almost 2km. Easy access and popular with swimsuited visitors, but there is also an official naturist section. Recommended by the Asturias Naturist Association (ANAPA).

Practical info
The beach is located 8km west of Ribadesellea, driving out of town on the N632 until the right turn to Vega and the beach.
Camping Playa de Vega is 400 metres from the beach.

Playa de l'Arena accommodation

Camping Playa de Vega
Tel: +34 985 86 04 06
www.campingplayadevega.com

Playa Conbouzas, Arteixo, La Coruña

This lovely unspoilt white sand Galician bay is a favourite with local naturists, attracting upwards of 500 naked bathers in summer. The beach is also known as Playa de Barrañán. Luis Cortes, a well-known Spanish nude beach researcher, rates it 'excellent'. At 200 metres long and facing the full force of the Atlantic, care is needed in the sea. This official nudist location has lifeguards, a beach bar, showers and toilets.

Practical info
Head to Arteixo 12km west of La Coruña and turn right at the traffic lights towards Caion. After 4km a large quarry on the left marks the place to park. Playa Conbouzas is the smaller of two beaches, a short walk down the track. Disabled access available. The Tourist Office in Arteixo will provide a map.

Playa de Castro de Baroña, Porto do Son

Our last beach in mainland Spain is another stunner on the dramatic west coast. Its name comes from the fascinating Celtic ruins at the northern end of the bay. The whole shore is officially nudist but has some clothed visitors too. Naturists prefer the more sheltered southern end of the beach.
Practical info
From Santiago de Compostela head south-west on the AC543 to the seaside town of Noia. Turn left along the AC550 coast road through Porto do Son to Baroña. Park by the bar named Castro de Baroña, near km-marker 58, and take the path 600m to the sea. Camping Os Castros (Tel: +34 981 82 48 33) is very close to the nude beach and the owner can sometimes offer a secluded naturist spot to pitch; just ask.

▲ Naturists in Spain are lucky enough to have nearly 700 beaches which are used in the nude, spread throughout the mainland and the Spanish islands. For more information, take a look at the Spanish Federation for Naturism's website www.naturismo.org. Picture above taken on Mallorca, supplied by www.radiantnude.com

Spain: mainland

The Balearic islands

Mix the vibrant colours of the Caribbean with the cheerful nude beach culture of Europe and you get Spain's wonderful Balearics.

The best of these is Formentera, an absolute gem of an island just off Ibiza, famed for its dazzling seas and fabulously relaxed nude beaches. In fact most of the coast can be enjoyed in your birthday suit and the laid-back attitude means peace and privacy are yours for the asking. Ibiza, on the other hand, is most famous as a party island, and many a clubber has found the delights of bathing naked a superb antidote to a night in the bar. Nude beaches here are popular and well-established.

Mallorca's famously pretty coastline also has plenty of long-established places for naked bathing, with many undeveloped bays and pine-backed coves offering peaceful seclusion. Menorca's nude beaches are slightly further off the beaten track, but well worth a visit for their stunning natural surroundings.

Formentera

Illetes and Llevant, northern peninsula

These two fabulous beaches run back to back along a narrow peninsula in the north of Formentera. Both have long stretches of soft yellow sand, dotted with pretty bays and little development apart from some handy beach bars. Llevant, the beach on the east side, is particularly popular with naturists, who use pretty much all of the 4km shore.

Playa Illetes, on the west, has sections where clothed bathers tend to gather exclusively but you're never more than a few minutes away from bare bodies. The tip of the peninsula, known as Es Trucadors, is the rockiest part of this coastline and so has the best snorkelling areas. It's well worth exploring all the coast along here – it has some of the best views of Ibiza and Playa Illetes in particular is dotted with pretty islands offshore.

One further advantage of these beaches is that you can cross the peninsula in a minute or two – which is handy if one side is a bit windy.

Practical info

Astbury Formentera, a leading accommodation agency on the island, has several attractive apartments to rent in the area. And the Hostal Sa Roqueta is a minute's walk from the start of Llevant's long nude coastline.

▲ The sparkling colours and relaxed nude atmosphere of Formentera are unique even for Europe. Picture on opposite page by Juan Picca

Spain: Balearics

Playa Migjorn, southern coastline

This stunning 10-kilometre stretch of golden sand and brilliant blue sea is pretty close to perfection, particularly if you're daring to bare all for the first time. Its easy mix of naked and dressed bathers means you can wear or not wear whatever makes you most comfortable. But on a sunny day the clear warm waters would convince just about anyone to skip the swimming costume and dive right in.

The beach is huge and apart from some pleasant bars and restaurants there are very few buildings along the beach. With plenty of rocky bays to lend seclusion or shelter if there's a breeze, you can sit for hours gazing out to sea and soaking up the peaceful atmosphere around you. The beach is easy to find and there are tracks leading to it from the island's main road for its entire length.

Practical info

There are some excellent places to stay along the shore here. The 4-star hotels Insotel Club Formentera Playa and the Hotel Riu Club La Mola are both just a few minutes' walk from nude bathing areas. The Talaya Bungalows are set in pretty gardens just 150m from the

beach, and some visitors hardly even dress for the walk to the sea. Talaya's agent Astbury Formentera has other accommodation in the area too. Another good option is the Pueblo Balear Casa Blanca. This traditionally designed group of nine apartments is right by a quiet stretch of beach. Finally the Hostal Ca Mari is a fine hotel in the middle of the beach just a few minutes from bare bathing.

> **Migjorn accommodation**
>
> Insotel Club Formentera Playa
> Tel: +34 971 32 80 00
> www.insotel.com
>
> Hotel Riu Club La Mola
> Tel: +34 971 74 30 30
> www.riu.com
>
> Talaya Bungalows
> Tel: +44 (0)1642 210163 (UK)
> www.formentera.co.uk
>
> Pueblo Balear Casa Blanca
> Tel: +39 348 5167706
> www.formentera-app.com
>
> Hostal Ca Mari
> Tel: +34 971 32 81 80
> www.guiaformentera.com/camari

▲ and facing page: the many faces of Migjorn beach, which runs for 10km along Formentera's southern shore. Pictures on facing page top left and centre, middle right and bottom by Juan Picca of Formentera Report magazine and island guide: www.formenterareport.com

▼ Just one of the spectacularly inviting bays at the northern end of Illetes

Spain: Balearics

Playa es Calo, north coast

This sandy beach is a great alternative to the longer Playa Migjorn on the other side of the island if there's a breeze from the south. Nudity is common for much of the year although less so during the peak season around August – Playa Migjorn is a two-kilometre walk or a short drive if the sight of soggy swimming costumes gets too much.

A rocky shoreline beyond the sands gives this stretch of coast some of the island's best snorkelling. There are several sandy bays to choose from, with a handy beach bar in the last one. Beyond here the coast is rocky but deserted if you fancy exploring further in your birthday suit. The beaches start a minute's walk from Es Calo, to the left if you're facing the sea past the pretty little harbour of fishing boats.

Practical info

There are some excellent places to stay in Es Calo and even right by the beach itself in the Ses Platgetes bungalows, where some holiday-makers choose to live completely naked. Astbury Formentera offers these and a wide range of others.

Es Calo accommodation

Astbury Formentera
www.formentera.co.uk
Tel: +44 (0)1642 21 01 63 (UK)

Formentera Report

When in Formentera, pick up a copy of the handy Formentera Report magazine, published by Juan Picca, whose images appear in this book. It has multilingual listings and up-to-date holiday info.

Other beaches around Formentera

Formentera's tranquil shores attract some of the most discerning beach lovers in the world. On most beaches people are either naked or unbothered by nudity, so you can find a place to strip off on some of the other beaches too. The main resort beach of Es Pujols is pretty much clad bottoms only, while the gorgeous bay of Cala Saona on the west coast is usually packed out with clothed tourists. Even so, plenty of nude bathers enjoy the rocky bays just round the corner to the north. Finally, the little island of Espalmador can be reached from the tip of the northern peninsula. Lots of bare bodies grace the sands here, while the mud pools at the back of the beach are often used for an all-over body mask. Be careful when you cross to the island though, the water is chest height.

▲ **Es Calo attracts plenty of bare bathers, but fewer in peak season**
▼ **After bare skin, mud seems to be the second most popular costume on many of Formentera's beaches**

Ibiza

Aguas Blancas

Cala Bassa and Cala Conta
• San Antonio

IBIZA

Ibiza town •

Es Cavallet

▼ Es Cavallet's popular sands have plenty of space for peace and quiet, particularly away from the dunes

Playa de Es Cavallet, southern coast

This long sandy nudist beach is very popular with the whole spectrum of Ibiza's holiday crowds: trend-setters, hedonists, gay visitors, young clubbers, party animals and pretty much everyone else, baring all among like-minded folk. Fortunately the beach is long enough to take everyone on board, stretching for well over 1km with bars/restaurants at both ends, and sunbeds and umbrellas for hire. It can get noisy at times near the bars and a few people treat the dunes

area as a cruising ground, which has driven away some of the normal naturist users to Ibiza's other beaches, particularly those with families.

Practical info

Travel south from Ibiza town, passing Playa den Bossa and the saltpans. The beach is clearly signposted and there is a car park that can get very full, meaning you might need to park on the approach road and walk a few minutes. Buses come here from town; alternatively it's a pleasant cycle ride.

Spain: Balearics

Aguas Blancas, Figueral, north-east coast

This string of pretty, light sandy beaches has calm clear turquoise water in good weather, but some raging surf when the sea is up. These shores are officially nudist and very family friendly. There is a good beach bar at the foot of the access road. The tall clay cliffs behind the beach can be used for plastering on bare bodies as a skin tonic. A slight drawback out of season – some of the beaches lose the sun later on because of the cliffs, so get there in good time if you want to make the most of your day.

Practical info

Travel 1km north from Figueral and there is a choice of rough parking areas on the descent to the sea. From the beach bar turn left (facing the sea) if you want the more secluded au naturel coves, while many families strip off to the right where the beach is bigger and next to the bar.

The informal 30-room Hostal Sa Plana, near Playa de Figueral, is surrounded by pine-clad hills and located 15 minutes' walk from the nude beach at Aguas Blancas.

> **Aguas Blancas accommodation**
>
> Hostal Sa Plana
> Tel: +34 971 33 50 73
> www.ibiza-hotels.com/saplana

Cala Bassa and Cala Conta, west coast

Situated across the bay from San Antonio on the west coast of Ibiza, these two locations listed in the previous edition of the World Guide to Nude Beaches are easily accessible and now attract a majority of costumed bathers, especially in high season. Skimpy swimwear is mostly de rigueur these days, but at quieter times discreet nudism at the sides of Cala Bassa is still possible for the brave.

At the slightly more remote Cala Conta there are two stretches of sandy beach, backed by rocky terrain, with a third smaller naturist beach at the far end (to the left) reached by steps hewn in the rock. Beach bars, sun beds, umbrellas and pedalos: packed in mid-summer.

Practical info

From San Antonio it's fun to go on the regular ferry that takes 15 minutes to Cala Bassa. It's further to drive or cycle along the coast road (8km); alternatively take the bus. For Cala Conta fork right along the signposted track shortly before Cala Bassa. The handy Camping Cala Bassa includes 'nudist beach' in its list of attractions.

> **Cala Bassa accommodation**
>
> Camping Cala Bassa
> Tel: +34 971 34 45 99
> www.campingsonline.com/calabassa

▲ Aguas Blancas has soft and inviting sands at the foot of the access road and beach bar. The coast gets rockier and quieter to the north (top picture, supplied by Andy Eke)

▲ Snap happy: bathers on Es Cavallet

▲ Naturist accommodation just 10 minutes from Es Trenc nude beach, Skinny Dippers has a pool and private gardens

Mallorca

Playa Es Trenc, near Colonia Sant Jordi

The best known and one of the prettiest nude beaches on the island. It has a long undeveloped shoreline with lovely soft yellow sand. The beach shelves gently into the turquoise sea – perfect for swimming. Low dunes and pinewoods complete this beautiful spot.

There are sunbeds and umbrellas for hire on part of the naturist section, or for more tranquillity just walk a little further. As skinny dipping becomes a commonplace activity for holidaymakers visitor numbers inevitably rise, but secluded beaches like this still have plenty of space.

Practical info

Take the lanes to the seaside hamlet of Ses Covetes. On entering the village look out for a left turn into a wide unmade track by the phone box. Arrive early and park here, otherwise

there is a large car park (fee) just before the village. Walk 200 metres along the track to the start of the beach, then another 300 metres to the nude area.

Many holidaymakers stay in Colonia Sant Jordi, from where it is possible to walk along the beach to the southern, clothes-optional, end of Es Trenc. New for 2007, Skinny Dippers near Campos has naturist self-catering accommodation in six studio apartments 10 minutes' drive from Es Trenc. Set in the grounds of a 100-year old Mallorca finca: a secluded retreat in private gardens with a swimming pool and sun terraces.

Es Trenc accommodation
Skinny Dippers
www.skinnydippersmallorca.com

143 ▮

Playa Es Pregons Gran, Colonia Sant Jordi

This wonderful little naturist bay has a crescent of fine yellow sand 180 metres long. The sea is transparent and looks more like the Caribbean – a paradise for 'kids' of all ages. There are no beach bars so bring your picnic and plenty of drinks. In our opinion, the jewel in the crown of the Es Trenc area.

Practical info

The route to the beach is a pleasant 15 minute stroll along the shore, heading north from Colonia. Start at the Hotel Marques Del Palmer, and it's the third bay along. The fourth bay, if you walk further, is the southern end of the main Es Trenc beach.

The Swiss-owned 4-star Hotel

Marques Del Palmer is in a lovely location at the water's edge on the outskirts of town. The hotel is adjacent to the attractive Playa es Marques, sometimes described as Estanys Playa. The Villa Piccola Apartments in Colonia is a small privately owned luxury development (4 keys), located opposite the Hotel Marques Del Palmer. The accommodation enjoys similar access to the nude beaches. Villa Marquesa Apartments (next door to Villa Piccola) provides basic holiday accommodation (1 key). The modern 4-star Hotel El Coto in Colonia is near Playa es Marques beach and a 900-metre walk from Pregons Gran nude beach.

Playa El Mago, Portals Vells

This delightful and picturesque little cove must be the smallest official nudist beach in Spain. It has soft golden sand and calm sheltered water ideal for swimming and snorkelling. However, it gets extremely busy and nude and swimsuited sunbathers spread out on

the smooth rocks surrounding the bay. There is a restaurant.

Practical info

Drive south from Magaluf towards Portals Vells, past the golf course and into the pinewoods. Take the left turn signposted Playa de Mago Restaurant.

▲ Breathtaking however you use them, beaches in the Balearics would satisfy anyone curious about nude bathing. This image shows two free spirits enjoying the sea around Mallorca; picture by Charlie Simonds

---

Es Pregons Gran accommodation

Hotel Marques Del Palmer
Tel: +34 971 65 51 00
www.universaltravel.ch

Villa Piccola Apartments
Tel: +34 971 71 71 22
www.villapiccola.com

Villa Marquesa Apartments
Book via Hotel Marques Del Palmer
(same tel and web address, above)

Hotel El Coto
Tel: +34 971 65 50 25
www.elcoto.de

Spain: Balearics

Playa Son Real, near C'an Picafort

This string of protected and undeveloped nude beaches stretches for 2km to the east of the main resort, and attracts both naturist and swimsuited users. Driftwood and occasional seaweed washed up along the shore help make this part of the coast feel remote. There are no facilities so remember to take refreshments with you.

Practical info
From C'an Picafort walk out of town along the beach past the last property, Hotel Son Baulo, and you can bare all within 350 metres. Or drive to Son Serra Nou and walk west towards C'an Picafort. The Es Baulo Petit Hotel in C'an Picafort, which caters mainly for German holidaymakers, has a naturist terrace.

Playa Sa Canova, Son Serra Nou

This is a vast and unusually isolated (in Mallorca) virgin beach not far from the previous location – Playa Son Real. A broad swathe of pale level sand stretches away in the distance. It can be exposed to prevailing breezes, so a wind shelter might come in handy.
Practical info
Drive to the wild village of Son Serra and turn right: walk eastwards on the shore to find peace and space. Alternatively, drive to Colonia Sant Pere and walk west away from the small urbanisation of s'Estanyol. The modern family-run Sa Punta de s'Estanyol Aparthotel at Sant Pere overlooks Sa Canova and has some rooms with individual secluded roof terraces.

▲ Nude bathers love Cala Mesquida's surf. It's an increasingly developed spot but has a long tradition of nude use. Pics from www.radiantnude.com

Son Real accommodation

Hotel Son Baulo
Tel: +34 971 85 01 14
www.fehm.es

Es Baulo Petit Hotel
Tel: +34 971 85 00 63
www.esbaulo.com

Sa Canova accommodation

Sa Punta de s'Estanyol Aparthotel
Tel: +34 971 18 37 04
www.sapunta.com

Cala Mesquida, near Cala Ratjada

A beautiful white sand beach with good facilities and superb swimming. The area has developed rapidly with new apartments and hotels, so the beach is very popular. Nude bathers tend to use the southern side of the bay, near the pill box. Influxes of swimsuited holidaymakers can sometimes overwhelm almost the whole beach, particularly during peak season. The extensive dunes behind the shore still provide seclusion for all-over tan seekers.
Practical info
Turn off the Arta to Cala Ratjada road at Capdepera, following the signs to Cala Mesquida. Park by the Viva holiday village and take the path to the beach.

Cala Varques (Coves del Pirata)

This stunning little gem is said to be one of the most picturesque beaches on the island, but it's not easy to find – which helps keep the crowds away. Almost-white powder sand, turquoise sea and a backdrop of pinewoods make it a bare beauty. There's an impressive cave to explore to the south of the cove.
Practical info
Take the road from Porto Colom

towards Porto Cristo (PM-401-4) and after about 11km look out for a left turn to Manacor (PM-401-5). Don't take the turn, but continue 200 metres and turn right on to a track signposted Cala Falco. In 1.5km there is a fence on the right which signals the place to park. Take the path past the fence for 200 metres to the beach – and bring your refreshments with you!

Calo d'en Rafalino, S'Illot, Porto Cristo

This unspoilt swimsuits-optional little cove has a tiny patch of fine golden sand bordering the transparent Med. Superb swimming, with easy access from S'Illot: take a picnic and shade.
Practical info
From the tourist centre of S'Illot

follow the coastal footpath to the south for 750 metres to Calo d'en Rafalino. Nearest parking at Cala Morlanda. The 3-star Hotel Temi at Cala Bona, 15 minutes' drive to the north, has a rooftop naturist terrace and Jacuzzi.

Other Mallorca beaches

The excellent and well illustrated 'Complete Guide: Beaches Mallorca and Cabrera' by Miguel Angel Alvarez Alperi (ISBN 8487933076 – available on the island), recommends a further six remote and undiscovered coves just to the south of Cala Varques for nude bathing. Access to each involves

a long walk varying from 2km to 4km, or a trip by boat. From north to south the coves are: Cala Sequer, Calo des Serral, Cala Pilota, Cala Magraner, Cala Virgili and finally Cala Bota. These beaches are some of the most unspoilt and least visited on the whole of Mallorca.

▲ Mallorca is a long-established destination for nude bathers. Cala Varques, pictured above, is off the beaten track and perfect for some peaceful back-to-nature relaxation. **Pictures by Charlie Simonds**

Calo d'en Rafalino accommodation

Hotel Temi
Tel: +34 971 81 33 81

▲ Unofficial nude sightseeing on Cabrera island, just off Mallorca. Picture: Charlie Simonds

Cala Presili and Playa de Capifort

MENORCA

Cala Macarelleta

Playa de Binigaus

Mahon •

Playa Son Bou

Spain: Balearics

Menorca

Playa Son Bou, St Jaime, south coast

The biggest sandy beach on the island, with a long tradition of nude bathing, shelves gently into the sea and is super for children. There are plenty of facilities on this busy blue flag beach. The nude area is on the western side of the bay, away from the two large hotels.

Practical info

Travelling along the main road from Mahon towards Ciutadella, turn left to St Jaime, just after the town of Alayor. After 6km park by the beach and take the boardwalk to the right (facing the sea). The nude area normally starts near the end of the sunbeds. You can't miss the twin high-rise family hotels Sol Milanos and Sol Pinguinos, built right by Son Bou beach. They are both 3-star and have a total of 600 rooms.

According to one brochure 'clothing requirements descend from the start of the hotels where bikinis and shorts are required, to the end stretch of the beach which is au naturel'. In other words the further you go the better it gets, only 15-20 mins' walk at most.

Playa de Binigaus, Sant Tomas, south coast

This lovely clothes-optional beach is increasingly popular. The 900m of yellow sand shelve gently into the sea and with low pine-clad cliffs behind the shore it is reasonably well sheltered: nooks and crannies provide extra seclusion. A beach bar opens in mid-summer. Beware of occasional strong currents. The neighbouring Cala Adeonato also has nude bathing.

Practical info

Travelling along the main road between Mahon and Ciutadella, directions to Sant Tomas are well signposted. Approaching the resort there is a roundabout where the main road turns left along the seafront into Sant Tomas. Instead, turn right here into a car park and walk down to the beach by the Es Bruc bar. Go west (right) along the shore around the headland for a few hundred metres until the swimsuits disappear and the bare bathing area stretches out before you.

Son Bou accommodation

Sol Milanos and Sol Pinguinos
Tel: +34 971 37 12 00
www.solmelia.com

147 ■

Cala Macarelleta, south-west coast

A picture-postcard cove which is completely unspoilt and has warm clear water lapping on the soft white sand. Surrounded by pinewoods and rocky headlands, this secluded inlet is well sheltered from the breeze, which also makes it a popular spot with visiting yachts. There is usually a mix of swimsuited and nude bathers enjoying the sun in their own way. In low season the tall limestone cliffs restrict the sun later in the day.

Practical info
Drive through the lanes south east from Ciutadella to Cala Macarella – the last 4km are bumpy. Walk from the car park and turn right (facing the sea). Scramble over the headland to the next bay, Cala Macareletta. It is not difficult, but not for the infirm.

▲ The stunning Cala Macarelleta beach on Menorca. Picture by Mr Bun, of the naturist travel website www.sunnybuns.me.uk

▲ The end of a sunny day on Mallorca. Pic from www.radiantnude.com

Cala Presili & Playa de Capifort, north coast

These two attractive virgin beaches in remote north-eastern Menorca are mostly enjoyed by naturists. They are not accessible by motor vehicle and so not so crowded. According to John, a recent correspondent: "Nice sand, warm water, rocks to snorkel over – a brilliant destination for an all over tan."

Practical info
From Mahon drive north on the PM710 Fornells road and a short distance after km-marker 8 fork right on to the PM715, signposted Cap de Favaritx. A kilometre before the lighthouse at the Cap, park on the road by a wide-gated track on the right. After a 10-15 minute walk down the track turn left to reach Cala Presili. Alternatively continue walking further along the track to reach Playa de Capifort.

H&E naturist

THE HEALTH & EFFICIENCY GUIDE TO NATURIST LIVING

The world's only **monthly** *naturist magazine!*

Naked News

Travel reports

Readers' letters

Competitions

Read by naturists and all who enjoy a naked lifestyle worldwide

H&E naturist magazine
**New Freedom
Publications Ltd
Burlington Court
Carlisle Street, Goole
East Yorks, DN14 5EG
United Kingdom**

www.henaturist.co.uk

newfreedom@btinternet.com

Tel: +44 (0)1405 760298

The Canary Islands

Northern Europeans and a good many North Americans love the Canary islands, particularly when it's winter back home. With perennial spring-like weather and laid-back style, this Atlantic archipelago off the coast of Africa attracts a huge number of sunseekers, many of whom come to enjoy the vast beaches in their birthday suits. From powder white to volcanic black, the sandy beaches are hugely varied and in some cases stretch for kilometers along undeveloped coast.

Fuerteventura with its glorious unspoiled shores and relaxed approach to nudity, unsurprisingly, attracts more all-over tan fans than the other islands. Not to be outdone, Lanzarote has its own well established naturist village, while Gran Canaria boasts the most populous nudist beach. On Tenerife there's a great choice of reasonable 4- and 5-star hotels offering dedicated naturist terraces for sunning in the buff. And Tenerife's little sister, La Gomera, can certainly hold its own, with a choice of skinny-dipping beaches.

Lobos
Lighthouse beaches
Corralejo
El Cotillo lagoons
Corralejo dunes
El Cotillo surf beach

Puerto del Rosario

Caleta de Fuste

FUERTEVENTURA

Playa del Viejo Rey

Playa Esmeralda
Playa Barca
Playa Risco del Paso
Morro Jable
Playa Esquinzo

Fuerteventura

Corralejo dunes, south of Corralejo town

The dunes provide a spectacular backdrop to a line of yellow sandy beaches with great views across the bay. Although popular, there is plenty of space for that away-from-it-all feeling. You will find a relaxed mix of swimsuited and nude bathers here.

Practical info

The main road south from Corralejo to Puerto del Rosario runs right by the beach and dunes 4km outside town, and there is plenty of parking by the side of the road. Buses and taxis are readily available.

Two large hotels are situated in the dunes area – Hotel Riu Oliva Beach Resort and Hotel Riu Palace Tres Islas are right on the shore. The beach is clothes-optional within 200m north or south of the hotels. Infiniti is a small British-owned development of high-quality apartments and villas on the outskirts of Corralejo with a rooftop

sauna and a solarium for nude sunbathing. A further 10km south of Corralejo, Villa Bougainvillaea at Parque Holandes has two bedrooms and a secluded pool with large terraces perfect for skinny-dipping and sunning au naturel.

Corralejo accommodation

Hotel Riu Oliva Beach
Tel: +34 928 53 53 34
www.riu.com

Hotel Riu Palace Tres Islas
Tel: +34 928 53 57 00
www.riu.com

Infiniti Apartments
Tel: +44 (0)1548 561289 (UK)
www.infinitivillas.co.uk

Villa Bougainvillaea
Tel: +44 (0)1787 281417 (UK)
www.islandseekers.co.uk

▼ The stunning sand dunes at Corralejo, a great place to run around naked, or simply soak up the sun next to the sea (opposite page). Pictures by Donald Stewart

Spain: Canary Islands

Spain: Canary Islands

El Cotillo lagoons beaches, west coast

A cluster of picturesque sandy coves divided by low volcanic rocks. The turquoise seawater pools are protected by offshore reefs, making them perfect for swimming and snorkelling. Recent construction of new holiday accommodation in the area has brought more swimsuited visitors, but the coves remain popular for developing an all-over tan.

Practical info

El Cotillo is on the north-west coast, 20 minutes' drive from Corralejo. There is a newly surfaced road heading north from the village towards the lighthouse. The beaches are on the left-hand side and are used clothes-optional from within half a kilometre, stretching into the distance. Parking by the beaches. There are buses from Corralejo to El Cotillo.

El Caleton apartments are on the beach in an unspoilt spot with 11 units 1km from the village. Nude sunbathing is available only steps from your door. Maravilla apartments are a few minutes' walk from the nearest clothes-optional areas. There is a small sheltered swimming pool (often used for skinny-dipping). El Balcon del Cotillo apartments and Cotillo Sun apartments are both on the beach half a kilometre from the village, and less than five minutes' walk to the clothes-optional areas.

> **El Cotillo accommodation**
>
> El Caleton
> Tel: +44 (0)1494 580728 (UK)
> www.chalfontholidays.co.uk
>
> Maravilla
> Tel: +34 609 54 54 26
> www.maravilla.at
>
> El Balcon del Cotillo
> Tel: +44 (0)1403 738866 (UK)
> www.sunseekerholidays.com
>
> Cotillo Sun
> Tel/Fax: +44 (0)870 770 5378 (UK)
> www.canariandreams.com

▲ Beaches on either side of El Cotillo: top shows the surf beaches, bottom shows lighthouse beaches

Lighthouse beaches, north of El Cotillo

These wild and remote coves towards the northern tip of Fuerteventura, next to the El Cotillo beaches, have glistening white sand. Although the sea crashes dramatically on the rocky headlands, the water in the coves is normally sheltered and calm. Ideal for finding your own peace and tranquillity.

Practical info

Take the road north out of El Cotillo for almost 2km, passing the lagoons beaches on the left. Approaching the lighthouse (Faro Toston), there is a sandy track off to the right. The coves appear within a few hundred metres. Ordinary cars might be seen negotiating the final part of the track, but soft sand and rough terrain make it more appropriate for off-road vehicles. The best beaches are nearer the lighthouse.

El Cotillo surf beach, west coast

A big and ruggedly attractive beach, popular with windsurfers. It is rarely busy and there is plenty of space for au naturel sunseekers. However, care should be taken when swimming because of the undertow.

Practical info

It is easy to find because it starts immediately south of the village, reached by a wide track. Parking is on the low cliff above the beach with an easy scramble down to the sand.

Playa Esmeralda, Costa Calma

This pretty golden sand beach lies on the sheltered side of the island, which makes it particularly popular for nude sunbathing and swimming. Sunbeds and umbrellas are available for hire.

Practical info

From Costa Calma take the minor road south out of the town and go left at the supermarket. The beach is 1km further, in front of Hotel Playa Esmeralda.

> **Playa Esmeralda accommodation**
>
> Hotel Playa Esmeralda
> Tel: +34 928 87 53 53
> www.h10.es

▲ Stone shelters help against the wind. Top pic by Donald Stewart

Playa Barca, Sotavento

A wide flat beach by the Hotel Gorriones, which stretches more than 20km south! There is a world-renowned windsurfing school here. The beach can be a bit exposed, but there are plenty of volcanic rock shelters. Nude kite flying is another popular activity.

Practical info

Take the main coast road south from Costa Calma and after 3km watch for the sign to the Hotel Gorriones on the left. The road goes down to the beach.

There is no development in the area other than the hotel, which is a large well-equipped complex. The beach is clothes-optional within 150 metres of the access, which is why many of the guests come here.

Playa Risco del Paso, south of Costa Calma

Possibly the finest beach on the island, Playa Risco del Paso boasts miles and miles of almost deserted golden sand. Fantastic sense of freedom for walking and relaxation dressed or undressed.

Practical info

Take the main road south from Costa Calma and just before a large bend in the road and a filling station on the right there is a short track on the left down to the beach.

▲ **Beach life on Fuerteventura. Picture top right shows Playa Barca, supplied by T Parker, pic above shows El Cotillo's lagoons beaches**

Playa Barca accommodation

Hotel Sol Elite Gorriones
Tel: +34 928 54 70 25
www.solmelia.es

Playa Esquinzo accommodation

Hotel Occidental Grand Fuerteventura
Tel: +34 928 87 36 00
www.occidental-hoteles.com

Hotel Fuerteventura Princess
Tel: +34 928 54 41 36
www.princess-hotels.com

Hotel Club Jandia Princess
Tel: +34 928 54 40 89
www.princess-hotels.com

Monte Marina naturist apartments
Tel: +44 (0)845 3458345 (UK)
www.pengtravel.co.uk

Playa Esquinzo, north of Morro Jable

This beautiful clothes-optional beach lies towards the southern end of the giant Playa de Sotavento. There is a selection of large modern hotels nearby, handy for the nude beach.

Practical info

Head north from Morro Jable along the main coast road. Gain access by any of the large hotels here – the beach is mostly clothes-optional a short walk either side of each building. There are a few more swimsuited bathers around than in the past because of the number of hotels – but don't let that deter you: there's space for everybody. The Occidental Grand Fuerteventura is a 700-room hotel with a nudist area

including a pool, sunbathing lawns, loungers, open-air spa, sauna and vitamin bar. Nearby, the Hotel Fuerteventura Princess has a dedicated naturist area with two glass-sided saunas, a steam room, outdoor showers and a pool overlooking the sea (said to be the best nude facilities of the three neighbouring hotels). Next door, its older sister hotel Jandia Club Princess has a small nudist area. Just up the road, the fully naturist Monte Marina apartments and swimming pool are built on an elevated site overlooking Playa Esquinzo. The beach below the apartments stretches for miles and is widely used by nude sunseekers.

Playa del Viejo Rey, La Pared, Jandia

A bracing beach on the wild south-west coast of Fuerteventura, ideal for that exhilarating nude stroll or sunbathing sans costume in the shelter of one of the coves. Rough seas make swimming hazardous.

Practical info

From Costa Calma take the main road north for 2km and look out for a left turn to La Pared. After 4km drive into the Hotel Costa Real car park and take the path by the side of the hotel on to the low cliffs, and then down the steps to the beach.

The 4-star Hotel Costa Real is situated on cliffs 300 metres from the sea. The hotel sauna and outdoor spa pool can be used nude. Rooms can be requested with a secluded terrace to allow private au naturel sunbathing.

Playa del Viejo Rey accommodation

Hotel Costa Real
Tel: +34 928 54 90 04
www.canariandreams.com

Tenerife

Red Rock beach, near El Medano

This beautiful sheltered and secluded beach is ideal for swimming and sunning all year round. Mount Teide, Spain's highest peak, provides a stunning backdrop. The beach is on the most southerly part of the island. Sun loungers are available for hire and there is a bar nearby. It's the most established and easily accessible nudist beach on Tenerife, well used and well loved.

Practical info

On the road from El Abrigo to El Medano there is a car park at the eastern end of Playa la Tejita. Walk towards the sea, keeping to the left until the bar at the end of the beach. There's a path behind the bar which takes you up and round a corner to a footbridge, and you're there – heaven! El Medano is the closest town, and Playa de las Americas is 20 minutes' drive away.

Playa la Tejita, near El Medano

This big, open and undeveloped beach can best be described as clothes-optional, with more nudist use year by year. It has very dark-golden soft sand and is great for swimming. With lots of space it is easy to find a quiet spot to yourself. Dressed and undressed sunseekers share the beach in harmony. It's sometimes breezy, in which case Red Rock (see above) around the corner at the eastern end of the bay might be a better bet.

Practical info

The car park at the eastern end of the beach is ideal, and there is another one at the other end of the bay, towards El Abrigo. A privately owned apartment at the Sotavento complex, on the western side of the beach, has a solarium suitable for au naturel sunbathing.

▲ **Red Rock beach. Picture by Mr Bun, of www.sunnybuns.me.uk**

Playa la Tejita accommodation

Sotavento Apartment
Tel: +44 (0)1494 580728 (UK)
www.chalfontholidays.co.uk

Playa Blanca accommodation

Gran Hotel Costa Adeje
Tel: +34 922 71 94 21
www.costaadejegranhotel.com

Sheraton La Caleta Resort & Spa
Tel: +34 922 16 20 00
www.starwoodhotels.com

Hotel Fanabe Costa Sur
Tel: +34 922 71 29 00
www.fanabecostasur.com

Hotel Noelia Sur
Tel: +34 922 71 72 10
www.dreamplacehotels.com

Playa Blanca (Diego Hernández), La Caleta

An attractive but remote beach, 30-40 mins' brisk walk from civilisation. The lovely south-west facing shore with views to the island of La Gomera feels a million miles away from the hurly burly of nearby Playa de las Americas. Expect to find a few dozen other bare bathers and a handful of hippies who camp at the 200-metre long beach.

Practical info

Approach on foot from the village of La Caleta taking the well-trodden path north climbing over two headlands or, from the village of El Puertito, head south along the coastal path. Take good footwear for this adventurous and scenic hike.

There are some new hotels at La Caleta, but for nude sunbathing at your hotel there's a good choice in Playa de las Americas, just 7km away. The 5-star Gran Hotel Costa Adeje, the 5-star Sheraton La Caleta Resort & Spa; also the 4-star hotels Fanabe Costa Sur and Noelia Sur – all have rooftop naturist terraces.

▲ The nude beach at Playa de las Gaviotas enjoys both a dramatic cliff backdrop and some on-site cafes. It's also handy for Tenerife's capital Santa Cruz

Playa de los Patos, Puerto de la Cruz

A wild place with soaring cliffs where the heavy Atlantic swell sends giant waves crashing on to the north-west facing shore. Jet-black sand and a challenging access make it ideal for the discerning and the determined nudist! Most likely your only company will be a dozen or so other intrepid naked bathers. No facilities or lifeguard on this 250-metre strand.
Practical info
Surprisingly, the beach does not appear on local maps. It lies 5km to the east of Puerto de la Cruz – head first for El Rincon and then follow the signs to the textile beach of Playa Bollullo, where there is very limited parking. Continue east along the coastal footpath for a kilometre. The final descent to Playa de los Patos is steep and requires considerable fitness and balance to negotiate.

While there are limited naturist beach opportunities in the north of Tenerife, nude sunbathing is readily available at a choice of hotels and apartments in the resort of Puerto de la Cruz.

The 4-star Puerto Palace has a secluded rooftop swimming pool, spa pool, showers and terrace dedicated to nude relaxation and skinny-dipping – recommended. The H10 Tenerife Playa and the Playacanaria Hotels also have naturist areas. The Maritim Hotel at Los Realejos near Puerto de la Cruz has a nudist sunbathing lawn in the gardens.

The older Parque Vacacional Eden Apartments have a nudist sunbathing terrace, sauna and pool on the roof.

Playa de las Gaviotas, near Santa Cruz

The profile of this clothes-optional haven has grown in recent years, to the extent that it was recently included in a listing of 10 best international nude beaches. We wouldn't go quite that far, but it's certainly handy for the capital of Tenerife and enjoys official naked status. Steep mountains rise up from behind the black 120-metre sandy shore, which is in the next bay to the famous artificial Playa de la Teresitas (all imported white sand). Gaviotas is popular among the gay community. The beach is easily accessible and has three cafes nearby.
Practical info
From Santa Cruz take the main TF112 coast road north-east to the fishing port of St Andres. After the Teresitas textile beach and the traffic lights, the route becomes a minor road, TF111, which climbs steeply up the hillside passing a mirador (viewing point with excellent vistas of both beaches). Drop down towards the village of Playa Chica, but then bear right to Playa de las Gaviotas – not to be confused with the next cove, which is Playa Chica!

Spain: Canary Islands

La Gomera

Playa del Ingles, Valle Gran Rey

This super, volcanic black sand beach lies on the western side of this subtropical island, and has long been popular with nude bathers. The naturist beach is just an 800 metre walk to the north of the main promenade.

Practical info

There are plenty of holiday apartments in the vicinity, while 2km to the south, just beyond Vueltas, Finca Argayall is a holistic retreat with home grown organic produce next to the sea. It specialises in all types of relaxation, meditation, massage and therapies such as Reiki and Shiatsu. Although textile, it is described as nude-friendly and the adjacent pebble beach – Playa Argaga – is clothes-optional.

> **Vueltas accommodation**
>
> Finca Argayall
> Tel/Fax: +34 922 69 70 08
> www.argayall.com

Playa de Tapahuga, Playa Medio and Playa de Chinguarime

These three small clothes-optional bays near the southern tip of the island have pebbles and coarse dark sand. They are close to the resort town of Playa Santiago.

Practical info

The bays are easily reached from the popular 4-star Hotel Jardin Tecina by walking east for 20-45 minutes along the zigzag coastal track. The further you go the quieter it gets. The hotel has a nudist sun terrace and is surrounded by gardens renowned for their flora and fauna.

> **Local accommodation**
>
> Hotel Jardin Tecina
> Tel: +34 922 14 58 50
> www.jardin-tecina.com

▲▼ The beaches around Playa del Ingles have a dramatic setting and plenty of unclad visitors enjoying it

▲ Papagayo beach on Lanzarote is warm enough for year-round bathing. Picture by Charlie Simonds

Lanzarote

Playa Famara

Charco del Palo

LANZAROTE

Arrecife

Puerto del Carmen

Playa Guasimeta

Playa Papagayo

Papagayo accommodation

Iberostar Papagayo Hotel
Tel: +34 922 07 03 00
www.iberostar.com

Natura Palace Hotel
Tel: +34 928 51 90 70
www.hipotels.com

Timanfaya Palace Hotel
Tel: +34 928 51 76 76
www.h10.es

Playa Guasimeta accommodation

Hotel Los Jameos Playa
Tel: +34 928 51 17 17
www.los-jameos-playa.de

Playa Papagayo, near Playa Blanca

Not one but a collection of beautiful and undeveloped yellow sandy beaches in the natural park on the peninsula of the same name. All of the beaches are clothes-optional to some extent, but Playa Caleta del Congrio is the one most bare sunseekers head for. Over 500 metres long and ideal for walking and sunbathing, the beach is popular and well used but there are no facilities, so take your own refreshments. Playa Mujeres and Playa del Pozo also have some nude bathers.
Practical info
From Playa Blanca follow the signs to Playa Papagayo. After 2km pay a small toll to enter the natural park. After a further 1.5km along an unsurfaced

road turn left at the sign to Playa Puerto Muelas. Playa Caleta del Congrio is the next beach to the right, on the eastern side of the peninsula. Large car park nearby.
There is a wide choice of places to stay in Playa Blanca including three 4-star hotels that have nude sunbathing terraces. The Iberostar Papagayo Hotel on the outskirts of the resort at Playa de los Coloradas opened in 2002. The au naturel terrace has super views. The Natura Palace Hotel has a nude area in the garden and an indoor Jacuzzi, sauna and Turkish bath which are costumes-optional. The stylish Timanfaya Palace Hotel has a nude sun terrace in a screened area of gardens.

Playa Guasimeta, near the airport

This clean, sandy clothes-optional beach is right beside the airport runway, but is pleasant and feels surprisingly well away from civilisation. There are a couple of beach bars but it doesn't get too busy. Swimming here is great.
Practical info
To get to Guasimeta take the turn for Playa Honda off the main road

between the airport and Arrecife, and after less than 1km you'll find a car park. Hotel Los Jameos Playa at Playa de los Pocillos, a few minutes drive from Guasimeta, has a secluded area in its acres of tropical gardens reserved for nude sunbathing. Sunbeds are provided as well as a freshwater shower.

Spain: Canary Islands

Charco del Palo, near Mala

This unique naturist village by the sea is open to all. There are plenty of sheltered and sandy spots for sunbathing, but the beach is tiny and best for paddling. But don't let that put you off because the rugged coastline is beautiful and there is a large man-made tidal swimming pool, which is great fun. Or you can swim in the sea from steps on the rocks. There are miles of sea walks along the low cliffs, where you can leave your clothes and your cares way behind.

Practical info

Travelling north, turn right off the coast road at the village of Mala, just after the small hospital. Follow the winding tarmac road for 3km to Charco del Palo. You can be bare almost anywhere if you wish, and many of the holiday properties have lovely skinny-dipping pools.

There's a wide choice of places to stay at the naturist village, including luxury villas, bungalows and self-catering apartments. Also three restaurants, bars and a supermarket. The Villa Salida del Sol is a three-bedroomed villa overlooking the sea, with two au naturel terraces. Villa Casa

Ronda has its own private swimming pool. Las Piteras apartments have a shared pool, whilst Charco Natural offers simple accommodation near the sea. Hotel Playaverde at Costa Teguise is 15 minutes' drive from Charco del Palo. The hotel has a terrace reserved for nude sunbathing.

Charco del Palo accommodation

Charco del Palo
Tel: +44 (0)870 770 5378 (UK)
www.charco-del-palo.com

Villa Salida del Sol
Tel: +49 5345 989 595
www.salida-del-sol.de

Villa Casa Ronda
Email: ronald.hagge@t-online.de
www.casa-ronda.de

Las Piteras Apartments
Tel: +34 928 81 15 49
www.laspiteras.es

Charco Natural Apartments
Tel: +34 928 52 95 95
www.charconatural.com

Hotel Playaverde
Tel: +34 928 82 60 70
www.playasenator.com

▲ The village at Charco del Palo is conveniently naturist, making it an easy place to enjoy the island
▼ By the tidal pool at Charco del Palo, Lanzarote. The pool water is replaced at high tide, and offers safe swimming on this rocky coastline.
Pictures by Charlie Simonds

Playa Famara, La Caleta

The biggest beach on the island and certainly the most dramatic, backed by 2,000-foot cliffs. There's lots of space and the northern half is ideal for nude sunning, swimming and walking. The little stone 'zocos', or shelters, provide protection from the breeze, as well as privacy for those who want it. The beach is popular with windsurfers.

Practical info

Take the road from Arrecife to Mozaga, and then turn right for Teguise. After 3km turn left for La Caleta and Playa Famara. After 15km you can't miss the beach, which is located just before the resort at La Caleta.

Some of the holiday villas immediately behind the beach have secluded patios which are suitable for discreet nude sunbathing. Plenty of privately owned apartments for hire in nearby La Caleta.

Gran Canaria

Playa de Maspalomas, Playa del Ingles

Hundreds of acres of sand dunes that might have come straight from the Sahara frame the beautiful long curved beach between Maspalomas and Playa del Ingles. It's 4km from one end to the other and over 1km deep. Along the shore it gets packed with holidaymakers, but there are specific places reserved for nude sunseekers. The bare areas, like the swimsuited ones, have sunbeds and umbrellas for hire. For a quieter spot, walk away from the sea into the vast expanse of dunes, but be careful not to get lost!

Practical info

The best way on to the beach is from either end: the walk from Maspalomas to the nudist area is slightly shorter. Just look for the many other people without clothes.

The largest resort area on Gran Canaria has developed around this huge beach, so there is no shortage of places to stay. For fully nudist accommodation, the attractive Magnolias Natura resort offers 28 bungalow apartments, a swimming pool, sun terraces, a bar and restaurant, which can all be enjoyed in the buff. The following hotels in Maspalomas, Playa del Ingles and San Agustin have nude sun terraces: Palm Beach (5-star); IFA Dunamar (4-star); Lopesan Catarina (4-star); Sandy Beach (4-star); Barcelo Margaritas (4-star); Caserio (4-star) Gloria Palace (4-star); Don Gregory (4-star); IFA Beach (3-star). Inland the 4-star Helga Masthoff Park & Sport Hotel at Los Palmitos, about 15 minutes' drive from Maspalomas beach also offers nudist sunbathing.

Spain: Canary Islands

▲ **Maspalomas is famous for its vast sand dunes. Picture by Charlie Simonds**

France

France's sparkling coastline, pastoral countryside and sunny weather draw visitors back year after year. For millions of holiday-makers, the chance to enjoy all this absolutely au naturel makes it unmissable.

The popularity of nude bathing in France goes back several generations. It's an accepted way of life and much of the country boasts the perfect climate for relaxing as nature intended. Quick to recognise an opportunity, a myriad of fabulous naturist holiday centres have emerged, particularly along the south-west Atlantic coast and next to the sandy beaches of the Mediterranean.

The French tourist industry could not make it easier to find that perfect spot at the seaside for bathing in the buff. Whether you're seeking a lively location with thousands of other nude bathers or you prefer the solitude of your own company, we've listed more than 50 beaches. There's bound to be one that's just right for your holiday.

Berck Plage — • Berck

Merville Plage
Hatainville Plage — • Cherbourg
St Germain sur Ay — • Le Havre
Breville sur Mer — • Caen
Plage des Chevrets
Mez-an-Aod — • Paris
• Brest — • St Malo
Plage de — Plage du Port Sud-Est
lost-Marc'h — Le Lourtuais

• Le Mans

Plage de Kerler
Plage de Kerminihy — • Tours
La Turballe Pen Bron Plage — • Nantes
Plage de Luzeronde
Les Lays Plage
Plage de Salins — FRANCE
Le Petit Pont — Pointe d'Arcay
Sauveterre Plage
La Grande Plage — • La Rochelle
La Cote Sauvage — Plage des Saumonards
La Grande Cote — • Clermont Ferrand
Plage de Saint Nicolas — • Royan — • Lyon
CHM — Euronat
La Jenny — • Bordeaux
Teste du Buch

Arnaoutchot — • Avignon
• Bayonne — Nice
Montpellier •
Béziers • — St Tropez
7 — • Marseille — 14
4 5 6 8 9 10 13
3 11 12
2
Perpignan • — 1

Mediterranean France
1. Bocal del Tech
2. Leucate Plage
3. Plage des Moutilles
4. St Pierre sur Mer
5. Serignan Plage
6. Cap d'Agde
7. Maguelone Plage
8. Grau du Roi
9. Piemancon Plage
10. Plage de Bonnieu
11. Le Jonquet
12. Les Grottes Plage
13. Le Layet Plage
14. Plage du Gros Pin

CORSICA
Bravone Plage
Riva Bella Plage
• Ajaccio
U Furu naturist centre — Villata
La Chiappa

Websites for naturist France

French Naturist Federation
www.ffn-naturisme.com (in French only)

France 4 Naturism
www.france-4naturisme.com

Organisation Naturist European
www.onenaturism.com

French National Tourist Office
www.franceguide.com
(search for naturism)

France

Mediterranean beaches

Bocal del Tech – Elne, south-east of Perpignan

This could be one naturist beach or two, depending how you view it. A long undeveloped sandy shore in the Reserve Naturelle du Mars Larrieu, divided by the mouth of the River Tech. During summer you can wade across the river with care. There are no facilities or lifeguards, but access is fairly easy and it's popular with families, couples, singles and gay visitors.

Practical info
From Argelès Plage head north on the D81 towards St Cyprien. Shortly after crossing the Tech river there is a track on the right which goes to a car park at the beach. There is also a slightly harder to find access road to the beach south of the Tech river.

Leucate Plage – Aphrodite, north of Perpignan

This is a superb nude beach of fine golden sand stretching for over 1km. The water is normally calm and the shore shelves gently into the sea, making it ideal for young families. Occasional breezes off the Pyrenees are welcome in the summer heat.

Three established naturist resorts share the coastline here, and have recently been joined by even more naturist accommodation in swish new villas – Les Jardins de Venus. However, there's still plenty of space for everybody on this extensive beach.

Practical info
Go north from Perpignan on the main N9 and turn right on to the D83, signposted Port Bacares. After 9km turn left on to the D627. Go through Bacares and Port Leucate, and the nude beach is on the right. Park on the road – easy public access lies between Aphrodite Village and Club Oasis.

Aphrodite and Oasis holiday centres provide modern naturist accommodation right on the beach. Club Oasis is the newer of the two and shares facilities with the bigger Aphrodite village. In addition to all the sports available, there is a harbour for naked sailors to moor boats and small yachts. Holidays available through Peng Travel (www.pengtravel. co.uk). At the other end of the beach the older Ulysse Nature has basic apartments and camping space. There is an historic artist's house, Cailloux d'Or, to rent in the centre of Fitou, a small village 10 mins' drive from the nude beach. The property sleeps five and has a completely private terrace and garden for all-over tanning.

▲ **The popularity of nude bathing on the Med has seen whole resort towns built for unclad holiday-makers, such as Cap d'Agde, above**

▼ **This golden sweep of sand makes one of France's finest naturist beaches and resorts, Leucate Plage. Picture on left by Charlie Simonds**

Plage des Moutilles and Le Clapotis resort

This excellent beach is handy for the inland naturist resort of Le Clapotis (7km), making it popular with the resort's guests. In addition to pale yellow sand stretching for over a kilometre there are large areas of sun-baked salt, suitable for parking. The beach is a lovely place to escape.

Practical info

The naturist beach is located on the southern outskirts of Port la Nouvelle, between Perpignan and Béziers. A track from town runs along the coast 500 metres from the shore. Continue until the sign for the naturist beach, or when you first spot the bare bodies.

Le Clapotis naturist camping is in an enviable location with its own private inland beach on the Etang de Lapalme lagoon. It's ideal for children and novice windsurfers. A large pool, extensive sports facilities, restaurant, bar, shaded pitches and modern mobile homes make for a superb nude holiday.

▲ Nude bathing is big part of beach culture in France. Pic at St Raphael by www.radiantnude.com

Le Clapotis accommodation

Le Clapotis
Tel: +33 468 48 15 40
www.leclapotis.com

St Pierre sur Mer accommodation

La Grande Cosse
Tel: +33 468 33 61 87
www.grandecosse.com

Serignan Plage accommodation

Serignan Plage Nature
Tel: +33 467 32 09 61
www.leserignannature.com

St Pierre sur Mer, La Grande Cosse, Narbonne

A lovely, long, undeveloped and official nude beach that has a wild feel. The sand is soft and clean, with driftwood often washed up and left to bake in the sun. The dunes, lakes and marshes behind the beach are a haven for birds and wildlife.

Practical info

Leave Narbonne on the D168, travelling east to Narbonne Plage.

Continue through the resort for 3km to St Pierre. There is a coastal track heading north out of the village which goes to the bare beach.

La Grande Cosse naturist camping and caravan site is 500 metres from the beach. The site is popular and well equipped, offering chalets and mobile homes for hire. There is an attractive pool, bar, restaurant and small shop.

Serignan Plage, near Béziers

This beautiful nudist beach lapped by the Mediterranean is particularly popular with families. There is a snack bar and lifeguard in season. Next to the beach is the Serignan naturist holiday centre.

Practical info

Exit the A9 motorway at Béziers East, and take the D64 towards Serignan. Follow the signs to Serignan Plage and walk south-west along the beach.

Serignan Plage Nature is a thriving nude resort right on the beach. You can hire a range of accommodation from pre-erected furnished tents to comfy chalets and mobile homes. There is a bar, restaurant, shop and even a casino and mini-club. Next door and with direct access, the stunning new Spa-Fitness Centre and pool has naturist sessions each morning.

France

Cap d'Agde, Between Béziers and Sete

The most famous nude beach and resort in France attract up to 40,000 people at any one time in peak season. More than 1km of level sand and calm sea make this a popular choice for countless European nudists, although it's rather different from most of the quieter and more natural resorts and beaches. All manner of seaside-based sports are available.

Practical info

Exit the A9 motorway at the Agde junction and take the RN312 expressway towards the main resort. On entering Cap d'Agde follow the signs to the Quartier Naturiste. There is a small charge to enter the resort. Alternatively, the nudist beach area can be accessed by walking south along the shore from the Marseillan Plage direction.

This naked city has apartments, villas, and a 3-star hotel, as well as camping and caravan accommodation. The whole naturist quarter is clothes-optional – so if you're curious it offers a unique opportunity to go to the bank, have your hair cut or fuel up the car all in the buff! There is also a marina within the resort.

▲ The entire town in the naturist part of Cap d'Agde, from banks to beaches, is clothing optional. Picture top right from Mark Ripon, other pictures by Paul Carlson

Maguelone Plage, south of Montpellier

This is another stunning undeveloped beach which draws praise from the naturist community. It's exposed (in more ways than one) and so may not be the best location if the Mistral is blowing. Mainly fine sand that goes on for miles, but also pebbles as well. Parking (fee) and easy access. A mobile canteen visits in peak season.

Practical info

From Montpellier travel south on the D986, crossing the lagoon to the seaside town of Palavas les Flots. Turn right out of town taking the minor road down the coast to Plage Maguelone. From the car park walk 350 metres south-west along the shore to the start of the nude area. Also accessible from Villeneuve les Maguelone with parking to the north of the lagoon. A mini-train takes passengers across a footbridge over the lagoon to the beach. Don't miss the last train back.

Cap d'Agde accommodation

Hotel Eve
Tel: +33 467 26 71 70
www.hoteleve.com

Agence Rene Oltra (apartments)
Tel: +33 467 26 33 78
http://perso.wanadoo.fr/.agence.oltra

Centre Helio-Marin Rene Oltra (camping)
Tel: +33 467 01 06 36
www.chm-reneoltra.com

Cap d'Agde tourist information

www.capdagde.com
www.agdenaturisme.com
www.naturist.de
www.cap-d-agde.com
www.capdagdefrance.co.uk

▲▼ Two faces of French naturism: urban Cap d'Agde (top) and tranquil Ile du Levant, pic by Paul Carlson

Grau du Roi, Espiguette, east of Montpellier

At 22km long this is reputed to be the biggest nude beach on the French Mediterranean coast! It is a place you can leave your cares and everything else behind. Good access means it's particularly popular with families. In mid-summer the beach gets very busy close to the car park, but a stroll along the shore will be rewarded with peace and tranquillity. Refreshment vendors operate in the more populated areas.

Practical info
From Aigues Mortes take the D979 south-west towards Grau du Roi, but before entering the town turn left on to the D62B for Port Carmargue. At the next junction turn left again, signposted Phare de l'Espiguette (lighthouse). Beyond the lighthouse there is a huge pay car park by the beach.

Piemancon Plage (or Plage d'Arles), near Arles

This is a wild strand in the heart of the Carmargue, near Salin de Giraud. The beach is almost 4km and officially nudist, but it requires a pleasant walk. The beach is managed by the local naturist club Camargue Soleil. It can be dangerous to swim, particularly close to the mouth of the Rhone.

Practical info
Leave Arles on the D570 travelling south-west, but shortly turn left on to the D36, which heads south-east (along the west bank of the Rhone) to Salin de Giraud. Collect any required provisions or water here. Continue through the village on the D36D and after 10km the road ends in a car park. The almost 1km walk to the beach is signposted. At the shore turn left (east) for the naturist area.

Plage de Bonnieu, Martigues, west of Marseille

An unusual bare beach – it's run by local nudists as a club. In summer they control the parking (with the agreement of the municipality) and will ask to see an INF or other bona fide naturist card. A cove of coarse sand and large flat rocks for sunbathing, it has an excellent family atmosphere and lots of activities, but the view of the nearby power station, it has to be admitted, is not the most scenic.

Practical info
Leave the A55 motorway at the exit Martigues Sud Lavera and follow the directions south to 'EDF Ponteau' (Electricity de France power station). The road becomes narrow – look for the signs to Martigues naturist car park.

Le Jonquet, near Cap Sicie, west of Toulon

The name Le Jonquet is used to describe seven beautiful sand and rocky naturist coves, some of which have fresh water springs, backed by cliffs scattered with pine trees. Access requires a walk and some scrambling, but that doesn't appear to deter families with children. Much loved for the stunning scenery and escapism. In peak season the largest beach may have a refreshment stall, supplied by boat.

Practical info
Travel west from Toulon to the resort of Le Seyne sur Mer and turn south in the direction of Les Sablettes. Continue heading south to the tiny hamlet of Fabregas where, from mid-June to mid-September, the forest road beyond is closed (gated) as a fire precaution: there is a car park by the roundabout. The onward track around the headland, known as Merveilleuse, provides a pleasant walk and then a steep but safe climb down steps to reach the first beach. Out of season it may be possible to park almost above the first beach.

Les Grottes Plage, Ile du Levant

A gem of a beach on this magical island, reached by an easy coastal footpath 10 mins' walk from the quayside. A small natural crescent of white sand slides gently into the turquoise sea, providing excellent swimming and snorkelling. Bare beachbums will feel like castaways at this lovely secluded cove.

Practical info
There are no private cars allowed on

France

the island, and the easiest way to get there is by ferry from Le Lavandou. The journey takes 35 minutes. The ferry timetable is at www.vedettesilesdor.fr.

More than 70 years ago Ile du Levant was the birthplace of nude leisure in France. Today, there is a tiny resident community and lots of holiday accommodation including apartments, villas and private hotels, as well as two rustic campsites. Minimal clothing is normally worn in the village of Heliopolis, but gardens, sun terraces and swimming pools can be enjoyed in the buff.

The pleasant Héliotel at the top of the island just near the village square is available through Chalfont Holidays (www.chalfontholidays.co.uk). The 8-room Hotel des Arbousiers is also a couple of minutes from the centre of Heliopolis and 20 mins' walk from the beach. Hotel Ponant is situated high above the sea and has spectacular views. Residence L'Escapade self-catering studios also enjoy great views and are located half way up the hill between the port and the village; well placed for walking to the nude beach – 15 mins.

> **Ile du Levant accommodation**
>
> Héliotel
> Tel: +33 494 00 44 88
> www.heliotel.info
>
> Hotel des Arbousiers
> Tel: +33 494 05 90 73
> http://membres.lycos.fr/arbousiers
>
> Hotel Ponant
> Tel: +33 494 05 90 41
> www.ponant.fr
>
> Residence L'Escapade
> Tel: +33 494 05 93 45
> www.escapade-levant.com
>
> **Ile du Levant tourist information**
> www.naturiste.com
> www.iledulevant.com.fr

Le Layet Plage, Cavalière, Le Lavandou

This is a picturesque little bare beach tucked in a sheltered cove at the western end of Cavalière bay, by Point Layet. The sand here is soft and yellow and the sea is normally as calm as a millpond. The smell of mimosa fills the air. There is a fascinating outdoor restaurant on a wooden terrace built out over the sea. This popular spot has a lovely atmosphere and gets very busy.
Practical info
Drive east from Le Lavandou along the twisty D559 coast road and in 5km, just before Cavalière, there is a series of coves on the right. Park near the cycle tunnel and take the signposted short flight of steps down to the beach. More nude bathing in the next cove just around the corner – towards Le Lavandou – Plage du Rossignol.

The pretty seaside resort of Cavalière (not to be confused with the bigger Cavalaire nearby) has plenty of places to stay. The Grand Hotel Moriaz, about 350m from the naturist beach, is a 3-star establishment. The stylish family-run Le Cap Negre Hotel has two stars and is close to the sea at the opposite end of the bay, about 20 mins' walk or 5 mins' drive from the nude beach. Rooms on the top floor have terraces with beguiling views of the bay.

> **Le Layet Plage accommodation**
>
> Grand Hotel Moriaz
> Tel: +33 494 05 80 01
> www.grandhotelmoriaz.com
>
> Le Cap Negre Hotel
> Tel: +33 494 05 80 46
> www.hotel-cap-negre.com
>
> **Le Lavandou tourist information**
> www.lelavandou.com

▲ Bathing the St Tropez way.
Picture from www.radiantnude.com

▲ Top: lovely Levant, the birthplace of nude holidays in France and where minimal clothing is worn in the summer. Picture by Paul Carlson
▲ Above left and right: the naturist beach at Beauvallon, right by the road but hidden by a sea wall. Pictures from Russel Kimpton

Plage du Gros Pin accommodation

Hotel Marie Louise
Tel: +33 494 96 06 05
www.hotel-marielouise.com

Camping Les Prairies de la Mer
Tel: +33 494 79 09 09
www.riviera-villages.com

Plage du Gros Pin, Beauvallon

This strand of white sand has a great location, overlooking glamorous St Tropez across the bay. A popular hidden beach that is superb for sunning and swimming au naturel. It is only a few steps away from the road and yet completely out of sight, and handily located between Port Grimaud and St Maxime.

Practical info
Follow the coastal N98 east from Port Grimaud, passing the Camping Les Prairies de la Mer. After a further 1km look out for a phone box above an open cove with lots of parked cars by the side of the road. Where is everybody? Walk to the breakwater on the left of the bay – they are all on the (hidden) nude beach, on the other side!

The charming 2-star Hotel Marie Louise at Guerrevieille, between Port Grimaud and St Maxime, has 12 rooms. It is a 10-minute drive from the naturist beach. Camping Les Prairies de la Mer is a lively site situated by the sea. It attracts a lot of British visitors and is 20 mins' walk from the nudist beach, or 3 mins in the car.

Atlantic beaches

Merville Plage accommodation

Nature et Soleil de Normandie
http://naturisme.chez-alice.fr

Merville Plage tourist information

www.ot-mervillefranceville.fr

Berck Plage, Berck sur Mer, Le Touquet

This wonderful wide sandy beach has lots of space. It's easy to find your own private spot for a truly back to nature rest. Surrounded by attractive dunes covered in wild flowers and marram grass, it is an official nude beach. Don't be surprised to see evidence of recent history by way of World War II fortifications. It's handy for the channel ports and ideal for a weekend trip from the UK.

Practical info
From Berck sur Mer drive north towards Bellvue on the outskirts of town. Pass the Thalassotherapy Hospital and shortly you will see a car park. Walk on to the beach and turn right (north) – a large sign indicates when you've arrived at the naturist area. There is a bar, restaurant and shop near the car park. Local information is available from the internet at www.opale-sud.com.

Merville Plage, north-east of Caen

An attractive official nude beach of light yellow sand, east of the mouth of the river Orme. Only 15km from Caen, you can watch the cross-channel ferries from Portsmouth arrive and depart.
Practical info
From Merville Franceville Plage take the D514 coast road west for 1km. A lane going north leads to a car park at the nautical base, and then it's a short walk to the naturist area. A local inland naturist club, Nature et Soleil de Normandie, accommodates camping and caravanning visitors.

Hatainville Plage, Carteret, near Cherbourg

Sometimes referred to as Les Moitiers d'Allonne, this lovely quiet and unspoilt au naturel beach, with miles of golden sand, is backed by rolling dunes. The sea goes out a long way here, making it a pleasant stroll in the buff to go for a dip. But beware of strong currents as there are no lifeguards.

Practical info
Travelling south from Cherbourg on the D904, turn right on to the D242 to Hatainville. Go through the town and 2km on to the coast at Les Moitiers. Park and walk south along the beach in the direction of Carteret. Tourist info www.barneville-carteret.net.

St Germain sur Ay, near Lessay

Acres and acres of wild unspoilt beach just waiting to be discovered. The whole shore is flat and the sea goes out a long way. Shellfish, shrimps and oysters can be found in the rock pools. Miles of walking in the buff to enjoy on this official nude beach.

Practical info
Drive south from Cherbourg for 50km, first on the D904 and then the D650. Just before St Germain sur Ay, turn right on to the D306 to St Germain Plage. Drive as far south as possible then walk in the same direction from the car park.

Breville sur Mer, north of Granville

A beautiful big sandy beach with pebbles and shells washed up at high tide. Although not officially nudist, it's been used naked for years. The bare area shrinks slightly in mid-summer when there are more swimsuited visitors. According to Michael, one of our correspondents, "generally, it is one of the best naturist beaches I know".

Practical info
Head north out of Granville on the D971 and turn left following signs to Breville Aerodrome. Just before the aerodrome there is a turning to the beach, with a car park by the shore. Walk south in the direction of Granville for about 250 metres – depending on season – to the naturist area.

▲ **Enjoying a fresh sea breeze at Hatainville Plage, where low tide reveals a wide sandy shore, top pic**

France

▲ The gorgeous golden sands at Le Lourtuais, Cap d'Erquy. Worth a visit on any sunny day, especially if you're staying at the Pallieter naturist site nearby; picture supplied by Pallieter

▲ A classic Atlantic beach: surf, endless sands and nudity. Pic by Mr Bun from www.sunnybuns.me.uk

Le Lourtuais accommodation

Centre Pallieter
Tel: +33 296 83 05 15
www.pallieter.fr

Le Lourtuais tourist information

www.erquy-tourisme.com

Plage des Chevrets, La Guimorais, St Coulomb

This naturist beach is in an area of picturesque coastline and has a fine sandy shore, about 10km east of St Malo, handy for ferries to the UK.
Practical info
Travel east from St Malo on the D201 coast road for approximately 10km in the direction of Pointe du Meinga. Park near the Pointe and it is a 10-minute walk to the La Guimorais nude beach, which is on the north-west side of the bay.

Plage du Port Sud-Est, Crique de Frehel

A west-facing sandy shore near Erquy, backed by steep cliffs and officially recognised for nude bathing. Access requires a walk down a steep goat path, but it doesn't seem to deter families from using this popular beach. Well worth the effort.

Practical info
Take the D786 east from Erquy and turn left on to the D34, signed to Cap Frehel. Go through Pleherel Plage, park at Trou du Poulifer and walk 15 mins down the track to the nude area, the west side of Cap Frehel.

Le Lourtuais, Cap d'Erquy

A stunning 500-metre rural beach with scattered rocks and backed by hilly pinewoods. Good sand, but a pleasant 15-minute walk downhill is required to access the shore. A mix of dressed and undressed beach users: plenty go au naturel. The sign says nudes to the left and costumed bathers to the right, but nobody appears to worry too much. The beach is popular with visitors staying at the excellent naturist campsite Pallieter www.pallieter.fr (see the inland France section on page 178 for a full description).
Practical info
From Erquy take the minor road north to Cap d'Erquy and the naturist beach is just to the east of the Cap. The road narrows, descends and deteriorates – it's time to walk the rest of the way. If possible use the more eastern of the two car parks. Au naturel bathing also takes place south of Erquy, below the cliffs between Ville Berneuf en Vallee Plage and Val Andre.

France

Mez-an-Aod, Pointe de Servel, Beg-Leguer

At the mouth of the Leguer river you will find a handy and well-established naturist beach with plenty of firm pale coloured sand. Excellent for building sandcastles and sunbathing in the buff. It is a particularly attractive and unspoilt location with a turquoise sea.
Practical info
Head due west from Lannion towards Beg-Leguer. Approaching the town, pass Beg-Leguer church and before the lighthouse turn left at the road with a stone marker. Park on the roadside and walk for 10 minutes west to a small cove surrounded by granite boulders. Then walk north over the rocks to the bay of Mez-an-Aod. Tourist info www.ot-lannion.fr.

Plage de Lost-Marc'h, Crozon

A huge unspoilt beach encompassed by rocky headlands at either end and just across the bay from Brest. Hundreds of acres of level sand, but swimming can be dangerous as it faces west and is exposed to the full force of the Atlantic. A widely recognised nudist location, but also used by swimsuited bathers in happy co-existence. The pretty countryside behind the beach is undeveloped and criss-crossed by footpaths. Many German visitors in summer.
Practical info
From the small town of Crozon head 3.5km south-west on local roads to the hamlet of Lost-Marc'h and walk 900m to the shore. Nude bathing also down the coast at nearby Plage du Palud, towards the point of Kerdreux.

Plage de Kerler, Fouesnant, near Quimper

The bare area extends along a lovely sandy spit which has been used nude for years. Following a campaign by the regional branch of the Federation Francaise de Naturisme (FFN) the beach received official naturist status in recent years. It's a beautiful spot and highly recommended.

Practical info
From Quimper travel south on the D34 to Benodet and turn left on to the D44 towards Fouesnant. In 3.5km turn right to Mousterlin. Plage de Kerler is accessed on the western side of Pointe de Mousterlin and stretches back towards Benodet.

Plage de Kerminihy, Erdeven

A remote but pleasant official nude beach of gently sloping sand and shingle stretching 2km north to the mouth of the Etel river. Easy access makes this beach a popular place for families, especially as the resorts of Carnac and Quiberon are near. We regularly get great feedback about it.
Practical info
Travelling north-west from Carnac on the D781 turn left in the village of Erdeven, signed to Kerminihy Plage. There is a huge car park not far from the sea – walk to the beach and turn right for the naturist area, which is clearly signposted. In addition to lots of ordinary campsites and holiday homes in the area, there is a simple naturist site, La Pinede (Centre Naturiste Bretagne Sud) near Erdeven, 7km inland from the beach. Take your own tent, campervan or caravan.

La Turballe Pen Bron Plage, near La Baule

A lovely long undeveloped peninsula backed by pinetree-clad dunes on the Atlantic coast, near the mouth of the Loire. The fine yellow sand and larger resorts nearby ensure this is a popular nude beach, used by locals and holidaymakers alike. The many seabirds make it a particular favourite with ornithologists.

Practical info
Travel north-west from La Baule to Guerande then take the D99 to La Turballe. Go south on the D92 past the 'Village Vacances Famille' following signs to Pen Bron Hospital. In summer the road is gated and requires a pleasant 10-minute walk to the beach. Tourist info: otsi.la.turballe.free.fr.

▲▼ **Contemplating another fine day on a French nude beach. Pictures from Paul Carlson**

Plage de Kerminihy accommodation

La Pinede
Tel: +33 297 55 61 55
www.cnbs56.com

Plage de Kerminihy tourist information

www.ot-erdeven.fr

France

▲ The French coast enjoyed as nature intended. Picture from www.radiantnude.com

▲ Sunflowers and sunworshippers: France has plenty of both! Picture supplied by Andy Eke

Plage de Salins accommodation

Cap Natur
Tel: +33 251 60 11 66
www.cap-natur.com

France

Plage de Luzeronde, Ile de Noirmoutier

This quiet beach between L'Epine and Herbaudière extends to almost 4km. It is probably the only place on the Ile de Noirmoutier with a long tradition of nude bathing. Extensive saltpans dot the landscape behind the shore.
Practical info
There are two routes on to the Ile de

Noirmoutier: a bridge, or for the adventurous a tidal causeway. Plage de Luzernade is on the west coast of the Ile, almost mid-way between L'Epine and Herbaudière, north of Pointe de Devin. Walk along the shore from either end to find peace, seclusion and fellow naked bathers.

Les Lays Plage – Barre de Monts, Fromentine

An attractive 7km stretch of coast just south of Ile de Noirmoutier with a fine sandy shore. Backed by pinewoods and completely unspoilt, it has long been popular with naturists. No facilities or lifeguards so take care in the sea.
Practical info
To reach the beach at Les Lays turn

off the main D38 between La Barre de Monts and Notre Dame de Monts, at the hamlet of the same name. Follow the tracks through the woods (Chemin des Lays) to a car park not far from the beach. Once on the shore move away from the access to find your own space to strip off.

Plage de Salins, Saint Hilaire de Riez

Another great nudist location down the road from the previous beach (Les Lays). Popular with families and holidaymakers staying at the nearby naturist resort of Cap Natur.
Practical info
A minor coastal road south from St Jean de Monts provides access to Plage de Salins at le Grand Bec.

Modern naturist accommodation at Cap Natur is less than 5km from Plage de Salins. Set in attractive pinewoods, there are apartments and mobile homes to rent and places for tents and caravans. Complete with a range of leisure facilities including a stylish indoor pool and an outdoor pool surrounded by sun terraces.

Le Petit Pont, Brétignolles

With more than 1km of sandy nude beach to enjoy, there is space for everybody on this beautiful stretch of coast between St Gilles-Croix-de-Vie and Les Sables d'Olonne. Completely unspoilt, the dunes behind the beach are covered with wild flowers and marram grass. The naturist area is tucked away between two natural outcrops of rock. Take care when swimming due to the strong tidal currents.

Practical info
Drive south from St Gilles on the D38 for 8km. Turn right on to a track by l'Auberge du Petit Pont, at La Sanzaie, on the outskirts of Brétignolles sur Mer. Park at the beach. Tourist information is available from www.bretignolles-sur-mer.com.

Sauveterre Plage, Olonne sur Mer

A stretch of this delightful and secluded sandy beach has been granted official naturist status by the local municipality. The beach is mainly undeveloped with pinewoods behind the shore. The recognised au naturel area extends for 300 metres. There are warnings about the danger of swimming here due to heavy Atlantic swells.

Practical info
From Sables d'Olonne travel north on the D32, then west on the D80 to Sauveterre. Turn into the forest and park near the sea. Walk 800 metres north up the beach to the nude area.

▲ Perfect place to escape: the coast around Pointe d'Arcay is a sanctuary for all true nature-lovers
▼ The Atlantic coast is particularly developed for naturism along the southern section, with large resorts such as La Jenny, near Bordeaux. Pictures supplied by the resort

Pointe d'Arcay, La Faute sur Mer, La Rochelle

A bird sanctuary – the Reserve Nationale de Chasse – lies behind this lovely wild beach, making it ideal for escapists and ornithologists. The further you go along the spit the more remote it gets.

Practical info
Approach by the D746 west through L'Aiguillon. There are two ways to get to the nude beach from here. You can park at the sanctuary entrance and walk 2km south along the beach. Alternatively you can continue driving along the lane and park at the end, then cut west through the woods to the beach.

Plage des Saumonards, Ile d'Oleron

This is an attractive nudist beach backed by dunes on the sheltered north-east coast of Ile d'Oleron, near Boyardville, facing the mainland. There are mussel beds to explore and a huge pine forest behind the shore. Patches of mud are exposed when the tide goes out. The nearby car park has a small cafe.

Practical info
Take the impressive free road bridge on to the island (D26). Continue along the same road for 5km and then turn right on to the D126 (north) to the little seaside village of Boyardville. Take the minor road into Saumonards forest towards Pointe des Saumonards and drive to the car park. It's a five-minute walk to the 500-metre naturist beach, which is signposted. Tourist information is available from www.oleron.org.

La Grande Plage, Ile d'Oleron

The fabulously open white-sand nude beach near St Trojan-les Bains has acres of space and a completely relaxed atmosphere – swimsuited and nude bathers enjoy the peaceful setting in harmony. During fine weather it feels more like the Mediterranean than the Atlantic and the quality of the light attracts artists from all over the country.

Practical info
Take the free road bridge on to the island (D26). At the end of the bridge drive on for a further 2km, then turn left, signposted to St Trojan-les-Bains. On the edge of the town turn right, on to the minor road D126 and continue to the beach. Walk 500 metres south (left) from the car park to the naturist area.

■ Two of the many spacious nude beaches on France's Atlantic coast, pictured opposite. Top is the Plage des Saumonards and bottom La Grande Plage, both on naturist-friendly Ile d'Oleron. Pictures by Charlie Simonds

La Cote Sauvage, La Tremblade

As the name suggests, this is a wild and remote beach, stretching over 12km between Ile d'Oleron and Royan. It is ideal for undisturbed sunbathing and for bracing long naked walks along the shoreline. It's a beautiful place, but also exposed to the full force of the Atlantic swell. So with no lifeguards, great care is needed in the sea – signs indicate there should be no swimming at all. There is a bar and restaurant at the northern end of the beach, by the Pointe Espagnole.

Practical info

From La Tremblade head north-west on the D25, through Ronce les Bains and into the forest. The road then turns south following the line of the coast. There are a number of car parks in the woods. Take one of the paths through the dunes to the beach. The nude area is south from Pointe Espagnole for 5km.

La Grande Cote, near Royan

Not far from La Cote Sauvage, between La Palmyre and St Palais, this attractive sandy beach is popular with families because it is more sheltered and has easy access. Acres of fine light golden sand slope gently towards the sea, making it good for skinny-dipping in calm weather. There is a sandwich bar serving refreshments on this official nude beach. Lifeguards in season.

Practical info

Travelling south-west from La Palmyre on the D25 towards St Palais, there is a car park in the woods on the left, 3km past the zoo. Take the pedestrian underpass and a pleasant walk through the trees (ligne 15) and turn right when the path reaches the shore. A correspondent warns not to leave valuables in vehicles anywhere in the area, which is unfortunately notorious for thefts. Tourist info from www.la-palmyre-les-mathes.com.

Le Petit Dauphin is a new naturist campsite (2006) at La Palmyre, which is open all year and handy for La Grand Cote nude beach. Modern mobile homes available to rent or buy.

▲ Beautiful sunsets on the west coast of France complete a perfect day. Pic by UK naturists from Heritage Club (www.heritageclub.org)

La Grande Cote accommodation

Le Petit Dauphin
Tel: +33 546 06 38 23
www.le-petit-dauphin.com

Plage de Saint Nicolas, Verdon sur Mer

This Atlantic naturist beach near the mouth of the Gironde marks the start of almost 100 miles of mostly clothes-optional shore stretching south, punctuated only by the seaside surfing towns where swimsuits are required. Plage de Saint Nicolas has a kilometre of sand officially sanctioned for nude bathing. Lifeguards in summer.

Practical info

Verdon sur Mer is near the tip of the peninsula on the Gironde estuary, just south of the landing point for the car ferry from Royan. Take the minor road north-west from the town through the forest to the Saint Nicolas lighthouse. It is about 10 minutes' walk from the car park to the naturist beach (which is signposted). Another recognised spot for au naturel bathing is at Pointe de la Negade, on the southern outskirts of nearby Soulac sur Mer.

Euronat, north of Montalivet les Bains

There is a glorious expanse of clean golden sand in front of the Euronat naturist resort. The seashore is open to the public and bare beachbums will feel especially comfortable in the company of so many like-minded souls. However, there's plenty of room to find your own space. Lifeguards supervise a section of the beach for swimming and surfing. Popular with families and attracting thousands of happy visitors at peak times of the year.

Practical info

From the small seaside town of Montalivet les Bains, drive north on the D102 coast road. After 3km the road turns sharply right, inland. Park and walk on to the beach – the main nudist area is to the right. The well-known naturist resort of Euronat is large and modern, offering camping, caravanning and luxury self-catering chalets. There are shops, restaurants, a big indoor pool and a spa with seawater treatments, all set in pine forest. It's a peaceful place much loved by visitors for its friendly atmosphere. A great place to try camping naked.

▲ The resort at Euronat is so big you can hire bikes to get to and from the beach. Pic supplied by Andy Eke

Euronat accommodation

Tel: +33 556 09 33 33
www.euronat.fr

▲ A regular seaside town has grown up at Euronat, with shops, bars, restaurants and even hairdressers all part of the relaxing, back to nature lifestyle. This stretch of coast, from Biarritz in the south to the Gironde river in the north is sometimes called one long naturist beach – although it is interrupted by occasional resort towns. Picture top right supplied by Euronat, top left by Paul Carlson

CHM accommodation

CHM Montalivet
Tel: +33 556 73 73 73
www.chm-montalivet.com

CHM, south of Montalivet les Bains

Another huge nude beach backed by dunes and pine trees, offering long bare walks and lots of personal space. There is a lifeguard and some great waves for surfing. Directly behind the beach is the naturist resort of CHM Montalivet – the first purpose built nude holiday centre in France, which opened in 1950. It's still just as popular today, and although updated there's a definite touch of 'shabby chic' adding to the heritage. General tourist information is available from www.ot-vendays-montalivet.fr and www.montalivet-info.com.

Practical info
The beach can be accessed by parking in Montalivet les Bains and walking south along the sand to the bare area. If you're staying at the naturist resort, the beach is on your doorstep.

CHM Montalivet Vacances Naturistes offers acres of camping and caravanning space as well as timber chalets for hire where you don't have to wear anything. There is a large outdoor swimming pool, a new aquatic fun park and lots of sports facilities available. There are several shops and restaurants on site.

France

La Jenny, Le Porge Ocean, near Bordeaux

On the same long stretch of beautifully unspoilt coast as Montalivet, but 50km further south. This is home to the peaceful and friendly La Jenny naturist resort, set in pinewoods behind the shore. The beach is in a remote spot with no towns nearby, so the bare area stretches for miles in each direction. There's no difficulty finding your own privacy here – it's a place to escape.

Practical info

Travel west from Bordeaux on the D107 via Le Temple/Le Porge, then follow the direction of Lège Cap Ferret/Arès on the D3 to La Jenny. The resort is also well signposted along the way.

There is a lovely smooth cycle track running through the woods along the coast (no cars allowed) from Lacanau

in the north all the way to Cap Ferret in the south, so it's easy to find any number of deserted beach spots for sunning in the buff. Further tourist information is available online at www.leporge.fr.

La Jenny naturist resort covers 300 acres and offers high quality self-catering accommodation in a choice of bungalows and houses in the woods. There are no tents or caravans. The estate has a spectacular outdoor swimming pool complex together with a good range of sports and entertainments. There is even a golf course. Popular with British visitors, well run and managed and a welcoming place for both first-time and experienced nudist holiday-makers alike.

▲ Happy holidays: pictures taken by members of UK naturist club Heritage (www.heritageclub.org) enjoying the fabulous sands of La Jenny, a popular naturist resort handy for Bordeaux

▲ Endless room to play on La Jenny's beautiful beach. Pic from the resort

La Jenny accommodation

Tel: +33 556 26 56 90
www.lajenny.fr

Arnaoutchot accommodation

Arnaoutchot
Tel: +33 558 49 11 11
www.arna.com

St Girons Plage tourist information

www.tourisme-vielle-st-girons.com
www.tourismelandes.com
www.touradour.com

▼ **The much-praised resort beach of Arnaoutchot. Pics by Charlie Simonds**

Teste du Buch, Plage de la Lagune, Arcachon

Thousands of acres of pale golden sand perfect for stripping off. It's not far from the must-see Dune du Pyla, which rises to almost 400 feet above sea level (the highest dune in Europe) and a stunning landmark for miles around. The official nudist beach, which is backed by pinewoods, is adjacent to a military area and observatory, a few kilometres south of the giant dune. There is good access and parking.

Practical info

From Arcachon head south on the D218 coast road, past the roundabout at Dune du Pyla (you can't miss it). After a further 5km pass the restricted military road on the right that goes to Pointe d'Arcachon, and take the next track on the right to parking by the beach. Walk 200m south on the shore. Unofficial bare bathing also reported close to the base of Dune du Pyla.

Arnaoutchot, St Girons Plage

Yet another outstanding nude beach on the Aquitaine coast, 80km north of the Spanish border, between Bordeaux and Biarritz. Arnaoutchot naturist holiday resort is located here and provides lifeguards on the shore to watch over the skinny-dippers. Seamless sunbathing is on offer as far as the eye can see up and down the beach.

Practical info

Travel north from Biarritz on the N10 to Castets. Turn left on to the D42 to St Girons. Left on to the D652 to Vielle St Girons, then right on to the D328 for Arnaoutchot. There is a public beach car park to the south of the resort.

Arnaoutchot naturist resort is a self-contained village with lots of accommodation to rent as well as space for tents and caravans. There are three pools, including one indoors. A health and beauty centre offers a choice of treatments. It's highly rated by regular visitors from around the world.

France

Naturist resorts inland

Héliomonde, Saint Cheron, south of Paris

Set in the vast forests of the Beauce countryside, Héliomonde is a perfect retreat for visitors wishing to combine a sightseeing trip to the romantic capital of France and a relaxing au naturel escape. The range of facilities include a heated swimming pool with paddling pool, sauna, gym, three tennis courts, volleyball courts, badminton, bowls, basketball, archery, ping-pong tables and a mountain bike track. The extensive and tranquil grounds (47ha) are home to roe deer and pheasants. There is a small shop and the restaurant is open all day. Camping sites, together with mobiles homes and chalets available to rent. Disabled facilities.

Practical info
Located 45 minutes from Paris; there is a local train to Saint Cheron, 2km from the centre. By road, take the A10 motorway – exit at Dourdan and head towards Saint Chéron. Continue to La Petite Beauce and Héliomonde is signposted.

Centre Pallieter, Plancoet, near St Malo

Not far inland from the rugged coast and stunning sandy beaches of northern Brittany on the Cotes d'Armor, the Naturist Centre Pallieter offers a well-managed campsite with the added benefit of modern chalets to rent. The friendly Dutch owners Arno and Andrine have developed the centre in tune with nature and keep it immaculately clean and tidy. There is an attractive small swimming pool, bar and a restaurant serving main meals in season. An easy drive from St Malo, Dinard, Dinan and a number of the naturist beaches listed in this guide.

Practical info
Take the D786 from Dinard to Plancoet and turn left at the roundabout opposite Hotel-Restaurant Relais de la Source, on to the D19 towards Plelan. After 3km Centre Pallieter is signposted.

Héliomonde contact details

Tel: +33 164 56 61 37
www.heliomonde.fr

Centre Pallieter contact details

Tel: +33 296 83 05 15
www.pallieter.fr

▼ **Pallieter and its superb nearby beach. The welcoming site is handy for visitors to Brittany and has been managed for a true back-to-nature experience. Pictures supplied by Centre Pallieter**

France

▲ The pool and traditional french buildings make Charente Soleil an attractive place to enjoy the rolling French countryside. Pictures supplied by Charente Soleil

▲ Green lanes at Le Colombier, a pretty naturist camping site in the Vendée countryside

Koad ar Roc'h contact details

Tel: +33 297 74 42 11
www.koad-ar-roch.com

Le Colombier contact details

Tel: +33 251 27 83 84
www.lecolombier-naturisme.com

Charente Soleil contact details

Tel: +33 545 38 41 05
www.charentesoleil.com

France

Koad ar Roc'h, Néant sur Yvel

You can't help but be impressed by the imposing chateau at the entrance to the naturist estate. This large unspoiled park (110ha) in the heart of Brittany is away from the coast but has a huge lake for swimming, fishing and rowing. There's so much space you can pitch your tent or caravan anywhere you like. Mobile homes and bungalows are available. There are guided walks, boules, badminton, a toy library and even concerts at the chateau to enjoy. Bar, restaurant and BBQ facilities.

Practical info

From Dinan travel south-east on the D166/D766. Pass Mauron and after 8km at Neant sur Yvel turn right (north) on to the D134 to le Bois de la Roache.

Le Colombier, south-east of Nantes

In the south of the Vendée region, Le Colombier Centre de Vacances offers naturist camping and caravanning on an attractive 50ha site. The domain includes meadows and a forest covering an entire valley, with a small stream and fishing pond. There is a wide range of family activities on offer and a large heated pool. Ready erected tents and mobile homes for hire. There is a bar and restaurant, the baker calls each morning and groceries are available in the village (1km). INF or naturist club cards are compulsory but can be purchased on arrival.

Practical info

Le Colombier and the village of Saint Martin-Lars is 6km north-east of Sainte Hermine, which is on the main N137 between Nantes and La Rochelle.

Charente Soleil, Saint Angeau, south of Poitiers

An exclusive naturist experience is offered by Brian & Erica Thomas at their traditional French property in the heart of the rolling countryside. Charente Soleil includes four stylish self-catering gites (cottages) and three en-suite double and twin rooms for bed and breakfast, all set in beautiful gardens. A central focus of the gardens is the sparkling 10-metre swimming pool surrounded by terraces with sun loungers. From May to the end of September clothing is optional – most guests take advantage of course, but the owners don't mind if some family members prefer otherwise. Evening meals on request.

Practical info

Charente Soleil is 10 minutes off the RN10 dual carriageway, which links to the autoroute system (A10) at Poitiers, 90km to the north.

L'Eglantière, Castelnau Magnoac

The Gers, a playful and shallow river, flows through the entire length of this highly regarded naturist centre and is enjoyed by young and old alike. The high peaks of the Pyrenees mountains lie a short distance to the south. Excellent facilities include a large pool, paddling pool, solarium, sauna, health centre and massage area, mini-club, restaurant, bar pizzeria and small supermarket. In addition to camping pitches, there are chalets and mobile homes to rent. The family activities list is almost endless: campsite bonfires, tournaments, dancing games, ghost hunts, shows, ecosystem river workshops with fishing, discovery hikes, cycling and canoeing.

Practical info
From Toulouse go west on the N124 to Auch. Take the N21/D929 south through Masseube to Castelnau Magnoac, where signs by the tourist office show the way to L'Eglantière.

▲ In the woods at l'Eglantière

Domaine Naturiste L'Eglantière info
Tel: +33 562 39 88 00
www.leglantiere.com

Lissart Centre Naturiste contact info
Tel: +33 563 56 39 04
www.lissart.com

Domaine de la Sablière contact info
Tel: +33 466 24 51 16
www.villagesabliere.com

Lissart Centre Naturiste, Tarn, near Albi

Moira, Bob, Ali and Andy all hale from the UK, but they have spent the last 10 years developing this lovely three-star family naturist resort in the south of France. At the heart of the centre is the ancient farmhouse, now converted to a comfortable apartment, library and TV lounge. It also houses a Jacuzzi, showers and sauna. Terraces with sunbeds surround the large swimming pool. Most of the 37ha of south facing woodland and fields are undeveloped and offer fabulous naked walks. Accommodation is available in the apartment, a bungalow and four mobile homes. Pitches for tents, caravans and motorhomes. There is an honesty bar but no restaurant or shop. The baker visits each morning.

Practical info
From Albi take the D600 north-west, through Cordes and on to Marnaves.

▼ Spectacular Sablière; pictures from members of UK naturist club Heritage (www.heritageclub.org)

Domaine de la Sablière, Barjac, Gard region

This is a real southern French 'midi' village, situated where the Cévennes, the Ardèche and Provence regions meet. Whether you are sports minded or simply want to relax, you will be spoiled for choice at Sablière on the sparkling river Cèze. The naturist centre swells to a thriving community of 1,500 naked souls in summer: it even boasts its own town hall. There are varied activities, with art and pottery studios, archery, a circus, children's clubs and much more. For an invigorating skinny-dip, choose between the panoramic pool or the meandering river. There is a choice of accommodation to rent if you haven't taken your own tent or caravan. Bars, restaurants and shops provide for every day needs. The lively atmosphere, beautiful scenery and long sunny days attract holidaymakers of all ages.

Practical info
From the north take the A7 motorway towards Avignon and leave at Bollène, Pont St Esprit. Take the D901 towards Barjac, then left on to the CD266 to St Privat de Champclos. Follow the signs to La Sablière.

France

France

La Genèse, Barjac, Gard region

Nestled in the heart of an oakwood forest, La Genèse is a haven of peace by the Cèze. It's another site that provides opportunities for boating, fishing, swimming or just cooling off in the river. The centre spreads up the side of the valley with some steep paths. There are camping pitches near the water's edge and chalets for rent further up the hillside. As well as a bar and restaurant, there is a choice of shops including a baker, green grocer, butcher and a newspaper kiosk. There are nearby Roman sites and the stunning gorges of the Ardèche and the Cévennes to explore. The resort is managed by the same company as CHM Montalivet on the Atlantic coast.

Practical info

From the north take the A7 motorway towards Avignon and leave at Bollène, Pont St Esprit. Take the D901 towards Barjac, but before reaching Saint Privat de Champclos, turn left on to the D980 through the Cèze gorge. After 3km turn right on the D167 to Mejannes le Clap.

▲ Belezy's pool and balneotherapy centre are just two of the attractions at this family-orientated resort. Pictures supplied by Belezy

La Genèse Domaine Naturiste info

Tel: +33 466 24 51 82
www.chm-montalivet.com

Domaine de Belezy contact info

Tel: +33 490 65 60 18
www.belezy.com

Domaine de Belezy, Provence near Orange

At the foot of Mount Ventoux among olive trees and lavender, this family-friendly naturist domain offers arts, crafts and cultural activities. Sunny Provence has inspired a multitude of painters and poets over the years. The centre has a large pool, a small pool and a paddling pool for toddlers. Sports facilities include two all-weather tennis courts, basketball, football, beach volleyball, archery and petanque. Or you could just unwind in the balneotherapy centre. The clubhouse has two music rooms with pianos, a library, a TV room and a tourist office. The shop sells bread and other essentials and there's a restaurant serving local specialities. A range of accommodation is offered, from ready-erected tents to paradise villas. Pitches are available for tents and caravans.

Practical info

Head south from Orange on the N7 and after 6km turn left on to the D950 to Carpentras. The D974 then goes north-east to Bedoin and Belezy.

▲ **Wonderful ways to start the day. Pics from La Source naturist holiday centre**

La Source, Cotignac, north of St Tropez

For a touch of naturist indulgence in the sun, the privately owned La Source estate offers luxury accommodation in the south of France. Peter and Gill Coates have spent five years lovingly restoring this ancient property in the Var region. La Source has featured in 'Homes of Distinction' magazine and provides stylish clothes-optional holidays. Bed and breakfast is available in one of the attractive en-suite rooms in the main house. Expect fresh flowers,

Egyptian cotton sheets, and fluffy towels in your room: sumptuous breakfasts served on the terrace. The delightful gardens, woodland and olive groves are all secluded and there's a 12m salt-filter pool. Massages, relaxation and beauty treatments are all available on site. The nearby village of Cotignac is a hive of activity in summer with live music, theatre and circus. Nude bathing at the lovely Lac St Croix 35 mins away, or the Mediterranean – just an hour away.

Origan Village, Val d'Azur, Provence

This excellent centre, virtually on the banks of the river Var, is renowned for its stunning views and naturist trekking in the surrounding hills and mountains. It is only an hour from Nice and the glamour of the Cote d'Azure, but feels a world away. Whether you are sports minded or simply want to relax, you will be spoiled for choice. The pools,

restaurant and many cultural and leisure workshops are all popular. You can even take a Mediterranean cruise in the buff. For accommodation choose between camping or renting one of the well-equipped chalets.

Practical info

From Nice head north then west on the N202 all the way to Puget Theniers.

▲ **Origan: stunning setting and handy for Nice. Pics by Paul Carlson**

La Source contact info

Tel: +33 494 04 67 31
www.just-bring-sun-cream.com

Origan Village contact info

Tel: +33 493 05 06 00
www.origan-village.com

Corsica

Bravone Plage, east coast south of Bastia

Bravone Plage accommodation

Piana Verde
Tel: +33 495 38 82 99
www.pianaverde.com

Bagheera
Tel: +33 495 38 80 30
www.bagheera.fr

Corsica Natura
Tel: +33 495 38 91 30
www.corsica-natura.com

Club Corsicana
Tel: +41 56 631 88 11 (Switzerland)
www.club-corsicana.com

Les Eucalyptus Camping
Tel: +33 495 38 87 17
www.eucalyptus-camping.com

A wonderful 5km of official nudist beach with light soft sand and clear blue sea. It's so popular that five different naturist resorts have been built along its length. Apart from snack bars and these naturist holiday centres there are no other developments along this unspoilt coastline.

Practical info

It is easy to find – simply drive 50km south from Bastia on the N198 coast road, or 80km north from Porto Vecchio on the same road. The beach and string of resorts are just north of Bravone.

The five naturist centres and their accommodation offered are: Piana Verde – apartments, Bagheera – bungalows, Corsica Natura – chalets, Club Corsicana – cabins, and Les Eucalyptus – camping.

France

▲ Sea scenes at Bravone naturist holiday centres including Piana Verde, bottom right, and Bagheera, all other pics

Riva Bella Plage, south of Bastia

Another lovely white-sand bare beach with sunbeds and umbrellas for hire. The evocative fragrance of the maquis is ever present. A bar serves drinks and light meals and there's a sailing school with wind surfers and dinghies. The beach is home to another established naturist resort.

Practical info

Signposted from the main N198 coast road, 7km north of the historic village of Aleria and 3km south of Bravone.

Riva Bella naturist resort has bungalows and apartments right on the beach. There is a wide choice of accommodation, even ready-erected 'Bengali' tents. Health and beauty treatments are available at the modern spa, including outdoor massages overlooking the sea.

Riva Bella Plage accommodation

Riva Bella
Tel: +33 495 38 81 10
www.rivabella-corsica.com

Villata, Porto Vecchio, south-east coast

A pretty au naturel shore overlooking Pinarellu Island and lapped by a tranquil aquamarine sea, on the south side of Porto Vecchio. The famous nudist film 'Travelling Light' was shot here in the late 1950s. Views inland include stunning mountain peaks, frequently snow-capped as late as June. At the south end of the bay there is a romantic natural rock pool for swimming or just soaking. The transparent water and rocky headlands make the sea here ideal for snorkelling. Villata naturist campsite is right by the beach so refreshments are available and there are sunbeds for hire.

Practical info

Travel north from Porto Vecchio, firstly on the D568 coast road, then the D468 towards Pinarellu. After travelling 10km from Porto Vecchio watch out for signs and a right turn to Villata (3km before Pinarellu).

The rustic Villata Naturist Centre has plenty of camping space and very basic wooden bungalows to rent. The estate is set in extensive pinewoods that cascade right down to the sea. The setting is attractive, with a complete 'away from it all' feeling, even though the exclusive seaside town of Porto Vecchio is not far away. A 15-minute drive inland will take you into the foothills, where skinny-dipping in clear mountain rivers can be enjoyed.

At the time of going to press there is speculation about the long-term future of the campsite and naturist beach – check before you go.

▲ Strolling the sands at Riva Bella

Villata accommodation

Villata Naturist Centre
Tel: +33 495 71 62 90
www.villata.com

▼ **All-day activity on the beach at Villata. Pictures bottom row and top left by Donald Stewart**

France

La Chiappa, Porto Vecchio, south-east coast

▲ Seclusion and stunning scenery at La Chiappa. Top pic by Paul Carlson

This series of secluded and private nude coves is home to the clothes-optional La Chiappa Vacation Village, to the south of Porto Vecchio. A daily admission fee is payable if you're not staying. There are lots of facilities on the main beach, and the whole area is in a protected zone. Plenty of coastline to explore au naturel.

Practical info

Travel south from Porto Vecchio on the N198 for 2km. Turn left at the signpost for Chiappa Lighthouse and Plage de Palombaggia. Continue for 8km on a twisty minor road to the resort.

La Chiappa Vacation Village attracts discerning visitors from across Europe. A big swimming pool right by the main beach and a tennis school are just two of many attractions at this well-equipped holiday centre.

La Chiappa accommodation

La Chiappa
Tel: +33 495 70 00 31
www.chiappa.com

U Furu accommodation

U Furu Naturist Centre
Tel: +33 495 70 10 83
www.u-furu.com

▼ Adventure in the raw at U Furu's lovely river. Pictures by Paul Carlson

U Furu naturist centre, near Porto Vecchio

This is the place to visit for a truly back to nature experience in the foothills of the Corsican mountains, but not too far from the coast and only 8km from Porto Vecchio. Stunning walking and scrambling in the buff. Explore along the route of the gurgling stream as it cascades through the grounds. There are lots of hidden pools to discover – ideal for a cooling dip in summer.

Practical info

The centre has space for camping and stone bungalows for hire. A lively snack bar and attractive modern swimming pool complement the usual facilities. Day visitors welcome.

France

Holidays au naturel: other French sites

The French have perfected the art of living naked on holiday. Both the seaside and the countryside have some of Europe's most lovely campsites where you can get fully back to nature. In fact there are nearly 200 naturist places that open their gates to visitors from around the world. In addition to those described in detail, this page includes some of the many other places where your birthday suit is always à la mode.

As with all naturists sites around the world, do remember to arrange your visit in advance. Naturism in France is hugely popular and many places are fully booked during the peak season.

The French National Tourist Office

does a superb job promoting naturist holidays, and has websites aimed at visitors around the world; visit its website at www.franceguide.com and search for naturism. The French and Croatian national tourist organisations are easily the most active when it comes to promoting their country's attractions to bare bathers, and their tourist industry benefits accordingly.

The French calculate that around 1.5 million people come to France each year solely because of its naturist facilities. How many others visit nudist beaches on a casual basis during their holiday is impossible to count. The busy and happy atmosphere of French naturist resorts and beaches says it all.

▲ Au naturel at Terra Naturis (top) and Lambeyran (above). Picture opposite: www.radiantnude.com

French naturist campsites and resorts

Aquitaine

Domaine de Chaudeau
Tel: + 33 553 82 49 64
www.domainedechaudeau.com

Domaine Laborde
Tel: +33 553 63 14 88
www.domainelaborde.com

Domaine Naturiste Château Guiton
Tel: +33 556 23 52 79
www.chateau-guiton.com

Laulurie en Périgord
Tel: + 33 553 06 74 00
www.laulurie.com

Le Couderc
Tel: +33 553 22 40 40
www.lecouderc.com

Le Marcassin de Saint Aubin
Tel: +33 553 28 57 30
www.best-of-perigord.tm.fr/heberge/vac_camp.html

Les Coteaux de l'Herm
Tel: +33 553 46 67 77
www.naturisme-dordogne.com

Terme d'Astor
Tel: +33 553 63 24 52
www.termedastor.com

Terra Naturis
Tel: +33 553 47 69 50
www.terranaturis.fr

Auvergne

Domaine de la Taillade
Tel: +33 471 23 80 13
www.taillade-naturisme.com

Ferme du Feyt
Tel: 33 471 62 25 56

La Serre de Portelas
Tel: +33 473 39 35 25
http://serredeportelas.ifrance.com

Les Fourneaux
Tel: +33 470 66 23 18

Limousin

Camping Aimée Porcher
Tel: +33 555 732 097
www.aimee-porcher.com

Camping Lous Suais
Tel: +33 555 69 56 94
www.loussuais.com

Creuse Nature
Tel: +33 555 65 18 01
www.creuse-nature.com

Le Moulin de Gany
Tel: +33 555 98 53 59
www.moulindegany.com

Les Saules
Tel: +33 555 69 64 36
www.lessaules.com

Languedoc Roussillon

Côte Vermeille Naturiste
Tel: +33 468 48 05 80
www.camping-cote-vermeille.com

Domaine de la Vitarelle
Tel: +33 468 26 61 98
http://vitarell.club.fr

Camping le P'tit Bonheur
Tel: +33 468 97 08 53
http://mon.camping.free.fr

Domaine de Lambeyran
Tel: +33 467 44 13 99
www.lambeyran.com

Domaine le Clols
Tel: +33 468 39 51 68
www.leclols.com

Domaine Saint Laurent
Tel: +33 468 60 15 80
www.naturisme-st-laurent.com

La Clapère
Tel: +33 468 83 36 04
www.clapere.com

La Combe de Ferrière
Tel: +33 466 45 52 43
www.la-combe.com

Le Martinet de l'Elze
Tel: +33 466 61 12 37
Email: martinetdelelze@libertysurf.fr

Le Mas de la Balma
Tel: +33 468 39 08 88
www.labalma.fr

Le Mas de Lignières
Tel: +33 468 91 24 86
www.naturisme-et-terroirs.com/lignieres1GB.htm

Le Ventous
Tel: +33 468 87 83 38
www.leventousnaturiste.com

Le Village du Bosc
Tel: +33 467 96 07 37
www.villagedubosc.net

Ran du Château de Fereyrolles
Tel: +33 466 24 51 64

Source Saint-Pierre
Tel: +33 467 57 76 95
www.campingstpierre.com

Midi Pyrénées

Camping Millefleurs
Tel: +33 561 60 77 56
www.camping-millefleurs.com

Devèze
Tel: +33 562 66 43 86
www.deveze.eu

Domaine de la Sesquière
Tel: +33 563 33 96 02
www.sesquiere.com

Domaine de Lalbrade
Tel: +33 565 31 52 35
http://lalbrade.free.fr

Le Clos Barrat
Tel: +33 565 31 97 93
www.leclosbarrat.com

Le Fiscalou
Tel: +33 563 30 45 95
www.fiscalou.com

Le Mas de Nadal
Tel: +33 565 31 20 51
www.masdenadal.com

Le Moulin de Faget
Tel: +33 562 65 49 09
www.moulin-faget.com

Les Aillos
Tel: +33 561 83 22 57
http://lesaillos.free.fr

Les Grands Chênes
Tel: 33 (0)5 65 41 68 79
www.les-grands-chenes.com

Les Manoques
Tel: +33 563 95 24 06
www.lesmanoques.com

Les Roches
Tel: +33 562 66 30 18
www.campinglesroches.net

Bretagne

Les Bruyères D'Arvor
Tel: +33 297 32 57 91
www.les-bruyeres-d-arvor-naturiste.com

France

Provence Alpes Côte d'Azur

Domaine d'Enriou
Tel: +33 492 74 41 02
www.domainedenriou.com

Castillon de Provence
Tel: +33 492 83 64 24
www.castillon-de-provence.com

Domaine de l'Escride
Tel: +33 494 48 97 24

Domaine des Lauzons
Tel: +33 492 73 00 60
www.camping-lauzons.com

Domaine du Petit Arlane
Tel: +33 492 74 99 35
Email: petitarlane@net-up.com

La Tuquette
Tel: +33 494 76 19 40
www.tuquette.com

La Haute Garduère
Tel: +33 494 67 95 20
http://membres.lycos.fr/
lahautegarduere

Le Haut Chandelalar
Tel: +33 493 60 40 09
www.le-haut-chandelalar.com

Le Vallon des Oiseaux
Tel: +33 492 76 47 33
www.levallon.com

Messidor
Tel: +33 442 61 90 28
www.messidor.fr

Tamier
Tel: +33 492 66 61 55
www.naturisme-tamier.fr

Verdon Provence
Tel: +33 492 77 12 25

Bourgogne

Domaine de la Gagère,
Bourgogne
Tel: +33 386 30 48 11
www.la-gagere.com

Rhône Alpes

Domaine du Grand Bois
Tel: +33 474 87 89 00

La Plage des Templiers
Tel: +33 475 04 28 58

Le Romegas
Tel: +33 475 28 10 78

Les Ramières
Tel: +33 475 27 40 45
www.lesramieres.com

Val Drôme Soleil
Tel: +33 475 40 01 57
www.valdromesoleil.com

Poitou Charentes

L'Oliverie
Tel: +33 549 94 61 05
www.oliverie.com

Centre

La Petite Brenne
Tel: +33 254 25 05 78
www.lapetitebrenne.com

Le Moulin de la Ronde
Tel: +33 254 49 83 28
www.moulindelaronde.com

Pays de la Loire

Le Bois de la Herpinière
Tel: +33 241 51 74 81
Email: boisdelaherp@aol.com

Ile de France

Regain
Tel: +33 344 87 35 90
www.scn-regain.com

The Greek islands

Ancient Greeks thought nude recreation and sport were the epitome of physical purity. Modern Greece still continues this noble tradition in places, with some of the most pristine and laid-back nude beaches in the world. A lack of hassle and vast numbers of secluded beaches mean nudity is possible at an endless choice of places, in all the island groups. Whether you're after spacious seclusion or packed nudist beaches, fine snorkelling or long flat sands, fully naturist accommodation or wild camping with goats for company – Greece is quite simply unmissable.

Though there are few official beaches, nudity is so widespread that even many ordinary beaches often have a few bare bodies respectfully using them at either end, particularly among rocky headlands. We list the pick of Greek nude beaches in this guide, and you can always ask in local tourist offices or check out individual islands on the web for even more options. The Greek islands have one of the most comprehensive nude guides around in the superb Cap'n Barefoot site: www.barefoot.info

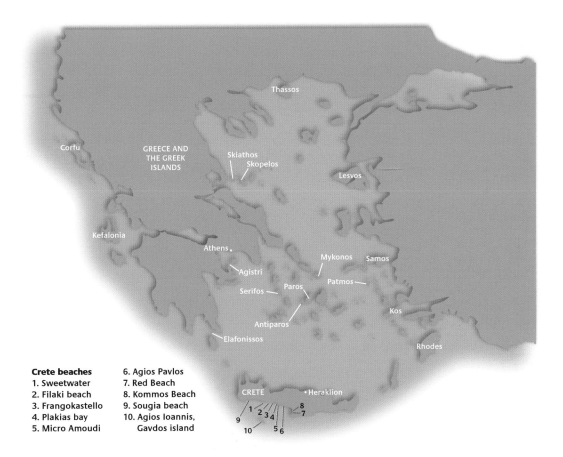

Crete beaches
1. Sweetwater
2. Filaki beach
3. Frangokastello
4. Plakias bay
5. Micro Amoudi

6. Agios Pavlos
7. Red Beach
8. Kommos Beach
9. Sougia beach
10. Agios Ioannis,
    Gavdos island

▲ Spectacularly fine bathing at Crete's Sweetwater beach, also pictured opposite. Friendly goats, a handy taverna, wonderfully clear water and hardly ever a swimming costume in sight add up to a glorious naturist experience. Picture opposite Fiona Ashley, above Charlie Simonds

Sweetwater accommodation

Xenofina's Hotel
http://xenofina.creteisland.gr/

Crete

Sweetwater beach, Loutro and Chora Sfakion

Dramatic cliffs, beautiful clear water and naturist-friendly wild goats are reason enough to come to Sweetwater. The beach consists of smooth pebbles and takes its name from freshwater wells at the back. It's a great place to get a tan and almost all visitors go naked. A taverna built on a platform in the sea is very handy; the beach is remote and has little natural shade.

Practical info

From Chora Sfakion town take the coast road west to Anapolis. Soon after Ilingas beach the road takes a sharp right bend back on itself to zig-zag up the mountain. Take the coastal footpath at the bend (marked E4) to continue along the shore. The beach is 30-45 mins' walk along a rough and rocky path above the sea. The path then leads on to the coastal village of Loutro, about 45 minutes away.

Alternatively take a 15-minute ferry ride from Chora Sfakion. Xenofina's Hotel in Loutro has a roof garden set aside for naturist sunbathing.

Nude bathing on Crete

Crete has long been considered one of Europe's finest nude beach destinations, and a huge influx of tourists in recent years has if anything enhanced that status. Nude beaches here get busier and busier, and the island itself, at 260km long, has plenty of space for everyone.

The biggest reason why naturists come here is the stunning and still largely unspoilt southern coastline. While ordinary tourists gather along the increasingly crowded northern coast near the airports, those who know best have the pick of the island and return home without tan lines. There is even a superb naturist hotel with its own nude beach.

The Greek islands

Vritomartis naturist hotel and Filaki beach

This striking pebble beach just outside the town of Chora Sfakion is used by the nearby naturist hotel Vritomartis, although any nude bather can come and join in. The hotel runs a beach bar and there are sunbeds and parasols for hire. It is a beautiful bay for naked bathing and fine snorkelling, with wonderful rock formations to explore.

Practical info

The beach is 900 metres from Hotel Vritomartis. As you drive into Chora Sfakion, the hotel is signposted on the left about 500 metres before the main town. From this street a lane on the left goes to the beach. There are buses from Hania to Chora Sfakion three times a day, which take just under two hours and will drop you at the hotel if you ask the conductor. Vritomartis Hotel and Bungalows is a high quality 3-star family-owned hotel. Its pool and outside areas are all nude during the day and the hotel has a free, regular minibus to Filaki beach. There are 85 rooms, half in the main hotel and half in bungalows set in extensive grounds. It's a lovely place ideal for all free spirits, not just keen naturists.

> **Vritomartis Hotel and Bungalows**
>
> Tel: +30 28250 91112
> www.naturism-crete.com

▲ At the Hotel Vritomartis and its neighbouring beach Filaki. For a truly relaxing naturist holiday on Crete, there's nowhere better. Pics top left and right Charlie Simonds, bottom left from the resort, other two from Fiona Ashley

The Greek islands

VRITOMARTIS
hotel & bungalows

we were born naked for a reason...

the only naturist resort in Crete**Greece**

restaurant • bar • pool bar • swimming pool • children's pool
playground • private beach • beach bar • tennis court
volley court • giant chess • live music • excursions

Vritomartis Hotel, Chora Sfakion 73011 Crete Greece
Tel: + 30 2825091112, Fax: + 30 2825091222
email: **info@vritomartis.gr**, URL: **www.vritomartis.gr**

www.nextstep.gr

The Greek islands

Frangokastello beach, by Frangokastello town

The town is worth visiting for both its dramatic coastal castle and its big sandy nude beach. The sea is gently shelving so is great for families, and at the very end are clay pebbles under a waterfall if you fancy some natural bodypainting. It's a lovely spot, often much busier than the ordinary clothed section of the beach but so large it never feels crowded.
Practical info
The nude stretch of beach is to the east of the town (to the left as you face the sea). To drive there head east from Frangokastello and 500m after leaving town turn right down the track marked Sunrise Taverna. Park and go down the steps then walk along the sands to the left for a minute or two. Fata Morgana Apartments is a modern development and taverna situated above the beach. To get to the nude beach it's a short climb down to the sand and then a walk to the left.

▼ Two of Crete's finest nude beaches. Top row shows the view down to Frangokastello's long and gently shelving beach. Bottom row shows the ever-popular cove of Micro Amoudi, which gets busier every year. Pictures top left and bottom left from Fiona Ashley, picture top right by Charlie Simonds

▲ Overlooking the magnificent bay at Plakias, a beach with all the facilities you could wish for. Top picture from www.barefoot.info, bottom picture from Fiona Ashley

Fata Morgana Apartments

Tel: +30 28250 92077
www.fatamorgana-kreta.com

Plakias Bay Hotel

Tel: +30 8320 31215 and 31315
www.c-v.net/hotel/plakias/plakiasbay

Plakias beach, southern end, Plakias town

A fabulous setting of cliffs, mountains and a huge sweep of golden sand make this beach a wonderful place for all-over tanning and snorkelling. The sea shelves gently, making it suitable for families, and showers are available. Refreshments are brought to the beach in season, and umbrellas are also available to rent. Many regulars come back year after year, enticed by the friendly atmosphere both on the nude beach and in the town.

Practical info

The nude area is the last section of the beach, to the left as you face the sea, and unsurprisingly is often the most popular part of the bay. Plakias Bay Hotel has 28 apartments and a reputation for good food, and is just three mins' walk from the nude area.

Micro Amoudi, by Damnoni beach

This is in fact two sandy bays, set between the much larger Damnoni and Amoudi beaches on either side. Sunbeds, parasols and a cold shower are available in the larger of the two bays (on the west or right as you face the sea). The smaller bay is therefore usually quieter, particularly as it involves a tricky climb down. The beaches are very popular and often there's not even a single swimming costume in sight, particularly in the larger bay. Many take comfort in the peaceful company of so many other bare bathers, and it just gets more and more popular every year.

Practical info

The bays are easy to find and a short walk from car parking. From Amoudi you go right as you face the sea, taking a short path uphill to take you to the nude bays. From Damnoni you go left along a track that's also suitable for vehicles if you're in a hurry to strip.

Red beach, Matala

There are two popular naturist beaches at the town of Matala. The first of these is Red beach, one of the Travel Channel's top 10 nude beaches in the world. It's not that easy to get to, which means splendid isolation but you need to bring your refreshments with you for the day. It was famous as a hippy beach in the 1960s but newer generations of nude bathers now gather here, as well as some textile tourists who also make the trip. The spectacular cliff face is studded with caves and great to explore.

Practical info
As you enter Matala town, take the left hand road just after the Hotel Zafirias. This sealed road gives way to a track which takes you over a headland to the beach. It's a moderate climb but safe enough even with children, and has some fabulous views along the coast.

▲ Views of Red beach next to Matala town. The walk to the beach, pictured left, has a superb view of the nude area and coast stretching into the distance. Picture on the right shows the cliff face, with caves to explore. Pictures from Fiona Ashley

Kommos beach, Matala

Just 5km to the north of Matala lies a second beach which nudists love for a number of reasons. It is a long stretch of sand with ample space to walk, explore or just be by yourself. There are turtle nesting areas here so respect the signs and as always do not leave a scrap of rubbish behind. Both ends of the beach have some developments, including a handy taverna at the southern end, so nude bathers gather in the undeveloped central section. Some trees at the back of the beach give shade, and a visiting refreshment van sometimes stops in the nude area. The wide spaces and high percentage of nudists give this beach a lovely, welcoming atmosphere.

Practical info
The beach, which is sometimes also spelled Comos beach, is about 5km away from Matala town itself, on the coast road to Pitsidia. It can be reached from both ends, but the easiest car park is at an archaeological site a few minutes south of the nude section. To drive here from Matala, head out in the direction of Pitsidia. Look out for the white walls of the Speed Cafe, and a campsite: there is an unsealed track to the left. Follow this track to a crossroads, where you turn right downhill and continue to the archaeological site. Head north, or right as you face the sea, to the nude beach.

▲ Hiring a boat to sail round the Greek islands is hugely popular and many dispense with the costume offshore. Picture by Charlie Simonds

Agios Pavlos beach, Agios Pavlos village

At the lovely little village of Agios Pavlos, worth visiting just for the views, there is a long-established nude beach over the headland. The walk down to the beach is a fairly steep sandy slope that gets hot in the sun. There is plenty of room for peace and quiet while you sunbathe and swim, and in recent years umbrellas have been available to rent. The beach is divided in two by a rocky outcrop: on the western side of this the sands stretch far away into seclusion. A heavenly spot with fine views along the coast.

Practical info
The bare beach is easy to find. Facing the bay at Agios Pavlos, walk over the headland on your right and down to the beach on the other side.

Sougia, east of Sougia town

This beautiful beach could not be easier to find. Bare bathing is popular and commonplace immediately to the east of the built-up area in Sougia town. The water is excellent for swimming and snorkelling, with safe natural rock pools for children. The beach is small pebbles, fine enough to make it comfortable for sunbathing. There is a happy mix of dress and undress on the beach, although the nude bathers often comfortably outnumber the clothed ones. Sougia is highly regarded among bare beach lovers as a largely unspoilt town in a beautiful part of the island. Further to the east, beyond a rock, is a more secluded area with springs and caves to explore. Tourist info, accommodation and much else of use to the visitor is available in English from www.sougia.info.

Practical info
Nude bathing starts at the very edge of the town: this beach is unmissable in every sense if you're staying in Sougia.

Agios Ioannis, Gavdos island

The island of Gavdos is officially the southernmost point of Europe. And appropriately enough for the bottom of the continent, it is a bare one. Indeed, the beach at Agios Ioannis is often entirely naturist, with a long and wide expanse of sand lapped by beautiful clear water. The island in general is well off the beaten track so it never gets heavily crowded – although the middle of August does see a big influx of visitors, to both the island and the nude beach.

Practical info
Ferries to Gavdos take about 80 minutes from Chora Sfakion or Paleochora on Crete. Once you get to the island, a bus goes from the small port every hour to Agios Ioannis, where it drops you at a taverna and small shop. You can stock up here and then walk the remaining 15 minutes west to the nude beach itself – turn left as you face the sea. Many free camp at the back of the beach, where there are sand dunes and trees.

▲ Above: the end of another sunny day on the beach at Plakias; pic from Fiona Ashley. Top pic shows Sougia, from www.sougia.info
▼ The bottom of Europe: Gavdos island's Agios Ioannis beach, on the left, is the continent's most southerly nude beach. Agios Pavlos, on the right, is one of Crete's most highly rated naturist beaches; picture from Fiona Ashley

Corfu

Myrtiotissa beach, near Pelekas, west coast

A beautiful nude beach with a freshwater spring tumbling off the tree-covered cliffs. A favourite place of writer Lawrence Durrell. Sunbeds and traditional Greek refreshments available. Although the track from the car park is very steep you will find plenty of like-minded company, both swimsuited and au naturel. Swimming and snorkelling are excellent. Nudists tend to use the south side of the bay.

Practical info
Take the road from Vatos to Glyfada and turn right immediately after Villa Myrto. Drive into the car park among the trees and walk down to the beach.

Villa Myrto has self-catering apartments set in olive and lemon groves. Myrtiotissa beach is a 10-minute walk. Villa Kapella at Vatos has good value self-catering studios and apartments 1.5km from the beach.

▲ Many a sailor's idea of a perfect welcome, on a nude cruise around Corfu. The island is also home to Myrtiotissa beach, pictured below left. Pictures by Charlie Simonds

Villa Myrto
Tel: +30 26610 95082
www.villamyrto.com

Villa Kapella
Tel: +30 26610 94563
www.corfu-villas-apts.com

▲ Some of Kefalonia's lovely nude beaches. Pics supplied by Vassaliki Club, an ideal place for bare souls on the island

Kefalonia

West Xi beach

▲ The Vassaliki Club naturist resort

West Xi beach, Lixouri, Paliki peninsula

A lovely clothes-optional beach of reddish-orange sand more than 1km long, which is completely undeveloped – there are no sunbeds or tavernas. Backed by clay cliffs, you may well have this sheltered haven to yourself. The swimming is excellent but take your own shade and refreshments.
Practical info
Drive south from Lixouri to the western end of the main Xi beach. Park and walk west over a small hill to the nude area. See kefhelm.tripod.com for local info. A family naturist resort – Vigla Natura Vassaliki Club – opened in

2007, situated 10 minutes' drive south-east of the island capital Argostoli. The attractive property run by Mark and Samantha from the UK has modern accommodation and delightful private grounds with a large pool. Their website has details of local nude beaches including the nearest, 2km from the resort at Avithos/Klismata.

> **Vassaliki Naturist Club**
>
> Tel: +44 (0) 870 8502420 (UK)
> www.viglanatura.com

Elafonissos island

> **Simos Camping and Bungalows**
>
> Tel: +30 27340 22672
> Mobile: +30 69777 18773

Megalo Simos, south-east coast

This tiny island – less than 600m from the southern tip of the Peloponnese mainland – is home to one of the most breathtaking beaches in Greece. According to Dana Facaros writing in the Sunday Times (London) "Megalo Simos is a dream beach". She adds that it is popular with nudists and suggests free camping is also possible. There are in fact two beaches separated by a small rocky outcrop – the larger one is more popular with bare bathers, towards the southern end. The sand is fine and golden: swimming is perfect.

An array of cedar trees, unusual in these parts, only adds to the serenity.
Practical info
Just 300km from Athens, the island is packed from mid-July to mid-August. Ferries go from Pounta to Elafonissos every half hour – crossing takes 9 minutes. Accommodation is available on the island, but it's also feasible to stay on the mainland and visit for the day. Recently opened Simos Camping and Bungalows is virtually on the beach (May – September). Local information at www.elafonissos.gr.

The Greek islands

Skiathos

Banana beach, near Koukounaries

▲ Happy days on Banana beach. Pic top left by Rod Burkey, pictures top middle and right by Andrew Winfer, picture at bottom from Greek island web guide www.barefoot.info

Banana beach is the collective name for three lovely sandy bays well known by nude bathers. The water is crystal clear and usually calm. The three small tavernas here look after the beaches and ensure they are kept spotless. In peak season bare beachbums will feel more comfortable on Little Banana, one of the smaller coves, as large numbers of clothed holidaymakers descend on the main beach. Little Banana is often described as the best nude beach in Greece, although there is plenty of competition for the accolade.

Practical info

There is a bus turnaround and car park at the end of the Koukounaries road, coming from Skiathos town. The track to Big Banana is signposted and takes 15 mins walking through the olive groves. From here it's a further 5-10 mins to Little Banana.

There is a great website for information about the beach and places for independent travellers to stay nearby at www.sunnybanana.com.

Other local accommodation that can be booked through tour operators includes: the Hotel Panorama, Golden Beach Hotel, Muses Hotel, Caravos Hotel, Maria Villa and Studios Periyali Studios and Strophilia Apartments.

SKIATHOS

Skiathos town

Koukounaries

Banana beach

The Greek islands

Skopelos

Velanio beach, Staphylos, south coast

A super bay of sand and fine shingle, described by Skopelos tourist board as 'the beach of the nudist'. Surrounded by pretty countryside, this beach does indeed attract nude bathers, who tend to use the area beyond the rocky outcrops. Swimming is superb.

Practical info
Travel south from Skopelos town for 4km to Staphylos. Park or alight from the bus near the Hotel Ostria. Walk down to Staphylos bay and at the other end of the beach simply walk over the headland to Velanio. The

family-run Hotel Ostria overlooks Staphylos beach. It is 750 metres from Velanio nude beach. The Poseidon Villas consist of maisonettes and flats located opposite the Hotel Ostria.

Hotel Ostria
Tel: +30 24240 22220
www.skopelos.net/ostria

Poseidon Villas
Tel: +30 24240 24153
www.skopelos.net/poseidon

Agistri island

Halikiada (Chalikiada) beach, Skliri, Skala

An attractive pebbly beach made famous in the 1970s as the site of 'Adam and Eve' naturist meetings, a testing ground for nudism in Greece. Many have recommended this location, including The Guardian newspaper's Greek correspondent Helena Smith who mentions it frequently, and Greek guidebook author Michael Cullen (Alistair Sawday 'Special Places to Stay'), both praising its nudist

credentials and unspoilt beauty. The tranquil beach with sparkling clear water is set in Agistri's largest bay and requires a bit of a scramble to access.

Practical info
It is easy to walk to from Skala harbour; go south-east and the path to the beach is just beyond the Agistri Club. You can stay nearby at Rosy's Little Village or Agistri Club. The island is less than an hour by high-speed ferry from Athens.

Rosy's Little Village
Tel: +30 22970 91610
www.rosyslittlevillage.com

Agistri Club
www.hotelsofgreece.com/saronic/agistriclub

▼ The secluded beach at Halikiada. Pic supplied by Rosy's Little Village

The Greek islands

Mykonos

▲ New horizons: Super Paradise on Mykonos is still used nude, but naturists tend to use other beaches now (picture on left shows Super Paradise by Kevin and Debbie Rudd)

Panormos beach, north-east of Mykonos

This is a delightful and quiet nude beach on Panormos bay. Two tavernas are at one end of the beach; nudity is the norm at the other. Can be breezy if the north wind blows. Lucy Gilmore, deputy travel editor of the Independent newspaper, was enthralled: "Whipping off my bikini, I reflected on names.

This, I decided, was the beach that should have been called Paradise."
Practical info
From Mykonos town drive north-east following signs to Panormos beach. The category 'A' Albatros Club Resort at Panormos is the only local place to stay, just a short walk along the beach.

Paranga, Elia & Agrari beaches, south Mykonos

There was a time when Paradise and Super Paradise beaches were the most famous places in the Aegean to get your kit off. But times change and while they still have a few devoted fans, nude bathers will discover a more enjoyable experience at one of the other bays nearby which can easily be reached by small boat (caique) from the busy but charming resort of Platys Gialos.
Practical info
Paranga beach is the first bay going

east, before Paradise. Then there's Elia beach, which is the furthest east the boats go, beyond Super Paradise. Agrari beach is a short walk back to the west from Elia. Swimsuits are optional at all three and there's likely to be a relaxed mix of dressed and undressed visitors.
Hotel Argo, a family establishment in Platys Gialos, is just 100m from the pier where caiques call often to ferry passengers to the south coast beaches.

Albatros Club Resort
Tel: +30 22890 25130
www.albatros-mykonos.com

Hotel Argo
Tel: +30 22890 23405
www.argo-mykonos.gr

Paros and Antiparos

Monastiri, Agios Ioannis, north Paros

There are lots of attractive little remote coves to explore in the area, many of which are suitable for nude bathing and exploring. There are no facilities or shade along this shore and the surrounding area is isolated and

undeveloped – it's escapist territory!
Practical info
The top of the peninsula can be reached by boat from Naousa, or by driving up the western side of the gulf, signposted from town.

The Greek islands

Lageri beach, near Naousa, Paros

▲ You don't even need to wear a snorkel or mask to enjoy some of the clearest waters in the Mediterranean, around the Greek islands. Picture by Charlie Simonds

A long narrow golden sand nudist beach considered by some to be heaven on earth. Completely undeveloped – no tavernas or even any roads nearby. The water is crystal clear, the sand is soft underfoot and the land behind the shore is covered in beautiful flora. Towards the southern end of the beach is best for au naturel sunseekers.

Practical info

Small boats that go regularly from Naousa are by far the favoured way to get to the beach, due to the lack of roads. It is possible to drive part of the way, travelling east from town towards Santa Maria, and then walk the rest of the way. Naousa itself is described as the pearl of Paros, full of historical antiquities, archaeological monuments and famous places such as the Acropolis of Koukounaries.

For accommodation, try Sakis Rooms; in a quiet elevated location overlooking a nearby beach and three minutes from town. Two good websites for local info www.parosweb.gr and www.paros-online.com.

Sakis Rooms

Tel: +30 22840 5217
www.sakisrooms.com

Porto Paros beach, opposite Naousa, Paros

This small crescent of fine golden sand is clothes-optional. Only 80 metres long and 7 metres wide, it attracts anything up to 30 sunbathers, most of whom are nude. It is lovely and clean, partly because there are no facilities other than waste bins. It is also easy to get to.

Practical info

Drive north from Naousa on the western side of the Gulf of Naousa.. Just past the Porto Paros Hotel there is a short path down to the beach. Alternatively, use a taxi boat from Naousa to Porto Paros and walk north for 300 metres.

Theologians beach, north of Antiparos town

This popular beach is unusual because it is one of very few 'official' nude beaches in Greece, and has been since the early 1970s. Although the sandy shore is less than 100 metres long, it is possible to carry on to the next beach. You can also go au naturel if you wade to the small offshore island of Diplo. Lots of opportunity for bare exploration and if it's windy there are dunes at the back of the beach. Refreshments and a mini-market are available at the nearby campsite.

Practical info

The beach is 700m north from the harbour in Antiparos village. Local information is available from www.antiparos-isl.gr. Camping Antiparos just west of the nude beach offers camping and bamboo huts for hire.

Camping Antiparos

Tel/Fax: +30 22840 61221
www.antiparos-isl.gr

Serifos island

Karavi and Livadakia beaches, near Livadi

SERIFOS

Livadi •

Karavi and Livadakia

Visitors to Serifos are quickly seduced by its charm – untouched by mass tourism it is renowned for its remote sandy beaches. The little port town of Livadi, and its attractive suburb of Livadakia to the south, make an ideal base for exploring the surrounding clothing-optional beaches.

Practical info

In low season nudists sometimes use parts of the beach in Livadakia, but Laura contacted us to advise that Karavi beach 15 mins' walk further south is a delightful spot for going nude. The shore consists of fine sand and there is a relaxed atmosphere with most visitors naked. Access to the sea requires care across slippery rocks before the sandy bottom. Reports of wild camping nearby. Accommodation gets booked up early in August. Local info www.serifos-island.com.

Lesvos

Molyvos Delphinia beach, Molyvos and Petra

This pleasant coarse-sand nude beach is close to the Delphinia Hotel. It is quiet and there are no facilities but the swimming is excellent and the beach is highly regarded for its good atmosphere and lovely views of Molyvos town.
Practical info
From Molyvos travel south towards Petra for just over 3km and look for Hotel Delphinia. There is a track down the side of the hotel signposted to the beach. At the shore turn left and walk to the end. The Delphinia Hotel and Bungalows resort is set in 87 acres of parkland by the sea. The nude part of the beach is a short walk to the south.

Delphinia Hotel and Bungalows
Tel: +30 22530 71315
www.hoteldelfinia.com

Sigri, on the west coast

Sigri town beach is not suitable for going nude, but there are half a dozen almost deserted bays within reasonable walking distance (or a short drive) of this pretty fishing village. Chris contacted us to recommend the area for an away-from-it-all experience. The mainly sandy beaches are never crowded and it's often possible to find one to yourself – even in August.

Andromachis, Faneromeni, Limena and Tsichlioda beaches attract bare sunseekers. There's usually a welcome breeze but little shade.
Practical info
A useful little guidebook *Sigri: Where the Road Ends* by Roy Lawrance lists paths to these beaches (available from the author: 87 Glebe Rd, Deanshanger, Milton Keynes, MK19 6LX, UK. Or email him: roylawrance@talktalk.net).

Skala Erossos, on the west coast

This long beach of yellow sand is one of the best on the island. It gets busy in summer and with lots of bare bathing, mostly in the area of the dried-up riverbed about 1km west of the town. On occasions, unfortunately, there are reports of folk gawping at the nudists so the location receives mixed reviews.

Practical info
To locate the nude section just walk along the beach from Skala Erossos, or take the road that runs parallel to it. Leave the car in the last parking area before the riverbed and walk north. Drinks are available from a nearby caravan on the beach.

▲ Take something soft to sit on and sandals for the beach if you're visiting Greece: a lot of the beaches have stones and sharp rocks at the water's edge. Picture by Charlie Simonds

Thassos

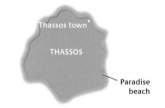

Paradise beach, south-east of Thassos town

This lovely beach is the most popular nudist spot on the island. Harry and Amy wrote to us recommending the soft white sand and gently shelving shore. "The sea all around Thassos is emerald green from the amazing Thassian marble which falls into the sea creating the colour." The beach has lots of clothed visitors at the southern end, especially at weekends, but to the north there's a large smooth rocky and sandy outcrop where people prefer to wear their birthday suits. There is a handy taverna at the southern end.
Practical info
The beach is 23km south-east of Thassos town along the coast road. You can drive down a track to the taverna.

▲ The nude end of Paradise, on Thassos island. Pic from Harry McKeown and Amy Clarke
■ Opposite page: escapism off the Greek islands. Pic Charlie Simonds

The Greek islands

Patmos

▲ The sandy, secluded and well worth the walk: Psili Ammos. Picture by Kevin and Debbie Rudd

Psili Ammos beach, south-west Patmos

James Knight, writing in the Sunday Times (London), recommended one of the only sandy beaches on the island of Patmos. Well off the beaten track and with plenty of shady tamarisks, "discreet naturism is part of the culture here". There is a handy taverna but little else at this lovely spot. The beach can get busy with swimsuited visitors in July and August, but there is room for all. Don't be surprised to see an occasional impromptu game of naked volleyball.

Practical info
Take one of the small boats that sail here from the harbour at Skala – the journey takes 40 minutes. Otherwise, it is a long hike from the port town, where most of the island's holiday accommodation is located.

SAMOS

Tsamadou beach

Samos town

PATMOS

Skala

Psili Ammos

Note: maps not to scale

Samos

Tsamadou beach, near Kokkari, north Samos

The only official nudist beach on the island, this picturesque shore has a mixture of coarse sand and pebbles. The beach is popular and divides near the small kiosk in the middle – nudes to the right and clad visitors to the left. Care is needed when swimming because the pebbles shelve steeply into the water and footwear is advised. There are toilets, showers, sunbeds and umbrellas for hire.

Practical info
Take the coast road from Samos town north-west for 9km to Kokkari. After a further 3km there is a taverna by the roadside at Tsamadou with adjacent parking (by a bend in the road). A steep but well-made path leads down to the beach. The Armonia Bay Hotel directly overlooks the beach and is only 5 minutes' walk from the shore. Local info www.samos-beaches.com.

▲ On the rocks in Rhodes: another unofficial nude beach on the island

Kos

Tropical beach, near Kardamena

A fine sandy nudist beach with sunbeds and umbrellas for hire. A taverna sells drinks and light snacks. The sea is clear and the swimming is good, although there is a line of sharp stones at the water's edge. Either wear sandals or use the makeshift access built by the bar owner when you go skinny-dipping.
Practical info
Take the coast road south-west from Kardamena for 3km. Pass the Lagas Aegean Village holiday complex and after 450m watch for a track on the left signposted 'Tropical Beach'. The Lagas Aegean Village is a large hotel ideal for families, 15 mins' walk from the beach.

> **Lagos Aegean Village**
> Tel: +30 22420 91401

Rhodes

Faliraki nude beach, south of Faliraki town

A well known and accessible nude beach, but a world away from the boisterous excesses of the nearby town. In places there are large outcrops of rock along the shore, but with good sandy areas behind for sunbathing. Taverna, toilets, shower, sunbeds and umbrellas are all available.
Practical info
Travel south from the town centre and turn left at the traffic lights, then bear left at the fork. At the next junction turn right past Muses Hotel and look for the signpost Nudist Beach – FKK Strand. The 3-star Danae Hotel is closest to the nude beach, less than 10 mins' walk.

> **Danae Hotel**
> Tel: +30 22410 85969
> or +30 22410 23340
> www.faliraki-info.com/danae.hotel

Tsambika beach, Kolibia and Arhangelos

A breathtakingly beautiful golden sandy beach surrounded by tree-covered cliffs and hills. The shore is sheltered and slopes gently into clear blue sea – perfect for paddling and swimming. It gets very busy and nude bathers use the southern corner of the bay – 650 metres from the car park and beach tavernas.
Practical info
Travel south from Rhodes town on the east coast for 25km, passing Faliraki en route. The turn for the beach is signposted 2km after Kolibia.

Kalathos beach, near Lindos

A mainly shingle beach stretching for an almost-deserted 5km to Haraki. There is a taverna and sunbeds for rent on the main clothed beach, but by walking north it's easy to find your own personal space far from the madding crowd. Swimming is good, but footwear is advisable for tender feet.
Practical info
Travel 3km north from Lindos to Kalathos and turn right at the sign for Ostria Taverna. At the roundabout turn left to the beach. Park and walk to the left (north). The Atrium Palace Hotel and Villas at Kalathos offers luxury accommodation within an easy walk of the nude area. It has a thalasso spa and indoor and outdoor pools. Each villa has its own private swimming pool.

> **Atrium Palace Hotel**
> Tel: +30 22440 31601
> www.atrium.gr

▲ **Open Rhodes: top picture shows Faliraki beach and above Tsambika**

The Greek islands

Portugal

Unthinkable just a couple of decades ago, nude bathing is now popular and commonplace right along Portugal's superb coastline, enjoyed by countless locals and holiday makers alike. It's no exaggeration to say that some of Europe's most discerning bare bathers make a beeline for the country's golden shores, attracted by the unspoilt seclusion that so many beaches enjoy.

Several of the Algarve's spectacular coves have become well-used nude beaches, and there are many other stretches of sand where you can sunbathe in splendid solitude. There is enough tourism in the area to provide a wide range of excellent restaurants, cafes, seaside towns and great places to stay, including some new naturist resorts. Heading up the Atlantic coast, Portugal's long sandy shore has nude beaches dotted all the way along it, with a particularly fine selection just to the south of Lisbon. For the latest on this lovely country's nude bathing, look at infolara.com/naturism/beaches/index.shtml and www.fpn.pt.

Rio Alto
•Porto
Palheirao
Cova-Gala
•Coimbra
•Figueira da Foz
Ursa
•Lisbon
PORTUGAL
Bela Vista
Meco beach
Praia do Monte Velho
Praia do Salto
•Sines
Praia do Malhao
Vila Nova de Milfontes
Alteirinhos beach
•Zambujeira do Mar
Praia das Adegas
Lagos
•Portimao
Praia das Furnas
Praia Grande
Caneiros
Island of
Tavira
Cabanas Velhas
Prainha beach

Portugal

Nudes in the news: as with the rest of Mediterranean Europe, going bare has become an accepted fact of life on many of Portugal's fabulous beaches. Picture opposite taken on Malhao beach in the Alentejo region, by Barnaby Hall
▼ Surf's up: unlike nude beaches in the Mediterranean, Portugal's are exposed to the Atlantic swell. Pictures below show Caneiros beach; picture on left by Charlie Simonds, picture on right from Quinta da Horta naturist holiday centre in the Algarve

Atlantic coast

Rio Alto, 8km north of Povoa de Varzim

This unofficial nude beach offers a wide stretch of near-white sand and dunes for sheltering from the Atlantic breeze. It's increasingly popular with naturists, both local and holiday makers, and is Portugal's most northerly nude beach.
Practical info
The beach lies between the seaside towns of Povoa de Varzim and Viana do Castelo. Driving north from Povoa de Varzim, look out for signs to Agucadoura, where you turn off to the left. Keep driving along here and head for the football field and golf course, which are next to each other; the nude beach is at the back of the golf course.

Palheirao, 22km north of Figueira da Foz

In the middle of Portugal's western coastline, in the Cantanhede region, lies this large sandy beach. Loved by naturists for both its open space and lack of hassle, Palheirao offers near-white sand and a very gently shelving beach, where pools appear at low tide.
Practical info
Despite offering solitude the beach is fairly easy to find. Driving north 20km from Figueira da Foz along the main IC1 highway, turn left at the town of Tocha to the seaside town of Palheiros da Tocha. About 500m before reaching the little beach town, or 6.5km after leaving Tocha, there is a turning to the right along an unmade road. Drive along here for 3.5km and take the first turning on the left. It's about 1km further to the shore and nude beach.

▲ Europe's most westerly point is marked in fitting style by one of its most beautiful nude beaches, at Ursa. It's a tricky climb down but worth it if you're able. Picture supplied by Portugal's naturist organisation www.fpn.pt

Cova-Gala, 4km south of Figueira da Foz

Barely a few minutes' drive south from the town of Figueira da Foz, on the other side of the Mondego river, is the sandy beach at Cova-Gala. Nude bathing is unofficial but commonplace here in this holiday area.
Practical info
The beach is very near the Orbitur campsite at Gala. Heading south out of Figueira da Foz, cross the river and turn off to the right when you see signs for the campsite, and park near here. There is a sandy path to the beach that runs along the north side of the campsite fence. Once you get to the sea, head south and join the other nude bathers.

> **Inland naturist places in north Portugal**
>
> The inland campsite at Quinta das Oliveiras is just 50km north-west of Coimbra, and a handy place to stay if you're exploring the rural heart of the country. Coimbra is less than 40km from the nude beaches around Figueira da Foz, and worth a stop to explore in its own right.
> Visit www.quinta-das-oliveiras.nl/en for more information about this pretty rural naturist retreat.

Ursa, 10km west Sintra

There are two good reasons to go to Ursa – the stunning unofficial nude beach and the Cabo da Roca, Europe's most westerly point. Some claim Ursa as Portugal's most beautiful beach – it's certainly beautiful enough to attract a good number of bare bathers despite the tricky walk down. Needless to say it's completely unspoilt and there is plenty to explore along the sand and rock coastline. Portugal's naturists rate this place very highly indeed.
Practical info
Just before you get to the cabo (cape in English) there's a track signposted to Ursa; some care may be needed on this dirt road. Park at the end and walk down to the beach. The path on the left is easiest but allow a good half hour to climb back up to your car. The beach is only a few hundred metres to the north of the cape itself.

▼ Stairway to nude bathing heaven: the steps down to Palheirao beach, in central Portugal take you to a wide stretch of undeveloped sands where nudity is commonplace. Picture supplied by Portugal's naturist organisation www.fpn.pt

▲ Looking along the sands at Meco beach. It is Portugal's most famous nudist venue and handy for the capital. Pic supplied by Portugal's naturist organisation www.fpn.pt

▲ The space to be yourself: Portugal's beaches are relaxed and largely undeveloped. Picture by Charlie Simonds

Bela Vista, Caparica, south of Lisbon

Very near to Lisbon, this huge official bare beach has 3km of white sand and dunes to lose yourself in. You can park right by the beach and in season there is a cafe. If you want to get away from other beach visitors, simply keep walking further south: like many beaches near cities it can attract some who don't respect the naturist ethos, but fortunately this beach is vast.

Practical info
From Lisbon drive south over the A2 toll bridge and turn off for Caparica. Head south along the coast road. There are turnings off here to beaches on the right; Bela Vista is the last one, after Praiado Rei, about 7km from Caparica. Drive to the end of this dirt road and park. The beach on the left as you face the sea is yours to bare.

Meco beach, Alfarim, south of Lisbon

This official nudist beach is just 12km south of Bela Vista, above. It's a popular and well-known destination for true beach lovers, attracting both tourists and locals alike. The sandy shore is backed by a high cliff and has springs that are said to be safe to drink – follow the locals. The white sand is resting place for a good number of bare bottoms on sunny days, and if you fancy a spot of bodypainting there's some fun green mud for skin treatment. The sea along this coast can be rough so take care in the water. This beach is

probably more fully naturist in atmosphere than Bela Vista, and is not much further from Lisbon.
Practical info
Take the main A2 highway south from Lisbon, and 12km after crossing the toll bridge turn right for Sesimbra, down the N378. After 6km turn right for Alfarim. It's then 12km to Alfarim, where signs direct you to the beaches (Praias). You can leave your car in the parking area for a small daily charge and head to the beach. The bare area is to the left as you face the sea, after the first spring.

Praia do Monte Velho, 13km north of Sines

Running along the coast south of Lisbon, before reaching the Algarve, there are a number of other fine nude beaches that are well worth a visit. First is Praia do Monte Velho, sometimes called Porto das Carretas. This wide beach of lovely white sand is easy to reach by car and there is a naturist campsite fairly nearby.

Practical info

This beach is 90km from Lisbon and 13km north of Sines. Take the sealed road heading off to Monte Velho beach from the town of San Andre. Drive to the end, park, and walk along the wooden path on to the sands. Turn left facing the sea, or south, and walk along to the established but unofficial nudist area.

The naturist campsite, Monte Naturista O Barao, is tucked away in the heart of rural Portugal, 30km inland from Sines and the naturist beach at Monte Velho. It's also handy for exploring the ancient landscape and towns of the Alentejo region. The site opened in 2005 and is being steadily developed by its English-speaking Dutch owners; check out the website for up-to-date info on accommodation and directions. The site is already attracting favourable comment from naturist visitors.

> **Monte Naturista O Barao**
>
> Tel: + 351 269 902 007
> www.montenaturista.com

▲ Monte Naturista O Barao, already a hit with naturists. Pic by the resort

Praia do Salto, Porto Covo, south of Sines

This official nude beach is a small but pretty cove of light golden sand tucked between two rocky headlands, just 14km south of Sines. A small freshwater spring at the back is great for rinsing off the salt – or for drinking if you forget to bring enough supplies.

Practical info

Heading out of Sines on the IC4 coast road, turn right after about 5km,

following signs all the way to Porto Covo. Drive through the village and at the end turn right, towards the sea. Follow the sealed road to the series of small bays. Salto is signposted, and it's in the middle of the two textile coves Cerro da Águia and Cerca Nova. All the beaches are very close together here but secluded by rocky headlands that make a spectacular setting.

▲ The path to Praia do Monte Velho through the sand dunes
▼ The official nude beach at Praia do Salto. Pics from Portugal's naturist organisation www.fpn.pt

Portugal

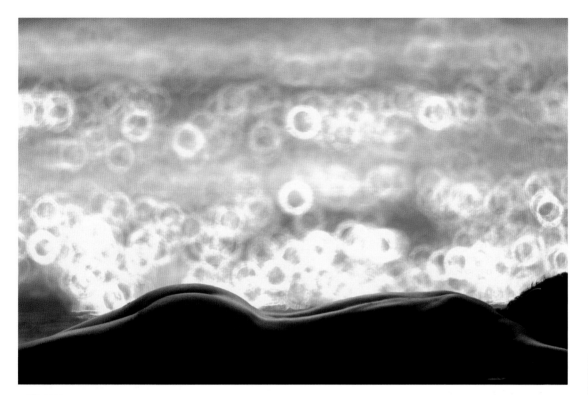

Other beaches and resorts south of Lisbon

▲ Top and middle pic show dazzling Malhao; top pic from Barnaby Hall, middle pic from Portugal's naturist organisation www.fpn.pt. Pic above shows the natural way to enjoy the lovely Naturest guesthouse

Naturest

Tel: + 351 283 933231
www.naturest-portugal.com

Two more naturist beaches on the coast between Lisbon and the Algarve should also be on any itinerary in this area, and there's a naturist guesthouse nearby too.

Praia do Malhao

The first beach is Praia do Malhao, about 20km south along the coast from Sines and not far from Praia do Salto. It's a beautiful beach backed by dunes, with springs of natural water where you can even wash after a day's sunbathing. This beach has been used naked for decades, and lies between Sines and Vila Nova de Milfontes. Driving along the coast between these two towns, turn off where you see signs for Malhao beach; the turning is a few kilometers north of Vila Nova de Milfontes near Sitava Camping. Malhao is a long beach popular with surfers. To get to the nude area drive north as far as you can and park, then keep walking along the sands to the north.

Alteirinhos beach

The second beach along this coast is the fabulous set of rocky coves at Alteirinhos beach, which is just to the south of the clothed beach and seaside town of Zambujeira do Mar.

There are several coves along here including one that is almost exclusively naturist at the far end. Access is tricky down some steep cliffs however and clothed visitors at the height of summer can make naturism in some areas uncomfortable – although there is talk of this beach gaining official nude status. To get to the beach head south out of Zambujeira, over the little river on the edge of town, and after about 1km there is a turning on the right that leads to a parking area and platform above the cliff. There is a wooden stairway down, and the nude areas are to the south, or left as you face the sea.

Naturest naturist guesthouse

Naturest naturist guesthouse is 40km inland from Alteirinhos beach. Set in tranquil countryside and enjoying a 9m swimming pool, the accommodation has been newly restored in a traditional 19th century house. Naturest is run by an English couple, who can give directions to other naturist beaches in the area including Praia do Salto and Praia das Adegas, on the Algarve. It's an environmentally friendly place too, and well worth a visit.

The Algarve

Praia das Adegas, 25km south of Odemira

Although on the west coast of Portugal, this beach is actually in the Algarve. It's an official nude beach which even has a lifeguard in high season. Almost exclusively nudist, the golden sands here attract a good crowd of visitors. It's a fairly long walk down some wooden steps to get to the beach, but well worth it according to regular users.
Practical info
To reach the beach, drive south along the N120 coast road from Odemira. Once you cross the bridge over the river Seixe, turn right and follow signs to Odeceixe beach, which is 3km away. Odeceixe beach itself is textile and the nude beach is a further 500m drive to the south, where you can park and walk down the steps. At low tide it is possible to walk here from Odeceixe beach by going round the headland. Otherwise it's the steps!

Praia das Furnas, Figueira, 15km west of Lagos

This wonderful nude beach is not to be missed if you're in this part of the Algarve. It's not the easiest place to find but naturists rate it very highly. A good idea is to stay at the local campsite of Quinta dos Carricos and ask them for directions; many naturists make a holiday out of these two places.
Practical info
To get to this beach, make sure it hasn't been raining recently as the track is unsealed and quite tricky to drive along. Driving west from Lagos, turn off the N125 coast road opposite Parque de Floresta, signposted to Salema. Then turn immediately right towards the village of Figueira. Drive through the village and when you cross a small concrete bridge, turn left down an unsealed track. At the first fork keep right, and at the second fork keep left. Cross another small bridge and turn left. You can park here and walk on to the beach.

The campsite Quinta dos Carricos is just a few kilometers away, next to the town of Salema. It is set in a national park and has apartments and caravans to rent in addition to camping pitches and most importantly a naturist area.

▼ Algarve scenes of cliffs, coves and caves: Praia das Adegas, on the top, and Praia das Furnas, on the bottom. Pics supplied by Portugal's naturist organisation www.fpn.pt

Quinta dos Carricos

Tel: +351 282 695 201
www.quintadoscarricos.com

▼ The nude beach at Praia das Adegas, below, feels less remote than some other Algarve beaches, with lifeguard – and mobile phone coverage. Pic by Barnaby Hall

Portugal

▲ Playing by the sea at spectacular Caneiros. The beach is not only easy to find, it is also used almost exclusively by naturists, making it highly popular among discerning beach lovers. Pics by Charlie Simonds

Cabanas Velhas, 8km west of Lagos

This is yet another beautiful, cliff-backed sandy beach with lots of space for nude bathing, beach games and generally taking in the peaceful setting. You'll need to bring your own refreshments. The sand is white, the sea warm in season and the cliffs ideal for careful scrambling. The one drawback is that the beach can attract a lot of clothed visitors too and if there are too many of them naturists will tend to head for Praia das Furnas along the coast.

Practical info
Drive west from Lagos along the main N125 towards Vila do Bispo. After about 7km turn left for Burgau, drive 2km to the village and go right at the road junction, signposted to Boca do Rio. Drive 2.2km and look out for a narrow lane on the left signposted to Cabanas Velhas. You can park right by the beach then walk down to the left. The Quinta dos Carricos campsite, mentioned in the previous listing, is also convenient for this beach.

Caneiros, Ferragudo town

This small but almost exclusively bare beach is easy to find and has a fabulous view of craggy offshore rocks. There's also a wonderfully creative naturist retreat just a few minutes' drive away. The beach is a delightful and safe place to swim or sunbathe on the yellow sands and watch the seagulls flocking to the rocky islets. You can hire a paddle boat from the neighbouring Ferragudo town beach.

Practical info
To get to the bare cove, simply walk round the rocks to the right (west) of Ferragudo town beach. Access can be a little tricky around high tide but the sea here is safe and warm. The beach is very near Quinta da Horta naturist retreat, described in the next listing.

Quinta da Horta, Ferragudo

If you want a fully naturist holiday in the Algarve sun, Quinta da Horta is a clothes-optional resort a short distance from the town of Ferragudo and nearby naturist beaches. It offers a range of naturist holiday cottages. Much loved by visitors looking for a simple and natural setting, it has its own studio and a range of art and craft courses.

The centre is set in an organic farm, which provides food for the gourmet meals, and has a small stable complex. Massage, yoga, health and holistic treatment holidays can also be arranged. There is a tennis court, swimming pool and sauna, together with a terrace for soaking up some of the 300 days of sunshine this region enjoys each year. It's entirely up to you whether or not you wear anything in the facilities and peaceful gardens.

> **Quinta da Horta**
>
> Tel: +351 282 461 395
> www.naturist-holidays-portugal.com

Island of Tavira, Tavira, 25km east of Faro

This beautiful half mile of official bare beach is very popular with tourists. The island of Tavira lies just across a short stretch of water from Tavira town, and has fine white sand and a warm sea. The island is part of the Ria Formosa natural reserve and has a campsite with cafes next to where the ferry arrives.
Practical info
To get here, take a short ferry ride from Tavira town's dock to the island of Tavira; the crossing takes less than 5 minutes. The beaches are on the seaward side of the island – you can walk across in a few minutes as the island is less than 500m wide. The nude beach is about 1km along the sands to the west, or right as you face the sea, although people strip off outside the official beach boundaries.

Other Algarve nude beaches

There are many other unofficial bare beaches on the Algarve, and many deserted beaches which people use without costumes too.
Prainha beach
Prainha, about 12km to the east of Lagos near Alvor, is a beautiful spot with cliffs, caves and a warm sea. To get to the nude beach go down the long stairway to the sands at Tres Irmaos beach and simply turn left as you face the sea, walking through some pretty coves.
Praia Grande beach
Praia Grande is an easily accessible cove that is even within walking distance of the resort town of Armacao De Pera. If you're driving, turn off the N125 at Pera and follow signs to Praia Grande. Keep going straight ahead when the sealed road finishes, and this dirt track will take you to a car park. Take the wooden path across the dunes, and turn right on the beach to find a well-used nude area after the rocks. If you're in Armacao De Pera, simply walk along the beach to the east, or left as you face the sea, until you reach the naturist area.

Madeira

Hotel Jardim Atlantico, south-west coast

Although there are no official bare beaches in Madeira, and hardly any other sort of beaches either, there is one hotel that is attempting to make up the deficit with a terrace for all-over tanning. The modern 4-star Hotel Jardim Atlantico is located 1,500 feet above the sea. There is a health spa and a nude sunbathing terrace.
Practical info
The hotel is at Prazeres, in south-west Madeira.

> **Other Algarve naturist places**
>
> Quinta da Vista is a pretty B&B run by naturists, with secluded gardens and a large pool. It is only 30 minutes' drive from two naturist beaches – the owners are more than happy to give directions.
> Quinta da Vista
> Tel: +351 282 444874
> www.algarvesun.eu.com

▲ Tavira's wide sandy shore attracts plenty of naturists during the Algarve's long sunbathing season. The beach is on the ocean-facing side of Tavira island, a short ferry ride from Tavira town. Pic by Bob White

▲ Above and opposite: the Quinta da Horta naturist centre and nearby nude beach at Caneiros, where the resort can arrange a beach barbeque. Picture above supplied by Quinta da Horta, all others by Charlie Simonds

> **Hotel Jardim Atlantico**
>
> Tel: +351 291 820 220
> www.jardimatlantico.com

Portugal

Croatia

Croatia's coast is unique. Aquamarine seas mirror verdant pines along the unspoilt shore, with a thousand sparkling islands dotted around pretty bays. Even better, there are hundreds of nude beaches just waiting to be enjoyed. Add historical interest such as the Venetian architecture and you get a perfect destination for discerning visitors.

The country endured a devastating onslaught during the 1990s, but quickly emerged from the troubles to reclaim its accolade as Pearl of the Adriatic. Investment has breathed new life into popular resorts and brought back happy holidaymakers to enjoy the delights of this special country. Low-cost flights have helped them on their way.

The authorities are supportive of nudist tourism, encouraging visitors to enjoy the huge number of au naturel resorts, or seek out their own secluded cove. Only one warning: take something soft to these beautiful pebble and rocky shores. Sand is in fairly short supply.

Istria

1. Kanegra beach
2. Solaris beach
3. Sveti Nikola beach
4. Zelena Laguna and Bijela Uvala
5. Funtana beach
6. Koversada beaches
7. Valalta beach
8. Maschin beach
9. Sveti Katrina beach
10. Camp Kazela
11. Rabac beach

Kanegra beach, Piran Bay, north of Umag

A pebbly nude beach with lovely clear water in a natural setting within the Kanegra Holiday Village. The popular resort has 232 bungalows and a campsite, which together provide a range of sports and other activities. There is also a swimsuited beach because the resort is not a nudist centre. A small charge is made for non-residents to use the bare beach and other facilities.

Practical info
From Umag drive 10km north on the coast road through Savudrija and shortly afterwards Kanegra Holiday Village is clearly signposted on the left.

Kanegra accommodation
Kanegra Holiday Village
Tel: +385 52 70 90 00
www.istra.com/istraturist

Solaris beach, Lanterna peninsula, Porec

This 2km long rocky naturist beach backed by attractive oak woods has man-made platforms for sunning. There are also shingle and pebble inlets. It is part of the Solaris nudist holiday centre. It is wise to wear sandals when swimming to protect your feet from sea urchins. Refreshments are available. There is a small admission charge for non-residents.

Practical info
Travel north from Porec on the main coast road for 12km. Clear direction signs to the holiday centre and the beach will be seen on the left side of the road.

Solaris Camping is a big naturist site with space for 2,000 tents and caravans. Apartments and pavilions are also available to rent, all within a few metres of the au naturel beach.

Solaris accommodation
Solaris Camping
Tel: +385 52 46 51 10
www.riviera.hr

Sveti Nikola beach, Sveti Nikola island, Porec

This island has a small and well-established naturist beach which, like many in Croatia, consists of limestone rocks with flat areas designed for sunbathing. There are places to access the translucent sea and the snorkelling is excellent. Sveti Nikola is just offshore from Porec, protecting the city's harbour, and has beautiful views.

Practical info
Regular ferry boats sail to the island from Porec harbour – the journey only takes five minutes. The beach is on the south side, near to the Hotel Fortuna, which is popular with British holidaymakers. The naturist beach is close to it, a short walk along the coastal path.

Zelena Laguna and Bijela Uvala, Porec

These two attractive nude beaches are close to each other and have ordinary (clothed) campsites next to them. The rocky beaches are terraced and have shrubs and lush grass behind them. Paved sunbathing areas have been provided.

Practical info
Travel south from Porec and in 6km follow the signs to Zelena Laguna.
Zelena Laguna Camping has a good range of facilities and an area of its blue flag beach is reserved for bare beachbums.

Bijela Uvala Camping is eco-friendly and located on an attractive peninsula. A section of its blue flag beach is available for nude relaxation.

The 3-star Hotel Parentium at Plava Laguna has a nude terrace for residents and the nude beach is a 2km walk along the coast.

▲ Many Croatian resorts offer naturist cruises, picture by Steve Thompson. Pictured opposite shows one of many hidden coves at Suncana Uvala in the Kvarner region. Pic from Fiona Ashley

Sveti Nicola accommodation
Hotel Fortuna
Tel: +385 52 46 51 00
www.riviera.hr

Zelena Laguna accommodation
Zelena Laguna Camping
Tel: +385 52 41 07 00
www.plavalaguna.hr

Bijela Uvala Camping
Tel: +385 52 41 05 51
www.plavalaguna.hr

Hotel Parentium
Tel: +385 52 41 15 00
www.plavalaguna.hr

Croatia

Funtana beach, Funtana village, Porec

A super nude beach on a natural peninsula with crystal clear water and little islets nearby ideal for swimming to. The usual rocky foreshore is backed by grass and trees and is part of Naturist Camping Istra. The large site with 1,000 pitches is well-equipped for tents, caravans and motor homes. You can camp right by the water's edge. Small admission charge for non-residents.

Practical info
The beach and campsite are signposted off the coast road, 7km south of Porec.

Koversada beaches, Lim Fjord, near Vrsar

A choice of rock or imported sand beaches at this famous nudist resort. The first and biggest naturist centre in Croatia, catering for up to 7,000 people, opened in 1961. There's also a small nude island reached by footbridge. A wide choice of accommodation, restaurants, bars and shops available. Plenty of space for camping. Volleyball, basketball, table tennis, and lots of water sports are on offer. There is an admission charge.

Practical info
Easy to find on the southern outskirts of Vrsar – follow the directions from the town centre.

Valalta beach, Lim Fjord, near Rovinj

An attractive bare beach across the water from Koversada and just up the coast from Rovinj. Valalta is another famous and long established naturist resort with lots of facilities including a super swimming pool close to the shore. A man-made sandy beach provides a comfortable alternative to the rocky coastline, of which there are several kilometres to explore au naturel. Apartments, pavilions and camping have a backdrop of vineyards and cultivated fields. It has received an award for 'Best Camping in Croatia' from the National Chamber of Commerce.

Practical info
To reach the resort, drive north from Rovinj for about 7km along the coast road. Valalta is well signposted.

Maschin beach, Red Island, near Rovinj

Maschin is the smaller of two islands connected by a short causeway. The whole nude islet is just waiting for intrepid naturist explorers. It is covered in pinewoods and has a picturesque shoreline offering a choice of places for all-over tanning. Visitors love it. During summer the nearby Hotel Sol Club Istria runs a snack bar on Maschin.

Practical info
Ferry boats from Rovinj take 15 mins to reach Red Island. Walk round the main island and across the causeway to Maschin.

The popular 4-star Hotel Sol Club Istria on Red Island provides quality accommodation in a delightful setting. It also has its own clothed beaches, but is only a short walk from Maschin.

▲ Warm sun at the end of a fine day at Valalta. Picture by Paul Carlson

Funtana accommodation
Naturist Camping Istra
Tel: +385 52 46 51 10
www.istra.com/funtana

Koversada accommodation
Tel: +385 52 44 11 71
www.maistra.hr

Valalta accommodation
Tel: +385 52 80 48 00
www.valalta.hr

Maschin beach accommodation
Hotel Sol Club Istria
Tel: +385 52 43 23 10
www.istra.com/jadranturist

▼ The Lim Fjord and sea at Valalta; Koversada is on the opposite side of the fiord. Pictures by Paul Carlson

Croatia

Sveti Katrina beach, Sveti Katrina island, Rovinj

A pretty au naturel area on a series of flat rocks at the edge of the water. This popular beach attracts plenty of nudes so get there early because the best spots are limited. Refreshments and toilets nearby.

Practical info
Use one of the shuttle boats from Rovinj harbour – the crossing to Katrina takes 5 mins. Then follow the footpath to the western side of the island, a 15 minute walk.

The Hotel Katarina is only a short stroll from the nudist beach.

> **Sveti Katrina accommodation**
>
> Hotel Katarina
> Tel: +385 52 80 41 00
> www.hotelinsel-katarina.com

Camp Kazela beach, Medulin, south of Pula

The campsite at Kazela is mixed, part naturist and part clothed. The nude section has mobile homes and large grassy camping pitches by the sea. An area of the pebble beach is reserved for naked bathing and is backed by sun lawns for soaking up the rays au naturel. There are sunbeds and parasols for hire. There's also an innovative new aquatic park with 12 mini swimming pools surrounded by sun terraces, but unfortunately swimsuits are required.

Practical info
The site is 12km south of Pula, and is signposted 2km from Medulin

▲ The award-winning and highly popular Valalta resort near Rovinj is particularly known for its large sandy beach – a rare treat in rocky Croatia. There's also a marina by the site and a huge range of sports available to guests. Pictures supplied by the resort

> **Camp Kazela accommodation**
>
> Tel: +385 52 57 60 50
> www.kampkazela.com
>
> **Rabac accommodation**
>
> Hotel Neptun & Aparthotel Pluton
> Tel: +385 52 46 52 00
> www.istra.com/rabac

Rabac beach, Rabac village, near Medulin

This lovely long clothes-optional beach where most go bare is at the end of a string of small bays backed by lush Mediterranean vegetation. Stretching over 1,500 metres of rocky shoreline interspersed with little pebbly coves, it has glorious scenery and great views across to the island of Cres. There are two snack bars just above the beach for refreshments – a swimsuit or light cover-up is required.

Practical info
The beach is easily accessible and has a large car park within 150 metres. Just take the coastal road out of the former fishing village heading east past the Hotel Neptun on the outskirts. The beach is reached shortly afterwards. Look out for the 'FKK' sign.

The 3-star Hotel Neptun is 300m from the nude beach, and Aparthotel Pluton next door is 400m away.

Kvarner region

Camp Politin, Krk town, island of Krk

An attractive nude resort for campers and caravanners on the outskirts of the picturesque capital of the island. Day visitors are welcome for a small fee. The popular swimming beach consists of fine shingle and pebbles. In addition, a large terrace overlooking the sea is furnished with sunbeds and parasols. There's even a naturist harbour to moor your boat. A bar, restaurant and shop are all on site. 250 camping pitches, but no accommodation to rent.

Practical info

It is a pleasant 25-minute stroll along the coast heading east out of town, or five minutes in the car. The Hotel Koralj is only 10 minutes' walk away and is owned by the same company, so admission to Politin is free to residents. Note that Krk island is connected to the mainland by a bridge south of Rijeka, so no need to use a ferry.

1. Camp Politin
2. Campsite Konobe
3. Camp Bunculuka
4. Baldarin beach
5. Camp Kovacine
6. Suncana Uvala
7. Kandalora beach
8. Stolac, Sahara & Ciganka beaches

Campsite Konobe, Punat, near Krk town

This appealing naturist resort is strung out along the pretty coastline – it has 500 carefully terraced camping pitches. There are many shingle and rocky beaches to choose from, all backed by natural woods. The distinct smell of fragrant herbs is ever present. The site has two restaurants, a supermarket and a range of sports facilities. You need your own tent, caravan or campervan.

Day visitors can park near the shore.

Practical info

The sailing resort of Punat is 8km by road from the town of Krk and well signposted. To reach Kanobe, continue through Punat and along the coast heading south for a further 3km. The entrance is on the right with another scenic kilometre winding down the private drive to the beach.

Camp Politin accommodation

Naturist Camp Politin & Hotel Koralj
Tel: +385 52 46 50 10
www.zlatni-otok.hr

Konobe accommodation

Campsite Konobe
Tel: +385 51 85 40 49
www.hoteli-punat.hr

▼ **Nice naked camping at Politin on Krk island. Pics supplied by the resort**

Croatia

Croatia

▲ **Famed for its naturist campsites, Croatia offers a warm welcome to au naturel visitors. Pic top left Camp Politin, other pics show the popular resort of Camp Bunculuka**

Bunculuka accommodation

Camp Bunculuka
Tel: +385 51 85 68 06
www.hotelibaska.hr

Baldarin accommodation

Auto-Camp Baldarin
Tel: +385 51 23 56 79
www.jadranka.hr

Camp Kovacine accommodation

Camp Kovacine
Tel: + 385 51 57 14 23
www.camp-kovacine.com

Camp Bunculuka, Baska, island of Krk

The pretty bare beach at naturist Bunculuka has stunning views across the water to the other islands and the mountains on the mainland. Set on steep slopes which tumbled down to the sea, the campsite accommodates 1,200 visitors and is packed with happy families during the summer. A handful of brand new mobile homes are available to rent, but they book up early in peak season. A range of shops and restaurants right on the nudist beach are handy for buying refreshments or more substantial provisions. Probably not suited to the infirm. And day visitors are required to park at the top of the hill! Well worth a visit though.

Practical info

The resort of Baska is 20km south of Krk town. The Camp Bunculuka naturist centre is 1.5km east of Baska, and is clearly signposted from the town; it can be reached by a pleasant coastal walk. A ferry goes from Baska to Lopar on the island of Rab.

Baldarin beach, Cres island

The Auto-Camp Baldarin campsite caters for 1,000 holidaymakers and has mixed dress codes. One part is a clothes-required section, but the other much larger part is naturist (no-clothes-required!) Most visitors bring their own tent or caravan, but there are 10 mobile homes available to hire. Excellent facilities and a naturist beach.

Practical info

Situated 3km south of Punta Kriza on the island of Cres.

Camp Kovacine, Cres town on Cres island

Rather like Baldarin (the previous entry), this is a holiday centre of two parts, with both naturist and clothed sections. An area of the beach is reserved for nude bathing.

Practical info

Situated on a pretty peninsula covered with olive and pine trees, and only 15 minutes' walk from the historic town of Cres. There's a grocery store, ice-cream parlour, restaurant and pizzeria. Playground with animation team for children. For those who enjoy sports, instructors provide coaching in scuba diving, basketball and volleyball.

Croatia

Suncana Uvala, near Mali Losinj, Losinj island

The name of the main beach translates as Sunny Cove and is mainly used by swimsuited visitors. Correspondent Fiona Ashley advises, "Take the concrete path to the left for 10-15 mins to locate the FKK section, which is clearly marked (small admission charge). There are flat rocks for sunbathing, so take something comfy to lie on." Toilets, shower and snack-bar. Many more au naturel spots nearby: Zlatna Uvala (Golden Cove), Srebrna Uvala (Silver Cove) and Cikat to mention just a few. In fact a network of well-marked footpaths through the aromatic maquis and pine forest should make it easy to find your very own deserted buff bay. Local walking maps from the tourist office.

Practical info
On the south coast of the island, 1.5km south-west of Mali Losinj, there are two sister hotels, both 3-star, within 200m of Suncana Cove – Hotel Aurora and Hotel Vespera, which are close to the Veli Zal sports centre. Note – the island of Losinj is linked to the island of Cres by a trestle bridge.

▲ **Superb bathing despite the lack of sand: the beaches around Suncana Uvala have flat areas for sunbathing and for entering the sea. Pictures from Fiona Ashley**

Kandalora beach, Palit, Rab town

This world famous nude beach is where the Duke of Windsor and Mrs Simpson swam au naturel in August 1936. It is often referred to as the English Beach and includes three coves, stretching for 1,500 metres in total. Bar and restaurant available.

Practical info
The beach is on the south of the Frkanj peninsula. A ferry from Jablanac on the mainland makes day visits possible. The Suha Punta holiday village is close to the naturist beach and has two sister hotels, Carolina and Eva.

Stolac, Sahara & Ciganka beaches, Rab island

Sandy beaches are a rare phenomenon in Croatia. However here at Lopar there are no less than 22 of them, including three undeveloped nude ones. The water is shallow, calm and clear making it ideal for families with young children.

Practical info
From the town of Rab drive north-west for 13km to the tip of the island. The naturist beaches are dotted around the Lopar Peninsula. Running from east to west they are Stolac, Sahara and Ciganka.

The Hotel San Marino Village at Rajska Playa (Paradise Beach) is close to the bare beaches – Stolac is the nearest, just a stroll away.

Suncana Uvala accommodation

Hotel Aurora & Hotel Vespera
Tel: +385 51 23 13 24
www.jadranka.hr

Kandalora beach accommodation

Hotels Carolina and Eva
Tel: +385 51 72 41 84
www.imperial.hr

Kandalora area tourist information

www.tzg-rab.hr

Stolac, Sahara and Ciganka beaches accommodation

Hotel San Marino Village
Tel: +385 51 72 41 84
www.imperial.hr
sanmarino@imperial.hr

NORTH DALMATIA

1
2 • Zadar
3 — • Biograd
4 5

1. Camping Strasko
2. Sabunike beach
3. Sveta Katerina
4. Camping Sovinge
5. Crvena Luka beach

North Dalmatia

Camping Strasko, Novalj, island of Pag

One of the largest campsites on the Adriatic, Strasko accommodates an amazing 10,000 visitors. Set among Dalmatian oak, pine and olive trees, it boasts a 2km beach. About a third of the site is reserved for naturists. There's a huge range of facilities and sports on offer including tennis and badminton courts, basketball and football fields, volleyball, table tennis, aerobics and aqua-aerobics, fitness centre, as well as bicycle, scooter and pedal-boat hire. Lots of shops, bars and restaurants. Mobile homes and tents to rent.

Practical info
The camp is in the north-west of the island 1km from the seaside town of Novalj. There's a 15-min ferry crossing from Prizna on the mainland to within 10km of Novalj. A road bridge from Starigrad Paklencia, north-east of Zadar, crosses to the southern tip of the island.

> **Strasko accommodation**
> Camping Strasko
> Tel: +385 53 66 12 26
> www.turno.hr

▼ Evening dip at Camping Strasko. Picture by Przemek and Joanna

Sabunike beach, Sabunike village, near Zadar

This is another rare (in Croatia) sandy and intimate beach for nude sun seekers. It is about 10 minutes' walk north along the coast from the village centre, while the main 'swimsuits'

beach is to the south of town.
Practical info
Travel north from Zadar for 13km to the village of Nin, then 3km west to Sabunike.

Sveta Katerina, offshore from Biograd

The little island of Sveta Katerina (St Catherine) is completely and utterly bare, on every bit of shoreline! There are rocky beaches and plenty of trees

which provide convenient shade.
Practical info
Taxi boats run from the quayside in Biograd.

Camping Sovinge, Tkon, Pasman island

Camping Sovinge is a picturesque naturist campsite catering for up to 200 bare souls on the south coast of Pasman island. Surrounded by olive groves and pine forest, there are two sandy beaches, something of a luxury in Croatia. The owner and his team offer a friendly welcome and the site is an active member of the Croatian Naturist Association.

Practical info
It is 2km from the fishing town of Tkon, easily reached by a short ferry ride from Biograd on the mainland.

> **Camping Sovinge accommodation**
> Camping Sovinge
> Tel: +385 23 28 55 42
> www.dnh.hr

Crvena Luka beach, Biograd, south of Zadar

This pretty beach of sand and pebbles is at Crvena Luka holiday centre. The naturist area is on the north side of the bay. The hotel, apartments and campsite welcome more than 1,000 guests at a time.
Practical info
From Zadar drive 25km south down the coast to the village of Biograd.

Continue through Biograd for a further 5km and watch for the signs to Crvena Luka resort.

> **Crvena Luka accommodation**
> Crvena Luka
> Tel: +385 23 38 31 06
> www.crvena-luka.hr

Croatia

Central Dalmatia

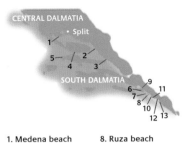

CENTRAL DALMATIA • Split

SOUTH DALMATIA

1. Medena beach
2. Nimfa beach
3. Dole beach
4. Paklina
5. Jerolim island
6. Sipan beaches
7. Sunj beach
8. Ruza beach
9. Slano beach
10. Cava beach
11. Lokrum island
12. Mlini beach
13. Croatia Hotel

Medena beach, near Trogir, north of Split

A typical Croatian pebble nude beach which is near the Medena holiday village. This popular strand has lovely views and there are restaurants and watersports at the nearby clothed beach.

Practical info
A regular bus from Split, 30km to the south, takes 30 mins and Split airport is only 7km away. The 3-star Medena Hotel is a short walk from the beach.

Nimfa beach, Zivogosce, Makarska

This rock and pebble naturist beach is set in picturesque scenery, very close to the hotel of the same name. It is open to guests and non-guests. The area is handy for the pretty tourist town of Makarska.

Dole beach, near Igrane, Makarska

This nude beach with crystal clear water is very popular and located at the western edge of the Dole campsite, a handy place to stay if you plan to spend some time at the beach.

Practical info
From Makarska travel south on the coastal highway. After 10km you'll pass through Igrane. Dole Camping is 3km further, on the right before Zivogosce.

Paklina, Zlatni Rat, Brac island

This popular beach is so pretty the Croatian tourist board often uses it in advertising. Paklina nude beach is on the western end of Zlatni Rat, which is often called the 'golden horn' because of its shape. A choice of watersports is available. There are more secluded coves for all-over tanning if you walk west beyond Paklina.

Practical info
Paklina is a short distance west of Bol town, on the south coast of Brac. Small ferry boats go from the town to the naturist beach or alternatively it is 30 mins' walk along the coast.
   Three hotels – Elaphusa, Borak and Club Bonaca (same company) – are less than 500m from the nudist area.

▲ Classic Croatian holidays. Above a naturist camp in the Hvar area, and below left and right pebble beaches are typical right along this coast

Jerolim island, offshore from Hvar

The whole of this rocky isle is a naked paradise – no clothes needed anywhere apart from the bar. Small ferry boats make regular crossings from the historic town of Hvar. It only takes 10 minutes.
Practical info
There are other naturist beaches and islands in the Pakleni archipelago, easily reached from town – just look for the boats advertising 'FKK', the German initials for bare bathing. Stipanska is another popular choice. There is no accommodation on the small islands but Hvar town is a beautiful place to stay and handy for the little ferries plying backwards and forwards to the nude beaches. Tourist info from www.sunnyhvar.com.

Medena accommodation
Medena Hotel
Tel: +385 21 88 05 88
www.hotelmedena.com

Nimfa accommodation
Hotel Nimfa
Tel: +385 21 60 50 82
www.hoteli-zivogosce.hr

Dole accommodation
Dole Camping
Tel +385 21 62 87 49
www.hoteli-zivogosce.hr

Paklina accommodation
Hotel Elaphusa, Hotel Borak and Hotel Club Bonaca
Tel: +385 21 63 52 10
www.zlatni-rat.hr

Croatia

South Dalmatia

Sipan beaches, Sipan, Elafiti islands

There are many small and pretty sandy coves where clothes-optional sunning and swimming have traditionally been the norm on this, the largest of the Elafiti islands. Prijezba is a particular favourite.

Practical info

Hotel Sipan at Sipanska Luka is an ideal base and has its own quay. The nearest sandy beach is 500 metres away, but the secluded au naturel coves are also nearby. It is 12km from Dubrovnik and just 1.5km from the nearest mainland.

> **Sipan accommodation**
>
> Hotel Sipan
> Tel: +385 20 75 80 00
> www.sipanhotel.com

Sunj beach, Lopud, Elafiti islands

This appealing sandy beach is a gem just waiting to be discovered. The long flat shore has safe swimming – perfect for children. Naked and swimsuited visitors happily share the shore dividing roughly in the middle, but nobody really worries. The stunning little island of Lopud is car-free, so a pleasant walk from the port is on the cards (1.5km). Mid-summer weekends attract Dubrovnik locals in droves – with costume-free folk seeking solitude elsewhere. Two beach snack bars: sunbeds and umbrellas for hire.

Practical info

Accommodation available on the island. Further info www.lopud.nl.

From June to August the ferry leaves the new Dubrovnik harbour of Gruz at 10am, but check the times in advance, especially the return!

Ruza beach, Kolocep, Elafiti islands

A beautiful sandy au naturel beach on the north-west coast of this car-free island in the vicinity of Villa Ruza, which is part of Villas Kolocep. One of the most southerly islands in Croatia.

Practical info

It is 6km from Dubrovnik and the ferry calls here three times a day.

> **Ruza beach accommodation**
>
> Villas Kolocep
> Tel: +385 20 75 70 25
> www.kolocep.com

Slano beach, Slano, north of Dubrovnik

Set in the same beautiful bay as the all-inclusive Hotel Osmine, where a secluded section of beach a short distance along the shore can be used for relaxing, sunbathing and swimming in the buff.

Practical info

The nude beach is a pleasant stroll along the coast from Slano village, 40km north of Dubrovnik.

▲ A happy mix of clothed and naked bathers make the most of Sunj beach's charming setting. Top picture: Valalta, by Paul Carlson

> **Slano beach accommodation**
>
> Hotel Osmine
> Tel: +385 20 87 21 00
> www.hotel-osmine.hr

> **Cava beach accommodation**
>
> Hotel Argosy and Hotel President
> Tel: +385 52 46 54 00
> www.babinkuk.com

Cava beach, Babin Kuk, Dubrovnik

A 300-metre long rock and pebble clothes-optional beach with good swimming, situated near the Hotel Argosy and Hotel President. Although there are no facilities in the nude area, the adjacent Copocabana clothed beach has refreshments available.

Practical info

Cava beach is 6km north-west of Dubrovnik town centre on the Babin Kuk peninsula and can be reached in about 20 minutes on the number 6 bus from Pile Gate, in front of the old town. Get off the bus at the last stop by the Hotel President, take the path past the hotel following the signs to Copocabana and on to Cava nude beach itself.

Croatia

Lokrum island beach, offshore from Dubrovnik

An established south-facing rocky nudist beach with smoothed areas for sunbathing. It is particularly popular because the number of clothes-optional beaches near Dubrovnik is relatively limited, so it gets busy in summer. There are quieter spots to be found by walking a little away from the main bare area. Occasionally breezy, but otherwise good for swimming – short ladders make it easy to get in and out of the sea.

Refreshments, showers and toilets nearby. The island has regional park status and is well worth exploring for the flora and fauna alone.
Practical info
Lokrum is reached by ferry from Dubrovnik old harbour, regular departures take 10 minutes to make the crossing. On landing turn left and follow the path signposted 'FKK Nude Beach', which is on the eastern side of the island. It's 5-10 mins' walk.

Mlini beach, Betirina, south of Dubrovnik

A lovely au naturel terrace has been built at the water's edge for all-over tanning in this secluded bay. It's said to have a friendly atmosphere. Welcome shade is available under the pine trees during the hottest part of the day. A real away-from-it-all feeling and a great place to recharge your batteries.
Practical info
Take the airport road south from

Dubrovnik and in 9km arrive at the pretty fishing village of Mlini. From the harbour follow the local coast road that goes south past the Hotel Astarea and ends just afterwards. It is then an 800-metre walk to the nude area.

The nearest parking is at the hotel. Alternatively, use a taxi boat from Mlini harbour – enquire at the Hogar coffee bar.

▲ Why not combine a cruise with some all-over sunshine? For details of naturist cruises along the Croatian coast and around the islands, take a look at www.nudecruises.nl. Pictures by Steve Thompson

Croatia Hotel, Cavtat, south of Dubrovnik

An attractive naturist area by the sea, perfect for sunbathing and swimming au naturel. Although out of town it has all the facilities of the hotel to hand.
Practical info
Cavtat is 18km south of Dubrovnik,

not far from the Montenegro border. The bare area is on the western side of the Sustjepan peninsula below the hotel, a 35-minute brisk walk from Cavtat town. An easy option is to drive or take a taxi to the hotel.

Mlini accommodation

Hotel Astarea
Tel: +385 20 48 40 66
hoteli-mlini@du.hinet.hr

Croatia Hotel accommodation

Tel: +385 20 47 80 55
www.hoteli-croatia.hr

Italy

Renowned the world over for its three millennia of history, sumptuous food and wine, outstanding landscapes and dreamy light, Italy has been attracting visitors for centuries. Bare bathing opportunities in this Latin homeland have traditionally been more limited than in neighbouring countries – but politicians and entrepreneurs have suddenly woken up to the value of the naked euro. This favourable wind of change heralds the possibility of new legislation to attract more freedom-loving tourists who prefer to relax in the buff.

Even without the bureaucratic change of heart, a steadily growing number of beaches are already being used as clothes-optional. For skinny-dipping travellers in Italy the pleasures of la dolce vita are definitely on the up. No fewer than three organisations represent naturists: the Naturist Italian Federation (FENAIT) www.fenait.org, the Italian Naturists Union (UNI) www.unionenaturisti.org and the Italian Naturist Association (ANITA) www.naturismoanita.it.

Guvano, Corniglia, north of La Spezia

This surprise hidden beach has nude bathing credentials dating from the early 1970s. It is situated on the Ligurian coast in the world famous Parco Nazionale Delle Cinque Terre (Corniglia is one of five renowned Roman villages on the Riviera di Levante). The dark coarse sand, pebbles and rocky shore attract an evenly balanced mix of swimsuited and bare bathers. Described as having a relaxed and 'alternative' atmosphere, this appealing cove remains as popular as ever with all-over tan fans. There is a modest fee to use the access tunnel and beach. Take your own refreshments for the day.

Practical info
From Corniglia station walk north-west and follow signs to a disused and privately owned railway tunnel. If the access door to the tunnel is closed, it can be opened automatically by pressing the buzzer at the side. The dimly lit walk takes 10-15 minutes before you emerge into the sunlight at the beach – expect to be relieved of a few euro for the privilege. There is a longer alternative path avoiding the tunnel, but involving a steep scramble. National park information is at www.parconazionale5terre.it.

Nido dell'Aquila, San Vincenzo, Tuscany

This long west-facing shoreline, backed by pine trees, has a 500m section favoured by skinny-dippers. Keen correspondent Marco describes it as 'one of the best nude beaches in Italy'. Technically its naturist status is unofficial, but that hasn't deterred growing numbers of au naturel visitors over the years. Golden sand and stunning views of romantic San Vincenzo to the north and the island of Elba to the south only enhance this favoured spot.

Practical info
Nido dell'Aquila (Eagle's nest in English) is set in the Parco Naturale di Rimigliano 100km south-west of Florence and 50km south-east of

Livorno. From San Vincenzo travel south on the coast road – Via della Principessa – for 5km and look out for camping 'Park Albatros'. Two derelict cottages nearby mark the start of a path through the woods to the beach, which is reached in a little over five minutes. At the shore turn left and walk south for 350m to the bare area.

The nude beach is only a short walk from Park Albatros, which has its own shops, restaurant, bar and bungalows for hire. Alternative accommodation and fine dining is available nearby at a restored Italian country house – Podere Tuscania – less than a kilometre from the beach.

Pizzo Greco, Isola di Capo Rizzuto, Calabria

Pizzo Greco is unique: it is the only fully naturist camping and caravan site in Italy that has its own nude beach. With yellow sand sheltered by low cliffs, this popular strand attracts dedicated buff bathers from far and wide. A gently shelving shore and crystal-clear water are the perfect ingredients for a delightful dunk. The well-organised Villaggio Camping Club Naturista has bungalows and caravans for hire, and pitches for visitors. Verdant eucalyptus trees provide welcome shade at the height of summer. A bar, restaurant and shop take care of everyday needs and there's a snackbar on the nude beach.

Practical info
From the Calabrian regional capital

Catanzaro, travel south to Catanzaro Marina. Turn left on to the E90/SS106 coast road travelling north-east. After about 30km a turn on the right is signposted to Isola di Capo Rizzuto. Pizzo Greco is in the Fratte Vecchie locality just to the north of Isola di Capo Rizzuto.

The international airport at Lamezia Terme, which is near the west coast about 75km away from the naturist resort, makes Pizzo Greco easily accessible from further afield.

Pizzo Greco
Tel: +39 0962 796222
www.pizzogreco.com

1. Guvano
2. Nido dell'Aquila
3. Pizzo Greco
4. Capocotta
5. Lido di Dante
6. Cala Gonone

Park Albatros
Tel: +39 0565 701018
www.parkalbatros.it

Podere Tuscania
Tel: +39 0565 705486
www.podere-tuscania.it

▲ Italy has fewer nude beaches than some of its neighbours, but the quality of the sea, particularly around the islands, makes for some superb nude bathing
■ Pictured on previous page: an early morning swimmer takes advantage of some peace and quiet before the tourists arrive to enjoy a skinny dip in Lake Garda. Picture by Christopher Gannon/Alamy

Italy

▲ When in Rome... forget the Versace bikini and head to Capocotta beach for some elegant all-over bathing on the soft sands. Picture supplied by naturist website www.geocities.com/birichino_nat

Capocotta beach, Lido Ostia, near Rome

Capocotta became Italy's first official nudist beach in the summer of 2000. Nude beach lovers had discovered this 3km stretch of coastline – backed by tall ancient dunes – long before then; but in those days frequently faced unwanted encounters with the police. Today a 250m section of the shore is designated for sunning and swimming in your birthday suit, although it still attracts a mix of folk wearing costumes among those who know better. During summer weekends the beach gets packed when residents of Rome – a short distance to the north-east – descend en masse. The local naturist association Uni-Lazio (www.unilazio.it) continues to lobby for an enlarged nudist area. There are toilets, showers, umbrellas, deck chairs, bars and a restaurant nearby.

Practical info
The recommended journey from the city is by underground train from the Piramide station in Rome on line B to Lido Ostia Centro. At Lido Ostia there is a number 7 bus every 12 minutes travelling south down the coast to Villaggio Tognazzi: alight after 9km at the Oasi di Capocotta beach bus stop. Parking in the vicinity is extremely limited, as in Rome itself.

Parco Del Gargano naturist club, Puglia

This rustic nudist club has stunning views of the distant Adriatic from its sparkling swimming pool. A real back-to-nature place with pine scented air, where tranquillity, peace and good friendship are the priorities. Space for campers, but don't be surprised to find yourself sharing your pitch with the local wildlife.

Practical info
The site is on the northern edge of the Parco Nazionale del Gargano, at Rodi Garganico. Contact the club directly to book a visit and for detailed directions. Although the site is close to the coast, there are no nearby nude beaches.

Parco Del Gargano Naturist Club
Tel: +39 08849 65333
www.gargano.net/naturist

Italy

Lido di Dante, Ravenna, Emilia-Romagna

This lovely Adriatic beach is surrounded by pinewoods in an undeveloped area well away from local industry and commerce. A kilometre of the long and sandy shore was granted official nude beach status in 2002. It now attracts upwards of a thousand naked souls at busy weekends. The three-star Camping Classe – half a kilometre from the bare area – has part of the site reserved for naturist holidaymakers.

The camping and beach are both handy for visiting the historic city of Ravenna just a 10-minute drive away.
Practical info
Lido di Dante is 6km south-east of Ravenna and well signposted; including the delineation 'FKK'. Watch out for Camping Ramazzotti and Camping Classe, where parking is available. The nude beach is 550 metres walk south along the shore from Camping Classe.

▲ The ancient Romans would have approved: a nude bather swims off the little island of Caprera, in north-west Sardinia. Unofficial nude bathing takes place at quiet stretches of coast all around this part of Italy. Picture by Paolo Curto

Club Le Betulle, La Cassa, 25km from Turin

This well-equipped and well-loved centre is set on the edge of the Lanzo valley. Surrounded by birch and oak trees, it boasts a large pool, Jacuzzi and sauna. Established in 1969: the first Italian nudist club recognised by the International Naturist Federation (INF). Chalets and caravans are available for holidaymakers.

Practical info
From the A56 Turin northern ring road take the SS24 west to Pianezza. Turn right (north) taking the road to San Gillio and on in the direction of Fiano. The village of La Cassa should be reached after a further 5km (well before Fiano): follow the local signs to La Betulle.

Camping Classe (part naturist)
Tel: +39 0544 492005
www.campingclasse.it

Camping Ramazzotti
Tel: +39 0544 492250
www.campingramazzotti.it

Club Le Betulle
Tel: +39 0119 842962
www.lebetulle.org

Terranera naturist club

Tel: +39 0564 954210
www.terranera.it

Camping Baia Sareceno

Tel +39 3387 816022
www.baiasaraceno.com

Camping Lo Scoglio

Email: loscoglio@loscoglio.net
www.loscoglio.net

Club le Peonie

Tel/Fax: +39 0784 96293
www.calagonone.com/hotel/
clubdellepeonie/clubdellepeonie.htm

Terranera naturist club, Montenero, Tuscany

This club, with the full name Terranera Naturist Agriturismo, is a 40-acre organic farm set amidst 1,000-year old olive groves, with a swimming pool, sauna, tennis court, horses, trekking paths and hot springs nearby. There is a large holiday home and a small number of campers can also be accommodated. According to the website – 'To live like Adam and Eve in paradise, who would not like that?'

Practical info

From Siena, Terranera is reached by travelling south-east on highway SR2. Exit at Paganico-Monte Amiata taking the road to Castel del Piano-Monte Amiata. Approximately 10km before Castel del Piano turn left to Montenero and follow the signs to Azienda Agricola Terranera.

Sicily

Lo Scoglio, Castel di Tusa, east of Palermo

This attractive campsite lies next to a pebble beach and translucent sea on the north coast of Sicily – and part of the long private shore is set aside for sunning and swimming in the altogether. The site has super views of the lovely Aeolian islands. Lo Scoglio is not far from the motorway and could prove a useful base for exploring further afield. Furnished apartments and bed and breakfast are also available. INF or club membership is required for naturist camping.

Practical info

From Palermo travel 75km east on the A20 motorway to the exit for Tusa. Head north to Castel di Tusa, then turn left (west) on to the S113 coast road: Camping Lo Scoglio is on the right after around 2km.

Nudist well-being

Across the bay from Naples, the pretty island of Ischia has been famed for its recuperative thermal springs for decades. Extravagant spa hotels have been developed around the coast to pamper jaded visitors. And no fewer than seven offer secluded nude sunbathing terraces:

Hotel Loreley
www.hotelloreley.it

Hotel Romantica
www.romantica.net

Hotel Terme Parco Maria
www.parcomaria.it

Grand Hotel Terme Di Augusto
www.termediaugusto.it

Hotel al Bosco
www.hotelalbosco.it

Hotel San Nicola
www.ischiadirecttours.com

Hotel Mirimare
(Apollon Sea Resort & Spa)
www.hotelmirimare.it

Meanwhile, 50km west of Venice, at Abanao Terme, the Hotel Leonardo da Vinci Terme & Golfe has an appealing nudist terrace in its attractive landscaped grounds (www.hldv.com)

Sardinia

Cala Gonone, Dorgali, east coast

Sporadic nude bathing occurs at quieter spots all around the stunning coastline of the island of Sardinia. At Cala Gonone parts of the long fine-shingle shore can be enjoyed without wearing a swimsuit. And a number of other pretty out-of-the-way beaches and coves in the vicinity attract plenty of freedom loving nudists. If you want to extend your nude holiday beyond the beach, Club le Peonie is a small naturist campsite 13km inland with its own swimming pool in the grounds of the Monteviore Hotel and Restaurant. Guests staying at the hotel are welcome to skinny dip in the pool and sunbathe au naturel in the campsite grounds.

Practical info

Cala Gonone is 106km south of the regional capital Olbia. Allow up to two hours for the journey by road – take the SS131, SP3 and the SS125 all the way to Dorgali. Turn left and follow the local signs to the beach at Cala Gonone.

Camping Baia Sareceno, Palau

This attractive campsite with its own beaches on the beautiful Costa Smeralda is not naturist, but it has a delightful secluded cove reserved for nude bathing and relaxation on the south side of the resort.

Practical info

Travel north from Olbia on the SS125 to the resort of Palau. On entering the town turn right (east); follow the signs to Camping Baia Sareceno. The site is just 600m from the centre of Palau.

Italy

The UK and Irish republic

One of the world's prime tourist destinations, for its history, culture and iconic landscape, Britain has long been overlooked as a place for naturist holidays. But a wealth of popular nude beaches and surprisingly positive attitudes towards beach nudity by the authorities are helping to change Britain's reputation for being stuck in the past.

The biggest drawback is not the weather – which hardly deters Scandinavian naturists on the other side of the North Sea – but a lack of any major naturist resorts. Even so, several clubs and smaller enterprises have done superbly well in filling the gap. There are more than 100 naturist places around the country, including a few that are within walking distance of unofficial nude beaches.

All told, nude bathing experiences in Britain have a rural and uncommercial charm of their own, while in the Irish republic, naturism is even more ad hoc, and only on unofficial beaches.

England
1. Sillery Sands
2. The Strangles
3. Pednevounder
4. Vault Beach
5. Downderry
6. Slapton Sands
7. Budleigh Salterton
8. Weston Mouth
9. Cogden Beach
10. Studland Beach
11. Eastney Beach
12. Blackgang Beach
13. Culver Beach
14. Shoreham
15. Fairlight Cove
16. Leysdown
17. Corton Beach
18. Holkham Bay
19. Ross Back Sands

Scotland
20. Cleat's Shore

Wales
21. Morfa Dyffryn
22. Whiteford Burrows

Irish republic
23. Brittas Bay
24. Inch Strand

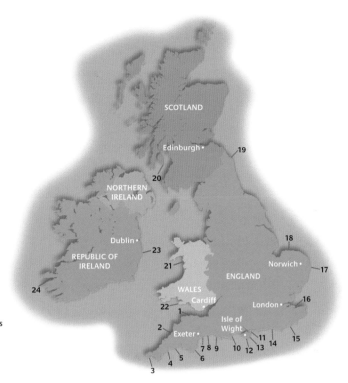

▲ The UK has much to offer naturists on holiday. Opposite is Durdle Dor on England's south coast: it is used nude at the furthest end of the beach, under the brilliant white cliffs, picture by Mark. Picture above shows the lovely and secluded Sillery Sands beach in north Devon

The Strangles information

Lower Poulza Post Farm (naturist) Jacobstow, Bude, Cornwall EX23 0BX
Tel: +44 (0) 1566 781520 (6pm-9pm)

Naturism in Cornwall

The NatCorn website run by Keith Gordon has details of Cornish beaches and clubs: www.natcorn.org.uk

England

Sillery Sands, east of Lynmouth, north Devon

This remote beach stretches for more than half a mile below dramatic cliffs on the edge of the Exmoor National Park. The shoreline consists of pebbles and coarse sand at this escapists' paradise. With a long tradition of nude bathing the few swimsuited visitors and the nude ones happily co-exist.
Practical info
Travel east from Lynmouth on the A39 coast road for just over a mile as it climbs Countisbury Hill. A small layby on the right-hand side (and about a third of the way up the hill) is the starting point for the footpath which leads to the beach. The path is steep but well maintained by the National Trust. The walk down takes around 15 minutes, but a little longer back up. Tourist info: www.northdevon.com.

The Strangles, Crackington Haven, Cornwall

A delightful place enjoyed by Thomas Hardy more than 100 years ago, though he no doubt kept his drawers on. The pebble and shingle shore gives way to large sandy areas as the tide goes out. Relatively sheltered by high cliffs and completely undeveloped, attracting a mix of swimsuited and bare bathers. A quick scramble over the low rocky outcrop at the north of the bay to Little Strand may be on the cards if there are too many clothed visitors on the main beach. Take care not to get cut off at high tide.

Practical info
Travel south from Bude on the A39 coast road to Wainhouse Corner and turn right to Crackington Haven. Take the lane heading south for a mile to the National Trust property of Trevigue, where there is roadside parking and the footpath to the beach. Follow the track down to the shore and turn right.

Naturist camping is on offer 5 miles from The Strangles at Lower Poulza Post Farm, with 40 secluded acres to explore. Local tourist info is available at www.visitcornwall.com.

The UK

Pednevounder, near Treen, Cornwall

This uniquely beautiful cove nestles at the foot of spectacular cliffs, which make access tricky but the views sublime. A golden sandy bay with bright blue water awaits anyone who can face the scramble down. The mix of clad and unclad bathers is about half and half – just the sort of laid back attitude that would put even a first time bare bather entirely at ease. The fine yellow sand, cyan waters and amazing rock formations in the bay could trick you into dreaming you're in the tropics, although a quick skinny dip in the sea will soon snap you out of any reverie.

Practical info

Park in the pay and display car park at Treen and walk down the narrow lane past Treen campsite to the coastal path. Don't take this main path, but cross it and follow the path branching off that goes much closer to the (very

steep) cliffs. A third very narrow but well used path leads off this down the rocks to Pednevounder. If in doubt, the picture on the right will help you identify the nude beach. It becomes a very steep scramble for the last section but if you have a head for heights the rewards are well worth it.

The 18th century Wisteria Cottage bed and breakfast, 4 miles from Pednevounder, is not naturist but the owners are naturist-friendly. Accommodation in the area gets heavily booked in summer.

Pednevounder accommodation
Treen campsite (textile) Tel: +44 (0) 1736 810273
Wisteria Cottage Tel: +44 (0) 1736 811021 www.wisterianet.co.uk

Vault Beach, Gorran Haven, Cornwall

A stunning bay of coarse sand and fine gravel which faces south-east. In an area of outstanding natural beauty, it enjoys a fine reputation for nude bathing, with dressed and undressed happily coexisting. The bare end is towards Dodman Point, while swimsuited visitors mainly use the opposite side of the bay. Take refreshments and shade with you. Although the descent to the shore is fairly steep, it is popular with families.

Practical info

From St Austell, take the road to Mevagissey, which can be a traffic bottleneck in peak season. Continue

south on the unclassified road to Gorran Haven, through the village and up the steep narrow lane to the National Trust car park at Lamledra. The footpath leads from here to the north-east end of Vault Beach. Walk along the sand to the south-west for the nude area.

Carlyon Bay Caravan and Camping Park is a 5-star family touring site near St Austell with a separate small field reserved for naturists (excluding August). Close to the north coast, Southleigh Manor has everything a naturist camper or caravanner could want. Log cabins also for hire.

▲ The South West is England's best region for beach holidays. Top two pics: Pednevounder. Bottom pic: Vault Beach, by Matthew Whyndham

Downderry, east of Looe, Cornwall

A series of three bays to the east of Downderry village, where the second and third ones are ideal for sunbathing naturally. The third bay is also popular with gay visitors. The sand is fairly coarse but the coves are completely undeveloped and provide good shelter when the weather is breezy. Care is needed to avoid being cut off at high tide.

Practical info

From the Tamar Bridge at Plymouth travel west on the A38 to the roundabout at Trerulefoot. Take the first exit following the A374 for 1.3

miles, before turning right on to the A382 (signposted Looe). After 2 miles, at Hessenford, turn left on to the B3247 and a further 3 miles on is Downderry. Parking is limited. Walk east along the road out of the village and as it swings sharply left inland, drop down the path to the beach. Walk along the sand (east) to the second bay, avoiding high tide to gain access.

The very convenient naturist Carbeil Holiday Park, half a mile from the village, has a swimming pool and space for tents and caravans.

Vault Beach accommodation
Carlyon Bay Caravan and Camping Park (small naturist area) Tel: +44 (0) 1726 812735 www.carlyonbay.net
Southleigh Manor (naturist) Tel: +44 (0) 1637 880938 www.southleigh-manor.com

Downderry accommodation
Carbeil Holiday Park (naturist) Tel: +44 (0) 1503 250636

Slapton Sands, Strete, nr Dartmouth, Devon

▲ Popular, pretty and hassle-free, sunbathers enjoy a long stretch of shore at Slapton Sands

Slapton Sands accommodation

Manor Farm Camping
Tel: +44 (0) 1548 511441
www.manorfarmstrete.co.uk

Hideaway
Tel: +44 (0) 1803 770549
www.hideawaybb.co.uk

This fabulous naturist beach attracts hundreds of swimsuit-free visitors. It's easily accessible and the shore has plenty of space for everybody. The views are beguiling. Rather than sand (as the name suggests) the beach consists of fine shingle. Popular with families, couples and singles of all ages and the atmosphere is warm and friendly. The sea is extraordinarily clear but the beach shelves steeply. Nudity is technically unofficial but there's no hassle: it's been a favoured bare bathing spot for more than 70 years. There is a hidden walled garden with picnic tables (not naturist) next to the car park – a children's paradise which is missed by many visitors. Toilets are nearby.

Practical info

Travel south from Dartmouth on the picturesque A379 for 6.5 miles through the villages of Stoke Fleming and Strete, continuing down the long hill to sea level. At this point turn sharply left off the main road into Strete Gate car park. In summer the parking fills early and once full alternatives are hard to find without a long walk. From the car park entrance a few steps lead down to the shore. Turn left (north) along the path at the back of the beach and in a few hundred metres small fishing boats and winches mark the beginning of the clothes-optional area. Bus 93 from Dartmouth to Plymouth goes right past Strete Gate.

Manor Farm, in the village of Strete, has pitches for naturist campers and caravanners. The spacious rustic site has a range of facilities, but perhaps the best thing is the relaxed approach taken by owner Kate Gill, who has reserved a third of her 6-acre site to be enjoyed au naturel. For those seeking a luxury B&B, Hideaway at Tamarisk Cove is on the outskirts of the village with direct access via steep steps to a traditionally clothes-optional cove. More accommodation and tourist info at www.slapton.org, www.strete.org.uk and www.dartmouth.org.uk.

The UK

Budleigh Salterton, near Exmouth, Devon

A long wide pebble shore backed by dramatic sheer cliffs of red sandstone. The nude beach here is officially recognised as clothing optional by the local authority. The pebbles are large so take something comfortable to lie on and footwear suitable for swimming. Delightful scenery and good access from the town centre make it a popular spot at this pretty seaside resort. There are no facilities on the beach so take refreshments.

Practical info
Budleigh Salterton is reached by the B3178 from Exmouth, or by the A3052 and B3178 from Sidmouth. From the main street (Fore St) turn into Rolle Road, next to Hardings the clothes shop. At the end of the road, walk down Steamer Steps to the shore and turn right (west) for 500 metres to get to the naturist area. Toilets by the steps. Limited parking nearby, but more availability within a short walk.

▲ A mix of modern attitudes and traditional English heritage puts Budleigh Salterton high on the list of places for naturist tourists to visit in the UK. Picture by Mark Ripon

Weston Mouth, east of Sidmouth, Devon

This remote, south-facing nude beach has gained many fans over the years. It has pebbles and shingle, with coarse sand at low tide. It requires about a mile's climb down from the car park, using a good footpath. The National Trust looks after the coast here. There are no facilities or shade. Good co-existence with the few swimsuited sunbathers and walkers in the area.
Practical info
Take the A375 north from Sidmouth and turn left on to the A3052 at

Sidford. After 2 miles turn right by the sign to the Donkey Sanctuary and the hamlet of Weston, where there is a small National Trust car park (additional parking at Higher Weston Farm). The footpath leads down through fields into Weston Combe and then there is a steeper descent to the shore. Most naturists turn right (west) on the beach and walk a short distance to the main nude area. There is an alternative path to the beach starting from Dunscombe.

Cogden Beach, West Bexington, Dorset

A lovely secluded bare beach of small shingle heaped up by the sea, the top of which hides the shore from the coastal path behind. Apart from some fishermen near the access points don't expect to see many other people, apart from a few nude bathers. There is no shade on the beach, but the car park at

West Bexington has a cafe and toilets.
Practical info
Cogden is towards the western end of Chesil Beach, a famous stretch of coast. The area used by naturists is easily reached by walking west for 15 minutes on the coast path from the car park at West Bexington.

▲ Happy seclusion at Weston Mouth beach. Picture by Charlie Simonds

Studland Beach, near Swanage, Dorset

This is the best known and most popular naturist beach in Britain. Managed by the National Trust, it consists of gently shelving fine pale sand backed by dunes and an extensive nature reserve. The sea is generally calm and offers excellent swimming. Refreshments are available from a mobile kiosk in the centre of the nude area, and ice creams are sold by a floating vendor. The whole scene is bustling but easy-going: it gets packed in mid-summer. The bare area is marked by green-topped posts and stretches for over 800 yards. National Trust wardens patrol on quadbikes and are on hand if assistance is required

(Tel: 01929 450259 or 01929 450500). Call them if you seen any inappropriate behaviour: there are a few selfish visitors at times, although they tend to stick to the dunes rather than the open beach. The National Trust has a visitor centre, restaurant, shop, toilets and showers at the huge Knoll Beach car park. Wheelchairs with balloon tyres for using on sand are available.
Practical info
Studland is on the north-eastern tip of the Isle of Purbeck, separated from Bournemouth by the entrance to Poole Harbour. A vehicle ferry crosses from Sandbanks on the Bournemouth side, or the village can be approached from

▲ Enjoying the sun at Studland Bay. Picture by Steve Thompson

The UK

▲ **Studland is the UK's busiest nude beach, with thousands of sun lovers**

The UK

Studland accommodation

Knitson Farm Camping
Tel: +44 (0) 1929 425121
www.knitsonfarm.co.uk

Dilly Dally's
Tel: +44 (0) 1258 840908
www.naturistbreaks.co.uk

St Annes Naturist Caravan and Camping
Three Legged Cross, Dorset, BH21 6SD
Tel: +44 (0) 1202 825529

BDOC
Tel: +44 (0) 1425 472121
www.bdoc.co.uk

Wareham using the A351, turning on to the B3351 at Corfe Castle. It is also well signposted from Swanage.

There are three popular routes to the naturist area. Our favourite is from Knoll Beach car park; just walk down to the water's edge and it's a pleasant 10-minute stroll along firm sand. The naturist area nearest the car park is particularly family-friendly. The second approach is to walk along the beach from the opposite direction, from the ferry landing at Shell Bay. The third route is to park on Ferry Road at Fire Point 6. A footpath across the heath to the nudist area is just over half a mile on soft sand. Arrive early to avoid traffic jams in summer. Dorset and Wilts Bus 150 from Bournemouth to Swanage will stop at any of the three places mentioned along Ferry Road.

Rural Knitson Farm camping is 10 minutes' drive from the beach: in addition to the ordinary site there is a small informal naturist field, but no facilities apart from water and waste. Dilly Dally's, near Wimbourne, offers naturist accommodation complete with swimming pool, hot tub, sauna and steam room. And close by St Annes Naturist Caravan and Camping at Three Legged Cross and Bournemouth and District Outdoor Club (BDOC) both have space for camping in the buff. Studland info: www.nationaltrust.org.uk.

Eastney Beach, Portsmouth, Hampshire

This popular and official city beach is in an area undergoing redevelopment. The beach is a few metres from the car park and a local bus route. The shore has shingle and coarse sand, so take something soft to lie on. The beach attracts a cross-section of visitors and has an active liaison group to look after naturists' interests during building work in the area (www.eastneybeach.org).

Practical info
It is at the eastern end of Portsmouth and Southsea seafront. Travel along the Esplanade and as it turns inland bear right into Melville Road. Continue to the T-junction with Fort Cumberland Road, where there is an adjacent car park. A path leads to the beach. Turn left (east) and the nudist area marked by a city council sign is within 100m.

Blackgang Beach, Isle of Wight

Long enjoyed by locals, this lovely south-facing naturist beach near St Catherine's Point has fine shingle. It shelves steeply, and with strong tidal currents care is needed when swimming. Super views and a sense of natural peace. Access requires a bit of a scramble and there are no facilities nearby.
Practical info
From Niton village, near the south tip of the island, turn into St Catherine's Road in the Undercliff and then along Old Blackgang Road to a car park. Take the path to the sea, turning left

(west) at the junction, which leads you over a previous landslip and, after a steep climb, down to the beach. Alternatively travel west along the A3055 coast road to Whale Chine, walk down to the beach and then left along the shore to the naturist area, a pleasant if strenuous 2 miles. In Brighstone, 15 minutes' drive away, naturist B&B, a self-catering chalet, sauna and massage are available at The Cottage. Naturist camping is available at Valerian Sun Club near Havenstreet, less than 10 miles from the beach. Tourist info: www.islandbreaks.co.uk.

Culver Beach, Sandown, Isle of Wight

Culver Beach is easy to access and near Sandown on the south-east coast. Chalk cliffs rise above the sand and shingle shore. The beach slopes gently and the water is clear so swimming is excellent. It's popular with naturists and often gets busy in summer.
Practical info
From Sandown, travel north-east along

the seafront (B3395) following signs to the zoo, which is almost a mile out of town. Park, walk on to the beach and turn left towards the white cliffs. It is just a 10-minute stroll along the shore to the bare area beneath the cliffs. Naturist camping is available at Valerian Sun Club near Havenstreet, less than eight miles from Sandown.

Shoreham, Portslade, Hove, East Sussex

Do not be put off by the grim approach to this beach. Although it is next to commercial activity, users describe the beach as delightful and it is screened from the docks by a high retaining wall. It's a pebble shore, so take a roll mat. Sand is revealed at low tide and the swimming in calm weather is good, but avoid going near the harbour mouth. There are no facilities but a stroll west reveals a bargain diner – a sort of beach bistro meets transport cafe. Many naturists prefer Shoreham to the very public Brighton nude beach nearby.
Practical info
From the centre of Brighton, travel west

along the seafront to Hove. Look for the windsurfing school at the lagoon (on your left) where the main road forks at traffic lights and veers inland. Proceed straight on at these lights and turn left at the mini-roundabout. Keep going as the road doglegs and snakes toward the dock area. A high concrete sea defence wall on the left marks the naturist area: walk along the pebbles from either end. There are 50 parking bays at the west end of the lorry park, but don't obstruct the commercial areas. Tourist info is available from: www.visitbrighton.com, www.brighton.co.uk and also http://tourism.brighton.co.uk.

▲ **South coast pebbles: top picture shows an unofficial nude beach at Taddiford Gap (see www.nuff.org.uk for info), bottom picture Shoreham. Pictures by Charlie Simonds**

The UK

Fairlight Cove, Hastings, East Sussex

▲ Views of Fairlight Cove, top right and middle left, and the surrounding coast, which is used naked for more than a mile on either side. Picture middle left by John Young

History was made at Fairlight in 1978 when the local council designated it an official naturist beach – the UK's first, although plenty of beaches were used naked well before then. Fairlight has had some access problems in the past due to coastal erosion, but regulars work hard to reopen it and at the time of writing it has very well built steps cut into the earth cliff. Naturists have returned too, and 100 or more bare bathers might gather on a sunny weekend. For updates on the state of the path and alternative access, visit the beach section of the NUFF website (www.nuff.org.uk). The bay faces south and has shingle with sand at low tide. The limestone cliffs and woodland backdrop make a beautiful place to relax as nature intended. If you walk beyond the main bay, be careful not to get cut off by the tide.

Practical info

From the A21/A28/A2100 junction in Baldslow (north of Hastings) take the B2083 (The Ridge) signposted to Ore. After about 3 miles turn right at the A259 (it's a T-junction with traffic lights and a traffic island). After 150 yards take the first, sharp left into Fairlight Road, signposted to the Country Park. After three-quarters of a mile stop at the picnic site car park on the left, from where it is a 25-minute walk to the beach. Cross the road and take the single-track road downhill. When you see the short row of brick houses, head right and follow a tree-lined gully (actually a dried up river bed used as a path). You basically follow this gully all the way down to the nude beach access; it crosses a wide walking track once you get into the woods, after which a small stream runs along the bottom. You'll have to cross a fence just before the woods end, after which the path starts its stepped descent to the beach.

The UK

239 ■

Leysdown, Isle of Sheppey, Kent

A breezy sweep of coarse sand and fine shingle on the edge of the Medway estuary, Leysdown bare beach is undeveloped and relatively uncrowded. Backed by grassy sand dunes, the 250m official nude area is well signposted at both ends by the Swale Nature Reserve. There are good views of Whitstable and shipping in the Thames. Swimming is possible, but the foreshore becomes increasingly muddy as the tide goes out.

Practical info
Access to the Isle of Sheppey is by the A249 and once over the river Swale, turn right after half a mile on to the B2231, signposted to Leysdown-on-Sea. Go through the town, following the road along the beach for almost a mile to a Y-junction by Muswell Manor, and turn left towards Shell Ness. The road deteriorates into a track, passing more chalets and cottages, for almost another mile. Park behind the nude beach, which is 100 yards away over low-lying grassy sand dunes. Tourist information is available from http://tourism.swale.gov.uk.

Corton Beach, north of Lowestoft, Suffolk

It's not the prettiest part of the Suffolk coastline, but this handy beach is officially recognised for naturist bathing. It's a well-used stretch of pebbles and shingle, with sand at low tide, just 2 miles from Lowestoft. The local tourist website www.visit-lowestoft.co.uk proclaims the nude beach as one of the area's attractions. The sloping shore makes access to the sea easy, and there is a row of groynes providing shelter from the wind. The beach is backed by a concrete breakwater, with a path that runs along above the nudist area.

Practical info
The beach is just south of the village of Corton. Take the A12 from Lowestoft to Great Yarmouth and turn off for Corton down the B1385. The road ends in a T-junction, where you turn right. Drive into the car park, marked by a sign saying 'Toilets' and 'Golf'. A concrete path from the north-east corner of the car park (left as you face towards the sea) leads across a road to the coast. Turn left and after 200 metres you'll see the signs indicating it's time to strip. Two naturist holiday sites, Merryhill Leisure and the Broadlands Sun Association, cater directly for bare bathing tourists and are within 20-30 miles of Corton naturist beach.

▲ Early evening at the end of another sunny day on Corton Beach. As the signs say, it's an official nude beach – the grammar might not be perfect but the decision to designate this a nude beach can't be faulted

The UK

▲ Enjoying the wide open spaces of Holkham Bay official beach. Pic top left by Matthew Whyndham, others by Steve Thompson

▲ The sea around Britain gets more tempting on the hotter days of the year. Pictures by Charlie Simonds

Holkham Bay accommodation

Bolding Way Holiday Cottages
Tel: +44 (0) 1263 588666
www.boldingway.co.uk

Holkham Bay, Wells-next-the-Sea, Norfolk

This stunning beach is vast – 3 miles long and over half a mile wide of beautifully unspoilt coastline. Getting to the bare area requires a moderate walk along pretty tracks and paths, so it's never overcrowded. Backed by pine woods and surrounded by Holkham national nature reserve (the largest coastal reserve in England), this tranquil haven is the perfect place for relaxing naturally. Helpful signs provided by the Holkham Estate and English Nature identify the nude area on the western side of the bay. The landowners are supportive of naturist visitors, but ask they use the open beach rather than the dunes, to avoid damaging the fragile plant communities.

The shore is almost flat so the sea goes out a long way: youngsters (of all ages) will love paddling at the water's edge, but note that the tide comes in quickly. Set on the East Anglian coast, the weather is often bracing. Wardens and occasional local police patrols look after the naturists as well as the other visitors. Take your own refreshments and a picnic for a great day out.

Practical info

Holkham is on the north Norfolk coast 2 miles west of Wells-next-the-Sea on the A149. In the village, opposite the entrance to Holkham Hall and by the Victoria Hotel, turn right (north) into Lady Ann's Drive and use the car park on the left. Continue on foot down the drive, turning left at the bottom, and follow the hardcore track. Pass a small saltwater lagoon on your left and proceed half a mile to the George Washington Hide. Take the wooden boardwalk which heads off from here and goes to the beach. At the shore turn left (west) to the signposted naturist area. The walk from the car park takes 20-30 minutes. Holkham is on National Cycle Route No 1 (see www.sustrans.org.uk) and is also served by the regular Norfolk Coasthopper bus.

Fifteen miles east along the coast, two of the properties at Bolding Way Holiday Cottages have private gardens secluded enough for naturist sunbathing, and are promoted to naturists by the owners. Tourist info: www.holkham.co.uk.

The UK

Ross Back Sands, Bamburgh, Northumberland

Blissful seclusion, endless soft sands and fabulous views make Ross Back Sands a lovely place to relax. It's not an official beach but there is enough space to allow respectful bare bathing, with dunes and sandy hollows for privacy. Even on a sunny weekend there may only be a few visitors. Nude bathers use the north section of the beach, overlooking Holy Island.
Practical info
Ross is not marked on some maps, but

it's fairly easy to find. On the A1, about half a mile north of the B1342 turning to Bamburgh, look carefully for a right turn to Ross, down a minor road. Follow the road and signs to Ross, where you can park outside the village. Continue along the road by foot until it becomes a driveway and then a path leading through fields and grassy dunes to the sea. Turn left and find a secluded spot all to yourself. Local information from www.visitnorthumberland.com.

Scotland

Cleat's Shore, Lagg, Isle of Arran, Ayrshire

Surprisingly, this away-from-it-all nude beach near the southern tip of Arran enjoys official status. The shore is fine sand interspersed with rock and shingle. Palm trees outside the nearby pub attest to the favourable effect of the Gulf stream. The views across Kilbrannon Sound to Kintyre are delightful. Look out for seals basking just offshore. Don't expect to find lots of other visitors, dressed or undressed, at this remote haven: you may well have the beach to yourself.

Practical info
The ferry from Ardrossan on the mainland takes just under an hour to reach Brodick on Arran. Take the A841 south, then west, for 18 miles to Lagg. It takes about 30 minutes in a car or 45 minutes on the local bus. Continue through Lagg and soon after the village a sign saying 'Cleat's Shore mile' points to a lane on the left. It's possible to drive down the gated track almost to the shore and park close to the buildings by the naturist section.

▲ A warm summer's day at Ross Back Sands – and no one in sight. This beautiful and unspoilt shore has views of Bamburgh castle (on the horizon in photo above) and of Holy Island in the other direction

Wales

Whiteford Burrows, the Gower, W Glamorgan

The Gower was the first place in Britain to be declared an Area of Outstanding Natural Beauty, and it's not hard to see why. To the north of the peninsula, at Whiteford Burrows, there are more than 2 miles of secluded sands backed by a nature reserve. Owned by the National Trust and leased to the Countryside Council for Wales, this lovely bay is surprisingly deserted. It's a fair walk to the remote parts of the beach traditionally used by discreet naturists. Strong currents in the bay close to the mouth of the river mean bathers should exercise extreme caution. The sand is soft and yellow and there are plenty of hidden hollows

to find a perfect spot for nude basking.
Practical info
Leave the M4 motorway at junction 47 taking the A483 south for 1.5 miles to the junction with the A484. Turn right here (second exit on the roundabout, signposted to Llanelli). After 2 miles turn left on to the B4296 for a few hundred yards, then right on to the B4295 to Llanrhidian. Continue on unclassified roads following the signs to Llanmadoc. There is a car park by the church. Walk down the gated track through Cwm Ivy and follow the path to the beach. Walk north (right) for 20-25 mins to find seclusion. Local info: www.llanmadocgower.co.uk.

▲ Welsh waves: a nude bather enjoys the surf at an unofficial naturist beach, Traeth Mawr. For more beaches in the UK, see the naturist guidebook Bare Britain, and check out www.nuff.org.uk. Picture by Charlie Simonds.
■ Opposite page: the spectacular Scottish Highlands offer some of Europe's finest scenery, and plenty of free space. Pictures by Stuart and Karla of www.nakedmunros.com

GREAT BRITAIN

PHOTO BY - RICHARD DANIELS

THE UK IS A PERFECT DESTINATION FOR YOUR NATURIST HOLIDAY, SHORT BREAK OR VACATION

EXPLORE the richness of Britain's history and traditions
ENJOY exciting and fun days out
EXPERIENCE the beautiful countryside and beaches

With a wide variety of naturist places to stay, ranging from self-catering accommodation, through Bed & Breakfast, to caravan and campsites and our large number of sun clubs, there's plenty of choice. We have lots of beaches used by naturists around our coastline.

A visit to Britain is a "must-do" activity for everyone - such is our place culturally and historically in the world. Naturist visitors can come and add on some naturist time too, basing yourself in a naturist place or enjoy the many naturist events that British Naturism also organises and participates in throughout the year – indoor and outdoor.

Whenever you plan to take off, make sure we're on your list.

Naturist holidays in the UK? Nothing's better!

www.british-naturism.org.uk
www.redletterdays.co.uk/eden

www.nudefest2007.com
Design - pmdesigns07@yahoo.co.uk

The UK

244

Morfa Dyffryn, near Harlech, Gwynedd

▲ Easily one of Britain's finest nudist beaches, Morfa Dyffryn has endless space for beach sports, sunbathing, or just strolling along the 1km of sands. Top picture by Charlie Simonds, bottom picture taken on a British Naturism beach day by Steve Thompson

Morfa Dyffryn accommodation
Benar Beach Camping
Morfa Dyffryn
Tel: +44 (0) 1341 247571 / 247001

This is Wales' finest nude beach and one of Britain's favourites. With an inspiring location in the Snowdonia National Park it attracts naturists from across the country and even visitors from overseas. Although Morfa Dyffryn has been a popular spot for stripping off since the 1930s, Gwynedd Council took the decision several years ago to make naked bathing official and designated more than 1,000 metres of coastline for enjoying in the buff. During hot summer weekends hundreds of holidaymakers enjoy the beach au naturel. The golden expanse of sand shelves gently into the sea, providing perfect conditions for swimming: water quality is excellent. The naturist area is a 15-20 minute walk along the shore from the car park and is particularly popular with families. There are no facilities so take your own refreshments, and a windbreak might come in handy. The extensive dunes behind the shore form part of a national nature reserve. Fine vistas across the bay to the Lleyn Peninsular and glimpses of distant mountain peaks inland.

Practical info
The A496 coast road between Barmouth and Harlech passes within a mile and a half of the beach. Between the villages of Talybont and Dyffryn Ardudwy turn seawards into Fford Benar Lane, signposted Traeth (Welsh for beach). A small chapel at the junction is a useful landmark. The narrow lane leads to a car park close to the beach and there are toilets nearby. A boardwalk has been constructed through the dunes on to the shore and a helpful display board provides directions for the naturists. Turn right (north) and after a moderate stroll along the sand signs announce the start of the nudist area. The Welsh Coast railway line from Barmouth to Porthmadog runs just inland, and the Dyffryn Ardudwy stop is less than 2 miles' walk from the bare area. Benar Beach Camping includes a small naturist area for tents and tourers. North Wales Tourism information: www.nwt.co.uk. Snowdonia National Park info www.eryri-npa.co.uk.

The UK

British naturist centres

Holiday centres around the UK

Opportunities for British holidays in the buff are many and varied. A growing number of venues are catering specifically for the nudist traveller, providing serviced accommodation, self-catering, caravans and camping. Whether it's a 4-star cottage at an award-winning naturist retreat like Pevors Farm in East Anglia, a back-to-nature venue in a unique coastal setting such as Tything Barn in Pembrokeshire, or a Cornish holiday centre like Southleigh Manor with all the facilities for a great family holiday.

Not to be outdone, many naturist clubs throughout the UK open their doors and welcome holiday-makers to stay over. Provided prior arrangements have been made to visit, swimming pools, sun lawns and sports facilities can all be enjoyed. On the outskirts of London, Spielplatz to the north and the Naturist Foundation to the south are both handy havens near the capital. Some of the more progressive clubs have even invested in high quality overnight accommodation. Claimed to be the largest family naturist club in the south of England, Heritage in Berkshire has a spacious new luxury log chalet complete with all mod cons for guests to use (see www.heritageclub.org).

On the right we have listed details of the most popular holiday venues and larger clubs that accommodate visitors, while on the opposite page we list many British naturist clubs that have some facilities for visiting naturists. For more details of naturist clubs in Britain see the guide book Bare Britain (www.barebritain.com).

Pevors Farm: UK naturism at its best. Pictures by Peter Brennon

Main UK naturist holiday centres

The following places are particularly geared towards the needs of visiting naturist holiday-makers.

Carbeil Holiday Park, Cornwall
Tel: +44 (0) 1503 250636

Little Crugwallins, Cornwall
Tel: +44 (0) 1726 63882
www.littlecrug-naturism.co.uk

Roselan, Cornwall
Tel: +44 (0) 1872 572765

St Annes, Dorset
Tel: +44 (0) 1202 825529

Southleigh Manor, Cornwall
Tel: +44 (0) 1637 880938
www.southleigh-manor.com

The Naturist Foundation, Kent
Tel: +44 (0) 1689 871200
www.naturistfoundation.org

Broadlands Sun Association, Norfolk
Tel: +44 (0) 1508 492907
www.broadlandssun.co.uk

Croft Country Club, Norfolk
Tel: +44 (0) 1354 638445
www.croftcountryclub.co.uk

Merryhill Leisure, Norfolk
Tel: +44 (0) 1603 881411
www.merryhillleisure.co.uk

Pevors Farm Cottages, Essex
Tel: +44 (0) 1787 460830
www.pevorsfarm.co.uk

Spielplatz, Hertfordshire
Tel: +44 (0) 1923 672126
www.spielplatzoasis.co.uk

Tything Barn, Pembrokeshire
Tel: +44 (0) 1646 651452

The UK

Naturist clubs allowing holiday visitors

The following UK clubs have holiday facilities of some description for visiting naturists. You will need to contact a club first to arrange your visit.

Tara, Gloucestershire
Tel: +44 (0) 1454 294256

Wyvern, Gloucestershire
Tel: +44 (0) 7754 417810
www.wyvernsun.com

BDOC, Hampshire
Tel: +44 (0)1425 472121
www.bdoc.co.uk

Diogenes, Buckinghamshire
www.diogenessunclub.co.uk

Heritage Club, Berkshire
Tel: +44 (0) 1344 775032
www.heritageclub.org

Invicta Sun Club, Kent
Tel: +44 (0) 1622 762903
www.invictasunclub.co.uk

Valerian Sun Club, Isle of Wight
Tel: +44 (0) 7931 281360
www.valerian.fsworld.co.uk

Blackthorns, Bedfordshire
Tel: +44 (0) 1234 782212
www.blackthorns.org.uk

Cambridge Outdoor Club, Cambs
Tel: +44 (0) 1353 741335
www.cambridgeoutdoor.org

Springwood Sun Club, Essex
Tel: +44 (0) 7789 044072
www.springwood.org.uk

Charnwood Acres, Leicestershire
Tel: +44 (0) 1530 243958

East Midland Sunfolk, Lincolnshire
Tel: +44 (0) 7734 882333

Nottingham Sun Club, Nottinghamshire
Tel: +44 (0) 7977 490428
www.nottinghamsunclub.org.uk

Sungrove, Lincolnshire
Tel: +44 (0) 1472 233712

Telford Naturist Club, Shropshire
Tel: +44 (0) 1952 610873
tncltd.freeservers.com

Ashdene, West Yorkshire
Tel: +44 (0) 1422 379500
www.ashdene.net

Valley Club, North Yorkshire
Tel: +44 (0) 113 250 3336
www.valleyclub.org.uk

White Rose Club, North Yorkshire
Tel: +44 (0) 1904 468293
www.whiteroseclub.co.uk

Yorkshire Sun Society, East Yorkshire
Tel: +44 (0) 1964 550699
www.yorkshiresun.co.uk

Lakeland Outdoor Club, Cumbria
Tel: +44 (0) 1229 821738
www.loc.ic24.net

Liverpool Sun and Air, Merseyside
Tel: +44 (0) 7967 884448
www.liverbared.co.uk

Manchester Sun and Air, Cheshire
Tel: +44 (0) 7821 805866
www.msas.org

Ribble Valley Club, Lancashire
Tel: +44 (0) 1254 878845
www.ribblevalleyclub.co.uk

Solway Sun Club, Cumbria
Tel: +44 (0) 1228 529764
www.solwaysunclub.co.uk

Western Sunfolk, Monmouthshire
Tel: +44 (0) 1635 40188
www.westernsunfolk.org.uk

Scottish Outdoor Club, Loch Lomond
Tel: +44 (0) 141 533 0233
www.scotnaturist.freeservers.com

Sunnybroom, near Aberdeen
Tel: +44 (0) 7794 711627

Nude bathing in the Irish republic

Although Ireland does not have any official naturist beaches yet, there are plenty of places to strip off. The Irish Naturist Association has details at www.irishnaturism.org.

▲ **Happy to be here whatever the weather: Merryhill naturist club in the UK, picture by Alan Avery**

Irish republic

Brittas Bay, near Mizen Head, Co Wicklow

Reputed to be the finest shoreline on the east coast, Brittas Bay gets particularly busy with visitors from Dublin. Two miles to the south of the main beach discerning naturists relax au naturel at this unofficial location. In fact more bare bathers enjoy this special place than anywhere else in the republic. With beautiful views, white sand, good swimming and space for a naked stroll – it's not hard to see why. No facilities so take a picnic.

Practical info
Travel south from Dublin on the N11 and 9 miles beyond Rathnew, turn left at Jack White's Cross (pub). At the next 'T' junction turn right following the coast, and in under 2 miles park by a group of fir trees and gateposts marked 'Buckroney'. Take the path to the beach, then go left (north) until fencing is visible up on the dunes – the naturist area stretches from here to the stream further along the beach.

Inch Strand, Dingle Peninsula, Co Kerry

The south-west coast of the country is renowned for its world-class beaches and Inch Strand will not disappoint – rated as one of the best. The 2-mile long beach is on the southern side of the famous Dingle peninsula and is backed by extensive dunes. It is part of a sandy bar that almost reaches across to Glenbeigh on the Iveragh Peninsula, to form Castlemaine's superb natural harbour. The entrance to the beach gets busy with textile visitors, but a brisk 15-minute walk south along the shore brings seclusion and open space for baring all – naturist nirvana.

Practical info
Travel 7 miles south from Tralee on the N70 to Castlemaine. Turn right on to the R561 coast road and Inch is reached after 12 miles. The main entrance to the blue flag beach is signposted and has parking available.

UK and Irish republic

Central Europe & Benelux

Although the Mediterranean has the biggest nude beaches, don't forget who comes and fills them each summer. North and central Europeans are huge fans of naturism and it's not surprising they also continue to enjoy their hobby back in their home countries.

Germany was the birthplace of the naturist movement 100 years ago and today almost every stretch of its coast has a nude section. The Dutch have outstripped their German neighbours: the country has the world's largest proportion of naturists among the general population. Even Belgium now has a legal nude beach – a century later than Germany but well worth the wait. Austria and Switzerland also merit a mention for their own lakeside nude bathing sanctuaries.

Although not exactly a mainstream destination for holiday makers, naturists are missing some fabulous bathing opportunities if they ignore the nude delights at the heart of Europe.

1. Breskens – West
2. Rotterdam Europoort
3. Hoek van Holland
4. Den Haag – Kijkduin
5. Den Haag – Scheveningen
6. Noordwijk
7. Zandvoort
8. Bergen aan Zee
9. Callantsoog
10. Den Helder

(Map of the Netherlands with numbered locations: Vlieland island, Schiermonnikoog island, Texel island, Groningen, Amsterdam, The Hague, THE NETHERLANDS, Rotterdam)

Nude bathing in the Netherlands

Surprisingly, there are more naturist club members per capita in the Netherlands than in any other country in the world. The Dutch certainly know how to make the most of those warm summer days when they do arrive, baring all in droves on local nude beaches and at dozens of naturist clubs up and down the country.

Nude bathing began to gain favour in the 1950s, but it was 1973 before the first official nudist beach was secured. Now most seaside towns have one and there are many more recognised au naturel locations on the extraordinary network of inland waterways. We list our favourites plus two excellent naturist holiday centres in this guide, while details of all the clubs and beaches in the Netherlands are available from the national organisation 'Naturisten Federatie Nederland' at www.nfn.nl. A useful source of information on naturist campsites in the Netherlands can be found at www.naturistholiday.info.

If you're in the country, the VVV Tourist Offices will happily point out local naturist places to you. More general travel information at www.holland.com.

We are grateful to British Naturism and the Naturist Federation of the Netherlands for providing additional information.

■ A naturist couple stroll through a park by a Danube nude beach near Vienna. Picture Ed Kashi/Corbis

The Netherlands

Breskens – west, Sluis, Zeeland

This huge expanse of unspoiled golden beach has a series of sea defences at wide intervals to protect the shoreline. Official naturist status was granted in 1985 – the first beach to gain the accolade in the south of the country. Traditionally it has attracted significant numbers of visitors from across the Belgian border: though slightly fewer since Belgium acquired its own nude beach in 2001.

Practical info
The bare area is reached by following the coast road west from the seaside town of Breskens, on the Scheldt river estuary (Westerschelde). Continue just past Nieuwesluis and via dune crossing 24 to the western extremity of the Zandertje. The nude beach is between marker posts 21-22. A pavilion snackbar is situated at Palm Beach 200 metres away. A new road tunnel – the longest in the Netherlands – under the Scheldt river opened in 2003 and has improved access from Vlissingen on the northern shore of the Westerschelde.

Rotterdam Europoort, Europa Way, Maasvlakte

Naturists delight in wandering this long breezy strand in the buff, often with no other companions but the sand, the sea, and if in luck, the sun. Handy for local city dwellers and visitors alike. During summer a mobile cafe parks by the access steps to the beach. The NFN naturist camping park Natukreek (web address www.natukreek.nl) is about 28km east (see listing on page 253).

Practical info
From Rotterdam follow signs to Europoort, then to Maasvlakte until a road turns off to the left marked Strand Slufter. Take the road to the end, and the nude section is to the right of the last set of steps. Plenty of parking nearby, but no public transport.

Benelux

Hoek van Holland, Gravenzande

There is a fine official nude beach on this North Sea coast perfect for simply relaxing and bathing as nature intended. The bare area is not especially large, but it boasts two snackbars providing refreshments and catering, which can be enjoyed au naturel. Showers and toilets available. This is another spot much enjoyed by Rotterdammers. Great views of the super-ferries arriving from the UK.

Practical info
The beach is north-east of the Hook of Holland towards Gravenzande. From Rechtsestraat turn to the right, then to the left. The nude area is between beach access Stuifkenszand and access Vlugtenburg, marker posts 116.12-116.62. Fairly convenient for buses and trains.

Den Haag – Kijkduin, The Hague

Kijkduin is one of two seaside resorts of the city of The Hague (the other being Scheveningen to the north – see next listing). With plentiful shops and hotels the resort is popular with German and Dutch visitors, as is the official sandy nudist beach. There is a long unspoilt strand backed by low dunes and naturists strip off in the area from post 108 on towards Monster. There are pavilion snackbars available within 200 metres of the nude section.

Practical info
From Kijkduin follow signs to Kijkduinpark Camping (clothes-required) at Ockenburg and locate the rear entrance across the road from the shore. Use beach access number 1, which is close by. Parking 800m along the road (Machiel Vrijenhoeklaan) behind the campsite. Just to the north is another nude beach, Westduinpark, between posts 104-105, next to the pavilion Moby Dick. Both beaches have reasonable access by bus.

Den Haag – Scheveningen, The Hague

This is an altogether larger resort than Kijkduin (previous listing) and has its own grand seaside pier and an FKK zone. Getting to the nude beach couldn't be easier – it's a pleasant 20-minute stroll north from the pier up the firm sand towards the town of Wassenaar. There's a snack bar, showers and toilets in the naturist section. Marker posts 96.5-98 indicate where it's OK to bathe in your birthday suit.

Practical info
Direct beach access between Zwarte Pad and Meijendelseslag. Parking by Zwarte Pad. A cycle track and secure bike storage are both nearby at beach access number 17. It is also handy for buses and trams.

The Kuur Thermen Vitalizee Spa (details on right) overlooking the sea and connected to the deluxe Steigenberger Kurhaus Hotel has mixed-sex clothes-free facilities.

■ The seafront at Scheveningen is a popular spot and though you can't go nude right on the town beach, you can strip off just a few meters behind it. Pictured is the Steignberger Kurhaus Hotel and on the left edge of the image is the Kuur Thermen Vitalizee Spa (the low, black building), which has mixed nude facilities. And the nude beach itself is a short walk north up the sands. Picture courtesy of the Netherlands Tourist Board

Nude spas in the Netherlands

It's not just the beaches that would keep a naturist happy – there are dozens of spa and wellness centres where costumes aren't necessary. Some of the best are listed below.

Amsterdam: Sauna Deco
A popular haunt for relaxing in the heart of the capital and as the name suggests it has a stunning art deco interior: an authentic atmosphere of Paris in the 1920s. Facilities include two saunas, a Turkish steam bath, cold plunge pool, hydro-jet massage and an outdoor terrace. Locals and visitors have no use for swimwear here.
115, Herengracht, Amsterdam
Tel: +31 (0) 20 623 82 15
www.saunadeco.nl

Amsterdam: Bliss Spa (Sauna de Keizer)
Located just outside the city centre, but recommended for its extensive modern facilities and au naturel ambiance. Steam room, sauna, hot pool, cold pool, chill-out garden and refreshments.
Keizergracht 124, Amsterdam
Tel: +31 (0) 20 622 75 04
www.blissspa.nl

Near Rotterdam: Elysium Spa
We have to include naturist-friendly Elysium, the Netherlands' largest and most exotic spa. It boasts a huge range of indoor and outdoor facilities and has a man-made beach, an indoor heated pool, an outdoor pool, outdoor salt pool, several Jacuzzis, three steam baths, six further types of baths, 12 different kinds of sauna, five separate meditation gardens, a relaxation area and a number of restaurants. Expect to enjoy most of the experiences in the buff.
Bleiswijk, 15km north of Rotterdam
Tel: +31 (0) 10 524 11 66
www.elysium.nl

Kuur Thermen Vitalizee Spa
Tel: +31 (0) 70 416 65 00
www.vitalizee.nl

A comprehensive guide to saunas in the Netherlands is at www.saunagids.nl (in Dutch language only).

▲ The dunes and beach at Bergen aan Zee are pretty enough to attract plenty of visitors – but fortunately there is space enough for everyone, and nearly 3km of nude beach too. Picture courtesy of the Netherlands Tourist Board

Noordwijk, south of Zandvoort

Renowned for its beaches and summer flowers, the seaside town of Noordwijk is also home to the European Space Research and Technology Centre. Heavenly bodies of a different kind enjoy an excellent nudist area on the shore outside the town centre, with a pavilion snackbar, toilets and cycle storage nearby. The place to bare all is between marker posts 78 and 79.5.

Practical info
Find the beach access at Duindeseslag towards Noordwijk. The closest parking is by the Staatsbosbeheer information kiosk on the Randweg, 1.6km from the naturist section. The well-known Hotels van Orange in Noordwijk has a super spa with nude swimming and use of the other facilities every Friday, Saturday and Sunday 6pm-11pm.

Zandvoort, 30km from Amsterdam

One of the best-known resorts in the Netherlands, where the city lies down by the sea in summer. The local naturist beach is 'world-class' and very popular on fine sunny days. It has a selection of no less than seven beach cafes, with sunbeds and windbreaks for hire. Showers, toilets and secure cycle storage. Marker posts 68-71 signal where you can leave your swimsuit behind. Super North Sea bathing here.

Practical info
Frequent trains from Amsterdam make the trip in 30 mins. Good access also by bus. Head south of town towards Langevelderslag, where the beachfront buildings end. There's a dune crossing for pedestrians and cyclists at marker post 68.5. Parking on the most southerly boulevard (Paulus Loot), and by the entrance to Friedhofplein – both 750m from the nude zone.

Bergen aan Zee, 50km north of Amsterdam

A lively summer destination with the highest (54 metres) and widest dunes in the Netherlands – rising behind the long nudist beach to the north of town – towards Schoorl aan Zee. This is a beautifully unspoilt location with plenty of space to be yourself on the shore. There are at least 25 campsites in the area, but the beach rarely feels crowded with holidaymakers because it's so vast. The bare area is between marker posts 29.45-32.25. There are

cafes not far from either end of the naturist section. Well worth a visit. Nearby Alkmaar is famous for its Dutch cheese market.

Practical info
The naturist beach is between Bergen aan Zee and Schoorl aan Zee, to the north. From Amsterdam, take bus number 168 to Bergen aan Zee and walk north. You can also approach from Schoorl aan Zee and walk south. Limited parking in the area.

Hotels van Orange
Tel: +31 (0) 71 367 68 69
www.hotelsvanoranje.com

Benelux

Callantsoog, Zijpe, North Holland

Callantsoog was named the first official nudist beach in the Netherlands, back in 1973. With a wide sweep of golden sand backed by extensive dunes, this unspoiled spot is well off the main beaten track. Nonetheless, plenty of discerning summer visitors make the effort to seek out this au naturel strand. Don't forget to bring a windbreak! There's a cafe near the north end of the bare area, whilst to the south the splendid 'Zwanenwater' wildlife sanctuary famous for its stork colony extends to 580 hectares.

Practical info
Walk 30 minutes along the beach south from town, or use the beach access at Kiefteglop, towards Sint Maartenszee. The naturist area is between marker posts 14.5-16.8. Parking nearby.

Den Helder – Falga Strand, Zandloper

An undeveloped wild nude beach backed by dunes and pastoral farmland at the northernmost point of the North Holland peninsula. There are no facilities here so come prepared. The naturist area is between posts 4.09-5.0.

Practical info
From the city of Den Helda travel south on the N502 coast road along Zandijk towards Julianadorp aan Zee. Parking with beach access at Zandloper, 500 metres to the south.

Texel island, south Frisian islands

Austerely beautiful, with stunning sand, this is the biggest of the Frisian islands, also reputed to have more sun than anywhere in the Netherlands. The dune landscape is a unique habitat for wildlife and about a third of the island is a nature reserve. Choose from two official nude beaches.

First nude beach
Near the ferry landing from Den Helder, the village of Den Hoorn has the first naturist beach – an exposed strand where you can cast your cares and your clothes to the wind. The bare area runs south from the Hoorndeslag (beach road) to marker post 9. Cafe and parking nearby at Witteweg. Just 2km away is the Loodsmansduin campsite, part of which is set aside for naturists.

Second nude beach
The second beach is at De Cocksdorp in the north, marker posts 26.4-27.4 – between De Krim beach access and the stream gully at the Slufter nature reserve. Parking at the Krimweg access up to post 28, where there's a cafe. A day with strong easterly winds would not be the best choice here!

▲ The wilder shores of the Dutch coastline have their own unique appeal for an unforgettable back-to-nature experience. Picture from the Netherlands Tourist Board

Loodsmansduin campsite
www.rsttexel.nl

Vlieland island, Friesland

North of Texel, this narrow island has a landscape of mostly dunes, interspersed with wooded areas and small meadows. The western side consists largely of sand and is known as the Sahara of the north. The good news for skinny dippers is that almost the whole coast is clothes-optional! Look out for a couple of spots which are clothes-required, by the marina, at Badweg by posts 50-51 and next to camping Stortemelk (dams 53-55). Everywhere else you can look forward to long naked walks: go as free as you like.

Practical info
Vlieland can be reached by ferry across the Wadden Sea from the Frisian town of Harlingen in 90 minutes.

Schiermonnikoog island, Friesland

Northernmost of the Frisians, friendly and traditional; very popular with cyclists and walkers in the undeveloped nature. The town council recommends two places that are best for bare bathing.

To the east, the FKK beach is at the end of the Reddingsweg as far as post 7. There's a beach cafe near the access. (Swimsuits are definitely required on the section of beach between posts 7-2)

Towards the west of the island, the remote naturist sands are south of the access at the end of Westerburenweg, as far as post 2. There are no facilities so take what you need – including a windbreak – for a grand day here.

Benelux

Dutch inland sites

▲ Holiday scenes at Flevo-Natuur, pics supplied by the resort

Naturist holidays in the Netherlands

In addition to the many naturist clubs across the country, there are two excellent holiday centres operated by the Dutch naturist federation NFN – Flevo-Natuur and Natukreek. Also, Zon en Leven is a group of nine simple rural naturist campsites: www.zon-en-leven.org.

Flevo-Natuur

Tel: +31 (0) 36 522 88 80
www.flevonatuur.nl

Natukreek

Tel: +31 (0) 18 141 49 24
www.natukreek.nl

Flevo-Natuur, 75km east of Amsterdam

Probably the largest and best-equipped naturist holiday centre in northern Europe, and which is open all year. Set in the lovely surroundings of the Hulkesteinse forest, Flevo-Natuur is the perfect place to escape the stress and strain of everyday life for a day or a week. There's an impressive indoor pool and sauna, an outdoor pool, a lake with its own beach, tennis courts, volleyball courts, football pitches, mini-golf, and extensive sunbathing lawns, to mention just some of the attractions. Sailing, windsurfing and swimming can be enjoyed at nearby Randmeren. Entertainment includes live music, discos, karaoke and bingo nights. A restaurant, bar, cafe and supermarket provide for everyday needs. High quality bungalow accommodation and lots of camping and caravan space. Day visitors welcome. Open to all, club membership not necessary, only ID.

Practical info

Flevo-Natuur at Wielseweg, La Zeewolde, can be reached in about an hour from Amsterdam using the E321 (A1) and E232 (A28) motorways.

Natukreek, Voorne island, west of Rotterdam

There's space to relax and enjoy the sun, wind and water at this beautiful camping park on the banks of Brielse Meer. Also, ideally situated for visiting the nude beaches at Europoort and Hoek van Holland (see earlier listings). If you are reasonably fit, the coast is within cycling distance. Freshwater swimming is on hand at the site and spacious play areas to keep young children happy. Luxury mobile homes are available to hire and there's plenty of ground to park your own tent or caravan.

Practical info

Travel west on the E15 motorway and at the end turn left on to the N57 south across the water. Once over Brielse Meer turn left again following signs to Natukreek.

Benelux

▲ **Bredene beach, full to capacity on a hot day. Pic by William Helsen**

Belgium

Bredene, Between Ostend and De Hann

This is a lovely wide nude beach of pale soft sand that is easily accessible and very popular. The naturist area was extended to 650 metres during 2006 to accommodate all the bare bathers wanting to strip off. Complete with cafes, lifeguards, windbreaks and beach chairs for hire, it makes the perfect destination for a family outing. Safe swimming and paddling in the English Channel. Press speculation is rife concerning possible approval of another Belgian nude beach to cope with demand, but no firm news yet.

Practical info

From Ostend take the N34 coast road north to the seaside town of Bredene. The bare area is adjacent to beach post number 6 and is well signposted. The nearest tram stop is at Bredene Renbaan (Hippodrome).

Nude bathing in Belgium

Belgium was just about the only country in Europe with a coast but no nude beach – until 2001. Belgian residents used to travel to France, the Netherlands, Germany or further afield to enjoy nude sunning and swimming at the seaside. But all that changed at the turn of the millennium when an official naturist beach was established at Bredene in the province of West Flanders. Since then sun worshippers and skinny-dippers have flocked to the au naturel shore and in 2005 the local mayor suggested making it bigger because it was so successful.

Belgium was also slow to gain its first nudist centres in the countryside, but not through a lack of demand. In fact the first club was opened on the other side of the border, in Holland, to avoid a local ban. Again, thankfully in these more enlightened days things have changed and there is now a choice of inland places to relax as nature intended. Details available from the Federation Belge de Naturisme (FBN), the national organisation (www.naturisme.be). One of the largest, best equipped and most progressive clubs is Athena, which has three locations: Ossendrecht, Meerbeek and Walmes (www.naturisme-athena.org).

Luxembourg

Camping De Reenert, Heiderscheid

Camping De Reenert is a lovely nudist holiday park in the natural upper Sauer region, north of Luxembourg city. Good quality facilities include an attractive swimming pool. Pitches for tents and tourers, and modern mobile homes for hire. Surprisingly, there's no charge for storing a caravan out of season between September and June (minimum usage fees apply – see the website for details).

Camping De Reenert

Tel: +352 26 88 88 1
www.fuussekaul.lu (click on the
Camping de Reenert link)

Camping Bleesbruck, Diekirch

This established family-run 4-star textile campsite has a separate, screened area reserved for nude camping, with 25 pitches available for unclad campers. There is a shop, bar and cafe with a terrace in the main part of the site. The resort is just 2km from Diekirch by the entrance to the Blees Valley Nature Park. It enjoys fine views of the Ardennes.

Camping Bleesbruck

Tel: +352 80 31 34
www.camping-bleesbruck.lu

Central Europe

Central Europe

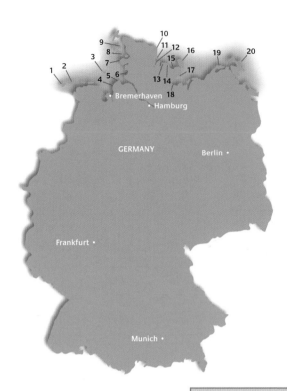

Atlantic coast
1. Borkum island
2. Norderney island
3. Helgoland
4. Wattenfreunde beach
5. Duhnen
6. Büsum
7. Zeltplatz
8. Pellworm and Föhr
9. Sylt (see map on page 258)

Baltic Sea
10. Glücksburg-Holnis
11. Weidefelder Strand
12. Eckernforde – Hohenhain
13. Wendtorferstrand – Bottsand
14. Behrensdorf
15. Weissenhauser Strand
16. Fehmarn island
17. Rosenfelder Strand
18. Timmendorfer Strand
19. Prerow Strand
20. Thiessow

Germany

Borkum island, East Frisian Islands

A short distance across the water from the Dutch island of Schiermonnikoog, Borkum has long sandy beaches, in fact 26km of them surrounding the whole island. A number of locations are clearly marked for nude bathing. One of the most popular – over 1,000 metres in length – is a short walk along the shore from Emden, the port where ferries arrive from the mainland. Toilets, showers, lifeguard and a children's playground are all to hand. Note: in summer large parts of the island are vehicle-free. Details of other places to bathe in the buff are available from the tourist office www.borkum.de.

Norderney island, East Frisian Islands

Visitors are asked to leave their cars on the mainland and use local transport, cycle or walk to explore the island. In summer a regular bus covers the 7km journey from Norderney town to the lovely naturist beach by the lighthouse on the north shore. Hundreds of acres of unspoilt white sand. Lifeguards, toilets, shower and snacks at the Oasis restaurant. The traditional and rather clever wicker wind-shelter-cum-couch (strandkorb), frequently seen on North Sea and Baltic coasts, can be reserved in advance through the local tourist office www.norderney.de. You can have one ready and waiting for your arrival at the FKK beach! Nearby accommodation at the family-run Villa Ney Hotel. The eastern half of Norderney belongs to the Niedersächsisches Wattenmeer National Park.

Practical info
The island is reached by ferry in about an hour from Norden on the mainland. It also has a small airport.

Villa Ney Hotel
Tel: +49 (0) 4932 91 70 www.villa-ney.de

Nude bathing in Germany

This is the birthplace of modern nudism or freikörperkultur (free body culture) – FKK. The concept of naked sunbathing and swimming as a health-giving activity sprang forth from Germany at the beginning of the 20th century.

Germany has two seaside coasts, the North Sea and the Baltic. In years past much of the shoreline would have been considered clothing-optional, but today bare beaches are signposted 'FKK'. They will be found on one side of the main resort beach or the other – and sometimes both! And don't worry about the weather either: at the height of summer the German Baltic coast enjoys as much sunshine as parts of the Mediterranean.

The multitude of inland opportunities for getting your kit off is legendry. At lakes and rivers across the land where the water's suitable for swimming, there's bound to be somewhere handy you can take a skinny-dip. Nude sunbathing in city parks is commonplace and covering up in a sauna is unheard of. Finally, there's a host of local naturist clubs to visit. Further information is available from the national organisation Deutscher Verband für Freikörperkultur www.dfk.org – in German, but easily translated using http://translate.google.com. The same goes for some of the other sites we've recommended. Additional holiday ideas at www.naturistholiday.info.

▲ One of the most interesting places to lose yourself and your swimsuit: Helgoland island has historical significance and vast beaches. Pictures supplied by the Helgoland Tourist Office

Helgoland, East Frisian Islands

This is a fascinating place – a small archipelago consisting of two main islands – located 70km from the German mainland. The larger of the islands is inhabited, but the smaller one, known as Dune, has just a handful of summer holiday homes for rent. A historically strategic outpost that in the past has been British and Danish. Once a Viking stronghold, but more recently during World War II a Nazi submarine base. No visiting vehicles are allowed, but minibuses and electric carts provide easy transport. The island has stunning sandy shores and the main naturist beach is no exception: clearly marked on the north coast. Some say it's like being in the South Seas – without the palm trees. Discreet mixed bathing (with and without costumes) is common elsewhere. Take the boat to Dune and play Robinson Crusoe for the day, or if you're feeling more adventurous book a beach chalet and stay for a while.

Practical info
Helgoland is reached by a two-hour ferry crossing from Cuxhaven at the mouth of the River Elbe, or by small plane. Tourist info www.helgoland.de.

Wattenfreunde beach and camping, Spieka

This remote foreshore and naturist campsite sit on low-lying ground in a protected area of the Wattenmeer national park, at Cappel Neufeld to the south-west of Cuxhaven. The site is unusual in Germany because strictly speaking it's clothes-optional and all are welcome – dressed and undressed. Sea swimming is only practical around high tide: amazing mudflats emerge as the water recedes. The sandy beach is divided into a swimsuited section and a naturist one. Each has its own volleyball pitch. The salt meadows are home to a wealth of flora and fauna. The camp has caravans for hire and is open from the beginning of May until mid-September. There's a restaurant and mini-shop selling fresh bread and essential provisions. Day-visitors welcome.

Practical info
Leave the A27 Bremen to Cuxhaven motorway at exit 3, and turn west on to the K14 heading for Nordholz. At the next roundabout take the L135 signposted to Spieka-Strände. From Spieka follow signs to Cappel Neufeld.

Duhnen, Cuxhaven, Lower Saxony

A stunning white beach with a long tradition of nude bathing, which is strongly promoted by the local tourist office. Today Cuxhaven is a popular holiday resort and port at the mouth of the River Elbe, but it was formerly a centre for German rocket development and testing during World War II, including the infamous V2.

Practical info
From Cuxhaven travel 3km north-west to the small resort of Duhnen. The FKK area is at the western end of Duhnen beach, just beyond the promenade and is clearly marked on the tourist office map www.duhnen.de. More tourist information is available at www.cuxhaven.de.

Non-naturist camping and modern holiday apartments are available in the resort, at Campingplatz Duhnen and Apartments Duhnen.

Campingplatz Wattenfreunde

Tel: +49 (0) 421 87 43 85
www.wattenfreunde.de

Campingplatz Duhnen

Tel: +49 (0) 4721 42 61 61
www.campingplatz-duhnen.de

Apartments Duhnen

Tel: +49 (0) 4721 40 02 00
www.appartementhaus-duene.de

Central Europe

Büsum, Heide, Schleswig-Holstein

A 700m lawn on a grassy bank above the foreshore is signposted for relaxing in the buff at the resort of Büsum. You can swim at high tide, but the retreating sea reveals extensive mudflats. Showers and parking.

Practical info
Take the A23 motorway north from Hamburg, turn off at junction 2 after Heide. Take the local road west to Büsum. Tourist info and places to stay: www.buesum-info.de/buesum-fkk.htm.

Zeltplatz, Amrum, North Frisian Islands

Blindingly white beaches surround this lovely island off the north-west coast of Germany. It has the benefit of a huge naturist campsite in the dunes adjacent to the nude beach, called FKK Zeltplatz. The well-equipped site is operated by the country's official naturist federation DFK and is particularly popular with families.

Camping equipment is available to hire and there are sports and play areas.
Practical info
The beautiful bare beach is near the lighthouse where there are hundreds of acres to be yourself. Cars are allowed on the island, but there is only one road! Ferry from Dagebüll on the mainland. Tourist info: www.amrum.de.

FKK Zeltplatz

Tel: +49 (0) 51112 68 55 00 (DFK HQ Hanover)
www.fkk-amrum.de

Pellworm and Föhr, North Frisian Islands

Two more islands in this group have nude beaches. On Pellworm it's actually a meadow next to the sea, with steps down to the water. The area is designated for sunning au naturel and there's a restaurant, kiosk and parking nearby. Pellworm FKK-Strand Hoern is at Nordermühle, on the north-west coast. Tourist info is available at www.pellworm.de.

Föhr nude beach
The island of Föhr has a beautiful white sand nude beach on the south-west shore, at Goting in the Nieblum area. Lifeguard, shower and beach chairs for hire. Tourist info www.foehr.de. Park at Badstrande (Klafwai), then walk west along the shore beside Gotingkliff to the large FKK zone. Can also be reached via Wikingwai.

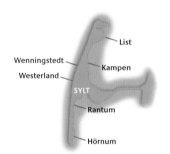

Sylt nude beaches, North Frisian Islands

Hörnum, Sylt's southernmost community, has a huge nude beach 15 minutes' stroll from the village – head west to the shore and then south down the extensive white sands. The campsite to the north of the village is not far from another bare beach. Boats sail to the islands of Föhr, Amrum and Helgoland. Tourist info www.hoernum.de.

Travelling up the coast, to the south of Rantum there are two excellent nude beaches – Samoa and Sansibar (Zanzibar), together with a beach sauna. The island is at its narrowest here, just 400 metres wide. Tourist and campsite info www.rantum.de.

Westerland, in the centre of the 40km long island, has its naturist area 45 minutes' stroll south down the shore. Nearby camping can be found at www.campingplatz-westerland.de.

Wenningstedt's 1km naturist beach, backed by low cliffs north of the resort, goes by the intriguing name of Abessinien. The local campsite has a

boardwalk west through the dunes with steps on to the shore, part of which is designated FKK. Tourist and camping info www.wenningstedt.de.

Further up the coast, the elegant resort of Kampen has 3km of nude beaches beneath low red cliffs, which reach north and south of a clothed central section. The northern FKK area by the village of Buhne has attracted much media attention over the years. Tourist info www.wenningstedt.de, camping www.campen-in-kampen.de.

List, in north Sylt, has breathtaking white beaches on the east and west coasts. The superb official naturist beach is due west of the village and starts 300m south of the swimsuits-required area (Strand bei der Weststrandhalle) by post marker 19. Parking, kiosk and toilets by the FKK zone access. A local bus runs from List to the shore. Ferries from List go to the Danish island of Rømø. Tourist info www.list.de.

Nude bathing on Sylt

Most northerly of the Frisian Islands, Sylt has a special place in the hearts of naturists. Way back in 1850 a certain Dr Jenner advised his patients to bathe naked in the sea at Westerland, the island capital. It caught on and since the 1920s Sylt has attracted hundreds of thousands of bare bathers. And with something of a sophisticated air, don't be surprised to bump into the occasional German celebrity here. Nudists are well catered for with cabanas, windbreaks, sunbeds, showers, refreshments, lifeguards, convenient lodgings and great nightlife. With 660,000 annual visitors, it's estimated 60 per cent enjoy free body culture (FKK) during their stay.

The island is joined to the mainland by a railway line on a causeway. Cars are transported to Sylt by train, and in 2006 direct low-cost flights started from a range of European destinations (see www.airberlin.com). Tourist info from www.sylt.de and www.sylt.strandtester.de.

▲ Sylt's iconic sunbathing chairs –
used on naturist and non-naturist
(pictured above) beaches alike. Pic
©iStockphoto.com/Philipp Baer

Germany – Baltic coast

Glücksburg-Holnis, Flensburger Fjord

This sheltered white sand beach has a gentle slope into the calm sea: very safe for young children. 250m of shore is available for bathing in the buff. Next to the beach, Ostseecamp Glücksburg-Holnis camping (clothed) has good facilities, especially for kids.

A very scenic area for cycling – bikes available to rent. Tourist information from www.gluecksburg-ostsee.de.

Practical info
Travel east on route 199 from Flensburg and fork left to Glücksburg, then follow the signs to the campsite.

Weidefelder Strand, Kappeln, Schönhagen

A 400m-wide expanse of soft golden sand has been reserved for naturist bathers. The shore faces east, shelves gently and offers excellent swimming. Nearby there's a cafe called 'Lobster' and plenty of parking (2 euro).

Practical info
From Kappeln take the bridge over the River Schlei and turn left on to the L286. Shortly after Olpenitz turn right at the crossroads into Weidefelder Weg and continue to the beach.

Eckernforde – Hohenhain, Eckernforde bay

Eckernforde claims to be the oldest seaside resort in Germany, established more than 170 years ago. The nude beach is on the south side of the bay, about 12km away. The bare area is almost 1km long, between the villages of Surendorf and Dänisch-Nienhof.

Practical info
From Kiel take the B503. Go right on the K19 to Sprenge, via Scharnhagen. Turn right for Dänisch-Nienhof. On entering the village turn left on to Eckernforder Strasse and next right into Strandkoppel, which ends by the beach.

Central Europe

Ostseecamp Glücksburg-Holnis

Tel: +49 (0) 4631 62 20 71
www.ostseecamp-holnis.de

Wendtorferstrand – Bottsand, Laboe

This lovely, unspoilt, white-sand nude beach shelves gently into the sea and is backed by low grassy dunes. It can attract thousands of bare bathers on fine sunny days in summer. A cycle track runs behind the beach.

Practical info
From Kiel take the B502 in the direction of Schonberg, but fork left to the Wendtorf Marina, where there is a car park. Walk 1.2km along the dyke to Bottsand. Tourist info www.bottsand.de.

Behrensdorf, between Kiel and Lubeck

A broad sweep of sand and pebbles in a romantic setting. The main access to the beach is textile but turn right and walk east: in no time at all the swimsuits disappear. You could walk up to 10km naked towards the village of Lippe. The shore becomes increasingly wild the farther you go. 'Camping Schuld' is close to the beach. Tourist info www.behrensdorf-ostsee.de.

Practical info
Travel east from Kiel on the B202 to Lutjenburg and turn left in the village and follow signs to Behrensdorf Strand.

Weissenhauser Strand, Wangels

This picturesque stretch of shoreline has 400m reserved for nudists. Behind the beach there's an impressive holiday centre with just about every conceivable facility. Clothes are required in the resort (except the spa), but the FKK beach is only a short walk to the west.

Practical info
Weissenhauser Strand is 6km north-west of Oldenberg in Hochwachter bay. Free transport from Oldenberg station for guests of the holiday centre.

Fehmarn island, between Kiel and Lubeck

Fehmarn island is one of the sunniest places in Germany – with two popular nude beaches. Both are next to award-winning camping and caravan sites. Wulfener Hals holiday centre is outside Burg, the largest town on the island and a short distance east of the bridge to the mainland. The fine white-sand naturist beach next to the site has a direct path to it. Wallnau holiday centre is on the west coast of the island. The sand and pebble beach directly in front of the camp is split in half: swimsuits on the right and birthday suits on the left.

Rosenfelder Strand FKK Camping, Dahme

This naturist camping and caravan site has 1km of sand and pebble beach. The beach faces east: sunrise over the Baltic is a spectacle well worth an early start. Visitors can bring their own tents and caravans and there are also mobile homes and chalets to hire. The camp is a member of the German Naturist Federation (DFK): INF or naturist club cards required, but the beach is open to all. If you prefer staying at a traditional centre, Camping Stieglitz is next door to Rosenfelder FKK and shares the same nude beach.

Timmendorfer Strand – Scharbeutz, Lubeck

This stylish resort attracts visitors from across the world. The official nude beach is on the north side of town towards Scharbeutz, part of a fine 6km strand with all the usual wicker beach baskets and other facilities. The Ostee Therme swimming complex next to the FKK beach has a completely naturist Sauna-Paradies area, including saunas, steam room and whirlpools. It even has a nude sunbathing terrace overlooking the sea.. The Maritim ClubHotel is close to both.

Practical info
Timmendorfer Strand is 15km north of Lubeck and 85km from Hamburg. Low-cost airlines recently began flights to Lubeck from France, Italy, Poland, Sweden, the UK and Ireland. Tourist info www.timmendorfer-strand.de.

▲ Spectacular cliffs on Germany's Baltic coast. The shore is surprisingly suitable for summer holidays, as it gets as much sun as parts of the Med during the hottest part of the year. Picture ©iStockphoto.com/ Guenther Dr Hollaender

Camping Schuld
Tel: +49 (0) 4381 41 65 45
www.schuldt-behrensdorf.de

Weissenhauser Strand Resort
Tel: +49 (0) 436 15 50
www.weissenhaeuserstrand.de

Wulfener Hals
Tel: +49 (0) 4371 86 28
www.wulfenerhals.de

Wallnau
Tel: +49 (0) 437 24 56
www.strandcamping.de

Rosenfelder Strand FKK Camping
Tel: +49 (0) 436 52 22
www.fkkcamping-ostsee.de

Camping Stieglitz
Tel: +49 (0) 4364 14 35
www.camping-stieglitz.de

Ostee-Therme and Sauna-Paradies
Tel: +49 (0) 4503 35 260
www.ostsee-therme.de

Maritim ClubHotel
Tel: +49 (0) 4503 60 70
www.maritim.de

Central Europe

Prerow Camping (Textile & FKK)

Tel: +49 (0) 382 33 - 3 31
www.regenbogen-camp.de

Camping-Oase

Tel: +49 (0) 383 08 22 86
www.jebensnet.de

Prerow Strand, Darss peninsula

This gleaming snow-white nude beach, with au naturel camping in the dunes, is much admired. Prerow campsite has two parts, one for nudes and the other for clothes. You can book caravans or ready-erected tents with under-floor heating! The site has great facilities and is popular with young visitors.

Practical info
From Rostock take the E22/B105 in the direction of Stralsund and turn left at Lobintz on to the L23 towards Barth. Approaching the village, fork left on to the L21 to Prerow. The naturist beach and campsite are on the north side of Prerow.

Thiessow, Rügen island

Another nude beach of fine white sand with a campsite next door can be found at Thiessow, on the pretty island of Rügen. This is the largest German island in the Baltic, linked to the mainland by a causeway. The FKK strand is in the beautiful Rügen-southeast biosphere reserve, on the outskirts of the village. Camping-Oase is across the road from the popular 2km nude beach (the northern side of the site is next to the bare area). Car parking 100m from the beach. Tourist info: www.ostseebad-thiessow.de. There are at least a dozen more nude bathing locations on the island – details from www.ruegen.de.

Practical info
From Stralsund on the mainland, cross the roadbridge and travel east on the E22/E251 to the island capital of Bergen. Continue east on the B196 to Gohren, and then south by minor road to Thiessow.

Wannsee, pictured right, is a huge lake where Berliners gather in droves on hot days. Both nude and clothed bathers enjoy the waters here. Picture by Rod Burkey

Nude bathing and spas in Berlin
Germany's capital is not short of places to catch a few rays in the buff, or to relax au naturel at one of the city's excellent saunas – particularly the Europa Centre Thermen (see below). Many of the downtown parks, as well as those on the outskirts, have places for sunbathing as nature intended and even skinny-dipping sans costume. Tourist info www.berlin.de (available in English).

Europa Centre Thermen
The largest sauna and spa in the heart of Berlin includes an outdoor sunbathing terrace and swimming pool. With its penthouse location and clothes-optional policy (except in the saunas – nude only) it provides panoramic views over the city whilst you relax and unwind. There are no less than eight different saunas and a range of wellness options. Visitors enjoying the sun in the buff are undeterred by nearby offices blocks overlooking the terrace.
Nürnberger Str. 7
Tel: +49 (0) 302 57 57 60
www.thermen-berlin.de

Berlin

Wannsee beach, Steglitz-Zehlendorf

A huge lake and park in the prosperous city suburbs that claims to have – at over 1km – one of the longest inland bathing beaches in Europe. Strandbad Wannsee is an open-air lido and the number-one bathing spot for western Berlin. Originally developed in the 1920s, an attractive FKK section at the north end of the beach is screened off from the swimsuits area. The shore shelves gently and is fine for children and adults alike. Beach chairs, snacks and refreshments are available. The lake is on the Havel river and covers an area of 2.7sq km. All types of water sport are enjoyed from dinghies to larger sailing craft. Easily reached by road or rail from the city centre (13km).

Practical info
Drive along the Havelchaussee (closed at night) to the Grosser Wannsee lake. From the Heerstrasse (beyond Scholzplatz in Charlottenburg) the road runs beside the river, through woods, arriving by the sand dunes. Parking is limited, so arrive early if you're driving.

Halensee park, Rathenauplatz

This pleasant green oasis and pretty lake in the heart of the city attracts hundreds of nude sunbathers to its sloping meadow. Picnicking is a favourite pastime. According to Rose de Sable, writing in the London Evening Standard, the experience was surreal, with high-rise office buildings plainly in view and the sound of occasional police sirens wailing in the distance. Convenient to get to, but don't expect total tranquillity – there's a city highway close by. Toilets, ice cream sellers and snack vendors in season. Facing south-west the banked lawn catches the sun throughout the day.

Munich

Englischer Garten

The best-known and most famous location for sunning in the buff is at the English Garden; bigger than New York's Central Park and London's Hyde Park. Between the Monopteros, a Greek-style temple and the Japanese teahouse lies the Schönfeldwiese (beautiful meadows) where nude sunbathing has been permitted since the 1960s. It is just one of a number of places in the park where folk cast off their clothes. Tourist info www.muenchen.de.

Nude bathing and spas in Munich

Germany's third largest city and prosperous capital of Bavaria deserves a special mention: it was the first city to allow nude sunbathing in its urban parks. Today Germans relax as nature intended in more or less discreet areas of city parks throughout the nation. Munich also has a superb spa complex with a fully nude area, the Therme Erding near the airport (see below).

Therme Erding
Within sight of Munich airport this vast leisure centre, one of the largest in Europe, includes a Sauna Paradise dedicated to nude relaxation and pampering. And with a host of indoor and outdoor thermal pools to be enjoyed as nature intended, it's much more than simply a sauna. There are three distinct themes within the bare area: Roman, Finnish and Tropical, all offering what must be some of the best nudist facilities anywhere.
Erding, 36km north-west of Munich
Tel: +49 (0) 812 22 27 00
www.therme-erding.de

Nude bathing in Austria

Millions of visitors are drawn to Austria each year by the stunning scenery, adrenaline pumping leisure activities and a wealth of architectural and historical sights. And for those of us who prefer to relax as nature intended, there's an abundance of places to take a skinny dip or nudist holiday. Sunbathing and swimming in the buff is widely accepted: lakes and rivers provide the FKK beaches in lieu of the coast in this beautiful land-locked country. More information is available from the Austrian Naturist Association – Österreichischer Naturistenverband www.fkk.at.

Naturists visiting the country also recommend the deluxe 4-star Hotel Thermenhof Paierl, which has some seriously impressive facilities for pampering and chilling out in its Spa and Sauna World. In addition to the usual relaxed dress code in the spa, the hotel invites guests to, 'enjoy the East-Styrian sun rays naked in front of the outdoor Celtic sauna'.

Hotel Thermenhof Paierl
Tel: +43 (0) 3333 28 01
www.thermenhof.at

Austria

Naturistenpark Lobau, south-west of Vienna

The capital's largest naturist club is situated less than 14km from the city centre and is easily accessible by public transport, bicycle or car. Bordering the Lobau National Park, it has space for tents and caravans – advance bookings required. There are plenty of activities to enjoy including a refreshing swim in the mill pool.

Naturistenpark Lobau
Tel: +43 1 280 42 54
www.naturistenpark-lobau.com

Central Europe

▲ Rutar Lido is one of the finest naturist holiday spots in central Europe, with great mountain views. Pictures supplied by the resort

▲ Naturism stops for nothing in the grounds of Gasthouse Lhurman, a naturist hotel set in a stunning location on the Ramasau plateau. Picture from Andy Eke

Rutar Lido, 22km east of Klagenfurt

Probably the best equipped nude holiday centre in Austria and, as in many parts of the country, complemented by fine mountain views. There is a choice of a hotel, self-catering apartments and pitches for up to 365 tents and caravans. Indoor and outdoor swimming pools, a sauna and naked walks in the surrounding pastures and hills are just some of the many attractions on offer. For winter sports enthusiasts the camp is open all year – with plenty of snow in winter.

Rutar Lido

Tel: +43 (0) 4236 2262
www.rutarlido.at

Danube Island – Donauinsel, Vienna

This long (21km) narrow island was created by the construction of a huge flood canal, which is sometimes called the New Danube. It runs nearly through the centre of Austria's capital. At the north and south ends of the island hundreds and often thousands of naked bathers enjoy the extensive nudist beaches. Surprisingly, almost a third of the total shoreline is considered clothes-optional. A mix of pebbles, lots of terraces and a few sandy spots provide opportunities for relaxing and swimming as nature intended: meadows and leafy woodland provide an attractive backdrop. Mobile caterers serve refreshments and ice creams, or you can use one of the handy barbeque pits to cook your own food.

Practical info

Cars are allowed on the island but parking is very limited. Better to use the excellent public transport network of buses and trams. Alternatively, there are good cycle routes – the bare areas are towards either end of this recreational mecca. The Gänsehäufel leisure park on the Old Danube also has a popular nudist beach. Baden Lobau FKK – in south-eastern Vienna – is yet another option, but cars are not allowed; take the 91A bus to Ölhafen Neue Donau.

Central Europe

Sabotnik & Müllerhof FKK camps, Carinthia

These two naturist campsites next to each other sit on the southern edge of lake Keutschacher. Adjacent meadows and beaches make it perfect for enjoying the sun and mountain air as nature intended. Wooden jetties built into the water provide ideal swimming platforms. FKK-Camping Müllerhof is the newer and smaller of the two and has a guesthouse for visitors who don't have their own tent or caravan. Both sites are family-friendly.

Karntner LichtbundTurkiese, Carinthia

Another naturist campsite on lake Keutschacher is located at the water's edge, further east along the shore from the previous listings. Enjoy fresh water swimming in the lake, or bask on the grassy banks soaking up the Austrian sun. The site is surrounded by attractive woodland.

Camping Pesenthein, NW of Klagenfurt

This impressive mixed campsite – part naturist and part textile – rises up from the shore of Lake Millstätter with pitches on several terraces, providing excellent views over the water. There are two swimming beaches, one for those who prefer to wear costumes and a larger one for those who prefer not to. Nude sailing and windsurfing are available, and if the weather falters a stylish pavilion provides a choice of indoor recreational activities.

FKK-Erholungszentrum Tigringer See, Carinthia

A holiday centre not far from Klagenfurt that boasts its own private lake for skinny-dipping. There is a guesthouse, self-catering apartments, mobile homes and pitches for tourers. And especially for children, the centre is home to a host of animals including: guinea pigs, rabbits, sheep, potbelly pigs, geese, a pony and a horse.

Gastehous Luhrmann, Ramsau, Styria

This enchanting naturist hotel is high on the Ramasau plateau, and is popular with visitors from far and wide. Offering comfortable accommodation in a stunning location, there is plenty to satisfy the most discerning nudist traveller: sunbathing lawns, a glazed indoor pool that can be opened up in summer, a sauna suite and new steam room. Open all year.

Zur Grünen, Winzendorf, Pöllau, Styria

Maria and Manfred Pailer run this smart countryside guesthouse and restaurant. Visitors have use of an intimate 'textile-free' wellness centre with indoor pool, and an outdoor skinny-dipping natural pool that is surrounded by extensive decking for taking in the sun.

Camping Rothenfels, Oberwölz, Styria

A compact campsite on the side of the valley with its own small lake. There's a choice of naturist and textile pitches. Part of the natural pool is reserved for nude swimming and sunbathing.

Freie Menschen, Volkersdorferstraße, Graz

This family oriented naturist club offers camping and caravan pitches for visiting holidaymakers. Several rustic chalets are also available to hire. There is a sparkling swimming pool and the grounds extend to eight hectares.

▲ A classic Austrian naturist holiday setting – mountains, lakes and fresh green meadows – await visitors to the Müllerhof FKK campsite, the nearest of the two naturist sites pictured on the shores of lake Keutschacher. Picture supplied by FKK-Camping Müllerhof

Camping Sabotnik

Tel: +43 (0) 4273 25 09
www.fkk-sabotnik.at

FKK-Camping Müllerhof

Tel: +43 (0) 4273 25 17
www.fkk-camping.at (German & Dutch)

Karntner LichtbundTurkiese

Tel: +43 (0) 4224 812 18
www.klb.at

Camping Pesenthein

Tel: +43 (0) 4766 26 65
www.pesenthein.at

FKK-Erholungszentrum Tigringer See

Tel: +43 (0) 4272 83 5 42
www.tigring.at

Gastehous Luhrmann

Tel: +43 (0) 3687 819 86
www.luehrmann.at

Zur Grünen

Tel: +43 (0) 3332 632 77
www.gruene-au.at

Camping Rothenfels

www.rothenfels.at
Tel: +43 (0) 3581 769 80

Freie Menschen

Tel: +43 (0) 3132 32 82
www.fkk.org

Switzerland

Club Gymnique Lumière Genève, Geneva

Ideally situated at Veyrier for a one-night stopover, or a stay of several days, only minutes away from Switzerland's famous Lake Geneva and the bustling centre of the city. There is a sparkling swimming pool and spaces for visiting tents and caravans. Additionally, dormitory accommodation is available in the large chalet clubhouse for travellers on a budget. INF or naturist club membership required.

Camping Club Léman, north-east of Geneva

This is a small private naturist club set in landscaped grounds of 1.8 hectares, close to the shores of Lake Léman. Facilities include a swimming pool, clubhouse with bar, small grocery shop and dormitory accommodation. Holidaymakers and visitors with an INF affiliated club membership card are welcome. There are no restrictions on alcohol and tobacco. Pitches are available for both tents and caravans.

Chläb (HESPA), Auenstein, west of Zurich

A pretty, terraced site with a profusion of trees and lots of open space that is home to the Chläb naturist club. There is an appealing pool with fine views and accommodation is available in the clubhouse. There is a small number of pitches reserved for visiting holidaymakers – but note that INF affiliated club membership cards are required.

Verein Natur & Sport, Lake Greifensee, Zurich

The Verein Natur & Sport (Gelnde Föhrli) club is in an attractive location close to picturesque Lake Greifensee, on the eastern outskirts of Zurich. The enormous pool with marked lanes is ideal for serious swimmers. Pitches are available for holiday visitors with an INF card.
Practical info
It's easy to get to by train: Nänikon Greifensee station is only just over a kilometre away (1,100 metres).

Wellness spas in Switzerland

A correspondent, Michael, has written asking us to highlight the many opportunities to indulge in an easy and truly natural bare experience at the popular wellness spas in Switzerland (and Germany, Austria and northern Italy). Enjoyable all year round, but especially after a day's skiing: they are invariably mixed and nude. It's not considered to be 'naturist', just the accepted thing to strip-off, relax in the sauna or Jacuzzi and socialise. It's a great introduction for anybody who is the slightest bit apprehensive about going to a nudist resort or beach. In particular, Michael and his wife recommend the Swiss hotels and resorts with extensive wellness facilities listed on the right.

Club Gymnique Lumière Genève

Email: info@clubnatur.ch
www.clubnatur.ch

Camping Club Léman

Tel: +41 21 801 83 98
www.snu-uns.ch/ccl

Chläb (HESPA)

Email: redaktion@heliosport.ch
www.heliosport.ch

Verein Natur & Sport

Tel: +41 44 941 20 59
Email: info@naspo.ch
www.naspo.ch

Hotels with wellness spas

Hotel Alpenhof, Zermatt

(outdoor Jacuzzi)
Tel. +41 27 966 55 55
www.hotelalpenhofzermatt.com

Hotel Julen, Zermatt

Tel. +41 27 966 76 00
www.julen.com

Ferienart Resort & Spa

Tel: +41 27 958 1900
www.ferienart.ch

Hotel Beatus, Merligen

(nude sun terrace)
Tel: +41 33 252 81 81
www.beatus.ch

Central Europe

Scandinavia & the Baltic

A long coastline and a short summer are two reasons why the north Europeans leap at the chance to strip off and enjoy the sunshine. Nude bathing is common and unremarkable, but far less commercially developed than in southern Europe: most of the time it's a quiet lake or stretch of beach that plays host to naked Scandinavians.

Attitudes are most liberal in Denmark, where you can use almost the entire coast naked as long as you respect other people and leave them in peace. Sweden's naturists claim more than 60 popular nude beaches, and like Norway has countless other quieter spots where bathers enjoy the fjords and lakes in their birthday suits. Finland probably has more nude bathers than anywhere else in the world, although they prefer home saunas and secluded lakes rather than group naturism. The Baltic sea generally is well used by naked souls, and all the countries bordering these chilly but refreshing waters have nude beaches. For more information see the superb web resource at www.naturistnet.org.

Sweden

Breviksbadet beach, Stockholm area

If you want a skinny dip in the Baltic while you're in Stockholm, there is an official nude beach to the north-east of the city, 6km from Åkersberga town. The beach is known as Breviksbadet and is about 35km from Stockholm city centre itself. There are areas of sand and rocks with a grassy region behind.

Practical info
From Åkersberga drive to the town of Djursholm and head to the coast along Soralidsvagen and then Tralhavsvagen roads. The road ends at a car park, from where it's less than 200m south (go left as you face the sea) to the naked area.

Lulviksbadet official beach, Luleå

This sandy stretch of shore is well-liked by local naturists and visitors alike. It's easy to find and close to the local airport. You can even camp wild at the back of the beach for a couple days, making it an attractive place to get away. With pine clad shores and islands offshore, even these northern reaches of the Baltic look tempting on a sunny day. Facilities are just a toilet and rubbish bins at the back of the beach.

Also of interest to naked souls is that the local town hosts what is claimed to be the most northerly naturist club in the world. Naturist Foreningen Nord is about 10km from the beach.

Practical info
To get to the beach, drive to the local Kallax airport, about 7km from the bridge out of Luleå town. Once you pass the airport (there's a plane parked beside the road so you can't miss it), continue for another 1.5km and stop at the car park on your left. There are two beach areas next to the car park; bare bathers use the one on the right as you face the sea.

Sandviken nude beach and camping, Filipstad

If you want to try lake swimming on your travels in Sweden, the nude beach at Filipstad is ideal for holiday visitors. Lake Yngen has beautifully clean water and the naturist beach and campsite are set on a sandy shore with pine forest around. There are large grass areas for sunbathing and the operators hire out boats to visitors. The campsite is run by the Värmland NF naturist club, and has places for 70 tents, with sauna and other facilities available. The beach is open to all visitors. Set in the middle of Sweden about 200km from Stockholm, the nearest large town is Filipstad, about 15km away.

Practical info
To get to Sandviken beach, drive from Filipstad along road 63 to the north-east. Then 5km past the town of Persberg turn off to the right for Sandviken, and the resort is less than 1km away.

Gustavsberg nude beach and camping, Nora

A popular naturist site, Gustavsberg welcomes visitors who come to enjoy the beautiful lake setting and peaceful campsite. Anyone can come and simply swim at the nude beach, although many overseas visitors stay and make a longer holiday of it. The whole site is naturist and there is a sauna at the edge of the lake for a truly Scandinavian treat.

The resort's website has plenty of information and pictures with an English language version too: www.gustavsbergscamping.com. In addition to tents and caravans there are also cottages and rooms to rent, with all the usual campsite facilities available free of charge to guests.

Practical info
The site is on the western shore of lake Norasjon, less than 1km north of the town of Nora and well signposted from the road. Gustavsberg is about 180km from Stockholm.

Nude bathing in Sweden

Swimming naked in Sweden is common and well accepted, but less commercially developed than in southern Europe. Sweden's naturists say that more than 60 beaches are regularly used by naturists, while there are countless other quieter spots where bathers enjoy the fjords and lakes in their birthday suits.

The country even enjoys some well-managed and attractive naturist resorts, something of a rarity in the rest of Scandinavia but entirely in keeping with the Swede's healthy attitude to the outdoors. To quote celebrity Swedish broadcaster Ulrika Jonsson in 2006: "I think you all need to holiday in Sweden and get your kit off! I highly recommend it."

Lulviksbadet accommodation

Naturist Foreningen Nord
www.naturistforeningennord.se

Sandviken accommodation

Värmland NF naturist club
Tel: +46 (0)590 21100
telia.com/~u16204354/

Scandinavia

Svanrevet official beach, Skanör

This huge white sand reef draws up to 1,000 naturists on the hottest days of the year, and is highly praised by nude beach lovers. The naturist area is the northern end of the Skanör peninsula, and is managed by the local council. Facilities are available in the town, which is a very short walk from the start of the nude beach. There is a naturist campsite nearby, called Solhejdan, which takes holiday visitors.

Practical info
Park on Kyrkgatan Street or near Skanör's town hall. At the end of Kyrkgatan Street a path leads to the coast. You will have to wade across some shallow water and then head north (right as you face the sea). Nudity starts after just 100m and continues for a further 5km.

▲ On the beautiful sandy spit north of Skanör, Svanrevet official naturist beach is hugely popular on sunny days, and just 55km from Malmö. Pictures by Marcus and Brenda Webb

Svanrevet accommodation
Solhejdan campsite
+46 40 962963
Email: svanrevet@naturistforbundet.se

Hökafältet official beach, Laholm

At the bottom of Sweden's west coast, facing Denmark, lies a pleasant stretch of sand that's officially designated nude. Just 60km north of Helsingborg, outside the town of Laholm, the beach is part of a long stretch of sandy coast that's popular with holiday-makers. The nude section starts to the north of the main Mellbystrand beach. The Marias campsite is very handy for the beach although it's not naturist. The beach is run by the local council, which provides a toilet but no running water.

Practical info
To get to the beach simply turn off the main E6 coast road on to road 24, for Mellbystrand. This is also the junction for Laholm, which is a few kilometers in the opposite direction. Follow signs to Marias camping and the nude section starts just north of here, to the right as you face the sea.

Knähaken official beach, Helsingborg

Very convenient if you're visiting Helsingborg, this lovely sandy beach is just 5km south of town and is looked after by the local council.

Practical info
The beach is easily reached from the town of Råå, a few kilometers south of Helsingborg. Simply head to the coast and drive north (right as you face the sea) for 1.5km. The nude beach starts just after the Råå Vallar campsite (a textile site that's handy if you want to stay within walking distance of the beach).

▲ Skinny-dipping in fresh water: a free stretch of lake is all it takes to enjoy the great and unspoilt outdoors as nature intended. Picture by Andy Eke

Sandhammaren nude beach, Ystad

One of Sweden's best beach areas according to some, Sandhammaren is a long stretch of white sand that is enjoyed by naked users at the far end, south of the main beach. With sand dunes at the back and pine forests behind, the beach lies at the southern tip of Sweden, about 25km east of Ystad itself. Be careful in the sea, there are dangerous currents along this stretch of the Swedish coastline.

Practical info
The beach is easy to find. Simply drive to the main Sandhammaren beach area and turn right (south-west) to drive along the shore. Go as far as you can then park and continue walking along the shore for a few minutes. The area where people strip begins just after a group of sheds and a weather vane. Assuming it's a sunny day just look out for other bare bodies and join in.

Hökafältet accommodation
Marias camping (textile)
www.camping.se/n18

Knähaken accommodation
Råå Vallar campsite (textile)
+46 (0)421 07680

Scandinavia

Norway

Ursetvika beach

Djupvika

NORWAY

Oslo
Svartkulp
Huk
Sandvika

Isefjær

Huk official beach, Oslo centre

Close to the city centre, and blessed by a sandy beach, the naturist area at Huk is a popular place for enjoying the sun and sea. Unclad bathers even have a small shop on the site offering refreshments. Other facilities include showers, drinking water and toilets. Like other city nude beaches around the world, Huk is very accessible and can attract the odd selfish visitor who causes hassle. Don't let them put you off: this beach was rated one of the world's top 10 by Teletext Holidays.

Practical info
The beach remains popular and lies just south of the city centre, at the bottom of the relatively undeveloped Bygdøy peninsula. To go by public transport, take bus 30 to the terminus at Bygdøy, and keep walking along the road for another 200m. If you drive here, there is a parking area right by the nude beach but the roads get very busy at weekends. The nude area is on the right as you face the sea, separated from the ordinary beach by a small bay.

Sandvika official beach, near Oslo

More secluded than Huk city beach, yet less than 15km from Oslo city centre, this sandy patch of shore is on the little island of Kalvøya to the west of the city. Access is easy as there is a footbridge linking the island to the suburb of Sandvika. Drinking water and toilets are available, and there is a picnic area amid sunbathing lawns.

Practical info
There is a car park in Sandvika by the footbridge, and a station in the town if you're coming by train from Oslo. Once you're on the island, turn left and walk about 600m to the eastern end. Sandvika has one of the country's largest shopping complexes, handy if you're waiting for a morning fog to lift.

Svartkulp lake beach, north of Oslo

A truly Scandinavian experience this, Svartkulp is a pretty little lake set amid pine forests to the north of Oslo. It's easy to reach, and is even within walking distance of the city's metro. There are flat rocks for sunbathing and good bathing in the clean lake water. The lake is officially set aside for unclad bathers, and lies just to the

east of the larger Sognsvann lake.
Practical info
To get here by metro, take line 3 (green) to the terminal at Sognsvann. There's a track heading north, signposted to Ullevålseter, which leads to both lakes. After 10 minutes' walk you will see a stone dam on the right, and Svartkulp lake is there.

Nude bathing in Norway

Norway's vast coastline is an uncrowded part of Europe, which makes it all the more easy to enjoy as nature intended. Scandinavia's no-nonsense attitudes to bare bathing apply to Norway and locals regularly enjoy the great outdoors in the buff. There are no laws against simple nudity and if you find a secluded lake or beach stripping off should be no problem if you respect other people.

In fact the open attitudes mean there are relatively few formal naturist places, although near populated areas such as Oslo they are well used. As with the rest of Scandinavia, naturist visitors are well served by the informative website www.naturistnet.org.

Going naked in the wild feels free enough at the best of times, but out in Norway's uncrowded countryside near a nude bathing lake is about as good as it gets

Ursetvika beach, Bodø

This sandy stretch of shore, beautifully set on the edge of a pristine fiord, has one rather important detail that sets it apart from all the other nude beaches in this guide, and indeed the world: it is inside the Arctic circle. While you wouldn't want to expose even your nose during the dark winter months, the location does mean that around midsummer's day the sun does not set at any point.

With no night for cooling down, air temperatures can easily climb to sunbathing temperature and even the water might start to look inviting on a hot day. It's an unofficial nude beach, and you can even camp wild round the back of it for a few days. This is a great place to get back to nature in every sense.

Practical info

The beach is on the eastern shore of Misværfjord, which lies about half way between the towns of Bodø and Rognan.

Coming from the main coastal road 17, turn off down road 812 and drive about 20km to the bridge that crosses Misværfjord. Take the bridge and on the far side, in the town of Støvset, turn right and drive along the fiord for just under 2km. You can park by the beach, which is set in a little bay and visible from the road.

Djupvika official beach, Trondheim

Very convenient if you're visiting Trondheim town, this beach is even accessible by public transport. With a lovely setting on Trondheimfjorden, to the north of the town centre, the mainly rocky beach has grassy fields behind and good swimming. Part of the beach here is officially set aside for nude users, and is well used on sunny weekends.

There are some lovely walks along this shore from here, including a

▲ Scandinavians seem to do nudity better than just about everyone. Top: lake bathing off a jetty in Sweden; picture from Getty Images. Above: skinny dipping in Finland

▲ The Baltic beckons, especially since you can enjoy it naked in Helsinki, from this beach on Seurasaari island, Finland

popular coastal path, and museums to visit in the area. Well worth a trip whether or not you fancy a quick skinny-dip in these northerly waters.

Practical info
The beach lies at the northern tip of the peninsula above Trondheim, easy to spot on any map. It is about 5km from the town centre, and you can park within 100 metres of the shore, near the hospital at Ringve. By public transport, take bus 3 or 4 to the school at Ringve, from where it's a few minutes' walk north to the beach. The beach is signposted and has toilets available.

Isefjær naturist centre, near Kristiansand

Few naturist holiday centres anywhere in the world can rival the lovely setting of Isefjær. Set at the end of a fiord in southern Norway, with a sandy beach and pine forests around, the resort is only open to members of accredited naturist organisations, linked to the International Naturist Federation (see www.inf-fni.org for details of your local naturist federation). The club is keen to make sure only bona fide naturists use the site.

The campsite is open during the summer months of June, July and August only and has space for around 20 visitors in tents or caravans, with a dozen chalets to rent. Apart from the ocean beach

there are plenty of things to do around the site including volleyball, cycling and boating. Campsite cooking and washing facilities, plus a sauna, are available.

Practical info
The club is located about 15km from the town of Kristiansand. Drive east from the town, over the fiord bridge on road E18. About 1km after the bridge turn right on to road 401 towards Høvåg. After about 10km turn left, following the sign to Isefjær, and drive another 3km until the road ends at the site.

Contact the centre first before visiting, even if you have an INF-accredited naturist membership card.

Isefjær accommodation

Isefjær naturist centre
Isefjær, N-4770 Høvåg
Tel: +47 37 27 49 90
Email: isefjaer.nnf@naturistnet.org

Pori beach

FINLAND

Helsinki

Pihlajasaari island · Seurasaari island

Nude bathing in Finland

Saunas are the focus of nude bathing here, but Finns tend to keep their nudity to family groups both in the sauna and adjacent lake. It means that an impromptu skinny dip somewhere quiet is entirely in keeping with the country's healthy attitude to bathing. So find a peaceful lake or beach and jump right in – or check out one of the few dedicated nude beaches.

Finland

Seurasaari island, Helsinki

This pine-clad island lies just offshore from Helsinki on the west of the city, and can be reached on a wooden bridge. It is home to a long-established sea bathing club, which screens off a rocky stretch of coast into a male and a larger female section. While great for taking a naked bathe in the Baltic, the division of the sexes is fairly meaningless when you swim out to sea as the whole shoreline becomes

visible. Even so men and women are happy to pay a small entrance fee and enjoy a proper swim.

Practical info
The island is easy to reach by bus 24 from the central train station in Helsinki, and there is a map indicating the bathing area when you get there. There's also an open-air museum on the island if the weather turns against skinny dipping.

Pihlajasaari island, Helsinki

For mixed-sex nude bathing, Helsinki is best served by the beach on Pihlajasaari island, which can be reached by a 12-minute ferry crossing from central Helsinki during the summer months. The nude beach is rocky and separate from the main beach; just follow the signs to 'Naturisti-ranta'.

Practical info
The island is a popular spot in the summer and worth a visit if you have some time to spare in the city. Ferries run frequently during the summer from Helsinki's Kaivopuisto port. You can stay overnight in the main campsite if you bring a tent (fees are collected each morning).

Scandinavia

Helsinki pool and sauna

The Yrjönkatu Uimahalli in central
Helsinki is one of the country's oldest
sauna and swimming complexes.
Recently refurbished, it offers a handy
venue for swimming and saunas, with
a superb 25-metre pool lined with
Roman style arches. Nudity is the
norm in both the pool and sauna,
although it's not a naturist
establishment as such: men and
women visit on different days and
you can wear a costume if you wish.

Practical info
Located a few minutes from the
central bus and railway station on
Yrjönkatu Street, the complex is
elegant, easy to find and affordable at
€4 per adult.

> **Yrjönkatu Uimahalli details**
> Yrjönkatu 21 b
> FI-00100 Helsinki
> Tel: +358 (0)9 3108 7401

Pori beach, Yyteri resort, near Pori city

The only official nude beach outside
Helsinki, Yyteri is a popular seaside
resort with 6km of white sand and
sea. A small section among the sand
dunes is designated for nude
bathers, with signs indicating where
you can strip.
Practical info
The city of Pori is on Finland's west

coast, about four hours by bus from
Helsinki. Access to the Yyteri resort
from Pori itself is very easy, with
buses and trains carrying sun-seekers
to the coast.
  For more information about the
area and details about camping and
other places to stay in Yyteri, see
www.yyteri.fi/eng.

▲ Saunas are a Finnish invention,
and they're very much part of
everyday life. Saunas are used naked,
although you should bring in a towel
or small cloth to sit on. Picture top
left by Charlie Simonds, top right
from Getty Images. For more
information check out the Finnish
Sauna Society at www.sauna.fi

Denmark

Sønderstrand, Rømø island, off Jutland

Hundreds of acres of white sand provide a popular haven for going bare. This was the first beach in Denmark to be granted official nude status, and it's still enjoyed by hundreds of freedom-loving folk today. A windshield would come in handy, as it would on all of Jutland's west-facing beaches, but it's a lovely spot for being at one with nature.

Practical info
The island is joined to the mainland by a causeway and the beach is on the south-west coast close to the port of Havenby. Head due west from town to the giant au naturel sands. A 45-minute ferry link from Havenby connects to List on the German island of Sylt. Tourist info www.romo.dk.

Houstrup Strand, west Jutland near Esbjerg

Here is an 800m official nudist beach of pale level sand backed by extensive dunes and marked by FKK signs. With the family-friendly Lyngbo Park naturist camp less than a 10-minute drive away, this shore attracts plenty of all-over sunseekers on fine sunny days. The dunes here are wildly romantic and the beach is vast.
Practical info
From Esbjerg travel north on highway 12 to Varde, taking the western ring road around the town. Then north-west on the 181 and follow signs to Henne Strand. The nude area is just up the coast on the south side of Houstrup. Esbjerg is Denmark's ferry port for visitors to and from the UK.

> **Houstrup accommodation**
> Lyngbo Park Naturist Camping
> Tel: +45 75 25 50 92
> www.lyngbo.dk

Nude bathing in Denmark

When it comes to sea bathing in the buff, Denmark must have the most laid-back approach anywhere in Europe, and possibly the world. With the exception of just two specific locations, the whole coastline is considered swimsuits-optional.

Since the early 1970s Danes have enjoyed the freedom to decide what to wear, or what not to wear, along more than 7,400km of coast. It is the smallest and southernmost of the Nordic countries and nowhere is more than 50km from the sea, so there's plenty of choice nearby.

There are four officially recognised public nude beaches in the country: on the island of Rømø at Sønderstrand, on the west coast of Jutland (the mainland) at Houstrup Strand north of Hennestrand, on the island of Lolland at Albuen and on the island of Falster south of Marielyst at Bøtø Strand. Elsewhere, the key to relaxing au naturel at the seaside is to be sensitive to others' comfort. Nudity that does not lead to complaints is entirely legal.

At Skagen, north Jutland, the mayor and the police chief advise that with 65km of beach there's room enough for everybody to sunbathe and swim in any fashion they like as long as people show mutual consideration. Holmsland Klit and Hennestrand, both on the west coast of Jutland, are the only two places swimsuits are mandatory.

Further information

www.dansknaturistunion.dk
www.naturistnet.org
www.strandguide.dk
www.visitdenmark.com

▲ Sandy scenes at Sonderstrand on Romo island. Pics from Romo tourist board

Lillebaelt camping and beach, Fyn island

This lovely family-orientated centre has modern facilities and its own nude beach. The water is clean and sheltered and there is a long bathing jetty. Fishing, sailing and windsurfing can all be enjoyed au naturel. There's a play area for children, a small shop and holiday cabins to rent. Open 1 May to 31 August. Day visitors are welcome.

Practical info
From Kolding on Jutland take the E20 motorway east and turn off at junction 59 for Middelfart. Take route 161 through Middelfart and turn right at Kauslande. Pass under the railway and then drive through the village of Gamborg, along the marina. Turn right at Fjordvej on to the gravel road to the campsite.

> **Lillebaelt accommodation**
> Lillebaelt Naturistcamp
> Tel: +45 64 40 33 59
> www.naturisme.dk

Bøjden Naes camping and beach, Fyn island

This narrow, pebbly shore with a bathing jetty is next to the Naturist Fyn campsite. This nude nirvana with grassed areas next to the water has a regular following of locals. Visitors with their own tents, campers or caravans are welcome. Situated in a preserved location and offering a real back-to-nature experience – although there is an internet connection! The site is open 1 May to 1 October. Day visitors need INF or naturist club membership.

Practical info
From Odense travel south on route 43 towards Faaborg, but before entering town turn right to Bøjden. Then take the turn on the left signposted to 'Naturistforeningen Fyn'.

> **Bøjden Naes accommodation**
> Naturist Fyn Campsite
> Tel: +45 62 60 17 02
> www.nf-fyn.dk

Albuen, Nakskov, Lolland island

An official nude beach along a remarkable spit on the far west coast of Lolland. This remote strand, more than 7km long, is the perfect place to escape the stresses of everyday life and commune with nature: a truly unspoilt destination. The spit forms a huge natural fjord (Søndernor) popular with sailors; the nudist beach is on the seaward side facing west towards the island of Langeland. Nearby clothed Camping Albuen Strand is only a modest walk from the bare area.

Practical info
Nakskov is the largest town on the island, 172km south-west of Copenhagen. From Nakskov continue south-west through Jordbjerg following the signs to Albuen. A minor road runs the length of the narrow sandy spit and more or less anywhere on the west side is okay to strip off. Tourist info www.nakskovinfo.dk and www.turistlolland.dk.

Bøtø Strand, Marielyst, Falster island

Local naturists who turn out in force when the weather is warm praise this lovely official nude beach on the Marielyst peninsular, near the southernmost tip of Denmark. It is said to be particularly child-friendly. The undeveloped east-facing sandy shore is backed by woodland and provides great swimming and sunbathing. The beach becomes more and more deserted the further south you walk.

Practical info
Falster island is connected to Sjaelland island and Lolland island by bridges. Nykøbing Falster is the island capital, 130km south-west of Copenhagen. Bøtø Strand is reached by taking highway E55 south from Nykøbing towards Gedser, but turning off to the left (east) at the signpost for Bøtø.

Park on the southern outskirts of the resort and walk down the beach away from town for naked bliss. Tourist info and accommodation www.marielyst.dk.

▲ Indoors and out the culture in northern Europe is very much in favour of nude bathing in a natural context. Top picture shows the favoured setting of Lillebaelt camping on Fyn island

> **Albuen accommodation**
> Camping Albuen Strand (textile)
> Tel: +45 54 94 87 62
> www.albuen.dk

Scandinavia

▲ Right: one of almost countless Baltic beaches where Danish bathers prefer to bare all. This is Dueodde beach on the island of Bornholm, which was voted best beach for bathing in the whole of Denmark in 2006. The beach wraps around the southern tip of the island and the western end is pretty much a full-time naturist beach; picture from Getty Images. Picture on the left shows a swimmer fresh from the Baltic; picture from Przemek and Joanna

Solbakken camp and beach, Sjaelland island

The largest and liveliest naturist club in Denmark is next to a stunningly attractive fjord near the north coast of the island. With 100 pitches the 18-acre site has plenty of space for visitors. Delightful swimming in the fjord from the jetty, but the beach is narrow and has a lot of stones. There's a sauna, clubhouse and timber cottages for holiday rental. It's a great area for cycling with lots of scenic routes to follow. Day visitors are welcome with an INF or club membership card, which can be bought at the site.

'Hellas', a clothes-free and family-friendly indoor swimming pool and spa with sunbathing lawns, is only 10km from the campsite www.hellasbad.dk (closed in July).

Practical info

Solbakken is easily reached in about an hour from Copenhagen by car or public transport. Take the motorway east from the city past Roskilde and turn right (north) on to highway 53 to Skibby. 2km south of Kirke Hyllinge turn left (west) at the sign 'Naturist Camping', then follow the signs to Solbakken.

Troldeskoven, Tisvildeleje, Sjaelland island

A wide-open beach of fine white sand that attracts lots of naturist visitors from Copenhagen and further afield. The area is noted for its natural beauty and large forests. The swimming is safe but there are no lifeguards at this rural spot. Backed by dunes and heath, the shore shelves gently into the Baltic.

Practical info

From Copenhagen travel north-west on highway 16 to Frederiksvaerk and then

north on the 205 and east on the 237 to Tisvildeleje. Park on the western outskirts of town and walk along the sandy path away from the built-up area to the nudist section. The beach can also be reached from the other side of the Tisvilde Hegn woods via a minor road (NR Olsensvej) from Asserbo. Park near the shore, then turn right at the beach. Tourist info www.helsinge.com and www.frvturist.dk.

Solbakken accommodation

Solbakken Naturistcamping
Tel: +45 46 40 51 07
www.solbakken-camping.dk

Scandinavia

▲ Debki beach in Poland has very fine, soft sand and a sparkling blue sea. Picture from Przemek and Joanna

Poland

Debki beach, north of Gdansk

A stunning stretch of fine light sand, sparkling clear sea and tall pine forests make this one of the Baltic's most attractive nude beaches. On a really sunny day the sea and sands look almost Caribbean – though the water temperature remains very definitely Baltic. It is long-established and fairly popular, although large enough to accommodate all the naturists without crowding. The beach is used naked for nearly 2km to the west. It's easy to spot Debki on a map – it's 65km north-west of Gdansk and just about at the very northern tip of Poland.

Practical info

To get to the nude area, head west through the village of Debki, cross the small river and keep walking. It's about half a kilometer to the nude area: there's a small fence which usually marks the point where people ditch their costumes. Be careful if you park in Debki itself: use official parking spaces only or you might find your car removed when you get back.

Rowy beach, 20km north of Slupsk

An almost endless stretch of undeveloped sandy shore makes Rowy one of the largest nude beaches in Europe. From the picturesque village of Rowy it's a full 25km along the shore to the next town, so there's plenty of space to find solitude. During high season some locals come and sell refreshments to the nude bathers. The beach is part of the Slowinski National Park, on a long sandy spit of land that separates two big lakes from the sea. It is undeveloped and a great place to explore, with UNESCO-protected sand dunes up to 56m high.

Practical info

To find the beach, head to the eastern end of Rowy, or right as you face the sea. Cross the little river that runs through the edge of the town, and keep walking for about 1km until you see bare bodies.

Nude bathing in the Baltic states

The Baltic states in general have a typically north European attitude to nudity on the beach: the coast is pretty much yours to enjoy as you wish as long as you don't hassle other people and don't strip near clothed and resort beach areas. All the countries here enjoy nude bathing facilities to some extent, and with so many uncrowded and sandy beaches it's not hard to find a quiet spot away from recognised naturist areas. Official attitudes in all Nordic states seem very relaxed about outdoor nudity in the right places, but do check if in any doubt.

Further information

More information on all of Poland's nude beaches can be found at www.naturyzm.info.pl.

The Baltic

▲ Vecaki beach near Riga, with several kilometers of golden sands stretching along a straight coast

Miedzyzdroje beach, near German border

Miedzyzdroje is a relatively upmarket beach resort that attracts plenty of foreign tourists. It's very close to the German border, which means a lot of visitors are German and come specifically because of the town's nude beach. This end of Poland's coast is the most southerly, meaning the water is usually a bit warmer here.

Practical info
It's a pleasant stroll along the sands to reach the nude beach. Turn left, or west, as you face the sea and walk along the coast for about 2km. The town is known as the Pearl of the Baltic and has very pretty bays and beaches right along the coast. It's connected to the country's rail network.

Ventspils

Vecaki

Riga

LATVIA

Latvia

Vecaki beach, near Riga

This popular beach can attract up to 2,000 naked souls on a sunny weekend, although it's often much quieter. It's a family friendly place, with many regular beach-goers organising events such as volleyball and petanque. There is a long, straight stretch of golden sandy beach backed by trees that stretches for several kilometers before you reach the next town.

Practical info
The beach is only 15km from Riga city centre and you can get there very easily by train. Take the Riga to Saulkrasti railway line and get off at Vecaki village. Walk to the beach, turn right along the sand, heading east, and the nude area is just 400m walk along the coast once you leave the village area. If you speak Latvian, see www.nudisms.lv.

Ventspils official beach, Ventspils city

This city has recently set aside a small stretch of its European blue flag beach for nude users, part of a town plan to attract more tourists. The area is near to the town centre and clearly marked with signs marked Nudistu Pludmale and FKK. Ventspils city itself is about 200km from Riga, on the country's

clean west coast, and well worth a visit for its historic buildings and 13th century castle.

Practical info
The beach is on the south side of town, left as you face the sea. Head to the Seaside Kemping campsite and go south along the shore until you see the signs.

▲ The only way to enter the Baltic: fast and without clothes! Pic from http://dunesspb.byethost7.com

The Baltic

Lithuania

Nida beach, Curonian spit

This busy and very large beach hit the headlines in 2006 when an EU commissioner was photographed bathing in the buff in the company of his female chief of staff. Nothing wrong with the fact he was naked – Nida boasts a long-established naturist beach that is hugely popular among German visitors in particular. It has plenty of sand dunes and space to stroll around. Nida is on a long spit of land that separates the sea from a huge lagoon, and is known for its UNESCO-listed sand dunes and pine forest.

Practical info

The nude beach here is at the southern end of the shore, heading in the direction of Kaliningrad, the Russian enclave. Turn left at the sea and walk down the sands, following the signs.

Estonia

Pärnu women-only nude beach

A well-known resource for Estonians and tourists alike, this stretch of sand by Pärnu town is exclusively reserved for women. The beach has fine golden sand and the nude area is marked with a sign saying 'Ladies beach'.

The fact that visitors have to leave their husbands at home along with their bikinis makes it a particularly easy place to try nude bathing if you're nervous, although plenty of single women use mainstream European naturist beaches without problem. UK travel company Teletext Holidays rates this as one of the world's top 10 nude beaches. It's certainly unique in being women-only, although there is sometimes talk of turning it into a regular naturist beach.

Practical info

To get to the beach simply walk along the sands from the town. The beach is not closed off, just marked with signs.

Russia

St Petersburg Dunes beach, Sestroretsk

Russians think nothing of stripping off to swim in this vast country's lakes, rivers and seas, but generally find somewhere alone to do so. There are one or two naturist beaches however and probably the most popular is to the north of St Petersburg, about 30km from the city centre and about 5km north of Sestroretsk. It can attract thousands of visitors over a hot weekend. Regulars often organise games of volleyball and other beach sports. The dunes that give the beach its name are fairly low, and give way to pine forest at the back. There are cafes near the beach, but none in the naturist section itself.

Practical info

The beach is about 1km south of the large Dunes Holiday Resort Hotel. The best way to get here from St Petersburg is to take a train to Sestroretsk. You'll then need to take bus 306 from the railway station to its terminus, which is a few minutes' walk from the hotel. The bus takes about 25 minutes. Transport and other information is available at http://dunesspb.byethost7.com.

▲ **Making the most of the long summer days near St Petersburg. Pictures from Dunes beach website http://dunesspb.byethost7.com**

The Baltic

East Europe

The countries of eastern Europe are becoming ever more integrated with the west, but when it comes to nude bathing they are already up to speed. While still relatively cheap, and a popular choice for holiday homes, naturists are discovering that the bare bathing opportunities are as good here as any to be found further west.

The beaches of Bulgaria and Ukraine's Crimean peninsula, for example, are well used to the sight of bare bodies plunging cheerfully into the Black Sea. With a climate to rival parts of the Mediterranean, holidays here can be every bit as enjoyable as a trip to more popular tourist countries.

Away from the coast, both the Czech republic and Hungary are rightly proud of their lakeside naturist holiday resorts. Spectacular scenery, modern facilities and a true naturist ethos permeate these sites and attract tourists from across Europe and further afield.

Eastern Europe

Bulgaria
1. Harmanite beach
2. Golden Sands
3. Albena and Kranevo

Ukraine
4. Simeiz
5. Koktebel
6. Tikhy beach

Hungary
7. Lake Balaton

Montenegro
8. Ada Bojana

Bulgaria

Harmanite beach and Hotel Villa List, Sozopol

Located at the southern end of Bulgaria's coastline, Sozopol is a popular tourist destination with a number of pretty coves and some ancient buildings to explore. And if you're after an all-over tan there is both a nude beach and a handy hotel with a nude sunbathing terrace. The beach is well known locally, and is located to the south of Harmanite beach, one of the town's main beaches which stretches from the town itself to the south. Simply walk along the sands and join in when you see bare skin.

Practical info

Also worth considering is the five-star Hotel Villa List, which has a nude sunbathing terrace on the roof, added to attract foreign tourists. The hotel also has a small spa including an indoor pool, spa bath, sauna and steam room. The hotel's website mentions the nude terrace on its German pages, but not yet on the English ones.

Golden Sands, 15km north of Varna

Golden Sands is one of a number of beach resorts along the coast to the north of Varna city. There is a nude beach here, and on a sunny day there will be plenty of tourists enjoying the sea in the altogether. Golden Sands is aptly named, and other attractions that draw visitors here include a pretty setting of wooded hills and a wide range of water sports along the gently sloping shore.

Practical info

To get to the nude beach, walk to the northern end of the town beach (left as you face the sea). Go past the Glarus Hotel and the yacht harbour and immediately afterwards the sun, sea and sand can be enjoyed in your birthday suit. It's just over 1km from the centre of this little resort town, or only a few hundred metres if you're staying in a hotel at this end of the beach.

Albena and Kranevo beaches

The long straight stretch of sand between the towns of Albena and Kranevo, at the northern end of Bulgaria, is well known as a nude bathing destination. The nude beach is popular and long established. Many web reports wrongly claim that the beach is more than 7km long: Albena and Kranevo are only 3km apart and the nude area lies in the secluded section between them.

Practical info

From Albena, simply head south, or right as you face the sea, and walk along to the undeveloped stretch of sand where bare bathers gather.

Nude bathing in Bulgaria

Although it's on the Black Sea, Bulgaria has a decidedly Mediterranean attitude when it comes to nude bathing. A large number of the ordinary beaches are used naked at the far ends, away from the crowds but near enough to the resorts to be an easy walk. And there are also some more well-established naturist places that are attracting a growing number of local and holiday visitors.

▲ **The old town of Sozopol on Bulgaria's Black Sea coast has a nude beach to the south of the town beaches, and a hotel with nude bathing facilities too. Picture ©iStockphoto.com/Geoff Berry**

Hotel Villa List

Tel: +359 550 2 22 35
http://hotellist-bg.com/en/

■ **Picture on previous page: by the Black Sea in Bulgaria: nude bathing is a regular part of beach life right along the coastline**

▲ Nude bathing, Crimean style: the Black Sea coast has plenty of wild places to enjoy some freelance naturism. Established naturist beaches include the beach at Simeiz, bottom left. It is used nude in two areas: at the edge of the resort beach (bottom right hand corner of the picture), and all around the pinnacle of rock by the sea. Pictures top row and bottom right by Ruslan Miheev

Nude bathing in Ukraine

Ukraine's Crimean peninsula is one of the most interesting destinations in Europe. With historical towns such as Sebastopol, ancient cave cities carved into cliffs and dramatic mountains rising sheer out of the Black Sea, there is enough to fascinate any curious traveller. And just to break up the sight-seeing it also enjoys several rocky nude beaches along its southern shoreline. Outside the Crimea, Odessa is another historical destination and also enjoys a small nude beach.

▲ Evening sun at Koktebel

Ukraine

Simeiz, 20km west of Yalta

Along the coast from the pretty and historical tourist town of Yalta lies a nude beach hidden among the rocks at the foot of a small mountain. Couples and families tend to congregate in the small rocky bays and inlets in the first part of the beach, and gay visitors further round, although access gets ever more tricky as you move among the boulders.

Practical info
As you drive along the coast from Yalta into the town of Simeiz, you might spot the huge sloping cliff face just beyond the town that slides down towards the sea. Locals call it Cat Mountain and it does indeed look rather like a cat crouched and about to pounce on an unsuspecting fish in the sea below. At the foot of the mountain, somewhere around the cat's whiskers, lies the nude beach. The town has two bays; the western one charges a fee for entry and has a few nude users, but to get to the main nude area simply walk a few minutes further west from here along the shore.

Koktebel, eastern Crimea

At the far end of the Crimean peninsula lies one of the most popular naturist beaches on the Black Sea. It's been established for decades and has a loyal following of visitors who return year after year. The beach is easy to find from Koktebel town, and enjoys clear water and a peaceful setting. The nude beach is more than 500m of small pebbles running along in a narrow strip to the east of the town beach. It can get very busy at the height of summer, with a cheerful crowd of true beach lovers.

Practical info
The nude area is about 25 minutes' walk from Koktebel town centre, or around half that from the promenade and boat jetty. Simply walk along the shore to the left as you face the sea. The busy nude area runs for 700m to a textile campsite, which is handy enough if you want to stay by the beach. After the campsite nudity starts again and continues along some quiet stretches of coast and bays, where many visitors camp wild.

Eastern Europe

Tikhy beach, Odessa

A small beach that gets very busy on sunny days, Tikhy is tucked away at the western end of Odessa. The pebble beach is only a couple of hundred metres long but a welcome relief from those who can't bear to swim in clothes. The sea is calm, protected by a submerged breakwater, and the crowd is a nice mix of sunlovers.

Practical info

The beach is about half way between the two coast areas called Delfin and Arcadia. It's round the back of a large spa/health resort called Chkalov, on Frantsuzky Bulvar (French Boulevard). To get here by public transport, take tram 5 from the railway station and ask someone to tell you when you get to Chkalov – or look out for the sign on the left. Walk through the gardens of this spa to the sea on the other side. The nude beach is a few minutes' walk down to your right as you face the sea, the last stretch of shingle beach.

▲ Naturists in Odessa have gained their own small stretch of shore at Tikhy beach, to the west of the city

Hungary

Lake Balaton campsites and nude beaches

The long shores of Hungary's Lake Balaton draw countless tourists every year, including many naturists. There are some modern resorts along its shores designed for naturist families in particular, with nude bathing and a range of accommodation. The lake itself is the largest in central Europe, 80km long and lying in the west of the country. One hotel here at the western end, the Villa Maria, welcomes naturist guests and has sunbathing facilities and a pool available for nude bathers.

One naturist site on Lake Balaton is Camping Levendula, on the north shore. It has more than 100 camping pitches, each one nicely bordered by a hedge, mobile homes to hire, and a modern shower and toilet block. Activities for children are arranged throughout the summer. Large enough to accommodate around 700 naturists at peak times, the resort is open from May to September.

Another naturist campsite taking advantage of Balaton's waters is Naturista Camping Balatonbereny, on the south-west tip of the lake. It also has more than 100 camping pitches and plenty of water sports including boats, canoes and windsurfing. It's also popular, with room for more than 1,000 visitors at peak times. There is a restaurant and mini supermarket.

Sziksosfurdo beach and camping, Szeged

Nestling in the very south of Hungary lies a popular and well-equipped naturist campsite on the edge of an attractive, tree-lined lake. There are sand and grass areas beside the lake and plenty to keep young and old alike active, including windsurfing, badminton, volleyball and of course swimming. There are camping and caravan pitches with electricity, log cabins and caravans to hire and two saunas.

Practical info

There is a small restaurant on site and even wireless internet access if you bring your laptop. The site is open from May to September, and detailed directions are included on its website.

Nude bathing in Hungary

Like every other central European country, Hungary enjoys some excellent nude beaches and naturist campsites. Lakeside beaches have been developed with modern facilities, offering some quality sites aimed at naturist holiday-makers from around the world. Numerous lakes around the country also see discrete nude bathing at times. There are even some lakes within 30km of Budapest that are used naked at Delegyhaza, although they tend to attract locals as they're not so easy to find.

Lake Balaton accommodation

Hotel Villa Maria
Tel: + 36 83 341 779
http://www.villamaria.de/

Camping Levendula
Tel: +36 87 544 011
www.balatontourist.hu (search for Levendula)

Naturista Camping Balatonbereny
Tel: +36 85 377 715
www.balatonbereny.hu

Sziksosfurdo beach and camping

Tel: +36 62 463 988
www.natours.hu

Czech republic

Sárka, Dzabán reservoir, Prague outskirts

Out to the east of Prague, and easily accessible by bus or tram, this large grassy beach is on the edge of a reservoir, used for swimming. The nude area, called Sárka, has some basic facilities including showers, toilets and refreshments. There is a fee of €1 to enter.
Practical info
The beach is on the north shore of the long reservoir lake at Vokovice, a suburb to the west of central Prague.

It's easy enough to spot the reservoir on any large city map, it is just to the north of highway 7 which leads out of the city. You can walk to the nude area if you take a tram or bus to Vokovice. Coming from Prague take tram 20 or 26 to Divoká Sárka tram stop. Enter the park next to the road and walk about 400m left around the lake to the north shore; the nude area covers about a quarter of the shore, from the middle towards the western end.

Opatovice nad Labem, 100km west of Prague

This beach enjoys the clean waters and golden sand of a former quarry. A few hundred metres are used naked, and it can attract hundreds of sunbathers at busy weekends. Grassy areas behind the sand make for convenient sunbathing, but there are no trees for shade in the nude area. There are refreshments on site and although it's

managed any entrance fee is voluntary.
Practical info
Half of the western side of the lake is used naked, from the south-west corner up. It's about 3km south-west from Hradec Králové town centre, just to the west of highway 37. There is a local train station called Opatovice nad Labem just 200m away.

Eastern Europe

The Czech republic may lack a coast but it has made good the deficit with countless lakes for swimming and relaxing. Naturists are not forgotten either, with nude beaches including Sárka, at the top of this page, and Opatovice nad Labem on the right. Pictures from naturista.cz/lokality

The former sand quarry at Melice, where nude camping is available behind the naturist beach. Picture from http://naturista.cz/lokality

Melice beach and camping, west of Prague

Naturist camping and a nude beach make this small site a good place to stay while exploring central Czech republic, especially as it is only 80km west of Prague. The beach is on a former sand quarry, and the campsite here is largely textile with a nude area by the beach. There is no shade at the beach, and although the nude beach is only about 50m long it does attract dozens of users at peak times. Refreshments are on the nearby textile beach. It's very affordable, at €1 per person and €1.50 for a tent.

Practical info
The lake is about 4km to the east of Prelouc town, and although there's a train at Valy, about 1.5km to the south, access is easiest by car. The nude area is right in the middle of the north shore.

Jezero, Podebrady, 50km west of Prague

The northern shore of this little lake is naturist, and there's an even smaller lake just to the east which is also used by nude bathers. There is a modest fee to enter the naturist area, and although the nude beach and grassy lawns are just 100m long it attracts hundreds of happy bathers in the summer months.

Practical info
The lake is just under 1km south of the historical spa town of Podebrady, on the other side of the river Elbe. It's only about 30 minutes' drive from Prague on highway D11. There's a footbridge from the town across the river, from where it's barely 200m walk south to the lake.

▲ Small but perfectly nude: the beach at Jezero, popular on hot days. Pic from naturista.cz/lokality

Antosovice beaches and camping, Ostrava

Right at the eastern end of the Czech republic, just a few kilometers from the Polish border, there are two naturist lake campsites almost next to each other. The first and oldest campsite is called SCSN Ostrava, and has 300m of sand and grass with volleyball, slide and rowing boats to hire. The second site, called Mzikovec, is a short walk north on another, smaller lake, where there is a camping meadow, volleyball and refreshments available on site.

Practical info
The beaches are about 8km north of Ostrava, the third largest city in the Czech republic. There are lots of lakes in this area, and the two with the nude camps are the ones immediately west and south of Antosovice village. For detailed directions and maps, as with all locations in the Czech republic, take a look at www.naturista.cz/lokality.

Milky Way Campsite, 120km south of Prague

This commercial resort – Mlècná Dráha in Czech – is actually run by a Dutch couple and is less than 20km away from the German border. Based around a large lake suitable for swimming and boating, the resort welcomes naturist tourists from around the world. It takes tents and caravans.

Practical info
The club is 12km from the nearest town, Vimperk, from where you head out north-west to the village of Zdíkov. Turn right on the outskirts of Zdíkov to Racov, where the campsite is based. Contact the club for more details.

Antosovice beaches accommodation

Sterkovna campsite
http://www.volny.cz/scsn.ostrava

Mzikovec campsite
www.natur-plaz-katka.unas.cz

Naturist campsite Mlècná Dráha

Tel: +420 388 426 222
www.m-d.nl

▲ Naturist camp Banovci in Slovenia, set in peaceful countryside. Picture from the resort

Slovenia

Camp Smlednik, Dragocajna, NW of Ljubljana

Near to the capital, this handy holiday park by the Sava River offers peace and tranquillity in attractive surroundings: a large section is reserved for nudist camping and caravanning. With a host of leisure facilities on site (mostly textile) and nearby lake Zbilje, Camp Smlednik is well placed for walking, touring, biking and mountaineering.
Practical info
Dragocajna-Smlednik is between Ljubljana and Kranj, 15km north-west of Ljubljana. From the capital take highway 211 and watch for the turn to Smlednik on the right (east). As you approach town, the site is signposted from the main road to the left (north).

Camp Smlednik
Tel: +386 1 362 70 02
www.dm-campsmlednik.si

Kamp Soncni gaj, Terme Banovci, Maribor

The Banovci Health Resort has its own campsite with 200 places. More than one-third of the spaces are reserved for naturists in a self-contained section of the park. Showers, washrooms and lockers are provided and there is a circular 15-metre nudist swimming pool filled by a thermal spring. The water comes from 1,500 metres underground and has natural healing properties.

Practical info
Banovci is situated close to the Austrian border between the towns of Maribor and Ljutomer, north-east of Ljubljana. The resort is well signed.

Kamp Soncni gaj, Banoci
Tel: +386 1 433 94 40 (tourist office)
Email: nationaltour@ntz-nta.si
www.ntz-nta.si/en (search for Banovci)

Montenegro

Ada Bojana, Bojana, Ulcinj

This remarkable nude beach and resort have been attracting naturist vacationers for more than three decades. Located right on the southern tip of Montenegro's Adriatic coast – in fact, a naked stroll down the shore will bring you to the Albanian border! The beautiful dark golden sands stretch completely undeveloped for almost 2km in a protected area of special ecological importance. Wildlife includes endangered species such as loggerhead turtles, jackals, spoonbills, pygmy cormorants, stone curlews and levant sparrowhawks.

At the opposite end of the beach, the resort centre is close to the mouth of the Bojana river. Here you can enjoy the outdoor bar in the buff and gaze at the unusual fishing huts on stilts with their nets suspended above the water: more reminiscent of the Far East than southern Europe. Swimming from the main beach away from the river is safe and ideal for children. Sports on offer include surfing, sailing, tennis, table tennis and horse riding. There are two restaurants and accommodation for 500 residents. According to the Montenegrin tourist board: "If you want to spend the holiday of your dreams dressed as Adam and Eve, Ada Bojana is definitely the right choice."
Practical info
The resort, which is reached by crossing a short bridge on to Ada Island, is 18km south of the regional capital of Ulcinj. Just follow the coast road south and Ada Bojana is well signposted. More tourist information from www.visit-montenegro.org.

Eastern Europe

Australia & New Zealand

Blessed by a perfect bathing climate and endless sandy shores, Australia has some of the world's finest places for baring all. This vast country is a place of unspoilt natural beauty, and nude beach lovers can enjoy the outdoors in their birthday suits all year round. Only the extra strong sunshine and unfriendly sea creatures mean you have to take extra care when joining in the fun. A few negative attitudes to nude bathing persist in one or two places, but there are enough official and well-established beaches to leave any free spirit spoilt for choice.

New Zealand on the other hand has no specific laws against being bare on the beach. As long as you're not disturbing other people, and there aren't any specific prohibitions against nudity, you can strip off on an empty beach. In fact, New Zealand's huge and largely unspoilt coastline has so many bare bathing possibilities it's hard to provide a complete guide to where other bare bathers gather: most remote beaches have been used naked at some time or other. It's a truly enchanting place.

Map labels: Cable beach, Cairns, AUSTRALIA, Alexandria Bay, Brisbane, North Belongil Beach, Swanbourne, Perth, Warnbro, Samurai Beach, Cobblers beach, Obelisk beach and Lady Jane Bay, Sydney, Werrong Beach, Maslin Beach, Adelaide, Armonds Beach, Melbourne, Beachport, Sunnyside North

▲ Making a splash: Maslin beach in South Australia became the country's first official nudist beach in 1975. Picture by Les Hotchkin
▼ White sand and a gentle sea make Warnbro an attractive option for Perth's nudists. Pic from Free Beaches Australia (www.freebeach.com.au)

■ It's not as if they need the practice, but Australians take their love of sports along with them even when they're visiting a nude beach. Picture opposite shows Swanbourne beach near Perth city centre, by Les Hotchkin

Western Australia

Swanbourne, Perth, near city centre

This is a popular and well-known beach, partly because it's so near the city centre and partly because it's a great stretch of sand. Although up to 1,000 happily naked souls gather here at the busiest weekends, there are 2km of white sand backed by grassy dunes so it's never overcrowded. Just about every person on the beach goes bare. You can buy refreshments from the nearby surf club, or from a vendor who sometimes drives along the beach serving naked customers. Beware the sea breezes though, they can be severe right along this stretch of coast.
Practical info
You can get here in 20 minutes' drive from the city centre; all you'll need is a city map. Simply drive to the end of Grant Street and park near the surf club here. Nude bathing starts a short walk to the north. If you're without a car or bike, the 207 bus goes from the city post office right to the surf club.

Warnbro, Rockingham, 50km south of Perth

Some naturists prefer Warnbro official nude beach, a short drive south of Perth, to the more urban Swanbourne beach. The beach is near the seaside town of Rockingham in the suburb of Warnbro. It has bright white sand and gentle waves suitable for children, although Perth's famous sea breezes mean a windbreak might be a wise investment if you're visiting any beach around here. Don't stray into the dunes behind the beach as essential stabilisation work is being done to protect the coast. There are around 2km of beach to enjoy before you reach Port Kennedy at the southern end of the nude section.
Practical info
To get to this nude beach, drive south from town on Warnbro Sound Avenue. Take a right turn down Grand Ocean Boulevard, the first turning after the open-air swimming pool in Warnbro. After about 1.6km take a right down Bayeux Avenue and park at the end of this road. The beach is a short walk away and the nude area is to the south, or left as you face the sea.

Australia

Cable Beach, Broome

Not only is this one of the world's longest nude beaches, many visitors also claim it's one of the world's very best. Certainly the 17km of fine white sand, lapped by a crystal clear sea, would encourage just about anyone to discard their swimming costume and luxuriate in the vast space of sunshine and solitude. It is also one of the relatively few official nude beaches to be located in the tropics, which means summer is extremely hot and humid, with temperatures nudging upwards of 35C. Winter is a more inviting prospect, with clear skies and temperatures a good 10C lower. Broome is more than

1,000km west of Darwin and 1,700 north-west of Perth in a direct line, and much more than a day's drive from either of them.

Practical info

The beach is easy to reach from Broome township. It's a 6km drive along Cable Beach Road to the car park. There is an access track leading to the beach and the nude area starts to the north, or right as you face the sea. If you have a four-wheel drive and know what you're doing, it's possible to explore the beach all the way up to the river mouth 17km away, which marks the end of this bare haven.

▲ Cable beach has endless space to explore, and only gets busy at the southern end near town, where textiles tend to gather. Picture on left Les Hotchkin, picture on right from Free Beaches Australia (www.freebeach.com.au)

> **More Australian nudist info**
>
> For more nude beach information take a look at freebeach.com.au or for naturist resorts try the Australian Nudist Federation at www.aus-nude.org.au.

New South Wales

River Island Nature Retreat, near Mittagong

Just 200km south of Sydney, this superb naturist resort is well regarded by both Australians and tourists alike. Set in a pretty valley about 200km south of Sydney, it boasts its own tree-lined lake and river for swimming, plus swimming pools and a spa nearer the accommodation. With 1,500 acres of land to enjoy, River Island is many times larger than some of the most popular European naturist resorts and you can roam freely. The resort is clothing optional, rather than strictly naturist, making it easy for visitors to do as they please. Accommodation options range from luxury cabins to grassy campsites, with all the facilities and even a cafe.

Practical info

The resort is about 40km from Mittagong. Drive south from Mittagong for 5km and turn off following signs to Wombeyan Caves. It's 34km along this road, the first half of which is sealed and the second half of which is good-quality but unsealed, suitable for all vehicles. Pass the Wollondilly Tea House and 2km later you'll see the large blue sign for River Island Nature Retreat. As always with naturist venues, contact them in advance.

> **River Island Nature Retreat contact info**
>
> Tel: +61 2 4888 9236
> www.riverisland.com.au

> **Other New South Wales resorts**
>
> Among other places recommended for nude-minded visitors are two naturist resorts in New South Wales. The Running Bare Retreat, near Narrabri, and Twin Falls, in the Port Macquarie area near Ellenborough, are both naturist centres open to holiday visitors. Running Bare Retreat is a mobile home and caravan park with cabins also available, along with a pool, tennis and badminton courts and bushwalks. Twin Falls is a naturist club that has space for holiday visitors, with cabins and camping. It also allows day visits, and facilities include about 100 acres of bush and rainforest plus a swimming pool. As with all naturist clubs, get in touch before planning your trip.
>
> Running Bare Retreat
> Tel: +61 2 6793 2169
> www.running-bare.com.au
>
> Twin Falls
> Tel: +61 2 6587 4455 (Australian daytime only)
> www.twin-falls.com

Australia

▲ Sydney's legal nude beaches include the small but secluded coves at Cobblers beach and Obelisk beach. Pics by Fiona Ashley

Cobblers and Obelisk beaches, Sydney

Cobblers beach is a small, secluded beach on Sydney harbour where bare bathing is officially welcomed. It's safe for swimming and is much loved by families because it has a grassy area for sunbathing, plenty of shaded areas and of course a lovely sandy beach. There is bush behind and walks through Middle Head to enjoy.

Practical info

Cobblers beach is on the north side of the Middle Head park area. To get here, go to the suburb of Mosman and drive along Middle Head Road. When the road meets Chowder Bay Road, take the next turning on the right after

30 metres, down a track with no name, and park here. You then need to walk back up the track and keeping heading north-east across the park for about 400m to the shore.

Obelisk beach

The other beach, Obelisk, is on the opposite, southern side of Middle Head and is larger. It's a white sand beach, popular with bare bathers including many gay people, and also has safe swimming.

Practical info

To get here, park in the same place as Cobblers beach and keep walking down the track down to the sea.

Lady Jane Bay, South Head, Sydney

Lady Jane Bay – also known as Lady Bay – has been a bare beach for more than 40 years. It was one of Sydney's first nudist beaches. Despite the name it's also very popular with gay men. The big advantage of this beach – that it's easy to reach – also means that it's not at all secluded and is sometimes used by visitors who don't even strip off.

Practical info

There's not much parking at Watsons Bay, but you can take buses 324 or 325 from Circular Quay. From Watsons Bay, go to the end of Old South Head Road, turn right down Robertson Place and walk to Camp Cove. There's a path from here to the beach.

North Belongil Beach, north of Byron Bay

▲ Sunny days at North Belongil Beach from Free Beaches Australia (www.freebeach.com.au)

North Belongil Beach accommodation

Byron Bay Beach Resort
Tel: +61 2 6685 8000

Byron Bay is an inviting stop for any visitor travelling between Sydney and Brisbane – and the local council has made sure it's an absolute must for bare bathers. There is a big sandy nude beach, sometimes called Tyagarah beach, with dunes behind and plenty of space. There's even a little lake just back along the road from the beach, where people also swim naked.

Practical info

It's easy to find. To get here, turn off the

Pacific Highway about 4-5km to the north of the Byron Bay exit, down Grays Road. The road goes into the national park and all the way to the beach – veer left where the road forks, about three-quarters of the way to the coast. Park at the end and you're there. Turn right as you face the sea for bare bathing. If you stay at the handy Byron Bay Beach Club, on the northern edge of town, it's an easy 500m walk north along the shore to the nude beach.

Australia

Armonds Beach, Bermagui, south of Narooma

Much cherished by local nude bathers and visitors alike, some say this is the prettiest nudist beach in Australia. It's set in a curved bay with rocks at either side, lined by native bush. If you're travelling between Sydney and Melbourne do stop and strip off. It's officially nude, and used all year round. There are no facilities but it's only a 10-minute walk from the car park. There is a superb website about the beach at www.freewebs.com/armonds.

Practical info

The beach is easy to find. Drive south along the coast road from Bermagui and Bermagui South. About 10km along – 3km after you've passed signs for Cuttagee Beach – take a left down Kullarro drive and park at the end. It's an easy track through the bush.

Werrong Beach, 40km south of Sydney

This official nude beach is set in a bay backed by bush-covered cliffs, on the southern edge of Australia's first national park, called the Royal. It's a steep climb to reach the beach but the 300m of yellow sand are well worth the effort. The walk down takes about half an hour and the climb back twice as long. There are rocks offshore so take care when getting in the sea. Bush camping is allowed in parts of the park but check with the visitors' centre first.

Practical info

To reach the park, head south from Sydney on the Southern Freeway. Turn left following signs for Stanwell Park, near Helensburgh, and turn left to Otford Lookout. Once you enter the park itself, stop beyond the shop and follow the footpath to Werrong Beach.

Samurai Beach, Anna Bay, Port Stephens

This is a great place: beautiful, unspoilt and well-used by delighted nudists. There is an annual sports day, which attracts a huge crowd of naked competitors. The beach is over 1km of golden sand and is also a good place for surfing and other beach sports. But it's not that easy to get to, being up to half an hour's walk under the hot sun from the car park unless you have a four wheel drive. Sky Travel ranks this one of the 10 best nude beaches in the world. Many visitors, particularly those with a suitable vehicle, would agree.

Practical info

This area is three hours' drive north of Sydney. The nude beach is to the east of Anna Bay town, near Nelson Bay, Port Stephens. From Anna Bay, drive along Gan Gan Road and look out for Middle Rock Caravan Park. Park near here and next to the caravan park is a track that leads for 1.5km through bush to this official nude beach.

▲ Top: Werrong official beach, picture from www.freebeach.com.au. Middle and bottom: the fabulous setting of Armonds Beach. Pictures from the beach's website (see listing) ▼ A happy community keeps Samurai special. Pic by Les Hotchkin

▲ Maslin beach, the first and still one of the best nude beaches in Australia. Picture by Les Hotchkin

▲ Maslin became Australia's first official 'unclad beach' more than 30 years ago. Picture by Pete Knight
▼ The naturist village of Sunland is right next to Beachport nude beach. Picture below from Les Hotchkin, picture at bottom from Sunland

South Australia

Maslin Beach, south of Adelaide

History was made in 1975 when Maslin became Australia's first legal nude beach. It's well known and fairly near the city, so it does attract many bare bathers – and some curious non-nude visitors. The white sand is backed by tall cliffs. Families may find access tricky but the safe swimming makes up for the walk, as do occasional visits by dolphins. The water is clear and great for snorkelling. There is a van that sells drinks and ice creams during summer weekends. Although it can get very busy, it is large enough for everyone to

find their bit of bare bathing peace.
Practical info
The beach is not the easiest place to find but a good map will help. Drive south out of Adelaide along Main South Road. After about 45km turn right into Maslin Beach Road, then first left into Commercial Road. Follow the signs to the car park at the end and walk down the 100 steps to the beach. If you want easier directions, simply drive to the main (clothed) Maslin beach and walk south (left, facing the sea) to the bare area.

Beachport & Sunland Holiday Village, Robe

As the only nudist resort in Australia by the sea, Sunland is a perfect destination for beach lovers to stay. It's about 300km south of Adelaide, and offers peaceful camping pitches, holiday cabins and caravans to hire. Facilities are self catering and you'll need to stock up on groceries before you arrive. The resort is planning to introduce a swimming pool and already has a spa, sauna, and miniten court. But by far the biggest draw for any bare soul are the 1.3km of beautiful golden sands a short walk away through the dunes. It's a legal nude beach and a good place for sea fishing too. The whole site has around 250 acres of dunes and bush tracks to explore inland from the beach.
Practical info
The resort is six hours' drive from

Melbourne or four and a half from Adelaide. It's easy enough to find its location on a map; Sunland lies half way between the seaside towns of Robe and Beachport, very near Lake St Clair. To get here from Robe, travel south out of town on the B101 Main South Eastern Road for about 20km, and turn right down the gravel Powells Road. Drive along for 6km to the crossroads, where you turn left (the resort is signposted from here). Keep going for another 3km and you'll see the entrance on your right.

Beachport accommodation
Sunland Holiday Village Tel: +61 8 8735 7115 www.sunlandholidayvillage.com.au

Australia

▲ Sports day on the lovely sands of Alexandria Bay. Picture by Les Hotchkin

Queensland

Alexandria Bay, Noosa, Sunshine Coast

This lovely, long sandy bay is in a pretty spot and highly popular with nude beach lovers for year-round sunshine. It's well over a mile from any roads and has been used naked unofficially for decades. Unclad bathers gather at the south end (right as you face the sea), and up to half the beach is used naked.
Practical info
You can approach the beach from two directions. If you're coming from Noosa Heads, start from the national park headquarters' car park and take the 3km scenic walk through the bush. If approaching from Sunshine Beach to the south, simply walk to the north (left as you face the sea) and take the track over the headland at the end. It's a nice walk, and Alexandria Bay lies just on the other side of the headland.

Victoria

Sunnyside North, 50km south of Melbourne

Victoria has a few official nude beaches, including this one at Port Phillip Bay. It's the most convenient for Melbourne and legally recognised, but it's a bit out of the way and not so busy. It's about 50km south of Melbourne, by the town of Mount Eliza on the Mornington peninsula.

Practical info
Drive to Frankston and follow signs another 8km to Sunnyside Beach, near Mount Eliza. The beach car park often fills up and you might need to park some way back on a busy day. On the beach, turn right as you face the sea round the rocky point to the nude area.

Mosaic Larry's, 45 minutes from Melbourne

Billed as a luxury naturist resort, Mosaic Larry's has been thoughtfully designed to provide a high-quality naturist destination in north central Victoria. There is a heated saltwater pool, tennis court and a well-equipped games complex. Meals, drinks and evening entertainment are all provided in the cafe, bar and nightclub area.
Practical info
The resort is just 45 minutes' drive from Melbourne, and can arrange airport transfers. For more details contact them first by phone or email.

Queensland resorts and B&Bs

There are several good naturist places in Queensland, inspired by the great climate and lack of official nude beaches. Many are listed at www.aus-nude.org.au, including Elephant Rock, to the west of Brisbane, Goody's Retreat, near Mackay, and The White Cockatoo near Mossman. Elephant Rock is a small retreat about two hours' drive inland from Brisbane, offering six rooms for hire, a pool, spa and 43 acres of bush to explore. Goody's Retreat is 35km south of Mackay, in the northern part of Queensland, and enjoys year-round sunshine. It has a campsite, vans to rent, with a pool that has lovely views of the surrounding hills. The owners can even point you in the direction of an unofficial nude beach just 30 minutes' drive away. And The White Cockatoo is a resort that goes naturist for six months of the year, from 1 October to 1 May. It has a large pool, enjoys a tropical climate, and is also near some beaches used unofficially for nude bathing. It's also easy to find: simply look out for the big White Cockatoo sign on the left as you drive into town from Cairns, 70km to the south.

Elephant Rock
Tel: +61 7 5463 5555
www.elephantrock-naturally.com.au

Goody's Retreat
Tel: +61 7 4956 4742
www.goodysretreat.com

The White Cockatoo
Tel: +61 7 4098 2222
www.thewhitecockatoo.com

▲ Playful spirits enjoying the curve of yellow sand that makes up Queensland's pretty Alexandria Bay. Picture by Les Hotchkin

Mosaic Larry's

Tel: +61 3 5793 8431
www.mosaiclarrys.com.au

▲ A natural setting with modern facilities make for an attractive holiday choice at Mosaic Larry's. Picture supplied by the resort

▲ One of the many lakes just waiting for a skinny dipper to break the surface at Jajarawong Country Cottages. Pic supplied by the resort

River Valley Naturist Resort, Echuca

Surrounded by native bush and bounded by the wide Goulburn river, this peaceful naturist hideaway is a great place to stay during a holiday in the Victoria region. With 34 acres tucked away near the historical river port of Echuca, River Valley is about 225km north of Melbourne. It's a naturist-only resort, with a swimming pool, sauna and spa, four tennis courts, volleyball and many grassy lawns for sunbathing. There is a two-bedroom house, cabins, caravans and camping facilities, and the site even welcomes day visitors. Contact them in advance.
Practical info
River Valley is 22km from Echuca; its website has a map and directions.

Jajarawong Country Cottages, Yandoit

This group of rural cottages situated in the bush is just two hours from Melbourne and close to the Spa Centre of Australia. There is camping on offer from October to Easter, and some superb lake swimming in one of five pool areas. The local area is alive with native wildlife, including kangaroos and kookaburras, and there are plenty of bushland walks in the 70 acre site. The resort is clothing optional, so it's up to you how much or little you wear. There is a bar and self-catering kitchen.
Practical info
To find this clothing optional oasis, drive to Yandoit town, which is near Daylesford in central Victoria. Leave town on Yandoit Creek Road and keep going for 4.4km until you see the Jajarawong sign and white gate posts.

Northern Territory

River Valley Naturist Resort
Tel: +61 3 5482 6650
www.rivervalley.com.au

Jajarawong Country Cottages
Tel: + 61 3 5476 4362
www.jajarawong.com

Top End Naturist Recreation Retreat
Tel: +61 8 8988 6185
www.members.optusnet.com.au/~tenrr

Top End Naturist Recreation Retreat, Winnellie

It may be at the top end of the country, but this naturist haven is well worth the trip if you're interested in exploring some of the nearby natural wonders – such as the Kakadu national park, two hours' drive away. The 100-acre site even has its own huge termite mounds. You can hire cabins or camp. Facilities include a swimming pool, various sports courts and even a small shop.
Practical info
The resort is 70km south of Darwin. Like many Australian naturist places it is nude-only rather than clothing optional. Contact them in advance to arrange your visit.

Australia

Rarawa Beach

Whangarei •

Uretiti Beach

Pohutukawa Bay

Orpheus Bay —

Little Palm Beach

Auckland

Opoutere

Katikati naturist park

NORTH ISLAND

Wanganui

Otatoka Beach

Hastings

Ocean Beach

Abel Tasman National Park

Mapua Leisure Park

Wellington •

SOUTH ISLAND

Christchurch •

Woodend Beach

New Zealand North Island

Rarawa beach, Northland, east coast

New Zealand

If you want some solitude and a bare beach in the most literal sense of the world, this blindingly white sand shore is well worth the drive. It's so remote you're unlikely to surprise anyone else who makes it here by bathing in the nude. There's certainly plenty of space to find somewhere by yourself. The sand is so dazzling white just about anyone sitting naked here looks like they've got a nice suntan in comparison.

Practical info

From Kaitaia drive north for 57km until you see the sign to the right for Rarawa Beach Access. It's about 4km from here to the sea. The nearest shops and petrol are at Houhora, 14km back towards Kaitaia. There is a camping ground at Rarawa.

▲ **Kay Hannan of naturist homestay Wai-natur, cycling near Mt Cook**

▲ Enjoying the sand and space of Uretiti, one of New Zealand's finest nude beaches. Pics by Pete Knight

Uretiti beach, South of Whangarei

Less than two hours' drive north of Auckland, this white sandy stretch of shore has some devoted fans who rate it among the very best New Zealand has to offer. It's not officially nude but is regarded as a naturist sanctuary by those who come to enjoy the elements as nature intended. There is a DOC (government-run) campsite at Uretiti beach. The nude area is to the south of the campsite, a few minutes' walk along the shore (turn right as you face the sea). There are dunes behind the beach to provide some shelter from the wind, but the sun here is unforgiving on a hot day so bring some shade and/ or plenty of sunscreen.

Practical info

This has to be one of the easiest beaches to reach by car, just off the main Highway 1 about 35km south of Whangarei. The Uretiti campsite is marked on maps and signposted from the highway. You can only park at the campsite if you are staying here, otherwise turn left down the track before the campsite entrance and park at the end. The shore is a minute's walk away, and the nude area itself a further 10-minute walk south.

Pohutukawa Bay, Auckland north shore

At the north end of Long Bay beach, this pretty beach has sand and good shade from the Pohutukawa trees which give the bay its name. It has good swimming and is remote enough for undisturbed bare bathing. If the tide is right in, simply take the path round the cliffs that separate it from the end of Long Bay.

Practical info

Long Bay is the last of Auckland's north shore bays, just past Torbay. There is good access and the bay is easy to find from Torbay: simply follow the main shopping road north. At Long Bay regional park, drive to the far end of the car park and it's a 20-30 minute walk north (left as you face the sea).

New Zealand

295 ■

Orpheus Bay, Auckland, west coast

The dark yellow/brown sand and overhanging trees give Orpheus bay an interesting, secluded atmosphere. The beach is backed by a steep hill overflowing with native bush. You can buy supplies in Huia itself; as with all New Zealand nudist beaches the seclusion means you need to bring your own supplies.

Practical info
From the west Auckland suburb of Titirangi, simply follow the signs to Huia, which is 14km away along the coast. As the road bends to the right and goes downhill into Huia town there is a sign to the left for Huia Point Lookout. Drive down this track and park on the grass. There is a well-trodden path on the left hand side of the parking area. It's slightly hard to spot the entrance to the path, but it's about 150m from the main road, well before you reach the lookout point itself. It won't take you long to find it.

▲ Beneath the pohutukawa trees at secluded Orpheus Bay, on the north-west coast of Auckland

Little Palm Beach, Waiheke Island

Waiheke is often called Auckland's island suburb, and is just 35 minutes by ferry from the city centre. It's well worth a visit for the beautiful countryside and vineyards – and of course to spend some time with the friendly nude bathers at Palm Beach. It's well used by locals, who are as welcoming as only Kiwis can be, clothed or not. The swimming is great: the beach is golden sand tucked beside a rocky headland that's ideal for snorkelling and exploring. In fact Little Palm is one of the few nude beaches in New Zealand where you're virtually guaranteed to find other nude bathers on a sunny day. It's a superb place to take time out from the city, and highly recommended.

Practical info
Catch the Waiheke ferry from Quay Street in central Auckland. Buses on the island meet the ferries: take the one for Palm Beach if you haven't got your own transport. At Palm Beach, simply walk past the rocks to your left, or over the low headland if the tide is in, and this popular bare beach is all yours. Ferry information from www.fullers.co.nz. Don't forget to note the return bus times before you walk to the beach.

▲ Geothermal wonder at Rotota Sun Club, above. Pic by Pete Knight. For club info see www.gonatural.co.nz
▼ A typically undeveloped sandy bay. Picture by Tourism New Zealand

New Zealand

▲ One of the many uncrowded sandy shores of beautiful New Zealand. Picture by Bob McCree

Opoutere, Western Bay of Plenty

This long sandy beach can seem virtually empty, even on sunny summer days. But it's well known to New Zealand's nudists for the fabulous bare bathing, and to other visitors for its nature reserve and peaceful location. It's a huge beach. Simply walk to the north (left as you face the sea) and keep going until you're either away from the clad beach users or among other nude bathers, although some people go skinny dipping pretty much anywhere along here at times.

Practical info

Opoutere is off a side road from State Highway 25, south of Pauanui and north of Whangamata. Drive past the few houses that make up Opoutere and follow the road to the parking area at the end; there's a sharp right at the very last bit where the road forks. There is a wooden footbridge that takes you into a pine forest. Sandy paths lead to the beach, about 10 mins' walk. There is a campsite and hostel at Opoutere, but buy supplies at Whangamata before you get here.

Katikati Naturist Park

Tel: +64 7 549 2158
Freephone in NZ: 0800 4567 567
www.katikati-naturist-park.co.nz

▲ Taking the plunge in New Zealand. Pics above from Kay Hannan of Wainatur. Pic on the right shows the peaceful sands at Opoutere

New Zealand

Katikati naturist park, Katikati, Bay of Plenty

A beautiful naturist haven worth considering if you're in the Bay of Plenty area is the Katikati naturist park. Its owners have created a unique holiday destination with camping and caravans for hire and extensive self-catering facilities in the centre of the site. There is a pool, sauna and spa and a pretty stream among the native plants. It's a heavenly place to strip off, and as long as you're happy to join in a bona fide naturist environment you can just turn up and book in. However, advance booking might be a good idea at busier times of the year.

Practical info
The resort is just over an hour's drive north from Rotorua. As you drive south-east out of Katikati towards Tauranga on SH2, turn right down Wharawhara road about 1.5km after you leave town. Drive along here for another 1.5km until you see the park signposted on your left.

> **Katikati Naturist Park**
>
> Tel: +64 7 549 2158
> Freephone in NZ: 0800 4567 567
> www.katikati-naturist-park.co.nz

Otatoka beach, north of Wanganui

This is what New Zealand beach naturism is all about. Otatoka beach involves a 6km drive down unsealed roads to a superb sandy shore with plenty of space for you to do your own thing. You can even free camp around the back of the beach and there are two simple toilets by the parking area. The beach is used unofficially by naked locals and visitors alike, and also offers good sea fishing. West coast beaches are notoriously dangerous in New

Zealand however so great care is needed with the sea itself.
Practical info
To get to Otatoka beach, drive north out of Wanganui on the Great North Road. Turn left into Rapanui Rd (opposite the BP service station) then after passing the turnoff to Mowhanau Beach turn left into Handley Road. Look for the sign to Otatoka Beach, where you turn left. The last 6km are unsealed. Park in the grass car park at the cliff top and walk down.

Ocean beach, Hawkes Bay

This long sweep of sand, bounded by a rocky headland, is a spectacular and uncrowded gem of a beach on Hawkes Bay, East Coast New Zealand. It has all the space you could possibly wish for, and many visitors take their 4X4 vehicles to explore the long shore. Nude use is common here – there is

more than enough room for everyone.
Practical info
From Havelock North drive east 4km to the end of Te Mata Road, turn right into Waimarama Road and go 11km. Turn left at the sign to Ocean Beach and drive the final 5km to the beach. Head left for the nude area.

▲▼ The unspoilt beauty of New Zealand never seems to end. Top pic this page shows Katikati naturist park's river. All other pics and opposite show the vast golden expanse of Ocean beach, pictured by Philip and Roberta Law

South Island

Mapua Leisure Park, Waimea Estuary

The beach here is attached to a unique holiday park where for two months of the year you can choose to enjoy the site wearing nothing. Some holiday-makers stay dressed, and of course many choose to strip off, particularly on the beach. The park is set in 25 acres of native woodland with a range of accommodation including motel rooms, cabins and chalets. The park has a swimming pool, tennis courts, cafe, sauna, spa, nine-hole golf course and much more. The clothing optional season is February and March, the best months in terms of weather for enjoying this part of New Zealand.

Practical info

From Nelson take State Highway 60 to Mapua. Turn right into the town, down Aranui Road, then take a left down Toru Street over the causeway to the leisure park.

▲ New Zealand has beautiful and uncrowded beaches all the way around its coastline. Picture by David Wall, supplied by Tourism New Zealand

> **Mapua Leisure Park**
>
> Tel: +64 3 540 2666
> www.nelsonholiday.co.nz

▲ The Abel Tasman national park has many little bays where visitors seldom intrude. Even many ordinary tourists are tempted to try skinny dipping while walking here. Pics from Casa Pacifica homestay, which offers boat trips in the area

Abel Tasman accommodation

Casa Pacifica
Tel: +64 3 540 3151
www.casapacifica.co.nz

Sounds Natural
Tel: +64 275 382 203
www.soundsnatural.co.nz

Wai-natur
www.naturist.co.nz/wai-natur.htm
Tel: +64 3 5722 681

▼ Freestyle skinny dipping New Zealand style. Picture on left by Pete Knight. Picture on right shows the sands of Woodend beach, near Christchurch, which are used nude at the northern end away from busy areas. There are dunes for sheltered and secluded sunbathing

Abel Tasman park, north-west coast

Not so much a beach as an entire coastline of yellow sandy bays, the Abel Tasman national park has all the space in the world for enjoying New Zealand naturally. The park is a beautiful reserve of native bush, golden beaches, sculpted granite cliffs and a much-admired coastal track that takes three to five days to complete. Nude bathing often takes place in the park's secluded coves, and some visitors have spent days in the park without meeting other people.

Practical info
There are four main entrances to the national park area. At the southern end you can enter at the towns of Marahau or Kaiteriteri, and in the north at the towns of Totaranui or Wainui (see www.doc.govt.nz for more info). Local naturist-friendly accommodation is excellent here: there are luxury villas with private gardens at Casa Pacifica, which offers a naturist boat trip to the park. Sounds Natural offers a truly unique naturist homestay on a houseboat, with naturist beach visits and bush walks. Finally Wai-natur also offers naturist accommodation in this corner of the South Island.

Woodend beach, north of Christchurch

One of many long sandy beaches that nude bathers sometimes use. You may be the only one undressed at times, but it's a huge expanse of coast and if you walk north there's plenty of space to sunbathe in peaceful seclusion.

Practical info
Heading north from Christchurch on State Highway 1, turn off for Woodend after 24km. Park at the end near the sands and walk north (left as you face the sea).

New Zealand

South Africa

With one main naturist beach in Cape Town and a few others dotted around the coast, South African naturists are blessed with plenty of open space and a favourable climate. Perhaps thanks to the Dutch influence there are some great organisations and guest houses taking full advantage. Add the fact that South Africans are normally soaking up the sun while winter grips the northern hemisphere, and you have a handy destination for Europeans and North Americans.

For more information about naturism in the country, check out the South African Naturist Federation's website at www.sanfed.com.

The rest of Africa is not known for its nude beach credentials, although in many countries people traditionally bathe or swim outdoors in the altogether. It's not naturism in any sense though, just a continuation of what everyone did before the Victorians invented the swimming costume and shipped it round the world.

Sandy Bay, Llandudno, Cape Town

▲ Nude bathers keep true naturist traditions going at Sandy Bay. Picture supplied by Villa Antoinette

Sandy Bay accommodation

Naturist Homestay
Email: gnatural@iafrica.com

Villa Antoinette B&B
Tel: +27 (0) 21 465 9623
www.villa-antoinette.co.za

Squire's Holiday Accommodation
Tel: +27 (0) 21 852 0184
www.squiresholidays.co.za

Sunset House
Tel: +27 (0) 28 254 9895
www.sunsethousegreyton.co.za

A beautiful beach with a long tradition of nude use, Sandy Bay is certainly South Africa's most famous naturist bathing spot. The beach sits in peaceful isolation, at least 20 minutes' walk from the nearest parking place. As the name implies, it has beautiful soft sand and some handy flat rocks to lie on. They also provide some shelter from the Cape's infamous south-east winds, but when there's a stiff breeze going the beaches around here might be best left for another day.

Like so many city beaches around the world, Sandy Bay does suffer somewhat from selfish visitors who abuse the naturist atmosphere. But naturists have overcome the same situation on other beaches and this beach should still be considered very much naturist territory. If you stay at one of the local naturist guest houses, the considerate owners will be only to happy to advise or possibly arrange an excursion with you.

Practical info

To get to the beach, drive along the coast road that winds around Table Mountain to the little suburb of Llandudno. Drive down Sandy Bay road, and stop where the road loops back. Parking in this area is limited, so

arrive early or be prepared for a longer walk. Take the coastal path down to the bay. Drinks are often available from a vendor in the parking area, but none on the beach.

Among Cape Town's many places to stay, some stand out a mile for their friendly attitudes towards naturists. One such place is Naturist Homestay, where the entire establishment is fully naturist with a pool and sauna. There are two rooms here, and the accommodation is even within walking distance of Sandy Bay beach.

Villa Antoinette B&B is at Verdehoek in the City Bowl, just 20 minutes' drive from Llandudno. It is run by naturists – but not naturist as such unless both of the two en-suite bedrooms are booked by people requesting nude use of the secluded terrace. Elsewhere in the city, Squire's Holiday Accommodation offers two cottages set around a completely private swimming pool and sunbathing area, where the naturist owner says you can bathe as you please.

Meanwhile, 100km from Cape Town, Sunset House at Greyton offers a two-bedroom cottage with private courtyard and outside shower that would suit naturist guests perfectly.

Kalypso Tours and NudistEcoPark

Kalypso Tours

Tel: +27 11 425 3533
www.kalypsotours.co.za

■ South Africa's Sandy Bay, the country's most famous nudist bathing spot, pictured opposite by the owners of Naturist Homestay
▼ A unique safari experience awaits visitors to the impressive and unique naturist game park run by Kalypso Tours. Pictures by the tour operator

Kalypso Tours opened for business in 2007, offering a variety of naturist trips – the centrepiece of which is a fully naturist eco-park just two hours' drive from Johannesburg. The Kudumanzi NudistEcoPark is completely secluded and allows nude use everywhere, including beside the river and waterfall by the eight-bedroom bush lodge. The park is in a malaria-free area, in case you're wondering about baring all in such an exotic environment.

The beautiful game park setting has

visits from giraffe, zebra, antelope and crocodiles, all of which can be seen on a naturist game drive organised by the managers. There are plenty of trails and hiking to enjoy around the park, and you can arrange your own private picnic by some of the lovely waterfalls. The park has a bar and holds a traditional barbeque in the evening.

Kalypso also organises other naturist tours in the region, including sailing on a luxury catamaran and visits to Sandy Bay and other naturist places.

South Africa

Naturist holiday services

Below is an index of advertisers in this guidebook. If you use one of the organisations listed here, do mention that you saw them in this book

▲ **Big business: naturism accounts for 15 per cent of the entire tourist industry in Croatia. Many millions have skinny-dipped along its shores**

The last word in nude guides

We are expecting to produce further nude beach and resort guidebooks, to keep the world fully up to date with the very best way to enjoy a holiday.

If you have any changes, new information, additional beaches or suggested resorts for our future publications, please drop us a line. Pictures of locations, with or without people, are always welcome too.

For readers in North America and South America, contact the US publisher:

The Naturist Society LLC
PO Box 132, Oshkosh,
WI 54903, USA
www.naturistsociety.com
naturist@naturistsociety.com

For readers in Europe and the rest of the world, contact the UK publisher:

Lifestyle Press Ltd
PO Box 1087, Bristol, BS48 3YD, UK
www.lifestyle-press.co.uk
info@lifestyle-press.co.uk